Hearing the Whole Story

Hearing the Whole Story

The Politics of Plot in Mark's Gospel

Richard A. Horsley

Westminster John Knox Press
LOUISVILLE
LONDON · LEIDEN

Book design by Sharon Adams
Cover design by Mark Abrams

First edition
Published by Westminster John Knox Press
Louisville, Kentucky

This book is printed on acid-free paper that meets the American National Standards Institute Z39.48 standard. ∞

PRINTED IN THE UNITED STATES OF AMERICA

01 02 03 04 05 06 07 08 09 10 — 10 9 8 7 6 5 4 3 2 1

Library of Congress Cataloging-in-Publication Data

A catalog record for this book is available from the Library of Congress.
ISBN 0-664-22275-7

Contents

Preface   vii

Introduction: Rethinking Mark in Context   ix

1 Taking the Gospel Whole   **1**
The Gospel in Bits and Pieces   2
Learning to Read Mark as a Story   6
A Story—and Audience—in the Public Arena of Significant Action   9
The Plotting, Outline, and Other Features of the Story   11
Ambiguities in Mark's Story   17
What Kind of Story Is Mark?   21
Restoring the Story to History and History to the Story   24

2 Submerged People's History   **27**
Was Mark Written for Us?   27
Galileans and Judeans under Imperial Rule   31
The Gospel of Mark as People's History   37
Giving Voice to Subjected People   44

3 Mark as Oral   **53**
The Limits of Literacy   53
Hearing Mark as Oral Performance   61
Mark as Oral Performance: The "Text"   66
The Difference That Hearing Makes   74

4 Disciples Become Deserters   **79**
Is the Gospel of Mark about Discipleship?   81
Hearing Historically   86
Hearing Politically   90

 5 **Getting the Whole Story**   **99**
    Discerning the Dominant Plot   99
    Jesus Is Leading a Renewal of Israel . . .   101
    . . . in Opposition to the Rulers   109
    Confirming the Dominant Plot   111

 6 **The Struggle against Roman Rule**   **121**
    Mark's Story Compared with Judean Apocalyptic Literature   122
    Jesus' Prophetic Speech in Mark 13   129
    The Battle with Beelzebul   136
    "My Name Is Legion"   141

 7 **Jesus vs. the Pharisees: Contesting the Tradition**   **149**
    Mark's Plotting of the Scribes and Pharisees   149
    A Quest for the Historical Pharisees   151
    Jerusalem-Based Torah vs. Popular Israelite Tradition   156
    Jesus Renewing Popular Israelite Tradition   161

 8 **Renewing Covenantal Community**   **177**
    The Community/Movement That Mark Addresses   178
    Covenant Forms and Covenant Renewals   183
    Renewed Covenant in Mark 10   186
    Covenant Renewal in the Rest of Mark's Story   195

 9 **Women as Representative and Exemplary**   **203**
    The Plotting of Women in Mark's Story   205
    Women as Representative Figures   208
    Marriage, Family, and Community in Mark   218
    Women as Paradigms of Faithful Ministry   225

10 **Prophetic and Messianic "Scripts" in Mark**   **231**
    The Dangers of Proof-Texting Mark's Christology   231
    The Origins and Manifestations of the Prophetic "Script"   236
    The Origins and Manifestations of the Messianic "Script"   243
    The Prophetic "Script" in Mark's Story   247
    The Messianic "Script" in Mark's Story   250

Appendix   254

Notes   257

Index of Sources   286

Index of Authors   294

Preface

I knew that my students were missing something in the New Testament course. Yet for several years I continued to structure the section of the course on Jesus and the Gospels along the lines that I had learned in graduate school. After an introduction to the "Jewish background" we focused on particular passages from the Gospels arranged according to topics. It finally dawned on me that what they were missing was some sort of overview of the story of Jesus. Of course!—since in studying Jesus and the Gospels we never paused to read a whole Gospel. Being literarily challenged, however, I prevailed on a teacher friend to come into the course to explain how we could read the Gospel of Mark as a whole story. Before long I was asking the students to outline the dominant plot and subplots of Mark's story and learned a great deal from their insights. In a two-day workshop on "taking the Gospel whole," the clergy participants became genuinely excited about the possibilities they saw for Bible study, religious education, and their own preaching when we focused on the whole story, and no longer on individual verses and "lessons for the Sunday." Among the aspects of Mark we "discovered" in class discussions and workshops were the multiple conflicts woven together throughout the story. And the dominant conflict in the story appeared to be the political-religious opposition between Jesus and the Jerusalem and Roman rulers, a conflict which, as I knew from my intensive study of the historical context of Jesus' ministry, was rooted in the very political-economic-religious structure of Roman Palestine.

Thus began many years of studying and teaching the Gospel of Mark as a whole story to be understood in its particular historical context. Step by step, new facets of the story and/or its context emerged that required serious rethinking of the received wisdom in the field of New Testament study. Meanwhile, many colleagues, similarly dissatisfied with the approaches we had been taught in graduate school, had begun exploring new literary approaches to Mark and other Gospels. Indeed, during the last two decades the "reading" and literary analysis of Mark and other Gospels has become a virtual growth industry. A few adventuresome pioneers have also explored what we have "discovered" was the oral communication environment of the original "performance" and "reading," or rather hearing, of Mark's story in the ancient Mediterranean world. I have learned a great deal from reading the books and articles of many colleagues and friends and I would like to express great appreciation for their mentoring in the exploration of Mark's Gospel. Especially important among these Mark scholars have been Pieter Botha, Rita Nakashima Brock, Joanna Dewey, John Donahue, Jonathan Draper, Robert Fowler, Howard Clark Kee, Werner Kelber, Burton Mack, Elizabeth Struthers Malbon, Stephen Moore, Ched Myers, David Rhoads, Vernon Robbins, Elisabeth Schüssler Fiorenza, Mary Ann Tolbert, Gerald West, Lawrence Wills, and Adela Yarbro Collins. Readers will find many of their ideas and insights incorporated here, although they cannot be held responsible for the ways in which I have qualified, twisted, and combined them.

Many of the analyses and explorations in the chapters below have developed in courses, seminars, workshops, and the composition of earlier papers, talks, and articles, for example at Union Theological Seminary, Pacific School of Religion, Harvard Divinity School, and the University of Natal, as well as at the University of Massachusetts Boston, and Society of Biblical Literature meetings. I am grateful for the stimulation of the participants in those sessions. Ellen Aitken, Joanna Dewey, Jonathan Draper, Stephen Moore, Marlyn Miller, Audrey Pitts, and Larry Wills were kind enough to read a draft of various chapters below and I am especially grateful for their critical suggestions. Finally, I greatly appreciate the stimulation of student friends Karyn Brownell, Tom Coburn, Sean Farrell, Leila Kohler, and Haywood Harvey in the development of some of the interpretations below, and the research assistance and editorial assistance provided by Beth Mullin and Ann DiSessa.

Introduction:
Rethinking Mark in Context

The Gospel of Mark has been discovered as literature during the last generation. The people who discovered that Mark is literature, however, are mainly theologians, and the Gospel they interpret is a modern Western literary mongrel—narrative theology written for private individual readers. As professional biblical scholars, they still read the story in terms of the standard schemes and concepts they have acquired from their Christian theological training.

One of the motives leading to the discovery of Mark as literature was the pioneers' recognition that the historical-critical methods of biblical study distanced the text from the interpreter. Getting "up to speed" in professional literary analysis, however, demanded so much energy that there was none left over to question and rethink the standard assumptions and scenarios of New Testament biblical studies in which they had been trained. Much of the recent interpretation of Mark is thus a hybrid of modern literary analysis and Christian theological concepts.

While literary analysts were busy interpreting Mark as literature, however, the received assumptions, categories, and approaches of biblical studies have been questioned. An overview of the fields of ancient Jewish history, ancient Roman history, Gospel studies, and critical analysis of ancient culture suggests that many if not most of the key determinative assumptions with which interpreters approach Mark have become questionable because of recent research, new insights, or shifts in perspective.

Problematic Assumptions and Practices

Among the most problematic habitual assumptions and practices for interpretation of Mark are surely the following:

a. Mark and the other Gospels have been customarily read or heard in individual verses or separate "lessons." In theological education, those lessons are isolated as "pericopes" for "exegesis" in preparation for preaching. The lectionary, in mainline Protestant churches at least, concentrates on one Gospel during a liturgical year, but still divided it up into separate lessons for each Sunday. The Gospel of Mark, however, is a story. If we always read it in fragments, we will never get a sense of the full story. It is high time to "take our Gospel whole," to deal with Mark as a complete story!

b. Given the separation of religion and politics that goes along with the "separation of church and state," modern Westerners have grown accustomed to thinking of Mark and other biblical literature as (only or primarily) about religion. Mark' story, however, is about politics and economics as inseparable from religion. It portrays a cast of characters in ominous power-relations, with the chief priests and Pilate wielding death-dealing political-economic power and the hemorrhaging woman and the poor widow in desperate economic circumstances. Jesus' exorcisms of "unclean spirits" turn out to be battles in a wider political struggle.

c. Given the historical and institutional grounding of academic biblical studies in Christian theological education, it is assumed that the Gospel of Mark contains theology. Whatever theological doctrine is supposedly found in Mark, however, is the creation of theologians. The Gospel of Mark itself can now be recognized as a story, full of conflicts, ostensibly about historical events in ancient Galilee and Judea under Roman imperial rule.

d. Given the Christian theological grounding of biblical studies, moreover, Mark is understood as an account of the emergence of Christianity, as a universalistic, largely Gentile religion founded by Jesus, from Judaism, the parochial religion led by the Pharisees. When Mark was composed, however, neither Judaism nor Christianity had yet emerged historically as identifiable and distinct "religions." Thus it is difficult to find anything distinctively "Christian" versus "Jewish" in Mark's story.

e. Many of those who recognize that Judaism as a monolithic religion did not yet exist historically when Mark was composed still think in terms of "sectarian" Judaism, that is, the Pharisees, the Sadducees, and the Essenes, now often identified with the Qumran community that left the Dead Sea Scrolls. These associations of ancient Judeans in late Second Temple times, however, represent only the tiny literate elite of the society. What about the other 90–95 percent of the people? According to ancient sources such as the Judean historian Josephus, society in ancient Palestine, as elsewhere in the Roman empire, was sharply divided, mainly between the powerful and wealthy rulers, on the one hand, and the mass of people on the other. Movements of protest or even rebellion persistently emerged among the people. That was the historical context of the story Mark tells.

f. Interpreters of Mark simply take for granted that the Pharisees who repeatedly challenge Jesus in Mark belonged in the Galilee setting of his ministry, and that as a "Jew" Jesus naturally went up to Jerusalem and the Temple there. At the time of Jesus' ministry and at the time Mark was composed, however, Galileans were not under Jerusalem's political jurisdiction. Herod Antipas had been the Roman-appointed ruler of Galilee for over thirty years by the time of Jesus' ministry. We have no evidence that the Pharisees lived in Galilee or that Antipas permitted the Pharisees, who were apparently based in Jerusalem, to exercise some sort of surveillance in Galilee. Indeed, Galilee had been under Jerusalem rule for only a hundred years, just prior to the birth of Jesus. Otherwise Galilee had a history very different from that of Jerusalem and Judea for over 800 years by the time of Jesus.

g. Modern Western readers tend to assume that Mark is addressed to individual private readers. Many of those who have recently discovered Mark as literature assume that it is to be read like modern prose fiction, with all the presuppositions of modern print culture. In the ancient Roman empire, however, only a tiny percentage of people could read, and printed books did not exist. Mark's story, therefore, was composed in an oral communication environment and would originally have been repeatedly performed orally to communities of listeners.

In addition to those major assumptions that have become problematic are many less important interrelated ones, such as that synagogues were religious buildings in which Judaism was practiced or that a standardized Jewish scripture already existed in widely circulated written form. Some interpreters still even refer to the nascent Hebrew scriptures as the "Old Testament," even though no New Testament had yet been defined. In the course of our rethinking of Mark and Mark's context, we will find it necessary repeatedly to replace such misconceptions, along with the more determinative assumptions listed above.

Many recent interpreters of Mark have recognized one or more of these unwarranted assumptions and are contributing important new approaches, insights, and perspectives. The adaptation of the techniques and methods of modern literary criticism has been particularly stimulating for recent interpretation of Mark. While a few lonely pioneers have pressed other interpreters to consider the ways in which the oral communication environment of Mark may affect interpretation of the Gospel, most interpreters simply continue on the assumptions of modern print culture. Most work on Mark and the other Gospels, moreover, continues on the standard old assumptions about the historical context, which more precise recent historical knowledge has rendered unwarranted and problematic.

It may be time, therefore, to attempt to "clean up our act" in more systematic and comprehensive ways. It may be time at least to attempt to quit working on the basis of a wide range of interrelated unwarranted assumptions and to grope our way toward more appropriate historical analysis and interpretation. Such an enterprise will be complicated and the steps taken below will necessarily be no more than exploratory, tentative, and provisional. We will regularly be reaching for comparative material, approaches, and insights from other fields, such as anthropology, historical sociology, ethnography of performance, feminist and womanist theory, political psychology, and the perspectives of subjected peoples in the modern world. Much of the exploration will simply require the practice of sound principles and methods of wide-ranging historical analysis and construction.

Steps in the Argument— the Sequence of Chapters

In this study of the Gospel of Mark, I will therefore be attempting to cut through many unwarranted interrelated assumptions and concepts to arrive at more appropriate literary and historical approaches, analyses, and constructions. Given the assumptions and prevailing views of Gospel studies and the many interrelated questions recently raised and insights recently gained, the sequence of steps in the investigation below seemed the most appropriate. Each step in this series of recognitions about Mark's story leads to the next one (or two or three). And each successive step in the investigation further complicates as well as confirms the previous ones.

1. Since Mark was composed as a story, we should be reading the whole story. This requires breaking old habits of reading it in separate verses and lessons, perhaps temporarily ignoring the later indicators of chapters and verses. Instead, we must get a sense of the overall drama of the multiple conflicts in the story as it unfolds through several steps of multiple episodes. Patterns of repetition and retrospective and prospective references in the sequence of episodes help the listeners hear the complete story. Mark, moreover, focuses on the particular history of Jesus, which it presents as the fulfillment of the previous history of the people of Israel.

2. When we grasp Mark's complete story it becomes evident that it was about and was addressed to the ancient equivalent of "third-world" peoples subjected by empire. It seems inappropriate therefore for Western Christians living comfortably in the metropolises of modern global empire to assume that Mark, like the Bible generally, was written for and to themselves. And it is equally inappropriate for modern colonized peoples who received the Bible from missionaries to assume that Mark is a European or European-American document.

Such assumptions need to be reversed, with the corresponding adjustments (major adjustments!) in attention to the context in which the story is heard and interpreted. A beginning can be made by attempting to relocate the story in the context of ancient Palestine under Roman imperial rule and to hear it as a story about subjected people, perhaps even giving voice to such people.

3. Since communications in the ancient world, especially among subjected peoples, were predominantly oral, Mark must have been performed orally to whole communities of people. Becoming critical of how our perceptions have been determined by modern print culture, we can attempt to hear the story as an oral performance by adapting recent studies in the ethnology of speaking and traditional oral narratives in other societies. Hearing Mark's story more in the live performance mode also means abandoning individualistic assumptions and entering as much as possible into a community of subjected people who would resonate with the story out of the Israelite cultural tradition in which they were rooted or with which they had identified.

4. If Mark's story was performed before a community, with some resonance with that community, then it seems unlikely that it was read as a story about individual discipleship. The understanding of Mark's Gospel as concerned primarily with discipleship, with the twelve disciples as the models, is the product of later Christian piety and theology. In Mark's story itself, the twelve do not come off very well. After Jesus calls and appoints the twelve and commissions them to help in his mission, they misunderstand and stubbornly resist the implication of his mission, and by the end of the story they betray, deny, and abandon him. We have almost certainly been missing the full story, mistaking a subplot for the main plot of the Gospel.

5. The dominant plot of Mark's Gospel focuses on Jesus, but it is not simple and not innocuous. Mark presents Jesus as a Moses- and Elijah-like prophet engaged in the renewal of the people of Israel through a sustained program of proclaiming of the kingdom of God and manifesting God's renewing power for the people in exorcisms and healings. Jesus further expands this mission to the village communities of Galilee by commissioning the twelve disciples to share in the preaching and exorcism, and he extends the societal renewal to other peoples in the villages of the surrounding territories. Almost from the beginning of the story, moreover, he carries out his renewal of Israel in pointed opposition to, and with the opposition of, the Pharisaic and scribal representatives of the Jerusalem rulers of Israel. The intense conflict reaches its climax when Jesus confronts the Jerusalem rulers in the Temple and they finally carry out their plot to destroy him by turning him over to the Roman governor for crucifixion. In an abrupt open ending, however, the vindication of the martyr-messiah clearly implies the continuation of Jesus' renewal movement in Galilee.

6. Mark's focus on historical conflict, between Jesus' renewal of Israel and the Jerusalem and Roman rulers, requires reexamination of the standard view of Mark as "apocalyptic." The latter concept, constructed synthetically a century ago from a somewhat literalistic and fantastic reading of certain ancient Judean scribal literature, implies an alienation from history and an orientation to some sort of "cosmic cataclysm." Even on a more focused comparison with particular pieces of Judean "apocalyptic" literature, Mark seems both less fantastic and yet more intensely caught up in the fulfillment of history. A close reading of Jesus' supposedly "apocalyptic speech" (Mark 13) and his conflict with the demonic forces in the exorcism episodes, indicates that both focus on Jesus' and/or his movement's opposition to the Roman imperial order and its treatment of and effects on subjected people—a further, wider dimension of the dominant plot of Mark's story.

7. Once we recognize the dominant plot of Mark's story, Jesus' renewal of Israel in Galilean villages in opposition to the Jerusalem rulers, the subplot of Jesus' controversies with the scribes and Pharisees falls more clearly into place. The old picture of the Pharisees as representative leaders of "normative Judaism" focused on the keeping of the Law and as leaders of the "synagogues" in Galilee must be abandoned as a construction of Christian theology. The conflict between Jesus and the Pharisees in Mark's story must be understood rather in terms of the differences in social location and geographical region between representatives of the Jerusalem rulers and the prophetic leader of a movement that originated in Galilean villages. The scribes and Pharisees accuse Jesus on the basis of their official Jerusalem version of Israelite (the "great") tradition, including both the "scripture" written on scrolls and their own "traditions of the elders." Jesus fires right back at them on the basis of popular Israelite (the "little") tradition, including the fundamental Mosaic covenantal "commandment(s) of God." Mark's Jesus caricatures the Pharisees as obsessed with purity and ritual but focuses his criticism on their economic exploitation and oppression of the poor (encouraging *korban* and "devouring widow's houses").

8. Recognizing that, in his controversies with the scribes and Pharisees, Mark's Jesus is not attacking but defending Israelite covenantal law opens the way to a more complete review of the relationship of Mark's story to Israelite cultural tradition. Indeed, an integral component of Jesus' program of renewal of Israel in its village communities is the renewal of Mosaic covenantal teaching. Mark presents Jesus' reaffirmation and adaptation of the Mosaic covenant as the basis of revitalized community life that is to be economically and politically egalitarian, with no manipulative aspiring after wealth and with leaders as the servants of all. Recalling the original ceremonial enactment of the Mosaic covenant as well as referring to his imminent martyr death ("my blood of

the covenant"), Jesus ceremonially renews the covenant in his final meal with the twelve as symbolic representatives of the twelve tribes of Israel.

9. Juxtaposed with the twelve, who become negative examples of leaders who stubbornly resist the egalitarian agenda of societal renewal, the women in Mark's story emerge as the paradigms of following and serving in the movement of renewal of Israel. Although the "subplot" of women begins slowly, Mark's story features a woman who has been hemorrhaging for twelve years and a twelve-year-old woman who is virtually dead as representatives of Israel responding to the power of renewal mediated by Jesus. The Syrophoenician woman is then instrumental in Jesus' agreeing that the renewal should include the surrounding non-Israelite peoples also. And at the climax of the story, after the twelve have all disappeared, women are the only figures who faithfully follow and serve and the only witnesses to the crucifixion and empty tomb— and the only links to the implied continuation of the movement in Galilee and outwards.

10. Finally, when we review the overall story, its plot and subplots, and note the particular ways in which it resonates with Israelite tradition, it is evident that the story is "in-formed" by particular (oral) "scripts" operative in the Galilean and Judean villages in which the Jesus movement represented by Mark emerged. Such "scripts" of popular movements led by new prophets like Moses, Joshua, and Elijah or by new "messiah-kings" like Saul, David, and Jehu can be seen in Josephus's historical accounts of movements contemporary with Jesus and Mark. Discerning the presence of these patterns in popular Galilean and Judean culture enables us to understand how Mark's story emerged and resonated with its historical context. And it enables us to understand how Mark's story developed from materials that had been shaped according to a popular prophetic "script" and criticized, perhaps even rejected, a popular messianic "script."

1

Taking the Gospel Whole

It is a fascinating story, full of intrigue, passion, and hope—intense struggle and painful death. In the remote villages of a "third-world" country a charismatic popular leader and his cadre worked village by village, dealing with the people's problems, revitalizing communities, organizing a movement, and proclaiming that a new social-political order was about to be established. The rulers in the capital city, concerned about his growing influence among the villagers, kept him under surveillance, and representatives of the rulers even formed a plot to destroy him. Finally the leader marched up into the capital city where he led a demonstration against the rulers, who were maintained in power by the dominant imperial regime. He boldly proclaimed that, because they had exploited and oppressed the people, they were about to be destroyed, as God established a new social order. The ruling elite, being careful not to take provocative action that might escalate the popular protest, sent out a paramilitary force by night that captured the people's leader and, after a sham trial or two, executed him publicly in an excruciatingly torturous and painful manner. Following his execution his followers, inspired by his martyrdom and convinced that he had not died in vain, continued organizing the people and revitalizing village communities.

At first take, this story sounds like one we heard in the news from Latin American and other "third-world" countries during the 1970s and 1980s. But this is a story that comes from the Bible, a story traditionally called "the Gospel according to Saint Mark." When third-world peoples hear this story they readily recognize the parallels between this story and their own life situations. North Americans and Western Europeans, however, have learned to read the Gospel of Mark very differently. Like the other Christian Gospels, it is by definition a religious story, about Jesus as the Son of God dying for our sins, or it is about Christian discipleship, challenging individual believers to follow Jesus despite their doubts and mistakes. In modern Western societies, religion has been effectively reduced to private individual belief, separated from real-life politics and economics, as institutionalized in the separation of "church" and "state." This peculiar modern Western development has limited the power and impact of Mark, which is not primarily about individual religious belief or discipleship but about struggles between and among people, indeed about the struggle for new possibilities in societal life.

The sketch of the Gospel of Mark in the opening paragraph above, of course, is only the simplest of summaries. The story as a whole is far more complex, with several serious conflicts overlapping and interwoven. At one level, the story turns on an almost "cosmic" struggle between God and Satan. The appearance of Jesus heralds the overthrow of Satan's rule through the superhuman forces of evil that have taken possession of the people. The Gospel presumes to present events of world-historical significance that are happening in the peasant villages and the capital city of a colonized country. The events constitute no less than the fulfillment of history long before prophesied by the prophets of Israel. Shortly after the authorities begin plotting how to get rid of Jesus, they also accuse him of working in the power of Satan. Right from the outset, Jesus challenges the authority of the authority figures by speaking and acting with an authority immediately evident to the people. When the authorities challenge his actions, he makes them look stupid in front of the people. Indeed, once he enters the capital city of Jerusalem, he attacks the rulers and their representatives relentlessly, as they in turn attempt to entrap and destroy him. The movement he launches spreads like wildfire among the people in Galilee and far beyond. Yet his own disciples, particularly the twelve whom he has called and appointed as his own envoys and representative leaders of the movement, utterly fail to comprehend what is happening. At the end of the story, they betray, deny, and abandon him. Meanwhile, although most of them go unnamed, women figure prominently in the story and appear as paradigms of faithful understanding of what is happening, in contrast to the faithless disciples.

The Gospel in Bits and Pieces

The Gospel of Mark could be exciting if we read the whole story. But the Gospel has usually been appropriated in bits and pieces.[1] Indeed until recently Mark was not even understood as a story. The persistence of previous ways of reading Mark continue to reduce its potential impact or even block access to the story. A brief review of what the Gospel of Mark has been understood to be and of how it has been read may help us move toward a more reflective and appropriate reading strategy. We begin with the three closely interrelated questions of (1) what the Gospel of Mark is in the first place; (2) what the wording of the text is, and (3) how we read, appropriate, and use it.

1. When today we read Mark as we would a short story or short novella, it seems obvious that it is a story—what kind of story may not be clear, but a story of considerable conflict and drama. Surely some people have read Mark as a story before, at least since the invention of the printing press and the development of widespread literacy. Both in biblical studies and among the general reading public, however, reading Mark as a story is a relatively recent experiment.[2] Indeed until very recently, Mark was not taken as a story, but as a collection of statements codified in chapter and verse or a loosely connected sequence of brief stories or lessons.

2. When we read Mark, moreover, we simply open up our Bibles and find Mark printed out, ready to read, and take for granted the existence of the text before us. That text, however, is one particular translation of the original Greek from among the many available. And both the original Greek text printed in critical editions and its (English and other) translations are modern scholarly products, and not what was written by an ancient writer supposedly named "Mark." Highly trained biblical scholars, expert in Greek, have "established" the text, and they periodically make revisions in it, based on their critical comparison of the ancient manuscripts of Mark or parts of Mark. On the basis of the Greek text thus established, individual scholars or teams of scholars then make the translations we read, sometimes striving for the best approximation of the Greek text's apparent meaning in English (or Spanish, etc.), sometimes following traditional Christian understandings of the text, and sometimes choosing more idiomatic representation in English in preference to "accurate" renditions of the apparent meaning in Greek. The possibility has been raised in recent years that Mark was not originally a text at all, written by a writer, but an oral story recited by a performer (see chapter 3 below).

3. How we are reading, appropriating, and using Mark is clearly related to how the text is conceived and arranged on the page. Mark is sometimes understood to be a collection of statements codified by chapter and verse, each statement printed as a separate paragraph, as in the King James Version of 1611. This arrangement makes it easy to cite separate verses taken from Mark—preachers in their sermons, parents in admonishing their children, and theologians or evangelists quoting "proof texts" for particular doctrines, e.g., that Jesus was "the Christ." Sometimes Mark is understood to be a collection of brief stories, as printed in the Revised Standard Version (or the NRSV) or in the Jerusalem Bible (or the NJB), which often include topical headings above each little "lesson." In this arrangement separate stories can be read in church as the scripture lessons for particular Sundays, preachers have handy "texts"

from the Word of God for their sermons, and scholars can easily categorize the stories into types, such as "healing stories" or "parables" as manageable "topics" for presentation and discussion in university or seminary classes. If Mark's story was originally an oral performance, of course, we as yet have few clues as to how it would have been heard.

How does it come about that the Gospel of Mark is understood sometimes as a bunch of statements and sometimes as a sequence of little stories or one longer story, that it has a given wording, and that it is read and interpreted in particular ways? From the variations just examined, it is evident that none of these matters is settled, stable, and secure. Why? Because what a piece of literature is understood to be, its wording, and the way it is read and interpreted, as well as what it can mean, are all determined by what have been called "interpretive communities."[3] The interpretive community with its distinctive viewpoints, reading conventions, and vested interests, might be a particular Christian denomination or the established professional guild of biblical studies, or an established national church. In the case of the King James Version, the interpretive community that established the text and appropriate interpretation was the circle of scholars sponsored by the English monarchy and responsible for the education of Anglican clergy in universities and theological schools. In the cases of the Revised Standard Version or the NRSV (used by mainline Protestant churches in the United States) and the Jerusalem Bible or the NJB (closely linked with the Roman Catholic Church), the interpretive community is the coalition of constituencies that form and support the professional guild of biblical studies (churches, synagogues, theological schools, colleges, universities, and professional societies).[4] This extensive "interpretive community," solidly established in important institutions, exercises pervasive power over biblical interpretation in society. A critical examination of some of the major ways Mark has been understood and read, however, may help in breaking the habits, overcoming the limitations, and questioning the interests of previous reading and interpretation.

Previous understanding of the Gospel of Mark as a collection of scriptural truths or as a set of scriptural lessons blocks the recognition that Mark is a story of intense and disturbing drama. Readers or hearers get no sense how the separated "verses" or "lessons" belong together in a complete story.[5] Children and adults alike who have a thorough acquaintance with stories such as "Little Red Riding Hood" or *Little House on the Prairie* or *A Christmas Carol* have no exposure to the whole story of Mark's Gospel. Most people hear or read thousand of stories during their lives, but never hear the story of Mark.[6] Besides keeping people from experiencing the whole story, reading isolated "verses" or hearing episodic "lessons" also obscures or distorts their significance in the broader context of the story. For example, in the very middle of

Mark's story Peter declares that Jesus is "the Messiah" (8:29). Shortly thereafter in the narrative, however, Peter rebukes Jesus for announcing that he has to go up to Jerusalem and be killed, and Jesus rebukes him right back, saying "Get behind me, Satan!" (8:33). Peter has utterly misunderstood what Jesus' ministry is all about.[7] Indeed, Peter never does "get it," and we would have to read the rest of the story to realize that.

After nineteenth-century scholars determined, by critical comparison with the Gospels of Matthew and Luke, that Mark was the first Gospel composed, it was assumed to provide a historically reliable account of Jesus' life and career. It was thus read not as a story important in itself but as a source from which Jesus' ministry could be reconstructed.[8] At the beginning of the twentieth century, however, Wilhelm Wrede demonstrated in a book named *The Messianic Secret* that Mark composed his Gospel with a particular design or plot centered on keeping Jesus' identity as the Messiah secret until the end of the story. Because of persistent interest in the historical Jesus, many readers are still tempted to take Mark's story simply as a window onto historical events. But that would be naive. No story or history is an "unbiased" or "objective" record of "the way things really happened." Even a modern videotape is taken from a particular camera-angle and "point of view." All stories have a point of view. We now recognize that what we call "history" consists of (re)construction focused on significant events by historians with particular interests and concerns. Like preachers of the gospel, Mark and other Gospels are attempting to persuade and teach, provoke and reassure. Like other stories, Mark's story is told from a particular point of view and has its own agenda.

For most of the twentieth century the dominant interests and prevailing interpretive practices in the field of New Testament studies have diverted attention from Mark as a whole story. Traditionally part of Christian theological studies and focused on educating the clergy to preach on biblical texts, New Testament studies tends to produce articles, books, and commentaries focused on the theological message (or historical value) of those scriptural "lessons" printed as separate paragraphs in Bibles,[9] rather than on a Gospel or epistle as a whole.

After disillusionment with Mark as a reliable historical account of Jesus' ministry, some critical scholars focused on isolated episodes from the Gospel and developed a method of analysis called "form criticism," designed to trace the development of particular types of stories in the life of the early communities of Jesus' followers. Mark's Gospel was viewed as simply a bunch of relatively unrelated "pearls" on a string, a series of separate little stories already developed in oral tradition. The only contribution of "Mark" was to link them within a largely artificial and extremely loose overall geographical and chronological framework. The Gospel of Mark thus became in fact an obstacle to historical knowledge. Only by tearing stories out of their seemingly secondary context could the scholar trace them to earlier stages and perhaps even discern some tidbits of the precious "authentic" words of Jesus himself.

By the middle of the twentieth century, scholars examining the Gospels began to suspect that "Mark," as the first "evangelist," had done far more shaping of the Jesus traditions he used than merely string the pearls end to end. They thus discovered "Mark" not as a writer so much as a theologian—not surprising, considering that New Testament studies was traditionally a branch of theology and had been cultivated mainly in theological schools. In a method called "redaction criticism" they examined how Mark had articulated a particular "christology" or understanding of "discipleship" in his selection and "editing" of oral traditions about Jesus. These readers of Mark are thus not interested in the story but in the theology they can distill by abstracting ideas from the story. By looking at "Mark" as an independent thinker, however, they prepared the way for recognition of Mark as a sustained story.

Learning to Read Mark as a Story

Because it presents the story of Jesus in a dramatic, immediate way very different from Matthew or Luke, Mark has attracted a great deal of popular interest and scholarly analysis that has virtually mushroomed in recent decades. Many of us began reading, and assigning our students to read, Mark as a whole story. One motive was simply boredom with the tedium of detailed philological study of the words and phrases in fragments of the text. Another was frustration with the alienating distancing of the Gospel involved in historical-critical study.

Once Mark and other Gospels were being read as stories, it is not surprising that readers began borrowing techniques and theories from the study of modern literature. Courses on "the Bible as literature" had been introduced in state universities skittish about having "religious studies" in the curriculum. And many biblical scholars had been English majors in college. Taking their cues from the New Criticism which had been prominent in literary studies from the 1930s to the 1950s, they rescued the biblical text from its historical context—and from the historical author as well. Meaning could be found within the text, taken as an autonomous world unto itself. New Critics, like biblical scholars, had tended to focus on text fragments. Some of its borrowers in biblical studies, however, trained a wide-angle lens on the Gospel of Mark (or John or Luke) as a whole. In an important step for biblical studies, some of those who borrowed literary criticism were finally attempting to attend to the Gospel of Mark (or another Gospel) as a complete story![10]

As practiced by interpreters of the Gospels, narrative criticism is a peculiar blend of literary criticism and theological interpretation, which are combined in ways that seem inappropriate to Mark. By and large, narrative critics assume that Mark and the other Gospels are like, and are to be read like, modern narrative fiction such as novels and short stories. Insofar as they (like redaction critics) are still assuming Mark was an author, they portray "Mark" as an autonomous modern writer, intentionally shaping his materials and crafting a distinctively new story. But an ancient composer such as Mark probably was heavily dependent on and worked carefully with traditional materials, as emphasized in previous biblical studies. Narrative critics emphasize that Mark's plot is full of suspense, like many modern novels. But Mark has many explicit indications throughout the story about how it will come out. Linear plots are characteristic of much modern fiction. But Mark's plot is not particularly linear, as some narrative critics point out.[11] While claiming to recognize how different ancient literature was from modern fiction, literary interpreters of the Gospels devote considerable attention to character development. But Mark's characters do not develop; they play roles in the plot(s), with little or no attention to their "character." Narrative critics suggest that Mark's story, like modern fiction, engages and grips the reader. But readers of Mark in my university courses and weekend workshops are not gripped by the narrative—perhaps either because they are overly familiar with its contents or are alienated by its supposedly authoritative status as scripture or are so utterly unfamiliar with Mark's "narrative world." In general, Mark's narrative appears much less complex than and significantly different from modern fiction. It appears inappropriate and unjustified to apply the overbearing methodological apparatus developed for interpretation of modern fiction to Mark's story, at least for the beginning steps in interpretation.

Narrative criticism also consistently betrays its origin and grounding in modern theological interpretation. Perhaps because it has been part of the Christian Bible, which by definition in the modern West is religious, Mark is taken as a primarily religious story. But the story concerns Jesus as a healer and political leader, portrays the high priests as well as Herod Antipas and Pilate in political roles, and depicts the Pharisees and scribes as fund-raisers as well as lawyers. Literary critics of Mark often read modern cultural assumptions and theological concepts into Mark's story.[12] If we are to read Mark as a story on its own terms, however, we cannot be applying abstract universalistic philosophical concepts such as "the human condition." Even defining the Gospel of Mark as the story of Jesus' life and death reduces the concerns of the narrative in accordance with Christian religious and theological focus. Mark's story is more complex than that. Understanding Mark's story as concerned mainly with "discipleship" also imports into the Gospel the interpreters' modern Western Christian theological orientation (as we shall see in chapter 4).

Interpreters of Mark have also adapted "reader-response criticism" (another spin-off from New Criticism) in a further effort to overcome the distance between the text and the reader established by extrinsic historical criticism. In reader-response the meaning is not something buried in the text waiting to be discovered and extracted but is established by the actively engaged reader in the act of reading.[13] While most other approaches assume the spatial orientation of print culture, reader-response emphasizes the temporal experience of reading a narrative. What comes later in the story may alter previous understanding based on an earlier part of the story. Insofar as the story develops and meaning changes as the reader proceeds, the story does not convey meaning as some sort of stable, discoverable content, but rather as event. To the extent that "meaning" in biblical studies has become identified as such content, perhaps the concept of meaning should simply be (at least temporarily) abandoned in favor of the effect of a story on the reader.[14]

Assuming that the reader of Mark is like the modern private individual reader of novels of short stories, reader response critics imagine the reader as unacquainted with the story to start with. Readers are assumed to be involved in a process of discovery of meaning in the temporal reading process. This is highly unlikely for readers of Mark, whether ancient or contemporary, since many aspects of the "Jesus story" were or are widely familiar. Contemporary readers, of course, presuppose religious education and/or popular media—however distorting these may be to Mark's story. It is a delusion of modern Western individualism to imagine that modern readers are all that free of the culture and interlocking communities in which they are constituted as people, communities that also provide one's "interpretive community." "Texts come before us as the always-already-read; we apprehend them through sedimented layers of previous interpretation."[15] Far from coming to the story as a "virginal reader" without textual experience, readers of Mark's story probably need to summon extraordinary efforts in resisting already familiar meanings in order to discover the distinctive story of Mark, freed as much as possible from all those layers of previous interpretation. The reader-response emphasis on the temporal process of reading may well be helpful to modern Westerners completely accustomed to print culture in appreciating the way in which Mark can be heard as oral performance, the way it must have been experienced by the original audience (see chapter 3).

Even more perhaps than narrative criticism, however, reader-response simply perpetuates the modern Western individualism of the subjective private reader. The supposed benefit of reading the Gospel of Mark like other narrative fiction would be that the reader would return from the world of the text transformed, or at least challenged. But the reader presupposed is the comfortable modern liberal individual whose convictions are so lightly held that a reading that turned out to be truly transforming would be rare indeed.

A Story—and Audience—in the Public Arena of Significant Action

It is ironic that many biblical scholars have turned to literary criticism as a source of salvation, since literary criticism developed out of the vacuum left by the modern social failure of the churches and theological studies, of which biblical studies was a part. Under attack by Enlightenment reason and anti-ecclesial resentment, Modern European religion and theology retreated—or were banned—from public life to the private sphere of personal belief. Sensing the demise of religion as a force capable of holding society together, cultural conservatives invented the study of literature as a replacement for religion.[16] Since industrialization and capitalism had reduced human relations to market exchanges, they sought personal and, innocently enough, social salvation in a separate sphere of the aesthetic. Art and literature, useless in the utilitarian world of politics and commerce, were the remaining vehicles of humanization. Literature was treated as "loftily removed from any sordid social purpose."[17]

Despite the fact that the great English novels of the late nineteenth and early twentieth centuries included references to political and social affairs—the economic resources of families portrayed, for example, often coming from English imperial ventures—literary criticism steadfastly avoided any treatment of such "sordid subjects."[18] New Criticism, which dominated literary studies from the 1930s to the 1950s, insisted on interpreting literature in quarantined isolation from its historical and cultural context. The effect was to exalt the text as a fetish with mystical authority, which made it all the more attractive to biblical scholars since that is exactly what they had traditionally done with fragments of literature from their canon.

Recent literary criticism of Mark and other Gospels is thus borrowing methods developed to appropriate literature as a socially conservative, pacifying force which, oddly enough, belongs in a sphere separate from real social life. Both narrative criticism in biblical studies and reader-response criticism generally appear to be developments of "aestheticism" in modern literary theory. As the great pioneer of literary criticism in New Testament studies, Amos Wilder, noted, aestheticism was the product of "the experience of personal alienation from the public arena of significant action . . . associated with the modern [Western] cultural crisis and its texts."[19]

The people who produced Mark, however, did not share the modern Western alienation of religion from political-economic life. Jesus' relationship with

God, his "Father," drives him directly into the "public arena of significant action," first in peasant villages and then in the principle public space of the capital city, the Temple courtyard. His pursuit of God's will is precisely what leads to his torturous execution by the occupying Roman imperial troops as a presumed leader of a popular insurrection against imperial and provincial rule.

Besides recognizing that Mark's story in particular is thoroughly political, however, we are coming to recognize that stories in general are political. A "fairy tale" such as Cinderella, for example, can hardly be thought of as merely aesthetic, unrelated to the "sexual politics" of culturally prescribed gender roles. Indeed, we have come to recognize that language itself is fundamentally social. Meaning is not merely "expressed" or "reflected" in language, but is produced in and by language. The notion of a private sphere of meaning is thus an illusion, since our personal experience is simultaneously, by definition, socially rooted and socially generated. In fact, language implies social life in a particular historical situation. The words or signs that constitute language, moreover, do not have fixed meaning, but are continuously used in multiple acts of communication by people involved in social interaction. And much of that social interaction entails competing interests and social-political conflict.

There is thus no language and hence no narrative that is not embedded and implicated in particular social-political negotiations and power-relations or even outright political struggles. A narrative such as Mark's story is a symbolic social communication that both represents and interprets particular people's experience, worldview (or "ideology"), and social-political-religious agenda. The narrative, moreover, is designed to communicate and persuade, it is "rhetorical." Literary criticism often separates analysis of the story from the way it is told, its rhetoric. But a story such as Mark's does not just have a plot, it was plotted. Its plotting, characterization, and settings are as much a part of its rhetoric or "discourse" as are its typical "rhetorical devices" such as metaphor and hyperbole.[20] To "get" the "whole story," and not simply its plot, setting, and style, we must appreciate its "politics."

The preceding discussion of language, moreover, has implications for us as readers-interpreters. For all its sophisticated analysis of how the "implied reader" reads a narrative, reader-response criticism has avoided (self-)criticism of the politics of modern readers. Besides exercising suspicion on the story and the rhetoric by which it is told, however, it is essential to exercise at least a little suspicion on our own viewpoint, including the social location and political interests as well as the cultural forms we simply take for granted. Our reading and interpretation are political insofar as we are human subjects. We are practically bound up with others and the material world, and these relations are constitutive of our life rather than accidental to it. The world is not an object "out there" to be rationally analyzed, set over against a contemplative subject; it is never something we can get outside of and stand over against. Recognizing that reading is always done from some particular historical location, we must conceive of "political perspective not as some supplementary method, not as an optional auxiliary to interpretive methods current today . . . but rather as the absolute horizon of all reading and all interpretation."[21] Precisely because it exercises political power in the interpretation of biblical literature such as Mark's story, it is particularly important for biblical studies to become more self-critically aware of its assumptions, agenda, procedures, and interests.[22]

The Plotting, Outline, and Other Features of the Story

Like any other story, the Gospel of Mark should be read as a whole story. While we may be fully aware that it lacks coherence and internal consistency at points, the Gospel should be read as a whole story, analyzed as a whole, and, as much as possible, understood as a whole. The particular parts and episodes make sense only as components of and in the context of the overall narrative. In order to avoid the distraction of the modern division into chapters and verses or paragraphs with topic headings, which interrupt the flow of the story, it should be read in a translation, preferably more than one, that does not contain such indications.[23] Moreover, since the Gospel was, almost certainly, originally recited or performed orally to a group of people (see chapter 3), it should be heard in oral performance, if not "live" before a group, then on a video.[24]

To become very familiar with Mark's story will probably require several readings or hearings, which I urge the reader/listener to do with sufficient blocks of time and without distractions. The following discussion of various aspects of the story may be helpful to readers/listeners, but not necessarily all at once. Real readers/listeners may rather want to become familiar with a few aspects at once, and in subsequent readings/hearings incorporate even more sensitivity to other aspects of the story.

It is important first to gain an overview of the story as a whole before moving into closer analysis of the particular aspects of the presentation and parts of the narrative. The best way to begin may be with the fundamental questions asked of a story in Literature 101 courses, however simplistic that may seem: setting, characters, plot. As we explore these basic aspects of Mark's story, we must keep in mind that plotting, setting, characters, the overall outline, narrator, etc., are not just there, but articulate a particular view of the interests and power relations that the story is about.

Setting. Broadly speaking, Mark's story is set first in the remote district of Galilee and then in the capital city of Jerusalem. At first Jesus performs exorcisms and healings and teaches in Galilee, then extends his activities into the villages of the surrounding regions of the Decapolis, Tyre, and Caesarea Philippi. After a journey through Judea to the south of Galilee, he enters the capital city of Jerusalem, where the final dramatic events of the story take place. Yet at the very end Jesus' followers—and the story's readers as well—are directed back to Galilee. In Galilee and the surrounding regions, Jesus' activities take place mostly in village assemblies or at unspecified points in the wilderness. In Jerusalem the dramatic conflicts and intense disputes take place in the Temple or in secret places outside the city.

Characters. Corresponding to the settings, Jesus interacts mainly with peasant villagers in Galilee and surrounding areas, while being regularly challenged by the Pharisees and scribes who come "down from Jerusalem." In Jerusalem he then comes directly into conflict with the ruling circles of chief priests, elders, and high-ranking scribes. Since the story always portrays the characters in interaction with one another, often in conflict, they cannot be abstracted from the plot of the story.

Plotting. To the modern silent reader Mark's story may appear to have no plot, or at least not in the sense of a linear development that builds through complications and suspense to a climax and closure. The dominant conflict, between Jesus and the Jerusalem high priests and their representatives, the scribes and Pharisees, does intensify when Jesus confronts them directly in the Temple. But that conflict is not plotted with complications and suspense. Rather, almost from the outset the power (authority) manifest in Jesus' actions is contrasted with "the authorities'" lack of authority (1:21–28). The Pharisees and scribes, moreover, confront Jesus in episode after episode toward the beginning. Before going far into the story we already know that the Pharisees and Herodians are conspiring to destroy him (3:6). This conflict then hovers over the narrative as Jesus takes one action after another to renew the lives of individuals and society at the village level over against the ruling circles who are supposedly in charge of the society. When Jesus heads up to Jerusalem the audience already knows that there will be a face-off. Except perhaps with regard to the intensity of the conflict, there is no suspense or surprise when Jesus mounts a demonstration against the Temple and a prophetic condemnation of the high priestly rulers, as well as the ruling institution itself. But of course, from Jesus' repeated announcements in the middle of the story, the readers/hearers already know the outcome of this conflict: that Jesus will be tried by the high-priestly rulers in Jerusalem and executed by the Roman governor.

While not linear and suspenseful, unlike many modern stories, the overall plotting of Mark's Gospel is surprisingly complex, with several subsidiary conflicts interwoven with the main conflict (which will be explored further in subsequent chapters). In the first half of the story, under the theme of the kingdom of God being at hand, Jesus engages in a sustained program of exorcisms, healings, and teachings among the villagers of Galilee and nearby areas. Many allusions to typical actions of Moses (sea crossing and wilderness feedings) and Elijah (healings and multiplication of food) indicate that Jesus' actions constitute a new founding or renewal of Israel. This renewal, moreover, is pointedly set over against the ruling institutions and their representatives, the Temple, high priesthood, scribes, and Pharisees. He also calls disciples, constitutes the twelve in representative roles, and commissions them as envoys to extend his own program of activities. Particularly at the beginning but continuing into the middle parts of the story, the Pharisees and scribes challenge Jesus, who repeatedly bests them in debate. In the middle of the story, Jesus comes into increasingly sharp conflict with the disciples, particularly the inner circle of Peter, James, and John, in juxtaposition with both his three successive announcements that he must suffer, die, and rise again and his insistent teaching about egalitarian social relations in the communities of his followers.

Once in Jerusalem, following his offensive attack on the Temple, Jesus sharply criticizes or condemns the chief priests, Pharisees and Herodians, Sadducees, and scribes in a succession of disputes. His announcement finally that the Temple is imminently to be destroyed leads into a long explanation of what his followers can expect and how they should respond in traumatic historical events that will follow. The Jerusalem ruling circles of chief priests and elders finally set in motion a plan to arrest and kill Jesus, and the interwoven conflicts of the story all come to a head simultaneously. At supper with his disciples, Jesus is anointed by an unnamed woman and announces that his disciples will betray, deny, and abandon him—which, despite their protests, they proceed to do. After agonizing over his impending martyrdom in prayer with his Father, Jesus is arrested by a paramilitary posse, condemned to death in trials before both the Jerusalem rulers and the Roman governor, and mocked and crucified by Roman soldiers. Toward the end, while the disciples have indeed all abandoned Jesus, some among the many women who had been following him witness his crucifixion. And then at the empty tomb, in the abrupt and open ending of the story, they are told that he will meet them back in Galilee.

Outline. Recent scholarly readers discern different outlines or structures implicit in Mark's story. A number of the variant hypotheses about the outline of the story, of course, are determined by certain theological assumptions or literary-critical schemes. While encouraging readers themselves to discern a narrative outline in Mark, I will risk presenting the outline I discern in the story (again attempting to resist being influenced by the now standard chapter and verse codification superimposed on the story while still using them for reference purposes). Because of the combination of setting, characters, and plotting, the overall story falls into two main parts, with the action beginning and developing in Galilee and surrounding regions before climaxing in the face-off between Jesus and the rulers in Jerusalem. In each part a long speech by Jesus interrupts the action temporarily and, in effect, divides the action into semi-separate campaigns or scenes. An apparent section in the middle of the story in which the (twelve) disciples appear to be blind to what Jesus is asking them to see is framed by two stories of his healing of blind people (8:22–26 and 10:46–52). The theme of the whole story appears to be announced in Jesus' opening pronouncement that the kingdom of God is at hand (1:14–15), with the prior episodes providing the opening or prologue of the story, while the empty tomb scene provides the surprising open ending. The outline could thus be delineated as follows (reluctantly using chapter and verse references and tentative phrases for the principal steps of the story):

1:1–13	opening
1:14–15	theme: "the kingdom of God is at hand"
1:16–3:35	campaign of renewal of personal and village life in Galilee
4:1–34	speech about the kingdom in parables
4:35–8:21/26	campaign of renewal of personal and village life in and beyond Galilee
8:22/27–10:45/52	action and teaching with an eye toward climax in Jerusalem
10:46/11:1–13:2	confrontation in Jerusalem
13:3–37	speech about the future
14:1–15:47	climactic events in Jerusalem (supper, arrest, trial, crucifixion)
16:1–8	open ending

While Mark's story unfolds in these principal steps, interrupted by the speeches, there are no sharp breaks between them. The action from campaign to campaign to Jerusalem confrontation is connected by many overlapping episodes and repetition of types of episodes and important motifs (see further the discussion of oral performance in chapter 3 below). Perhaps the clearest cases of overlapping episodes and repetition come in the middle of the story. The healing of the blind man in Bethsaida (8:22–26) completes the previous campaign while framing the subsequent step of the story. The healing of Bartimaeus (10:46–52) completes that step of the story while leading the journey onward to the entry into Jerusalem. Indeed the two parts of the story are smoothly connected as the middle section of the narrative flows almost imperceptibly into the explosive confrontation in Jerusalem. Besides the three predictions of Jesus' suffering and death, Jesus begins the journey in 10:1, continues in 10:32, pauses briefly in Jericho and then resumes his journey in 10:46. At 11:1 he is still underway with his followers, just "drawing near" to Jerusalem, and finally at 11:11 he enters Jerusalem and the Temple where the ensuing climax plays out. Other connections between steps in the story are also evident, such as the prediction of the Temple's destruction (13:1–2) which concludes the confrontation in the Temple and sets the scene for the speech about what to expect in the future, after which 14:1–2 picks up on the action underway just before the speech. In another obvious connection with the confrontation section, which ended with a story about the poor widow exemplifying how the scribes "devour widow's houses," the ensuing step in the story begins with a story about a woman anointing Jesus. This episode also points ahead to the open-ended scene of the women witnessing the empty tomb and being directed back to Galilee, where the whole story began.

Distinctive features. Within this overall outline Mark's narrative displays a number of distinctive features. Relatively brief episodes are related one after another, linked only by "and" or "and immediately," words often eliminated in translations in the interest of less awkward style in modern English. The same types of stories are frequently repeated and future events explicitly predicted or anticipated so that the audience is regularly looking backward and forward throughout the story. In contrast to much modern fiction, causal links between successive episodes are largely left implicit as the overall narrative presses forward, driving to its purposive goal. At several points Mark makes narrative "sandwiches," inserting one episode into the middle another, so that they are experienced together and interpret each other. We will discuss more of Mark's narrative features in chapter 3 on Mark as an oral performance.

Subplots. The different steps in the overall narrative are held together by several major subplots and themes. It is surely significant that the theme of "messiah" appears explicitly only in Peter's declaration (8:29) at the middle of the story and in Jesus' trial and crucifixion at the end (14:61; 15:32). Jesus declares that the "kingdom of God" is "at hand" at the start of his mission, discloses its "mystery" to the disciples, and announces that it will soon come "with power" (1:12–15; 4:11; 9:1). Jesus calls the disciples at the very beginning and soon appoints the twelve and sends them out to broaden his mission; but they begin to misunderstand and at the end betray, deny, and abandon Jesus (1:16–20; 3:13–19; 6:7–13; 4:35–10:45; 14:1–16:8). The scribes and Pharisees almost immediately come down from Jerusalem to Galilee to challenge Jesus, even conspiring with the Herodians to destroy him, then persist in their challenge in the middle of the story, and finally conspire again with the Herodians to entrap him during the climactic face-off in the Temple (1:21–28; 2:1–3:6; 3:22–28; 7:1–13; 10:2–9; 12:13–17). Toward the middle of the story women appear as exemplary figures in Jesus' renewal of Israel and the Syrophoenician woman bests Jesus in debate; then toward the end, after a woman anoints Jesus prior to the last supper, and the twelve all disappear, women become his only followers who witness the crucifixion and the empty tomb.

Lines of causation. Running through the story are two lines of causation that may seem incongruous to modern Western readers. On the one hand, Jesus and his followers are free agents who act on what appears important in the historical contingencies that present themselves as the story progresses. Jesus responds to requests for healing; friends or relatives bring a man to Jesus for healing; a woman takes a bold initiative to be healed. Although already under surveillance and subject to a plot by representatives of the rulers, Jesus steadily expands the range of his activities. Finally, although he (like the audience) knows that John had paid with his life for his prophetic pronouncements against King Herod, Jesus himself, like one of the Israelite prophets of old, boldly enters the capital city of Jerusalem to proclaim and demonstrate God's judgment against the oppressive rulers and ruling institutions. And, although he skillfully avoids arrest for several days because of his protection by the crowds during the day and hiding outside the city under cover of darkness, the rulers finally capture him by hiring an inside informant to betray him. Anticipating what the outcome will be, Jesus makes a conscious decision, in his agonizing prayer, to hold to his course. This plotting of events and actors' behavior all seems familiar enough to modern readers as the successive results of actions taken in contexts of contingent historical circumstances.

Yet another line of causation is woven into the story that seems incongruous, at least to modern Westerners. Indeed, Mark itself presents the same sequence of actions and reactions just summarized in terms of unavoidable necessity: "The son of man *must* suffer many things . . . and be killed" (etc.; 8:31; 9:31; 10:33–34). The same inevitability appears in the narration of events predicted before they happen, such as the disciples' betrayal, denial, and abandonment of Jesus. The seeming incongruity is only lessened somewhat but does not disappear when we recognize that politically naive modern Western readers are simply unattuned to how certain actions in the context of certain sets of political-economic power relations will almost inevitably result in certain outcomes.[25]

Narrator. The narrator in Mark is omniscient, telling the whole story from one overarching point of view in the third person, not as a character in the story. Roaming freely through time and space, the narrator is an implied invisible presence in nearly every episode. The narrator even reveals the thoughts and emotions of the characters and supplies explanatory comments and privileged information to the audience.[26] Mark's narrator uses the protagonist (Jesus, who shares the omniscience, 2:8; 12:15) to articulate the dominant con-

ceptual point of view in the story and to sift and subordinate the other characters' point of view.[27] That Jesus' teaching has little effect on his hearers in
the story itself suggests that it is aimed at the audience, as evaluative and interpretive commentary on the action, particularly where it is signaled by "truly I
say to you," "whoever . . ." statements, and statements about "the son of
man."[28] The narrator thus appears virtually indistinguishable from the
"author" of the story. And as the narrator is close to Jesus, so the trusting and
well-informed audience is also close to Jesus.

Ending. The open ending of Mark requires special comment. To most modern readers, familiar or unfamiliar with biblical stories, it is a shock to realize
that the story ended so abruptly: having seen that Jesus' tomb is empty and
been told that he would meet them back in Galilee, the women "said nothing
to anyone, for they were afraid." This seemed so strange, even to the early
Christians familiar with the other Gospels' stories of Jesus' resurrection
appearances to his followers, that Mark was supplied with alternative, more
"appropriate" endings that appear in some ancient manuscripts. To appreciate
Mark's story, however, modern readers must resist being influenced by those
alternative endings and the endings of the other Gospels. Mark's surprise,
abrupt, open ending, is specially important for our understanding of the story,
for it keeps the audience engaged with the story. Indeed, it has the effect of
inviting the audience, already included in the narrator's confidence and sharing in Jesus'—as well as the narrator's—point of view, to become involved in
the continuation of the story.

Ambiguities in Mark's Story

Many modern Western readers have come to expect Mark and other biblical
literature, as "the revealed word of God," to be straightforward and unambiguous in its statements and meaning. It is difficult to entertain the possibility
that "biblical" writings might use language ambiguously, ironically, or sarcas-
tically. But Mark's story is simply full not only of ambiguity, but of incongruity
and double meaning. We would miss the richness and subtlety of the story if
we fail to recognize and appreciate many incongruities in a whole spectrum of
interrelated rhetorical devices such as metaphor, irony, and paradox that are
deployed in Mark. In all of these rhetorical tactics Mark uses language figuratively, requiring the audience to "figure it out," since it cannot be taken only
at face value.[29]

Metaphor. Perhaps the simplest to recognize are metaphors (and similes),
comparisons which derive their power from the juxtaposition of dissimilar
things. John announces that while he has baptized people with water in the
Jordan River, Jesus "the mightier one" will "baptize you with the Holy Spirit."

Later in the story "baptism" is used as a metaphor for Jesus' anticipated martyrdom. The "kingdom of God" is the controlling metaphor of Mark's story, and it remains no less a metaphor when we realize that in Mark it means that God is literally in the process of coming to rule the people, with clear implications of condemnation and exclusion of the actual Jerusalem rulers and Roman rulers currently holding power.[30] The numerous metaphors in Mark's story include nicknames, as when Jesus gives Simon, the leader among the twelve, the nickname "Rock" (*Petros* in Greek, 3:16).

It has become customary to speak of the many complex, often narrative metaphors used by Jesus in the Gospels as "parables." Jesus uses them extensively, not simply in the parables speech and the attack against the high priesthood in the climactic confrontation in Jerusalem. "Those who are healthy have no need of a doctor, but those who are sick. I have come to call not the righteous but the sinners" invites the audience to make a judgment in response to the Pharisees' challenge of Jesus' eating with "toll collectors and sinners." "The wedding guests cannot fast while the bridegroom is with them" makes a comparison with the festive time of the presence of Jesus' preaching and healing that is being presented in the narrative. The way the parables function in the narrative is explicitly stated in the parables speech: "With what can we compare the kingdom of God, or what parable will we use for it?" (4:26, 30). Some have seen the longer "explanation" of the parable of the sower in terms of types of hearers (4:13–20) as the interpretive key to the whole Gospel.[31]

The importance of parables as extended metaphors throughout Mark's story suggests that other aspects of the narrative may have double meaning in a somewhat similar use of language. For example, Jesus' cursing of the fig tree, juxtaposed sandwich-style with his prophetic demonstration against the Temple, makes clear that the Temple is about to "wither" because it has not borne fruit (11:12–23). That the demon which possesses the man so violently in Gedara/Gerasa turns out to be named *Legion*, the Latin term for a division of the Roman army, suggests that the possessed man is also symbolic of the subjected people more generally, whose lives and land have became occupied by a violent alien force, the Romans. When *Legion*, now cast out of the man by Jesus, then enters the herd of swine and plunges headlong into the *Sea*, to the West, whence the Roman legions had come, the double meaning is not lost on the audience (5:1–20). Other healing and exorcism stories are also symbolic. The two healings of the blind that frame the section in which the disciples seem so utterly "blind," besides offering episodes of real healing, also suggest that at least some people "see" what Jesus is doing and talking about (8:22–26; 10:46–52). And that the women healed in the "sandwiched" healing episodes are both characterized with the number *twelve*, which would evoke the thought of the twelve tribes of Israel, suggests that, besides being particular healed women, they are symbolic of the healing of the whole people of Israel (5:21–43).

Irony. While metaphor simply draws a comparison, irony expresses both aspects of an incongruity. Irony involves both a seeing and a "seeing through." Some ironies in Mark are simply "verbal ironies," which the audience can "see through" almost immediately. In response to the scribes and Pharisees' charge that his disciples do not observe "the traditions of the elders," Jesus retorts in sarcasm (irony), "*Well* do you set aside the commandment of God in order to keep your [the elders'] tradition!" Judas, one of the circle closest to Jesus, betrays him, and betrays him with a kiss. Other verbal irony may not become clear until later in the story. Besides being a metaphor, "Rock" is an ironic name, seen at the dramatic climax of the story when, after protesting that he will remain true to the end, Simon first falls asleep while Jesus is agonizing over his coming crucifixion in Gethsemane and then denies Jesus three times while he is on trial for his life. Similarly, the extended metaphor about the doctor, the healthy, and the sick appears to be also ironic, for surely Jesus and the audience do not really understand the Pharisees as "healthy," i.e., righteous. The audience knows that Jesus is mocking his accusers. At the climax of the story, in which Jesus has uttered prophecy after prophecy, including those condemning the Temple and high priesthood, the high priests command him to "prophesy" at his trial (11:15–18; 12:1–12; 13:1–2; 14:65). Mark even employs double ironies. While Jesus is suffering on the cross, the chief priests and elders mock him as "the messiah, the king of Israel" (their words are ironic because they believe that to be false, since he is obviously a failure and an imposter). But insofar as the role of the anointed king of Israel was to restore the people in opposition to their foreign rulers, Jesus has just been doing precisely that in the preceding narrative.

These last examples come close to "dramatic irony," which persists and reverberates through the narrative, engaging the audience in reflection on the incongruity. The narrator presents much of the subplot of the disciples in a series of ironies. When the twelve ask Jesus to explain the parables, he declares, "To you has been given the secret of the kingdom of God, but for those outside, everything comes in riddles in order that 'they may . . . not understand.'" If it is not already clear from that juxtaposition of the disciples' failure to understand despite having been given the secret, then it becomes clearer and clearer later in the story that the disciples behave like outsiders, as they embody the seed sown on "rocky ground," the ones who (like their leader "Rock") "hear the word," but when trouble arises, immediately fall away (4:16–17). The disciples, who have already, despite their incredulity, seen Jesus feed five thousand in the wilderness, again a few episodes later cannot possibly imagine how one could "feed these people with bread here in the desert"

(6:30–44; 8:1–4), and they still do not have a clue even after the second miraculous feeding (8:14–21). Shortly thereafter, even after Jesus has insisted that they receive children, the disciples turn them away (9:37; 10:13).

Paradox. The most extreme form of incongruity or double meaning in Mark is paradox. A paradox is a contradiction that is nevertheless true in some way. Paradoxical statements are often oxymorons. For example, the scribes accuse Jesus of "casting out demons by the ruler of demons," which he sharpens in his retorts: "How can Satan cast out Satan?" The chief priests' mockery of Jesus on the cross, that "he saved others [but] he cannot save himself" forces the audience to ponder that paradox, presumably by thinking forward to the longer perspective of the empty tomb and the ongoing struggle of the movement that identifies with the crucified but now raised Jesus. At points, after Jesus uses paradoxical statements as teaching devices, Mark has Jesus explain the paradoxical statements in the ensuing statements. "For those who want to save their life will lose it, and those who lose their life for my sake and the gospel's will save it." The paradox points to the situation of repression and persecution of the audience of Jesus' followers (the movement) to which the Gospel is addressed. Steadfast loyalty and solidarity (with Jesus' own martyrdom for the cause) is possible since eventually the current crisis of the political struggle will be resolved in God's judgment. The paradoxical situation will be resolved (only) in the future (judgment).

The double meanings woven into the fabric of Mark's narrative lead us to recognize that, much to the dismay of those who would mine Mark as a vein of unambiguous christological statements, what have been taken as "titles" of Jesus may be, in effect, metaphors. In Mark "son of man" appears only as a self-reference by Jesus or as a future figure "coming with the clouds of heaven," and never as a "christological title" of or for Jesus. Does the story really present Jesus as the "king of the Judeans/Israel"? The term is spoken or inscribed only by the rulers or soldiers who condemn or execute Jesus. The chief priests' mockery is indeed ironic. But that does not mean that Mark's narrator presents Jesus as "the Messiah" or the "king of the Jews." Mark clearly rejects the idea that the messiah is the "son of David" (12:35–37). In that and in other ways, Mark does not portray Jesus as the messiah recognizable in any contemporary Judean literature. So is Mark presenting Jesus as the messiah while redefining what *messiah* means, as is often claimed, or is Mark suggesting that Jesus was not in any recognizable way the anointed king of Israel?

Mark's narrative is simply full of dramatic paradoxical turns as well as metaphors and ironies. Jesus proclaims the kingdom of God but winds up executed by order of the imperial governor. He is declared God's beloved son at the beginning, but dies apparently forsaken by God in the end. He is represented as "king of the Judeans" precisely after he is tried and handed over for crucifixion by the high-priestly rulers of the Judeans. The authority figures in the story have no authority among the people. The very disciples recruited, appointed as the twelve representatives of Israel, and given the secret of the kingdom of God fail to understand what is happening and finally betray, deny, and abandon the one whose project they were commissioned to advance. No wonder that modern interpreters keep coming up with oxymorons themselves to characterize Mark's story—as that of a "crucified Christ" or a "martyr Messiah" or "discipleship" modeled on those who betray, deny, and abandon. More to the point is that Mark's story, precisely through such multiple paradoxes and other incongruities in the narrative summons the audience to live out such paradoxes in their own engagement in and response to the story.

What Kind of Story is Mark?

When we read Mark, what kind of story are we reading? Given the individualistic orientation of modern Western culture, it tends to be taken as biography. Recent literary criticism, focusing attention on the story itself and countering the previous tendency to mine Mark's text for its theology, has reinforced the view that Mark is a biography of Jesus. A closer examination of the pattern and function of Mark's story and the literature to which it has been compared requires us to rethink the question of Mark's "genre."

Comparisons of Mark with pre-Markan materials concerned with Jesus have turned up no evident pattern from which Mark can have developed. The term *gospel* itself, in its earliest usage, referred to preaching about Jesus, and was not applied to literature about Jesus until the second century.[32] That Mark evolved in linear fashion from the "early Christian *kerygma* (preaching) about Jesus is no longer convincing, partly because an intermediate stage or pattern between brief episodic stories such as healings or parables and the full story of Mark appear to be lacking."[33] The old notion that Mark consists of a passion narrative with a long introduction now seems much too simplistic.

Most recent discussion of the genre of Mark has therefore focused on literature in the Hellenistic Roman world that could have provided a model for Mark's story. Because no particular type of contemporary literature is all that similar to Mark in convincing ways, no clear consensus has emerged among the various possibilities of biography, history, novellas/romances, and hero narratives. Literary critics concerned with genre are fairly candid that they are looking for somewhat vague sets of unexpressed expectation generated by existing literatures in a culture. They identify particular genres not in neat, mutually exclusive forms, but on the basis of multiple partial criteria.[34]

Similarities between Mark and Hellenistic-Roman biographies, or "lives," have attracted particular attention. A closer examination of Mark's story, however, suggests that many of those similarities are only apparent and very partial. In fact, the differences between the "lives" and Mark's story seem more fundamental. Hellenistic-Roman lives were written of three types of famous figures: kings, generals and other prominent political figures, famous poets or orators, and famous philosophers.[35] Far from fitting any of those types, Mark's Jesus is a charismatic peasant prophet. Hellenistic-Roman lives use the episodic narratives of sayings, anecdotes, and miracles to illustrate the hero's character or virtue. But it seems highly doubtful that Mark's purpose is to portray the character of Jesus—or, in more theological mode, Jesus as "Messiah" or "the Son of God."[36] Mark rather uses the healings, exorcisms, feedings, and teachings to portray Jesus as God's agent in the manifestation of the kingdom of God among the people.[37] The literary function of the Hellenistic-Roman "lives" is to display the dominant cultural values as exemplified in the hero. But Mark presents Jesus as a protagonist who, in bringing special revitalizing powers to the people and challenging the dominant order, inaugurates a change in the historical situation.[38]

Lumping Mark together with the other narrative "Gospels" may also involve a procedural problem. If Mark is understood as the first "Gospel," followed and adapted by Matthew and Luke, then the narrative "Gospel" genre was developing and changing. Moreover, Matthew and Luke display similarities with Hellenistic-Roman lives in certain ways that Mark does not, such as their inclusion of miraculous birth stories. Hellenistic-Roman lives of statesmen and philosophers may indicate how ancient (and modern) readers familiar with them may have understood Mark, but not the genre that Mark was following and adapting. Recent reflections on genres suggest that indeed they develop and change.[39] If Mark's story was the first "Gospel" then we should be sensitive for the ways Mark innovatively combined old and new elements into a new kind of story to which Matthew and Luke gave a more composite "classic" form.

Recent literary analysis of Mark as similar to modern fiction seems almost to obscure the fact that the story is about historical events. Literary analysis of genre, of course, includes not simply form, but content and function as well. In reaction against the nineteenth-century reading of Mark as referring transparently to historical events, and assuming a post-Enlightenment "scientific" criterion of truth, biblical scholars rejected Mark's narratives, especially the miracle stories, as "myth," not "history." Theological interpreters retreated defensively to the view that Mark's Gospel is merely a proclamation of a gospel message about Jesus. Even if certain pre-Markan material had connections with historical events, Mark's story itself is an imaginative construction devoid of historical value. Mark's "narrative world," however, is clearly not fiction in the sense of an imaginary or invented world. Nor is Mark's story simply biography. It is also about the movement that Jesus is spearheading, ostensibly headed by the twelve, and about an extreme crisis in the history of a subject people living under foreign imperial rule, and about a struggle between God and demonic forces. Mark even presents the history of the movement Jesus is spearheading as part of the far longer history of the people of Israel that is known in written historical records (what later became the Hebrew Bible). Indeed, Mark claims to be telling of the fulfillment of history, as Jesus himself announces at the outset (1:14–15) and reassures the disciples in his second long speech toward the end about what they should expect in the imminent future. In this connection, Mark refers to world-historical events that were about to unfold, in the widespread Judean and Galilean revolt against Roman rule and the Roman army's brutal devastation of the people and destruction of the capital city of Jerusalem and its Temple.

Given that Mark was apparently the first "Gospel" story (the first instance of a newly evolving genre) and that it repeatedly refers, explicitly as well as implicitly, to events and stories in the history of Israel, we should explore the ways it drew and built upon narrative forms in Israelite cultural tradition. Most obvious, at first glance, might be ways in which Mark's narrative draws upon narrative traditions of the prophets Moses and Elijah, the most prominent figures in popular Israelite tradition as the founder and renewer of Israel, respectively. It has been clear for some time, as readers of the Gospels shed narrower Christian doctrinal schemes, that Mark does not portray Jesus as founding a new religion, Christianity, in rejection of an old one, Judaism. Mark is rather telling how Jesus launched a movement of renewal among Israelite villagers that spread among villagers in the surrounding areas. It seems possible that, in terms of its function, Mark's story is the grounding history of origins of (one branch of) that Jesus movement as a renewal movement of the people of Israel and other subject peoples over against the Jerusalem rulers and Roman imperial rule.

Modern Western readers may have difficulty taking seriously Mark's seemingly presumptuous claim to be recounting the fulfillment of history. Indeed, modern Western readers, including biblical scholars, have long since consigned Mark's story to the category of religion. At most Mark might be a kind of "salvation history." Real history consists of events in the "public arena of significant action" as reconstructed by real historians, such as Herodotus and Thucydides or the Jewish historian Josephus in Western antiquity. But it is unnecessary and even inappropriate to seek an ancient generic model of "history" in order to conclude that Mark is a historical story.[40] We would be again imposing the assumptions of modern Western culture. Recently Indian historians presenting "subaltern studies" have complained that in its imperial arrogance, Western culture imagines that only the Western imperial nations have history. Movements among the ordinary people that attempted to resist British imperial domination of India, for example, were dismissed by Western historians as merely "religious" movements. To continue to categorize the Gospel of Mark as merely "religious" would simply continue to deny it entry into the "public arena of significant action"—and to ensure that it is a pacifying and comforting story, not a disturbing one.

Restoring the Story to History and History to the Story

Reacting against historically oriented biblical studies, recent literary interpreters tend to sever Mark's story from its historical context, presuming that the "story world" can be explored as an autonomous world unto itself. They are following and repeating their mentors in New Criticism, who insisted on treating the literary text in isolation, in their reaction against the excesses of previous extrinsic criticism. Mark can thus be enjoyed in uncomplicated separation from the world of its origins as well as from the real world of embodied readers.[41] Literary critics also often imagine virginal readers. As noted above, however, real readers in a society full of print and other media and already influenced by the biblical heritage of that society, have plenty of textual experience directly or indirectly related to Mark's story. But just think of what a virginal reader sent alone into the narrative world of Mark's story would be missing, how innocent and uneventful her or his reading experience would be. Should we intentionally continue to read and understand Mark as uninformed readers?[42]

In order to "get" more of the "whole story," to even begin to understand much of what it is about, modern Western readers desperately need to know about the historical situation from which it comes and which it addresses. This is true for a number of reasons. Although we have a great deal of familiarity with bits and pieces of Mark's story simply from living in a culture in which the Bible, and especially lore about Jesus, has played a central role, we are seriously uninformed about history. The result is not as innocent or neutral as uninformed readers finding things in the story that they do not and cannot understand unless and until they become more historically informed. It is more serious, distorting, and self-limiting than missing a few beats or not "getting" a few innuendos and implications.

Without an awareness of history and historical difference and distance, we tend to assimilate what we read into our own familiar experience. We simply domesticate Mark's story, or find in Mark what we already know. Those already well-imbued with modern Western individualistic Christian faith and theology, for example, find just that in Mark. It is a story about discipleship!

It is even addressed to me! If they are called "chief priests" they must be "leaders," indeed "Jewish leaders," and they must be "religious leaders" as opposed to the "political" authorities such as the Roman governor or Caesar. "Render to Caesar the things that are Caesar's and to God the things that are God's" must involve the difference between politics and taxes, on the one hand, and religious commitment on the other, as in the modern separation of church and state. A "synagogue" must be a religious building where Jews gather to worship their God. Almost all of those examples involve serious misinformation, partly based on mistranslation rooted in the limited knowledge and historically distorting theological schemes of previous generations of biblical scholars.[43]

The meaning of a story, as well as a word or phrase, depends on a meaning context. Unless we simply want to assimilate the story into our own modern Western historical meaning context, then we must know a good deal about the ancient historical meaning context of Mark's story, the context to which it was responding and in which it was told. Knowing something about that historical situation before hearing the story and further investigating it as we hear the story again and again should deepen and enhance our understanding of the story—including the degree to which we begin to realize what we do not understand about the story. Furthermore, insofar as the events portrayed and their world-altering significance are important in and to Mark's story, we will be interested not just in knowledge about the historical context of the story, but about the events narrated in the story.

Finally, given the pervasive irony, ambiguity, and double meaning woven into Mark's story, we clearly also need knowledge of the historical context to understand the innuendos, nuances, and implications. One might even say that modern Western readers' whole relationship to Mark's story is ironic. We who enjoy lives of plentiful resources and relative privilege because we reside in the modern imperial metropolis have as a "classic" or as "scripture" a story about resistance to an ancient imperial order composed from within and for a movement among peoples subjected to that empire. The next chapter will explore precisely the origin and purpose of Mark's story in historical context.

2

Submerged People's History

Its plot and setting indicate that the Gospel of Mark is about a subjected people in a strange, distant, "Oriental" country. The story does not take place in Rome or Athens, the ancient equivalents of New York City or London, or in the countryside of Italy, the ancient equivalent of Iowa or Nebraska. Rather, the story takes place in Palestine, the ancient equivalent of modern Iran or Afghanistan. Mark's story, moreover, is oriented toward the rural villages of a remote district of the country, Galilee, and is hostile toward the capital city Jerusalem, from which rulers sponsored by the Roman empire maintained a tenuous control of the populace. Ancient Romans and Greeks would not have known where Galilee was, just as modern Americans had no idea what was going on in remote Iranian villages prior to the eruption of the Iranian revolution against the Shah, whose rule was sponsored by the United States.

Was Mark Written for Us?

Mark as a story about a renewal movement among a people subjected by empire has been obscured in its reading as Christian Scripture in the modern Western world. Virtually "by definition," as part of the Holy Bible, the Gospel of Mark is understood as religious literature. Probably most reading of the Bible in general and of Mark in particular is done collectively in church services and individually in devotional exercises. In Europe and North America, moreover, the Bible and its interpretation have become increasingly institutionalized as religious. We find the Bible and books about the Bible in the "religion" section of bookstores or in the religion section of libraries. College and university courses in biblical studies are offered in religion departments. Interpretation of the Bible as an academic field developed and remains grounded in theological studies and theological schools dedicated to the train-ing of ministers and priests.

Even a minimal acquaintance with Mark's story and the difference between the historical situation in which it was composed and our own as modern read-ers will suffice to illustrate how some of the ways Mark has been understood religiously or theologically simply do not fit the story.

The Gospel of Mark is commonly understood in terms of Christ dying for people's sins or as a presentation of Jesus as the Son of God. Theologi-cally oriented interpreters study Mark to extract its "christology," its pre-sentation of Jesus as the Christ/Messiah and the Son of Man. In Mark's story, however, the protagonist does not die for others' sins. And, as suggested at the end of chapter 1, Mark's story is ambiguous, perhaps even ironic, in the way it presents Jesus as adapting the role of "messiah" and speaking about the "son of man."

Much recent theologically based interpretation of Mark simply assumes that Mark is a story about Christian discipleship, in which the ambiguously portrayed disciples function as provocative paradigms for the repentant disci-pleship of the reader. Mark presents the disciples so negatively through the middle and especially the end of the story, however, that it is difficult to see how the reader could possibly identify with them (see further chapter 4).

Not surprisingly, given its scriptural function as one of the principal found-ing documents of Christianity, Mark is understood as a story about the origins of the supposedly universal and spiritual religion of "Christianity" from the supposedly legalistic and narrowly ethnic religion of "Judaism." Unfortu-nately for this "reading," neither "Judaism" nor "Christianity" existed yet as an identifiable "religion" at the time Mark was composed. It is seriously mis-leading, however, for modern Westerners to read Mark as a religious story or a story about (the origins of a) religion, for religion means something very dif-ferent in modern Western societies than it did in most other societies. In the United States in particular, with the official separation between church and state, we assume that religion is separate from politics and economics. In most traditional societies, including ancient Galilee and Judea, however, religion was inseparable from politics and economics.

We may begin to realize that standard reading habits, the perspective and concepts through which we read the story, are blocking our discernment of what the story may be about. Is it possible that when Jesus proclaims that "the kingdom of God is at hand" in Mark 1:14–15 he means that literally, not metaphorically, and exclusively, such that the imperial rule of Caesar was on the way out? Is it possible that the "Ten Commandments" cited in Mark 10:17–22 are more about economic relations in society than about worshiping God or individual morality?

Once we recognize the limitations of the situation from which we read Mark, perhaps it would help to consider other perspectives. The contrast with which we began just above, between Mark as a story about a movement among imperially subjected people and Mark as a scriptural story of salvation, cannot but remind us of the modern juxtaposition of the Bible and imperially subjected people. The Bible, including the Gospel of Mark, played a key role in Western colonization of Africa and Asia. As Africans have pointed out, when the Europeans came, the Europeans had the Bible and the Africans had the land, but after a while the Europeans had the land and all the Africans had left was the Bible. Many Africans were taught by Europeans in mission schools and theological seminaries to understand the Bible in European terms as about personal spiritual salvation. But Africans also heard other voices in the Bible, heard stories and messages that the colonizers could not hear, and "saw" aspects of biblical stories that most Europeans and North Americans could not see. Most important perhaps, they recognized that the story takes place in the ancient equivalent of a colonized or "third world" country such as their own and that the story climaxed in the execution of the leader of an indigenous people's movement by the imperial military governor.[1]

With regard to Mark, and perhaps other biblical literature, what the field of biblical studies has done is similar to what other Western academic fields have done to (formerly) colonized people's history and culture. History that matters, that is politically and economically important, is the history of the dominant (European and American) nations, the imperial powers. Other peoples are even dismissed as "peoples without history."[2] Those peoples do have histories. And although it is difficult for Western scholars who belong to the cultural elite to imagine, even peasants have repeatedly proven capable of generating movements, with their own leadership and often in direct opposition to their own "native" as well as imperial rulers. But because Western history is what counts as history, the histories of subjected peoples have been submerged, kept hidden from view.

"More civilized" European and American nations, of course, have often extracted not only economic resources from the subject countries, but also imported their "cultural" resources, such as their "religion." The imperial countries have long been fascinated by the exotic "Oriental" or "Eastern" religions, such as "Buddhism," "Hinduism," "Sufism," and, more recently, "shamanism"—interestingly all "religions" supposedly without political implications. When movements of resistance occurred in subjected countries such as India, they were simply dismissed as of little political significance because they were merely "religious" movements. More recently, if obviously religious people such as priests and nuns were involved in resistance or revolutionary movements, they were simply labeled "communists." As we are learning from recent movements in Iran, Afghanistan, and elsewhere in the Middle East, however, such "religious" movements have rather ominous political implications and, in fact, can hardly be dismissed as if they were "merely religious" or mere religious facade for a political movement.

Once we recognize that the Gospel of Mark and other New Testament literature are about people subjected by an ancient empire, we may begin to see what has happened in modern biblical studies. What may have been an indigenous people's movement and its leader were taken as being primarily "religious." Since what mattered, what emerged from that movement was *a* religion, Christianity, i.e., its own religion, Western historical biblical studies constructed the movement and its literature as the history of its own religion.

Interestingly enough with regard to the Gospel of Mark in particular, this process of reduction to religion and appropriation by the dominant ancient Western metropolis, i.e., Rome, began quite early. Within a century after Mark was composed the "tradition" had developed that the Gospel of Mark was written in and for the church in Rome by Mark, the interpreter of Peter who wrote down "accurately but not in order" all that he remembered of what was said or done by the Lord. Not coincidentally Rome was quickly becoming the dominant church in Christianity, and Peter, the "Rock" on which Matthew's Jesus said he would build his church (Matt. 16:18–19), was supposed to have been the first bishop of Rome. Until recently, at least, established biblical studies has accepted this tradition.[3] The result is that Mark's portrayal of a Galilean prophet's sustained confrontation with the Jerusalem rulers and their Roman sponsors was reduced to incidental stage-setting for the passion and crucifixion of Christ, which became the basis of established Christianity in the West. When Mark is reduced to a religious story for individual modern Western readers, moreover, Jesus' sustained public campaign of preaching and healing in remote village communities and his execution by the Romans as a rebel leader becomes a mere backdrop for the devout individual disciple's struggle between guilt and repentance, between doubt/denial and recommitment.

In today's supposedly "postcolonial" and "multicultural" world it should be possible to take another look at biblical literature such as the Gospel of Mark. The Gospel is a story about a movement among ancient Galilean and other peasants addressed to Greek-speaking people who must have identified with that popular movement led by Jesus. Starting with the setting of Mark in a "colonized" or "third world" country, the obvious first step is to gain some sense of ancient Judeans and Galileans as people subjected to empire. Then we can reread the story to see if we discern a history of people who have been previously submerged. Finally, it may be possible to discern whether, as asked recently by "third-world" scholars, the Gospel of Mark addresses subjected people and gives voice to their concerns.

Galileans and Judeans under Imperial Rule

For centuries prior to the time of Jesus, the people of Israel had languished under the rule of one foreign empire after another. Yet memory of the time when Israel was a free people was still very much alive among the people. This is vividly evident in the Gospel of Mark. For example, during the climactic events of the story, Jesus and his disciples observed the feast of Unleavened Bread, the Passover, the meal that celebrated Israel's origin in the exodus events, their liberation from subjection and slavery to the Egyptian empire. However, that Roman troops were in Jerusalem to keep order during the Passover and that Jesus was crucified by order of the Roman military governor illustrate even more dramatically that Israel was still subject to empire. Indeed, Mark's story is full of references and allusions to Israel's origin, historical experiences, and current imperial subjection. We must briefly review the history of the people of Israel in order to even begin to understand "where it is coming from."

Memories of the wondrous origins of Israel in the exodus and wilderness wandering are evident at key points in Mark. Jesus' sea crossings and feedings in the wilderness in the middle of the story recall the formation of Israel as a free people under the leadership of Moses, who led the escape from slavery in Egypt through the Reed Sea and fed the starving people in the wilderness on the way to their land (Exod. 3–17). The recitation of the basic "commandments of God" to the young man who inquires about "eternal life" recalls the giving of the Mosaic Covenant as the constitution of Israelite society (Exod. 19–24). The twelve tribes of Israel then lived in village communities on their land for many generations in justice and equality directly under the covenantal rule (kingdom) of God, with no Pharaoh or other human king demanding tribute or forced labor (Judges 2–9). When the Philistine rulers of the city-states on the coast threatened to bring Israel under their domination, the young David, the prototypical messiah ("anointed one"), led the people in successful resistance (2 Sam. 2–5). When they enter Jerusalem crying "Blessed be the kingdom of our ancestor David, which is coming," Jesus' followers allude to that liberating popular kingship of the messiah David.

David, the Lord's "anointed," however, built an imperial monarchy, first conquering the Canaanite city of Jerusalem as his capital and then subduing the resistant Israelites themselves with the aid of his foreign mercenary troops (2 Sam. 5–22). His son Solomon imposed forced labor on the Israelites to build the original temple in Jerusalem. Unwilling to submit to such oppression, the ten northern tribes of Israel in the areas of Samaria and Galilee rebelled against Jerusalem's rule and formed their own kingdom (1 Kgs. 5:13–18; 12)— and their descendants did not again come under Jerusalem rule until a hundred

years before the birth of Jesus. When king Ahab attempted to impose Canaan-
ite-style rule and its accompanying royal fertility religion, Elijah led widespread popular resistance, with miraculous feedings and healings of the
suffering people, of which Jesus' healings and feedings are obviously reminiscent (1 Kgs. 17–19; 21).

The northern Israelites were conquered by the Assyrian empire and
thereafter Galilee and Samaria were placed under separate imperial administrative divisions of a succession of imperial regimes. Similarly the city of
Jerusalem was conquered by the Babylonian empire and the people of Judah
were placed under imperial administration. By the time of Jesus, the people
of Israel had lived under the rule of foreign empires for centuries. Imperial
rule affected the lives of the people in both blatant and subtle ways. The
empire determined the very arrangement by which the Judean priestly aristocracy controlled the land and people of Palestine. The Persian imperial
regime sponsored the building of the "second" Temple for "the god who is
in Jerusalem" (Ezra 1:3) when they restored the Judean ruling class to power
from their previous exile into Babylon. The Persians also encouraged the
composition of the Torah (the Law, the Five Books of Moses), which became
the (colonial) constitution and law book of the Judean temple-state. The
arrangements made by Persian officers such as Ezra and Nehemiah required
the people to render up various "first fruits," "tithes," and other dues to the
priestly aristocracy maintained in place by the imperial regime (e.g., Neh.
10:35–39).[4]

As we know from a wide range of Judean prophetic and apocalyptic (revelatory) literature, the "Second Temple" and the ruling high-priestly family
were never very widely accepted even among the scribal circles who worked
for the priestly aristocracy in various connections (e.g., Mal. 3–4; *1 Enoch*
94–102; and many passages in the Dead Sea Scrolls). Since their own position
of power and privilege depended on their cooperative relations with the imperial regime, the Judean priestly rulers were often tempted to compromise with
the empire in ways unacceptable to the people and to scribal circles engaged
in the cultivation of Israelite traditions.

The Persian empire seemed benign compared to the Western empires that
took power in the aftermath of Alexander the Great's conquest of the ancient
Near East. The Seleucid regime that took control of Judea around 200 B.C.E.,
particularly Antiochus Epiphanes IV in the 170s and 160s, pressed Greek cul-
tural-political forms as well as the usual economic demands upon Jerusalem
and the Judean people. When Antiochus forced Judea into the "Catch 22"
alternative of abandoning their God and traditional covenantal way of life or
being killed, he touched off two important developments among the Judean
people.

First, desperate to understand how God had allowed them to come into such straits, they sought special revelations (*apocalypses* in Greek) through dreams and visions. Through "apocalyptic" (or "revelatory") visions such as those in the book of Daniel (chaps. 7–12) they became convinced that God was still in control of historical events and had not abandoned them. God would eventually—soon, in fact—judge the oppressive beastly empire, restore the people in their land, and vindicate leaders of the people who might become martyred in the course of their resistance to imperial tyranny. Since God could not possibly be directly responsible for their oppression and suffering, Judeans attributed the worst evils they were experiencing to superhuman spirits or demons. Thus, as we know from the Dead Sea Scrolls as well as the Gospel of Mark, the people came to believe that Satan or the Prince of Darkness and his minions of demonic "unclean spirits" were temporarily wreaking havoc in human affairs. But God would soon act to defeat the superhuman forces of evil and restore the people to wholeness and freedom.[5]

The second important development that Antiochus's repressive attack on the Judeans provoked was a popular resistance and rebellion that persisted among the people for three centuries. In fact, Judean/Israelite resistance was distinctive among ancient peoples subject to Western empires. Perhaps convinced through the revelatory visions that, despite appearances, God would reestablish a society of justice, the people persisted in prolonged guerrilla warfare against Antiochus's army of war elephants (1 Macc. 6:35, 46). The original success of this Maccabean Revolt in regaining the people's independence was remembered by subsequent generations of Israelites who mounted resistance to empire. The Hasmonean family that led the Maccabean Revolt, however, soon set themselves up as high-priestly rulers. Imitating the imperial patterns they had led the rebellion against, they also took control of the rest of Palestine, destroying the Samaritans' temple at Gerizim and subjecting both the Idumeans to the south and the Galileans to the north to "the law of the Judeans" (Josephus, *Ant.* 13.257–58, 318–19). Thus, for the first time in over 800 years Galilee came again under Jerusalem rule, as if it were merely a pawn in the geopolitical game of imperial politics, barely forty years before the Romans took over Palestine.[6]

The Roman conquest of Palestine was particularly hard on the Galileans. Whenever the Roman armies conquered and reconquered the area, they started in Galilee, with devastating effects. For example, in Magdala—home town of Mary Magdalene, one of the three women who witnessed Jesus' crucifixion and empty tomb (Mark 15:40; 16:1–8)—the Romans enslaved thousands of people roughly fifty years before Jesus was born (Josephus, *Ant.* 14.120; *War* 1.180). This would have been a disastrous experience for people in the villages around the eastern shore of the Sea of Galilee that would have been remembered vividly at the time of Jesus' ministry which was centered there (according to the Gospel of Mark). The Galilean people, like their Judean cousins to the south, however, repeatedly mounted widespread resistance to domination by the Romans or their client rulers. After the Romans designated Herod as the "king of the Jews" in 40 B.C.E., the Galileans were the fiercest in resisting his attempt to take over his kingdom with the help of Roman troops. They rose in revolt three times in three years before Herod could finally "pacify" the district.[7]

After Herod died, both Galilean and Judean peasants attempted to reassert their freedom, acclaiming one of their own as "king" in each district. In western Galilee they attacked the fortress in Sepphoris, partly to reclaim their own goods that had been seized and stored there. When the Roman troops retook control of Galilee, they enslaved the inhabitants in the area (*War* 2.56, 68; *Ant.* 17.271, 288–89). Thus in Nazareth and other villages around the city of Sepphoris, just about the time Jesus was born, Galileans suffered another trauma of conquest and enslavement. Again thirty-five years after Jesus' ministry, the Galilean and Judean people erupted in widespread revolt against Roman rule, a revolt that the Romans suppressed with great slaughter and mass enslavement of the people and severe devastation of villages. At that time they also destroyed Jerusalem and the Temple. The principal insurrectionary forces were popular movements from the countryside, such as the Zealots, a coalition of peasants from northwest Judea. The largest force, from southern Judea, was led by another popular messiah named Simeon bar Giora, whom the Romans ceremonially executed as king of the Judeans. The Judeans, but not the Galileans, again mounted a massive revolt sixty years later in the Bar Kokhba Revolt of 132–35, which was led by another messianic figure named Bar Kokhba.[8]

The persistence of the Galileans and Judeans in repeated insurrection was almost certainly a response to the impact of Roman rule on their lives. It would be difficult to separate the political, economic, and cultural aspect of that impact. The Roman client King Herod taxed the people heavily to fund his massive building programs of temples and whole cities built in honor of Caesar Augustus as well as his own lavish Hellenistic-style court. He also launched a massive rebuilding of the Jerusalem Temple in Hellenistic style which was a dramatic transformation of the previous temple into one of the wonders of the Roman world. Under the direct Roman rule in Judea, the High Priests were appointed by and served at the pleasure of the Roman governors. Although most "scribes and Pharisees" acquiesced in the imperial chain of domination, it may not be surprising that after mid-century some of the more disaffected scribes formed a cadre of terrorists, the Sicarii ("Dagger-men"), who surreptitiously assassinated members of the high-priestly families who collaborated too objectionably with the Roman authorities.

Throughout the lifetime of Jesus, Herod's son Antipas (and not the Roman governor and the Jerusalem high priests) ruled Galilee. This arrogant Rome-educated ruler, in the first twenty years of his reign, proceeded to build not one but two capital cities in the tiny territory of Galilee, one named after the new emperor Tiberius. Some recent scholarly speculation about the Galilean context of Jesus and Gospel materials has suggested that lower (southern) Galilee in general had suddenly become a cosmopolitan culture of large cities featuring Hellenistic philosophers and the eager participation of nearby villagers. Such a picture runs counter to everything we know about Galilee in particular and the hostile relations between city and villages in the Roman empire generally. Rather, the construction of two new cities, even the relatively small ones in Galilee, must have placed a considerable tax burden on the populace. Moreover, in Galilee where the ruler had never resided before, Herod Antipas and his tax-collectors were suddenly based within easy striking distance of every village in the countryside. One or another of these new Roman-style cities was thus now within view of every village. Is it any wonder that the Gospel of Mark never mentions Jesus entering either of these cities and mentions Herod Antipas only as the tyrannical "king" who arrested and executed John the Baptist? Roman indirect rule in Judea and Galilee was not exactly popular. The Judean historian Josephus, who spent a year in Galilee supposedly organizing defenses against the anticipated Roman reconquest in 66–67 C.E., recounts story after story of the hostility of the Galilean peasantry against the cities of Sepphoris and Tiberias.[9]

The persistence of the Judeans and Galileans in resistance to Roman rule must have something to do with the Israelite tradition in which they stood, with its memory of the foundational event of the exodus from slavery in Egypt and the giving of the covenant on Sinai, both led by the great prophet Moses. Northern Israelites such as the Galileans also would have remembered the great prophet of resistance and renewal against king Ahab's attempt to impose foreign forms and customs, i.e., Elijah. The memories of prophets such as Moses and Elijah were very much alive among the people. Josephus offers accounts of several prophetic movements among the people that were clearly informed by these memories. As a new Moses or Joshua, a prophet named Theudas led his followers into the wilderness to the Jordan River where he promised that the waters would be divided in connection with God's new act of liberation. And as a new Joshua at the battle of Jericho, an "Egyptian (Jewish) prophet" led his followers up to the Mount of Olives opposite Jerusalem, where they were to see the walls of the city fall down and their Roman conquerors disappear. In both cases the Roman governor sent out military forces to wipe out the movement.[10]

Fundamental to Israelite tradition was living directly under the kingship of God, with no oppressive human rulers. That principle was pointedly articulated in the first commandment of the Mosaic covenant: No god other than Yahweh, who was understood literally as the king of Israel. Hence there could not legitimately be any human king, foreign or domestic. That this fundamental principle of Israel's faith was decisively operative at the time of Jesus is most tellingly manifested in the movement that Josephus calls the "Fourth Philosophy." Although one of the principal leaders was from the town of Gamala, east of the Sea of Galilee, it was centered in Judea in 6 C.E., where the Romans had just imposed direct Roman rule, after the reign of Herod the Great and his son Archelaus. Led by Pharisees and other teachers particularly well-versed in the Mosaic law, this movement advocated resistance to Roman rule by refusing to render up the tribute to Rome. Their basic argument, of course, was that since Israelites had God as their ruler and master, they could not possibly "render unto Caesar," which would be tantamount to serving another Lord and master (*War* 2.118; *Ant.* 18.3–9, 23–25).[11] When the Pharisees and Herodians attempted to entrap Jesus into uttering a politically dangerous statement in Mark 12:13–17, they would have known full well that according to the covenantal tradition of Israel/Judea, now subjected to direct Roman imperial rule, it was *not* "lawful to pay taxes to the emperor."

In short, the Galileans and Judeans among whom Jesus led the movement that forms the subject of Mark's story had thus been subjected to foreign empires for many centuries. Roman imperial conquest and periodic reconquest in the generations before and during Jesus' lifetime and the early decades of his movement were particularly devastating for the Galilean people. Roman imperial rule and Roman imposition of Herod as king while maintaining the temple-state and high priesthood, meant three layers of rulers over the people. And it meant three layers of rulers demanding their produce: tribute to Rome, taxes to support Herod and his building projects, and tithes and offerings for the Temple and high priesthood. During the lifetime of Jesus, the Rome-imposed ruler Herod Antipas must have intensified the economic exploitation of the Galileans in order to fund his massive building projects, the two capital cities of Sepphoris and Tiberias.

The Galileans and other Israelite people, however, inherited a long tradition of resistance to oppressive foreign rule. Their sacred traditions included memories of the origins of Israel in rebellion against such rulers and stories of messiahs leading popular revolts and prophets such as Elijah leading popular resistance against oppressive and/or alien rule. It is not surprising, therefore, that throughout the period in which Jesus and his movement emerged a number of popular messianic and prophetic movements arose to challenge Roman and Jerusalem rule.

The Gospel of Mark as People's History

In presenting Jesus as spearheading a movement in the villages of Galilee and nearby areas, Mark is telling about the history of subjected people, a history previously buried from historical view. However, the very possibility of discerning that Mark may be about people's history entails being able to cut through or get out from under the heavy weight of standard assumptions and a deeply embedded interpretive conceptual apparatus that has prevented us from seeing this before.

Cutting through Problematic Elite
and Western Christian Views of History

Two broad general factors may help explain why Mark could not have been seen as a story about people's history before in Western academic circles. One is simply that nearly all literature is the product of the elite, since only they possess literacy. The literate, of course, tend to write from their own elite viewpoint, for which peasants and peasant movements are uninteresting—unless of course they make trouble. Nearly all recorded history, therefore, consists of the history of the ruling elite and their literate clients. Peasants and slaves, like women, have been generally excluded from history. What has gone unnoticed until recently, however, is that some parts of biblical literature such as the Gospel of Mark are exceptions to the rule about what gets written and preserved. Mark's Gospel, like the Song of Miriam and the Song of Deborah and many stories included in the books of Exodus, Joshua, Judges, and (occasionally) the books of Samuel and Kings, appears to be about people's history.

The second broad factor that helps explain why Mark has not been recognized as people's history is the essentialism that pervades Western thinking about peoples and nations. Peoples, especially *other* peoples, are understood to have a distinctive character or essence. Despite minimal awareness, for example, that even the English are a hybrid historical product of Angles, Saxons, Normans, and Celts, "the English" have certain distinctive and essential cultural traits. Even more do "Arabs," "Africans," "Chinese," (East) "Indians," and "Jews." This essentialism not only obscures that most people are historical hybrids of various peoples; it also obscures the class divisions and other divisions and power relations that determine most of the dynamics of lived history.

This essentialism also dominates historical and historical literary study. In academic circles especially the ancient "Greeks" are idealized as the source of Western "humanism," an adulation that almost systematically avoids the embarrassing recognition that the great "Greek" cultural achievements were made possible by escalating economic dependence on slave labor. Modern Christian biblical studies has projected a less positive essence onto ancient

Palestinian people of Israelite heritage, lumping them into the category of "Jews" or "Judaism." Recently Jewish scholars themselves have protested that at least we must speak of "Judaisms" or "sectarian Judaism." But even pluralizing the category of "Jews/Judaism" obscures the regional, class, and social role differences that pervade ancient historical realities and that are prominent even in our limited historical sources, such as the Judean historian Josephus and the Christian Gospels. Mark's story, for example, does not speak of the people in Galilee as "Jews" or in any way characterize something that could be identified as "Judaism." Given the long history of popular resistance to centralized Jerusalem rule in Israelite tradition and the interrelated differences in regional history between Galilee and Judea (sketched in the previous section), we would expect conflict, not consensus, between Galilean villagers and Jerusalem rulers.

Compounding the obscuring effects of the traditional elite's lack of interest in peasants and modern Western essentialism, the Christian theological schemes noted at the beginning of the chapter have obscured our historical vision and make us unable to hear what Mark's story is telling us. The following survey, in one brief section of one chapter, cannot be very comprehensive. But we can at least attempt to continue to peel away problematic assumptions and concepts as we recognize several key aspects of the people's history that Mark presents.

Jesus Heads a Popular Movement among Villagers in Opposition to the Rulers

Mark portrays Jesus as spearheading a widespread movement among the villages of Galilee and the surrounding areas. Two modern Western assumptions in particular seem to block recognition of the program that Jesus is pressing in his activities in the villages, his appointment of the twelve, and his series of sea crossings, exorcisms, healings, and wilderness feedings.

First, the disintegration of forms of local community in industrialized and urbanized modern societies reinforce a Western individualistic understanding of life. The early English and Dutch settlers in America attempted to replicate the village community and even patterned their community life after the Mosaic covenant they found in the book of Exodus and the Sermon on the Mount. Industrialization and urbanization, however, undermined the village community economically. And the advent of centrally controlled communications by the mass media atomized the populace even further in its individualism. In any traditional agrarian society such as ancient Palestine, however, the village community comprised the fundamental form of social organization above the family. Individual life was embedded in family and village life. Each village, more or less self-sufficient economically, was a semiautonomous self-governing community. The rulers, who lived comfortably in cities on the crops they expropriated from the villages, generally left the villagers to run their own community affairs as long as they rendered up their taxes, tithes, tribute, and/or rents.

Second, besides having little sense of the village communities in which the vast majority of traditional peoples lived, modern Westerners assume the separate existence of religious institutions. We are acquainted with Christian churches and Jewish synagogues as optional, multiple, voluntary associations, institutionally separate from political institutions such as cities and towns and states and economic institutions such as corporations and farms. Without thinking about it, we project our own experience back onto the time of Mark and Jesus. In ancient societies, however, religion was inseparable from political-economic life. The Greek term *ekklēsia* referred to the assembly of the whole citizen body of a city-state, with its combination of religious and political functions. It did not suddenly become an exclusively religious term when Jesus' followers used it to refer to the communities of their movement. The term *synagōgē* (and the Hebrew terms *knesset* and *qahal*) also referred to an assembly. Mark uses the term for the assembly of the people of a village. The village assembly constituted the form of self-government as well as community cohesion. It took care of matters such as the water supply as well as communal prayers. Archaeologists' failure to find "synagogue" buildings that can be dated before late antiquity indicates that at the time of Jesus Galilean villages had not yet begun to construct buildings (i.e., "town halls" or "community centers") for their assembly meetings.[12]

It is thus historically far off the mark to imagine (1) that (Mark's) Jesus was addressing his teaching and healing only to individuals while remaining oblivious to social relations and community life, and (2) that the synagogues were Jewish religious groups that rejected Jesus, after which his disciples organized a new religion known as the Christian church. Thus when Mark portrays Jesus as "entering a synagogue" he is not attending a religious service of "Judaism" in the local synagogue building. In Mark the synagogues (= assemblies) have no connotation of the old religion "Judaism" that is supposedly rejecting Jesus or that Jesus is supposedly moving beyond in the course of the story. Far from being the leaders (or clergy) of the synagoges, moreover, the Pharisees and scribes are not even members of the local synagogues, because they do not live in the villages. Jairus, the *archisynagōgos* (Mark 5:21–43), is merely a "head" or "leader" of the local assembly, and decidedly not a "ruler of the synagogue" (and hence not a "Jewish leader"). And when the people of Jesus' hometown assembly take offense at his extraordinary prophetic powers and burgeoning fame—after all he was just one of them!—he is not being "rejected" by (a "synagogue" representing) "Judaism." As stated above, Mark is simply not about a breaking away from "Judaism" and a ministry of Jesus that prepares the way for a new religion, "Christianity."

Perhaps we can now hear a key aspect of Mark's story in more appropriate historical terms. Mark presents Jesus as building a movement based in villages of Galilee and adjacent areas. For the first two-thirds of the story, Jesus proclaims the good news of the kingdom of God and performs healings and exorcisms in the villages of Galilee and surrounding areas, working from a headquarters in the fishing village of Capernaum. In the course of the story we can discern several cumulative aspects of this village-based movement.

1. Mark's Jesus addresses his program of teaching and healing to village communities, not individuals. He does not found new communities because the communities were already there, as the fundamental form of social life in an agrarian society. Significantly, Mark portrays Jesus not as simply hanging around encountering a few people at a time, but as entering directly into the local assemblies on the Sabbath where most all villagers would have been gathered for discussion of community affairs generally as well as prayers (1:21, 39; 3:1). He carries out his teaching, healing, and exorcisms in the middle of those village assemblies. Similarly, he dispatches the twelve two-by-two into villages where, staying in a local household, they were apparently organizing as well as preaching the kingdom and exorcising demons. In an interesting indication that the village community, and not individuals, was the focus of their work, these workers are to "shake the dust off their feet" as a testimony against a whole "place" or village that refuses to hear welcome them (6:7–13).

2. Mark's Jesus was building a movement across many village communities. It would have been usual for an outsider to be invited or welcomed into the community in this way. Village communities in traditional agrarian societies usually do not associate and cooperate except in times of crisis. But Jesus is already known to be bringing special powers of healing, and Mark stresses the importance of his principle message of the kingdom of God and his teachings about marriage, economic equality, and democratic leadership, all fundamental village values. His sending out the disciples to expand his own preaching and healing clearly indicates a broad program of outreach and movement organizing across many villages.

3. In Mark's story Jesus does not enter, even seems to avoid, the two capital cities: Sepphoris, only a few miles from Jesus' home village of Nazareth, and Tiberias, across the Sea of Galilee to the south from Capernaum. In fact, both of these cities would have seemed like foreign bodies imposed on the Galilean social landscape. They had only recently been built by "king" Herod Antipas, whom the Romans had appointed to rule Galilee, and were probably resented as the sites from which and for which they were heavily taxed. In the middle of Mark's story Jesus extends his activity of teaching, exorcism, and

healing from the villages of Galilee to the surrounding areas. Again, however, he avoids the urban areas and works only in the villages. He presumes to move across frontiers into territory subject to other rulers, such as the "region of Tyre" and the "villages of Caesarea Philippi" and the "region of Judea" (7:24; 8:27). Even more unusual than cooperation with a peasant movement among villages in a given area is a popular movement that extends into many villages across wider areas and across political frontiers ("borders" are a modern political reality). Including all its "religious" aspects such as Jesus' extraordinary powers of healing and exorcism, Mark's story presents Jesus as spearheading a widespread popular movement based in local village communities, a movement that extends beyond Galilee to the villages of surrounding areas.

4. Mark presents Jesus as spearheading this popular movement not as a politically innocuous religious revival, but in direct opposition to the rulers and ruling institutions. Indeed, Mark has him carry out an obstructive demonstration in the public courtyard at the center of the Temple, the ruling institution of Judea, and pronounce God's condemnation of both Temple and the incumbent rulers (11:15–18; 12:1–12; 13:1–2).[13] That is a blatantly revolutionary act and that is the reason Mark gives for the condemnation of Jesus at his trial before the high-priestly rulers in Jerusalem. Established biblical studies still obscures this by its persistent anachronistic separation of religion and political-economic relations. To modern Western readers the Temple is a religious institution and the high priests and scribes are "religious leaders." Jesus' prophetic action and pronouncements in the Temple constitute the "cleansing of the Temple" to prepare it for Gentiles as well as Jews to "worship." However, not only were the high priests the political-economic as well as religious rulers of Judea, maintained in their power and privilege by the Romans, but they and their scribal representatives were definitely not "leaders" with an "authority" among the people (as Mark indicates in 1:21–28). Within two decades after Jesus' blatant prophetic denunciation of the Temple and high priests, as described by Mark, even a scribal group, ominously dubbed the "Dagger Men" in the Latin-derived term *Sicarii*, began assassinating members of the high-priestly elite who collaborated too closely with the Romans.[14]

5. Indeed, Mark presents Jesus' manifestation of a kingdom different from the established one (i.e., God's) as a challenge and threat to the rulers in Jerusalem and Galilee from the very outset of the story. The people respond to Jesus as having an authority/power that they do not recognize among the "authority" figures (1:21–28). Early in the story, the Pharisees as representatives of the Jerusalem rulers and the Herodians as representative of Herod Antipas, the Rome-appointed "Tetrarch" of Galilee, are conspiring to destroy him (3:6). After the high priests finally succeed in capturing Jesus outside Jerusalem, the Roman governor executes him, according to Mark's story, on the

charge of posing as the "king of the Judeans." And the Romans execute him by crucifixion, the form of execution by torture that the Romans used for rebels against the imperial order. Mark represents Jesus as a provincial rebel executed by the military governor of the Roman occupying forces in Judea.

6. Mark, furthermore, clearly suggests that the movement Jesus started continued after he died as a martyr for the movement. In the remarkable open ending of the story the audience, along with the women who find the tomb in which Jesus was buried to be empty, are directed back to the rural backwater of the villages of Galilee where the risen Jesus has supposedly gone ahead of them—apparently to pick up where Jesus and the twelve had left off in advancing the movement.

Adherence to Indigenous Tradition and Fulfillment of a Subject People's History

Mark presents Jesus and his movement both as uncompromisingly based on Israelite covenantal traditions and as the fulfillment of the history of an imperially subjected people. Both of these aspects have been obscured by Christian theological reduction of Israelite history in general to the history of religion in which "Judaism" is superseded by "Christianity" through the ministry of Jesus (as noted above). To hear the historical story Mark is telling, we need to listen again carefully in the context of world history, then and now.

To most observers of world history in the late twentieth century, the collapse of the Soviet Union and end of the Cold War meant that the capitalist West, the United States, Western Europe, and allied capitalist nations, had prevailed. The president of the United States even declared the advent of a "New World Order," what to third-world observers is the global capitalist order that articulates and spreads predominantly "American" culture throughout the world.

Similarly at the time of Jesus, to most observers who reflected upon the course that history had taken (such as the Judean historian Josephus) it was obvious that history was moving through the Romans. They had taken over the Mediterranean world city-state by city-state, people by people, with what must have seemed like a relentless inevitability. The most "civilized" areas such as Greece had submitted to Roman rule and become an integral part of the Roman imperial order. They easily incorporated elements of Roman political culture into traditional Hellenic culture. In urban areas of the eastern parts of the Roman empire the people had long since assimilated to the Hellenistic imperial culture brought by Alexander the Great and his successors, culture that the Romans left intact and built upon when they took over. The history of most peoples subjected by Rome simply came to an end. They were able to continue cultivating their cultural heritage only by detaching it from political independence and the political institutions by which they had previously conducted their own affairs. More often than not, subjected peoples' cultures, their gods and distinctive stories, became identified or fused with those of the dominant culture.

In stark contrast to this general pattern of subjected peoples under the Roman empire, Mark's Gospel not only (1) takes its stand squarely in the tradition of one of the peoples subjected to Rome, but also (2) tells the story of the fulfillment of the history of that people.

1. Far from accepting Roman rule and compromising the traditional Israelite way of life—i.e., accepting Roman domination of politics and economic life while reducing the Israelite tradition to a separable sphere of religion—Mark's Jesus insists on the original Mosaic covenant as the only guide for the people's social-economic life. In fact, he is so uncompromising with Western rule in his adherence to the distinctive Israelite tradition that he may remind modern readers of what are often called Islamic/Muslim "fundamentalists." The latter insist upon strict adherence to the Qur'an in both political-economic affairs and in relations with the dominant Western culture that is being pressed upon them. Mark portrays Jesus as similarly strict in his articulation of standards for his movement. Jesus flat-out excludes the possibility that a rich person, who would have to be someone in collaboration with the Rome-imposed political-economic "new order" in Palestine, can "enter the kingdom of God" (10:17–25). Such a person would, virtually by definition, be in violation of God's basic "commandments" in the Mosaic covenant: "thou shalt not defraud, . . . you shall not steal." Mark's Jesus, moreover, refuses to compromise with Roman rule in the most dangerous way. The Pharisees and Herodians attempt to entrap him by asking whether it is "lawful" (according to Israelite tradition) to give tribute to Caesar (Mark 12:13–17). They know full well, of course, that it is unlawful, against the first commandment, "You shall have no gods other than me [Yahweh]." That is precisely how they hope to entrap Jesus with their question, for his adherence to the covenantal commandment of God, that tribute is against the Law, would justify his arrest for fomenting a revolt, since the Romans considered failure to pay the tribute tantamount to rebellion. Cleverly avoiding a direct answer, Jesus insists upon Israelite law over against imperial rule: "giving to Caesar what belongs to Caesar" means they should not pay the tribute, since according to Israelite tradition everything belongs to God and nothing to Caesar.[15]

2. Mark also presents Jesus' actions and program as the fulfillment of the history of Israel, an astounding claim for a movement among an imperially subjected people. In the Passover celebration and other modes of cultivating their tradition, Israelites kept vividly alive the memory of Israel's deliverance

from oppressive foreign rule under the Egyptian Pharaoh. Those memories then informed long-standing hopes for a new exodus in which the people would again be delivered from alien rule. At the very beginning of the Gospel, Mark has John the Baptist declare, in the words of the prophet Isaiah, that Jesus is leading that new exodus: "Prepare the way of the Lord." Similarly, Israelites cherished memories of the great wonder-working prophet Elijah, who had led the people's resistance to the oppressive rule of king Ahab. Elijah was expected to come in the future to restore the people again. After the comparison of Jesus with both Moses and Elijah in the "transfiguration" vision, Mark has Jesus declare that Elijah has already come, pointing apparently to John and his "baptism of repentance" (9:2–13). In his prophetic demonstration condemning the Temple, Jesus in effect declares that the famous prophecy of Jeremiah that God would destroy the Temple because of its oppression of the people was (again) being fulfilled (Jer. 7; Mark 11:17). And at the climax of his trial before the high-priestly court, Mark's Jesus cries out that Daniel's equally famous vision of Israel's sovereignty being restored is about to be fulfilled: "You will see the Son of Man seated at the right hand of Power, and coming with the clouds of heaven" (Dan. 7:13–14; Mark 14:62).[16]

In sum, once we peel away unwarranted historical assumptions, it becomes clear that Mark is telling a story about people's history, a history that had been previously submerged under the weight of the dominant Roman imperial order. Mark presents Jesus as spearheading a movement based in village communities that both brings ordinarily separated villages into contact with each other and unites them in solidarity against their local and imperial rulers. Over against the "master narrative" that history was moving through the imperial power of Rome, moreover, Mark portrays Jesus and his movement as rooted in the history of Israel, an imperially subjected people. Indeed, Mark's story claims that Jesus' program and movement are the fulfillment of that subjected people's history.

Giving Voice to Subjected People

That Mark tells a story about a people subject to the Roman imperial order, of course, does not necessarily mean either that the story was addressed to subjected people or that the story gave a voice to (or spoke for) subjected people. Since Mark was composed in Greek,[17] not the Aramaic spoken in Galilean villages, it must not have been addressed to communities in Galilee itself, where the people almost certainly spoke Aramaic. Yet Mark was composed in ordinary people's Greek, not literarily sophisticated Greek. So it would seem that the Gospel was addressed to ordinary Greek-speaking people outside of Galilee. Most people in antiquity could not read (as we will discuss further in the next chapter); Mark was eventually written. So, although most literature was recited aloud to a group of people, at least one of the communities who used the Gospel included someone who was literate. Whether the story was directed to subjected people and whether it gave voice to those people, however, must be determined from the story itself.

Cutting through Previous Christian Constructions—Again

The principal problem in such determination, however, may not be that the story does not give clear indications but that we readers located in the modern imperial metropolis may have difficulty discerning those indications. It may therefore help again to take into account some of the more obvious reductions and misinformation that modern Western readers often impose on the story. Again it is most important to recognize that Mark is not about the origins of a new universal religion, "Christianity," out of an old parochial religion, "Judaism." As ancient sources indicate, the dominant division in the ancient world in which Mark originated was not between "Jews" and "Gentiles" or between "Jewish" and "Hellenistic" or "Roman," but between the imperial and local rulers, on the one hand, and the subjected peoples, on the other.

A parallel historical case illustrates the importance of cutting through the modern Western essentialism that obscures the historical dynamics of ancient Palestine under Roman rule. The widespread insurrection in 66–70 is known as "the Jewish Revolt," as if it were a "nationalist" struggle of the Jews generally against the Romans. If we read the accounts of the Judean historian Josephus, however, we find "Galileans" and "Idumeans," along with *some* "Judeans," peasants and some ordinary priests, pitted against other Judeans, the priestly aristocrats and Herodians, and the Roman army. That is, the Galilean, Idumean, and Judean peasants, along with ordinary Jerusalemites and some ordinary priests, fought against their Judean and Roman rulers.

Correspondingly we must question the standard interpretation of Mark as an expression of "Christian universalism" over against "Jewish particularism" and as an overcoming of a supposed division between "Jews" and "Gentiles." The Pharisees are taken as the "leaders" of "Judaism" in its obsession with particularistic ritual and purity laws, which Jesus ignores or even breaks. The tenants in the parable of the vineyard (Mark 12:1–12) whom the owner will destroy are taken as "the Jews" generally (many of whom were indeed destroyed in the Roman reconquest of 69–70). The "others" to whom it will be given must therefore be the Gentiles, who thus receive the Jews' heritage (an idea now called Christian "supersessionism"). Shortly thereafter Jesus instructs the disciples to proclaim the gospel "to all nations" (13:10). This supposed extension beyond "Jewish particularism" to inclusive Christian universalism is then seen prefigured in the Markan journeys back and forth across the Sea of Galilee from the "Jewish" (western) side to the "Gentile" (eastern) side. Finally, according to this modern Christian theological reading, the resurrected Jesus "going ahead of" (leading) the disciples to "Galilee" is meant as a symbol for the mission spreading out from Jerusalem to the Gentiles (as in the book of Acts).[18]

Mark's story, however, does not in any way fit or support this modern theological scheme. This can be seen if we simply correct several previous misreadings on the basis of more precise historical evidence and more careful readings of Mark.

1. Mark's Jesus does not oppose and is not opposed by "the Jews" generally, but only by the Jerusalem rulers. From Mark 11:27 through 12:12 Jesus is in confrontation with "the chief priests, the scribes, and the elders," i.e., the Jerusalem-based rulers of Judea. At the end of the parable of the tenants, Mark says explicitly that "they realized that he had told this parable against them and wanted to arrest him" (12:12). The parable pronounces not the condemnation of "the Jews" generally but only of the high priests, scribes, and elders. So "the others" to whom the vineyard (Israel) will be given would presumably be other tenants, presumably Israelite and other villagers represented by the Jesus movement.

2. There is no basis in the story for the idea that in moving back and forth across the Sea of Galilee, Jesus is somehow combining Jews and Gentiles into a universal religion. Mark gives no indication that the Galilee side of the Sea was populated by "Jews," a vague, essentializing translation of the Greek term *Ioudaioi* that obscures historical regional distinctions current at the time of Jesus and Mark. The Judean historian Josephus regularly refers to the people of Galilee as "Galileans," as distinct from those of Judea, whom he calls "Judeans" (*Ioudaioi*). Indeed, Mark's only use of the term *Ioudaioi* outside of the episodes of the trial and crucifixion of Jesus appears to be a regional reference to "Judeans," in connection with the Pharisees and scribes "who had come from Jerusalem" (7:1–3). The title "king of the Judeans" in the episodes of the trial, beating, and crucifixion of Jesus is used only by outsiders, the Roman governor and soldiers (Mark 15:2, 9, 18), who lumped all Israelites together as "Judeans." The chief priests use instead the pan-Israelite term "the Messiah, the king of Israel" (15:32).

3. Correspondingly, Mark does not portray Jesus as attacking a supposedly parochial and particularistic "Judaism" in general. The modern scholarly picture of "Jews" at the time of Jesus as obsessed with purity codes and ritual observances derives mainly from extremely fragmentary evidence for the Pharisees, who were interpreting laws designed to protect the purity of the

priestly class serving in the Temple. The Pharisees and the scribes in Mark, who "come down from Jerusalem" (3:22; 7:1–3), are not members of Galilean village communities and not representative of the people. We have no evidence, in Mark or elsewhere, for any exclusivist nationalist or religious consciousness among ordinary Galileans and Judeans. Given the contingencies of its previous history, the villagers of Galilee, while predominantly Israelite, must have been a somewhat ethnically mixed population anyhow. Moreover, Mark's Jesus defends rather than breaks the Israelite Law. Jesus insists upon the "basic commandments" of God, the Mosaic covenantal law, against the Pharisees' application of it, particularly in their "tradition of the elders," as we shall explore in chapter 7 (see esp. 7:1–13). Once we recognize that the term *Ioudaioi* is a regional (not a religious) reference, then it is clear how different Galilean villagers' (and Jesus movement's) social codes and practices were from those of "the Pharisees and all the Judeans" based in Jerusalem (see further chapter 7).

Addressing and Giving Voice to Subjected Peoples

Far from presupposing a sharp break between "Judaism" and the Christian mission to the Gentiles, Mark presents a striking continuity of Jesus and his movement from the villages of Galilee to those in the surrounding areas. And those villagers in the surrounding areas apparently identify strongly with the Israelite tradition in which Mark's story is rooted and which Mark portrays Jesus' movement as bringing to fulfillment. This strongly suggests that Mark is addressed to and gives voice to precisely such villagers in areas beyond Galilee—people who see the fulfillment of Israelite tradition in their own inclusion in the Jesus movement that is expanding precisely among their village communities. This will become clear from a series of observations.

1. Mark presents a gradual extension of the Jesus movement beyond supposedly Israelite villages of Galilee in continuity with, indeed virtually as an extension of, Jesus' renewal of Israel in its village communities. By contrast, Matthew presents a grand, programmatic change in strategy between Jesus' mission during his ministry and the mission of the disciples after Jesus' crucifixion and resurrection. In the original mission charge to the disciples, Matthew's Jesus instructs them to go only to "the lost sheep of the house of Israel" (Matt. 10:5–6). Not until the final scene of the Gospel does the risen Jesus commission them to "make disciples of all nations/peoples" (Matt. 28:19). The corresponding change is even more programmatic in Luke's writing. The literarily and culturally sophisticated Luke, who composes a second volume in the Acts of the Apostles, lays out a world-historical scheme of how the (now explicitly "Christian") movement was extended from its origins in

Jerusalem (not Galilee) in the opening chapter of the Gospel to the apostles' mission to the various nations, climaxing in Rome toward the end of Acts.

Mark has no such "universal" or imperial horizon in view. Nothing in Mark's story warrants reading Jesus' "going before" the disciples into Galilee as only a figurative and not also a geographical reference (14:28; 16:7). In those directions, rather, Mark's Jesus indicates that the movement that started in Galilee with Jesus' proclamation that "the time is fulfilled, the kingdom of God is at hand" (1:14–15) continues past its narrative end (16:7–8) with the hearers/readers as well as the disciples directed to go back to Galilee to continue the movement that Jesus started. Jesus' indication that the disciples must proclaim the gospel to all the peoples (13:10) fits well with that open ending as well as with earlier sections of the story, where Jesus himself had already extended the program of preaching and manifestation of the kingdom of God to the peoples of other areas around about Galilee such as Tyre and the Decapolis, and not simply to Judeans.

In contrast with Matthew in particular, Mark's story presents no dramatic shift between Jesus and the disciples' mission to Israel and the "Christian" mission to the Gentiles. Mark presents a striking continuity of Jesus and his movement from the villages of Galilee to those in the surrounding areas. Indeed, it seems as if, in his plotting of Jesus' and his disciples' journey in the middle section of the story, "on the way" to the face-off with the rulers in Jerusalem, Mark is pointedly including the people that Jesus has reached beyond Galilee. The journey section of the story starts at the farthest reach of Jesus' campaigns in the villages of Caesarea Philippi, moves back through Galilee and the Capernaum "headquarters" in particular, and finally moves through "the region of Judea and beyond the Jordan" to Jerusalem (8:27; 9:30, 33; 10:1). It thus seems clear that Mark's Jesus builds outward from his original Galilean base to surrounding peoples in continuity with and as an extension of his renewal of the people of Israel.

2. Mark's story also assumes a continuity between the Israelite tradition that forms the basis and much of the content of the story and the hearers of the story beyond Galilee and other Israelite areas. Mark seems simply to assume that the audience will resonate to the many explicit references and subtle allusions to Israelite history as well as to the Israelite covenantal tradition that Jesus reestablishes as the basis of community life. Mark supplies translations of the occasional Aramaic terms and a parenthetical explanation of distinctive Pharisaic (and "Judean") practices (e.g., 7:3; 15:34). So the audience must not be thoroughly familiar with Galilean and Judean culture and affairs.

Yet it seems clear that Mark is not teaching the Israelite tradition to those who are just learning about it. Rather the people Mark addresses must have possessed considerable acquaintance with the Israelite tradition already in order to understand the many and varied allusions woven throughout the narrative. Moreover, among other messages it gives, the Syrophoenician woman's besting Jesus in debate suggests that the non-Israelite peoples involved in the movement wanted to share in Israel's tradition (even the crumbs from the table!), in fact, desired to identify themselves with Israel's history and tradition.

Also, the audience, with a substantial but not thorough knowledge of Israelite tradition and Galilean political-economic-religious affairs, must have been able to resonate to many of the story's episodes by analogy with their own political-economic-religious affairs. They must have had some experience similar, for example, to the Pharisees, as representatives of the Jerusalem rulers, attempting to extract economic resources from the villages as *Korban* or "dedicated" to support the Temple (7:9–13). They must have resonated by analogy to Jesus' insistence that they need not resort to an established temple-and-priesthood to receive "forgiveness of sins" (2:1–12). In other cases they could probably resonate directly to Jesus' teaching rooted in Israelite tradition. It might be immediately evident, for example, how the importance and inviolability of the marriage bond for community life could be expressed by appeal to the Israelite creation stories (created "male and female" and "one flesh," 10:2–9). Thus the people Mark addressed were seriously acquainted with Israelite tradition and strongly identified with the history of Israel now coming to fulfillment in Jesus' prophetic action and village-based movement.

3. That Mark's audience identified so strongly with the story's grounding in Israelite tradition and history against the Rome-designated Jerusalem rulers suggests that they must have been ordinary people. That Mark represents Jesus as working strictly in villages, particularly when he enters areas beyond Galilee, suggests further that Mark's audience consists primarily of village communities.

There are a number of other indications, moreover, that Mark addresses village/peasant communities. Mark's Jesus not only refutes and "puts down" the representatives of city-based rulers, but insists upon radically egalitarian social-economic-political relations in the community life of his own movement (see esp. 10:17–25, 35–45).[19] This would resonate more readily with peasants still living in village communities than with "rootless" people whose bond with their family inheritance of land had been broken. The former, whose hold on their family inheritance was threatened, would have been eager to renew the village ideals of egalitarian "moral economy," with the traditional mechanisms of keeping each family economically viable in the local community.[20] Rural sharecroppers and rootless urban poor, on the other hand, would already have been forced by economic necessity into the position of clients of wealthy and powerful patrons. Thus, for example, Jesus' response to the young man who inquires how to gain eternal life—and from his great wealth has obviously been defrauding peasants by charging them interest on their debts—would have resonated mainly with peasants whose tenuous hold on their family inheritance was increasingly threatened by their indebtedness to such figures. We know from the letters of Pliny, the Roman governor in northwestern Asia Minor over four decades after Mark, that a movement of Christ-believers was active in villages as well as towns. So there is no need to confine the options for Mark's much earlier audience to the principal cities of the empire such as Rome or Antioch or Alexandria, as is often done. An audience of villagers provides a better fit for several key aspects of the story.

4. Mark's audience, moreover, seems to have a rather subtle savvy about the political-social-psychological situation in the village life Jesus addressed. In the most dramatic and violent exorcism episode (5:1–20), after Jesus casts out the demon, it is possible to recognize in the name "Legion," with its obvious allusion to the Roman army, that the alien force that had "possessed" the man with such devastating consequences was (related to) Roman imperial domination. And according to the story, once "Legion" entered the swine, the herd rushed down the steep bank back into the sea, with the obvious allusion to the Mediterranean Sea from which the Roman legions had come to take possession of the land and people in the first place.

5. It is also far easier to imagine village communities as the audience for Mark's sharp criticism of the twelve as arrogant or pretentious leaders of the movement (see further chapter 4). Traditionally more egalitarian village communities rather than urbanites accustomed to daily interaction with people of rank and status would resonate with Jesus' blunt rejection of James and John's request to be appointed to positions of prominence in the movement (10:16–28, 35–45). That Mark's Jesus rejects not only the scribes and Pharisees, representatives of the Jerusalem rulers, but even ambitious leaders within his own movement, parallels behavior of other peasant, village-based movements. The contemporary Judean historian Josephus indicates that the popular insurrectionaries in the summer of 66 C.E., near contemporary with Mark's audience, rejected the attempts by the more "scribal" "Dagger Men" to take over the leadership of the revolt. Modern third-world peasant movements similarly not only reject leadership by urban intellectuals but become suspicious of their indigenous leaders who appear to have taken on airs or perhaps compromised the movement's agenda.[21]

There thus appear to be several indications within Mark's story that the audience consists of village communities of a Jesus movement in areas around Galilee. The reasoning above may appear to be a bit circular: A story about Israelite peasants would resonate best with other peasants, therefore the audience must be peasants. An urban alternative, however, involves serious problems of how a story with such a radically egalitarian agenda could have been received by a more socially mixed audience that included some members further up the social scale. Such a community can be imagined as receiving Mark's Israelite tradition and egalitarian episodes only as already fixed contents of a Gospel tradition the authority of which one simply accepts. But Mark's story breathes a vital antiauthoritarian spirit alive in a dynamic popular movement. Mark's hearers are most easily understood as village communities. Indeed it is tempting to believe that the audience is, in effect, "written into" the story, i.e., located primarily in the areas mentioned in the narrative, such as the region of Tyre or the villages of Caesarea Philippi (7:24; 8:27). The Greek-speaking audience's location so close to "Israelite" territory such as Galilee would make it all the more intelligible how they could easily become familiar with Israelite tradition and identify with Israelite history.

That its audience consists of ordinary Greek-speaking people in the eastern parts of the Roman empire, most likely villagers, suggests that Mark's Gospel story does indeed give voice to subject people. They identify as their own story Mark's history of Jesus spearheading a movement of revitalized, autonomous, egalitarian community life over against the Roman and Roman-appointed rulers, for which cause he was killed as a martyr by the Roman rulers. The recent recognition that Mark's story was almost certainly performed orally in meetings of such communities, to be explored in the next chapter, strongly reinforces this conclusion.

3

Mark as Oral Performance

Scholars have recently been intensely debating how they should read the Gospel of Mark. But what if the original "readers" of Mark could not read? What if the story was being heard? What if the Gospel story was being performed by a storyteller?

Modern Westerners have simply assumed the existence of books and reading, particularly in educational circles.[1] After all, students in the finest schools and colleges learned great ideas out of the "great books," and it was the ancient Greeks who wrote those "books." Most important, in church and Sunday school we learned to read the Bible, *The* Book, which is made up of many "books" such as Mark. The Bible is sacred scripture, sacred *writing.* Scripture scholars spend their whole lives studying and interpreting these sacred writings. They teach prospective ministers in theological school to analyze the writings closely, in order to base their preaching solidly on the *text.* Modern scholars who devote their lives to study of "the Classics" and Scripture simply assume the existence of print culture. They assume that the classics and the biblical "books" were composed in writing, and that ancient Greeks, Jews, and Christians could read them. After all, the Jews, followed by the Christians, were people of the Book. They created and cultivated sacred books, Scripture.

The Limits of Literacy

Limited Literacy and Oral Communication

Outside of a few aristocrats and scribes in ancient Greece, Rome, and Israel, however, virtually no one could read and write. The great "writing" prophet Jeremiah could not write. He had to dictate his prophecies to a scribe named

Baruch (Jeremiah 36). Nor could king Jehoiakim read. He had to get Jehudi, one of the few royal officials who was literate, to read Jeremiah's prophecies from a scroll. In classical Athens, where the leisurely lifestyle of the elite was based on slavery and colonization, the rate of minimal literacy may have climbed to between 5 and 10 percent of the overall population. Under the Roman empire, the rate of minimal literacy was almost certainly under 10 percent. Evidence from Pompeii in Italy suggests that perhaps no more than 2 or 3 percent of the residents had some ability to write. The vast majority of people in ancient societies were illiterate.[2]

The best evidence for the Roman empire comes from Egypt, where writing was used more than elsewhere in the empire, making literacy there unrepresentatively high. Literacy was rare in the villages. Even the village scribe, unique to Egypt and historically subject to an elaborate governmental bureaucracy, did not have to be literate. A village clerk in Ptolemais Hormou named Petaus, for example, apparently never did learn even to sign his name independently; he always copied a model. Large numbers of papyri indicate that the vast majority of male and almost all female artisans and farmers were illiterate. Few among the indigenous Egyptian population knew even minimal Greek, and the vast majority, the peasants, knew no Greek and were presumably illiterate in their own language(s).[3]

Literacy corresponded with social location in classical Greece and the Roman empire generally. Partly if not largely for controlling the inheritance of property, the wealthy and powerful Roman elite used written records to record large-scale loans, wills, and marriage contracts. Written correspondence also accompanied long-distance trade which served mainly the lifestyle of the wealthy. Aristocrats of pretension had to cultivate a modicum of literary culture. Yet, while generally literate, the urban and provincial elite of the Roman empire often had their specially trained slaves handle their correspondence and read aloud to them rather than writing and reading themselves.[4] For the vast majority of people in antiquity, however, writing was simply unnecessary in everyday life, whether in the processes of food production or in local weddings and funerals. Shopkeepers and artisans in the towns had little use for writing and peasants had almost none, even in bureaucratic Egypt. Nearly all buying and selling and modest transactions were conducted orally in face-to-face interaction.[5]

Literacy was no less limited and oral communication no less dominant in ancient Jewish society, despite the wishful reading of ancient sources by modern biblical scholars.[6] Passages cited from the ancient Judean historian Josephus to prove that Jewish children were taught to read indicate rather that the teaching and learning of the laws was carried out by public oral recitation (at Sabbath assemblies). Those passages thus indicate both that Jewish communities were largely illiterate and that communication of the most important matters was oral. The concept of writing in these passages, moreover, is magical: by *hearing* the sacred laws taught aloud, the laws would become "engraved on their souls . . . and guarded in their memory" (*Ant.* 4.210; 16.43; *C. Ap.* 2.175, 178, 204; cf. Philo, *Legatio ad Gaium* 115, 210).[7] Rabbinic texts that were previously claimed as evidence for the people *reading* (e.g., *m. Ber.* 4:3; *m. Bik.* 3:7; *m. Sukk.* 3:10) in fact refer to the people *reciting* certain psalms and prayers from memory. Rabbinic references cited to attest general literacy and the ubiquity of schools in fact refer only to the tiny rabbinic circles themselves (*m. Šabb.* 1:3).[8]

In Judea and Galilee around the time of Jesus, as in the rest of the Roman empire, literacy was concentrated in the political and cultural elite. Officials in the Herodian administrations in Jerusalem and the Galilean cities were presumably literate in Greek, although probably not in Hebrew and Aramaic. Working primarily in the latter languages, the scribes and Pharisees constituted the professional literate stratum of the Jerusalem temple-state. The vast majority of people, the Galilean, Judean, and other villagers, were largely illiterate. One recent study places the literacy rate in Roman Palestine as low as 3 percent.[9]

The Relation of Writing to Oral Communication

If the vast majority of people in the Roman empire were illiterate, then we must obviously rethink the relationship between the Gospel of Mark and its audience. We can no longer impose modern assumptions about literacy and books onto the Gospel. The first step perhaps would be to ask about the relationship between literature and its audience in the predominantly oral communication environment of the ancient Mediterranean world.

Nearly all of what we think of as "literature" in Greek and Roman antiquity was oral: it was performed or recited, not read—certainly not read by an individual silently. Greek and Latin dramas of course were performed publicly in elaborately staged productions with actors and chorus in city theaters. All types of poetry, whether performed in a public venue or a private banquet, were chanted or sung. The words comprised only a part of the whole performance, which included accompaniment on a musical instrument and perhaps dance as well. Plays, poetry (= music) of all kinds, and even histories were performed on particular occasions for which they were customary: dirges at funerals, elegies at private symposia, hymns at public religious festivals, and victory odes and encomia at games.[10]

Written texts also existed for most of these types of literature that were publicly performed—although not necessarily to be read. Indeed, recent studies of Greek poetry, drama, epic and even philosophy have illuminated the function of the writing down of such "literature" in the broader context of its continuing oral performance and aural hearing. A very fluid relation existed between composition, performance, and text. When Aristophanes describes poets in the process of composition, he makes no mention of pen and papyrus (*Acharnians*, 383–479; *Thesmophoriazusae*, 95–265).[11] Composition apparently happened in the poet's head or in the processes of rehearsal and performance. A written copy was probably made only afterward. And such a copy recorded only one aspect of a total performance that was a combination of words, music, and perhaps dance. A written text functioned as an *aide-mémoire*, a silent record of a much richer experience. Even ancient philosophy, which seems to us such dense discourse, was oral, with written texts being an echo of spoken lessons, perhaps a teacher's summary or a student's notes.[12]

Although a great deal of literature was written down, however, there was little reading, for a number of reasons. In contrast with modern "print culture" since the invention of the printing press by Gutenberg, there were no "publishers" and no "mass-production" in antiquity. Papyrus rolls and scrolls made of skins were extremely expensive. Literary works were copied by hand, a laborious, time-consuming process. Since no spaces were left between words on the scrolls, it was very difficult to follow texts with the eyes, let alone to locate particular passages.[13] Reading aloud from an ancient manuscript would have required considerable familiarity with the content.

Even if the words of ancient poetry or drama may in some cases have been transmitted with the aid of texts, traditional performance continued for centuries, each successive generation learning from the previous one. The existence of written texts did not necessarily disrupt the continuity of oral performance and certainly did not displace or "kill it." If we have eyes to see, in fact, the style of ancient literatures in writing merely duplicated the orally composed and performed poetry literatures. The culture of oral recitation and performance did not die out and give way to a written culture or "book culture" in Greco-Roman antiquity. Even complex narrative history continued to be publicly performed.[14]

"Literature" thus continued to be experienced orally-aurally, through public performances or recitations at private banquets.[15] "There was no such thing as 'popular literature' in the Roman Empire. . . . Greek romances [being] the light reading of a limited public possessing a real degree of education."[16] Ordinary people did not need to read to experience "literature." They could listen to storytellers relating Aesop's fables, poets singing their poems, or historians recounting their histories in public places, particularly at festivals (Dio Chrysostom 20.20; Quintilian, *Inst.* 5.11.19).

The relation of oral performance and written texts in the Roman empire differed little from that which prevailed earlier in Greek cities. Long after written texts existed, oral performance continued its prominence and dominance. Recent studies show that a sophisticated and extensive use of writing in elite cultural circles coexisted with and provided certain assistance to what is to us an amazing dominance of the spoken word. Complex and often dense "literature" was regularly heard rather than read by its audience. The written word functioned mainly in the service of the spoken.[17]

Sacred Scrolls and Oral Communication in Judea and Galilee

The development of sacred writing on scrolls, i.e., "scripture," in Judea played a role in the appropriation and cultivation of cultural tradition that was distinctive among ancient societies where oral transmission of culture dominated.

Whereas the ancient Athenians inscribed new laws on stone erected as impressive public memorials of the legislation, along with curses sanctioning their authority, the presiding priests and scribes in Jerusalem wrote the laws legitimating the temple-state on parchment scrolls. The memorials to the sacred laws were all the more awesome for being housed in the sacred precincts of the Temple, thus shrouded in mystery, hidden from view of the people.

The story of Ezra's "reading" of "the book of the Law of Moses" reveals the distinctive function of such sacred scrolls in Judean society in which oral communication still dominated. In a founding ceremony of the "second" Temple community under Persian imperial sponsorship, an assembly of Judean elite just returned to Jerusalem from exile in Babylon, the scroll of the Law of Moses was displayed as a numinous sacred object of veneration, almost iconic (Neh. 8).[18] Standing above all the people, "Ezra opened the scroll in the sight of all the people . . . and when he opened it, all the people stood up . . . , answered, 'Amen, Amen,' lifting up their hands" (Neh. 8:4–6). The "reading," however, was oral and the Levites then "interpreted" the law, which apparently involved a good bit more than translation from Hebrew into Aramaic. This awesome display of the sacred scroll of the Torah served to authorize a great "reform," innovations in traditional practices, changes of the customary (oral) "laws" of the people, all introduced by the former ruling elite now restored to power in Jerusalem.

It is likely that sacred scrolls became more familiar to Judeans through their regular presentation and oral recitation by the high priests (Deut. 31:10; Josephus, *Ant.* 4.209; *m. Soṭah* 7:8). Such ceremonial exaltation, display, and "reading" served to enhance the sacred aura of the scrolls—a sacredness and mystery that continues in the Sabbath reading in synagogues today. In the first century C.E., Torah scrolls existed in at least some Judean and Galilean towns.

The Jewish historian Josephus tells of a heckler in the Galilean town of Tarichaeae holding up a copy of "the law of Moses" and of a scroll burned by Roman soldiers in a Judean village (*Life* 134–35; *War* 2.229). Yet because scrolls were so costly, and ordinarily in the custody of priests and scribes, it is unlikely that very many Judean or Galilean village assemblies (*synagōgai*) at the time of Jesus possessed Torah scrolls—or for that matter an assembly building in which they could be kept.

The dominant way of cultivating Israelite cultural tradition—which included but was much broader than what is usually called "biblical" tradition—continued to be by memory and oral communication. Judean texts themselves indicate that even the literate elite, such as the Essenes at Qumran, the Pharisees, and the Rabbis, cultivated Israelite cultural traditions primarily in oral modes.

The community that produced the Dead Sea Scrolls found in the Judean wilderness at Qumran were scribes and priests who possessed scrolls of Judean biblical writings and left many scrolls of their own literature. The latter, however, point to the intense oral life of the community. Members of the community composed and recited hymns and blessings at communal meals and meetings (e.g., 1QSa 2:21–23), they composed and recited hymns (e.g., 1QH), prayers, and blessings (e.g., 1QSb =1Q28b; 4Q408; 4Q503; 4Q507–9), they delivered sapiential exhortation (e.g., 4QS184–5), and they rehearsed holy war (1QM). Most of the scrolls they produced describe or are written copies of (often regular) oral performances and rituals. Since the leaders of the community were performing or practicing virtually all of the ceremonies and teachings covered in the Community Rule on a regular basis, they would hardly have needed to consult a "manual" very often.[19] The covenant renewal ceremony described at the beginning of the *Community Rule*, for example, would have been enacted orally whenever new members were inducted. Community members engaged in the communal life for years hardly needed to read a scroll of their "Community Rule" to know that "they shall eat in common and bless in common and deliberate in common" (1QS 6:3).

The Pharisees, who must have been literate, were known for their promulgation and transmission to the people of "regulations (*nomima*) from the teaching of the fathers which were not recorded in the laws of Moses," regulations that comprised part of the official law of the Judean temple-state (Josephus, *Ant.* 13.297; cf. 408–9).[20] In Rabbinic circles as well, oral communication even of Torah predominated.

> Written texts were preserved. . . . Yet their use in instruction was discouraged. Rather, the exposition of Sages' teachings took place in a highly ritualized setting designed to recreate and represent an origi-

nal imparting of oral tradition from Moses to his disciples. . . . Within such a milieu, written texts enjoyed an essentially oral cultural life, subject to all the vagaries of oral transmission as they [we]re memorized and transmitted in face-to-face performance.[21]

Thus, although scrolls of the Hebrew scriptures not only existed, particularly in elite circles, and held a sacred aura and authority, nearly all communication in Judean and Galilean society, including knowledge of the sacred traditions of Israel, was carried on orally.

Oral Cultivation of Israelite Cultural Tradition as Evident in the Gospel of Mark

If the cultivation of Israelite tradition was oral even among literate groups such as the "scribes and Pharisees," then it was certainly oral in village communities and popular movements. We must seriously revise the assumptions and generalizations of modern biblical studies about the presence and function of texts in the context of Jesus' ministry and the development of Gospel traditions. To continue to imagine that the source of Jesus' "knowledge of scripture" was hearing "scripture read aloud" is historically unrealistic.[22] It is highly unlikely that village assemblies possessed the extremely costly and cumbersome parchment scrolls of "scripture." It is also unlikely that someone in the village had acquired the necessary scribal training to be able to read them aloud.[23]

The key basis for the modern belief that Jesus and his followers were literate users of texts is the portrayal of Jesus in the Nazareth assembly on the Sabbath, taking in hand the scroll of Isaiah and easily finding the passage, "The Spirit of the Lord is upon me . . ." to "read" (Luke 4:16–20). This passage, however, is now recognized as Luke's projection of literacy onto Jesus, along with a particular christological scheme onto the launching of his ministry in Galilee. No such scroll or "reading" appears in Mark's picture of Jesus teaching on the Sabbath in his hometown assembly (6:1–2). Matthew may well have been working from written texts in his explicit "formula quotations" of scripture. By contrast, Mark gives virtually no indication that he is using written texts. The evidence in Mark is all the more impressive, since we would have expected that later copyists in the possession of written texts of the Jewish Scriptures in Greek (the Septuagint) would have conformed the references in Mark and Q to standardized textual wording. Yet, as is clear from ancient manuscripts of Mark, that did not happen.

The Gospel of Mark itself provides important evidence that cultivation of Israelite cultural tradition was oral. Ironically the key evidence lies in the references to Israelite cultural traditions that have previously been characterized as quotations of or allusions to particular *texts* of scripture.[24] Many references to Israelite traditions in Mark never should have been taken as quotations of or allusions to scripture (i.e., written texts) in the first place. Some of those are simply references to Israelite traditions, such as Jesus' entry into Jerusalem on a colt (Mark 11:2–8), Jesus' reference to David and his men plucking grain (2:23–28), and the "passion narrative" with its numerous allusions. Others are references to what characters in the story had said, and not to a written text (10:4; 11:9–10; 12:36). And others, such as "honor your father and mother," are the most fundamental and memorable principles that would have been well known to ancient Judeans and Galileans, just as key principles of the Bill of Rights can be cited from memory by patriotic citizens of the United States (e.g., 7:9–10; 10:19). Even in cases that are presented explicitly as citations, clearly the words come from memory, not written texts. For example, Mark 1:2–3 ostensibly quotes Isaiah, but in fact begins with a recitation of Exodus 23:20 and Malachi 3:1. The likely explanation is that such a composite recitation comes from popular cultivation of Israelite prophetic tradition rather than consultation of texts.

Especially passages introduced with the terms "it is written (in the prophet . . .)" and "scripture" (*gegraptai* and *graphē*, respectively) have usually been read as indications of a textual quotation. This must now be reconsidered in the light of the dominance of oral cultivation of Israelite tradition and the distinctive function of sacred writing in Judea. In ancient Greece and Judea the writing of laws or decrees on public monuments or on scrolls stored in the Temple was symbolic of the *authority* of what stood written, even though it was seldom consulted. This principle should be extended to references to scripture in Jewish and early Christian literature, most of which do not follow the written texts as we know them from the best manuscripts of the "texts" supposedly cited. These references were appeals to the *authority* of scripture, which is by definition written (and could presumably be consulted) on scrolls.[25]

Recognizing "as it is written" as a reference not to the written text but to the authority of the Israelite biblical tradition, as "written," leads us to yet another previously unrecognized dimension of Jesus' apparent citations of scripture in Mark. Jesus' "citation" of scripture is polemically aimed at the official cultivators and guardians of the sacred writings. When he "cites" Isaiah against the scribes and Pharisees (Mark 7:6) and Jeremiah and a festival psalm against the rulers of the Temple with the term "it is written" (Mark 11:17; 12:10), he throws back at the literate elite the very authority that they themselves claim as legitimation for their own power and authority. Similarly, the references in Mark 9:12–13 appeal to the general authority of scripture (with no particular references given), over against the scribal authorities on scripture. In 10:3–5 Mark throws a citation of Moses back in the face of the Pharisees, and in 12:18–27 he refers to the written text of Moses against the Sadducees who accept the written Torah as the only authority. Thus in most of the references to scripture in Mark, Jesus is citing it over against the rulers and their scribal representatives who claim it as the authorization of their privilege and power over the people.[26]

This brief survey of Mark's references to Israelite traditions, including his references to "it is written," thus indicates that even in the composition of this Gospel Israelite traditions were known in memory and cultivated orally. This should not be surprising. Just because ordinary people in traditional societies were illiterate does not mean they were ignorant of cultural traditions. In fact just the opposite. Preliterate peoples actively cultivate their own cultural traditions. The Galilean villagers among whom Mark's story develops, including Jesus and his followers, would have known and actively cultivated their Israelite traditions, such as the basic covenantal "commandments of God" (see 7:9–13), observance of the Sabbath, stories of Moses and Elijah (see further especially chapters 7, 8, and 10 below). Nor should it be surprising to find a narrative that derives from a popular movement working from memory in an oral mode of communication. Despite their possession of written scrolls, even the literate elite cultivated their traditions orally, as we know from the later Jewish rabbis.

Hearing Mark as Oral Performance

This survey of Mark's references to Israelite traditions brings us face to face with the question of composition and reception of the Gospel. We can no longer ignore the fact that nearly all literature from the ancient Mediterranean world, from poetry and speeches to history and philosophy, were performed orally. They are what is now called "oral-derived" texts. Even after performed materials were written down, they continued to be recited or performed orally.[27] Texts were written and used primarily for the purpose of facilitating oral communication. If read, they were read aloud, hence re-oralized in recitation. The mode of reception and understanding ("hermeneutics") implicit in such oral-derived literature would thus have been oral-aural.

Implications for a Modern "Hearing" Strategy

Since most literature from antiquity originated and continued in oral performance, and since literacy was so limited, particularly among ordinary people, the Gospel of Mark also must have begun and continued in oral performance. It is relatively less important to know whether the story was composed (out of oral traditions) in performance, dictation, or in writing. At some point it was written down, becoming an oral-derived text. It is most important to recognize that, given the close relationship between text and performance in the ancient world, Mark was performed and heard in communities of people. Mark was thus a "text" that was recited repeatedly even after it was written down in one or more copies. The earliest actual manuscripts that the English translations found in our Bibles are based on are probably third-generation copies.[28] But the Gospel of Mark continued to be performed long after it was written down. The church leader of the early second century named Papias preferred the oral over the written gospel long after the Gospels existed in written form (Eusebius, *Hist. Eccl.* 3.39.4).[29] We know from many cases in early Christian literature from the second century that Jesus' sayings continued to be recited orally long after the Gospels were written.[30]

Recognition that the Gospel of Mark printed in our Greek and English New Testaments is an oral-derived text—that the Markan narrative must have been performed orally in a predominantly oral communication environment—seriously alters our relation to the text in front of us. Reading Mark as a mere text reduces what was a living tradition of live performance to a fossilized skeleton of what it was or could be. Reading Mark as a mere text would be like merely reading the libretto of Mozart's *Magic Flute* instead of attending a performance. Or, in a more apt analogy, reading Mark as a mere text would be like reading the words of an ancient Greek drama without reconstructing the performance situation with our informed historical imagination. If we want to understand Mark as an oral-derived text which functioned in oral performance, then we must seek greater sensitivity to oral performance, particularly in the historical situation of Mark's origins. It would surely help "to strip away too 'bookish' an approach to the written texts, and to emphasize the value and circumstances of the performance."[31]

In contrast to silent, solitary reading in modern print culture, moreover, recitation of a story or even reading from a written letter was usually a communal experience of a group in the ancient Mediterranean world.[32] Thus even texts functioned "as constituents of a collective cultural enterprise or of a communal memory."[33] Recitation or performance of oral-derived texts was a relational, interactive event. Although "reader response" criticism includes the role of the reader along with that of the author, it still assumes a silent solitary modern reader. We require a more relational approach in order to discern the ways in which a performed story interacted with a communal audience. Recited narratives or communally read letters were embedded in communities and their particular historical and social circumstances, far more than a biblical scholarship focused on a solitary silent reading of printed texts has imagined. Indeed, the communal reception, like the performance, was empathetic and participatory rather than distanced and reflective (let alone "objective"). Performance and reception of Mark in particular were probably embedded in a context of political-religious struggle as well. Thus we must also consider the likely concrete historical social context inseparably from composition-and-performance.

Theory of Oral Performance

Standard biblical studies have not positioned us at all well to come to grips with Mark or any other biblical "text" as oral performance, mainly because biblical studies have been so exclusively focused on written texts with the assumptions of print culture. Studies of other oral-derived texts such as Greek epics and medieval European poems and anthropological studies of contemporary oral performances are more promising sources for approaches that may be helpful on Mark as oral performance. These studies are interrelated with important work done in sociolinguistics in the last generation.[34]

Working in a Christian religious tradition that has made a virtual religious fetish out of biblical words, verses, and lessons or "pericopes," standard biblical studies has focused on extracting the meaning of those text fragments. Once we recognize that a biblical "text" was performed for a community in a particular historical-social context, however, we should begin by asking not *what* is meant by words and verses, but *how* the performed "text" conveyed meaning to the audience.[35] Standard biblical studies assumes somehow that the text itself contains meaning which the scholarly interpreter must discover and/or extract. Once we recognize that the "text" of Mark was performed in a community located in a particular historical-social context, then all of those dimensions of communication must be held together. The "text" did not mean something in itself but was an act of communication of performer to audience in a particular context. The narrative evoked meaning among the audience on the basis of their situation and experience, including their cultural tradition. In modern literature, the writer individually manipulates inherited or idiosyncratic materials in a new direction or from a new perspective, thus conferring meaning on a fresh new literary creation. By contrast, the performer of an already familiar story, working through standard rhetorical patterns and strategies long familiar to the audience, summoned conventional connotations of cultural traditions in evoking in the audience a meaning that was inherent. Such inherent meaning cannot be stated by the modern interpreter in so many words because it is relational, it must be appreciated situationally.

Perhaps the key to how the performer evokes meaning in reciting a "text" to an audience is that a given term or phrase or image or statement summons up a whole range of connotations and experience. In such "metonymic" referencing the part stands for or evokes the whole in and from the shared cultural tradition or life-world of the performer and audience. To appreciate how such "metonymic" (part-represents-whole) referencing works we can simply think of typical cases in our own experience as hearers. For an American who has learned United States history well, hearing the phrase "We hold these truths to be self-evident" summons up not only the whole "Declaration of Independence" and "American Revolution," but the values that she and supposedly the whole society hold dear. For someone who lived through the 1960s to hear a recording of the distinctive voice and inflection of Martin Luther King say "I have a dream" evokes all sorts of images from the civil rights movement and the resistance to it: sit-ins, marches, police brutality, and the shooting of King himself, perhaps a vivid feeling of a whole formative period of American history.

Similarly, for the audience of the performed Markan narrative, stories of sea crossings or feedings in the wilderness would evoke the memory of the exodus and wilderness journey to the promised land, the formative events of the people of Israel. Hearing that the name of the demon cast out was "Legion" (the alien, Latin word for the largest divisions within the Roman army) would summon the feeling of being a people conquered by the Roman troops, perhaps even a memory of a Roman massacre or mass enslavement. The implication for modern readers who want to "get in touch" with the way Mark's narrative resonated with the audience is clear: to become as familiar as possible with the cultural tradition and life world of Mark's hearers.

The key to *how* meaning happens in oral performance is thus the way in which parts of the message resonate in the hearers as they reference metonymically the hearers' cultural tradition (and social situation). With the aid of sociolinguistic analysis of communication we can sense more precisely *how* meaning happens in this way. Three interrelated analytical aspects of this interrelationship between the audience and the metonymic referencing of the cultural tradition are particularly important in understanding oral performance: "text," or what precisely the performer performs; "context," or the setting or situation in which the performance occurs; and "register," or the kind of communication appropriate to the particular type of communication context. The remainder of this chapter will be devoted primarily to analysis of the "text" of Mark. But since the communication "context" and the "register" of the performance are so integrally related, some discussion of the latter aspects may help us understand the "text" of Mark.

Context. Hearers of a recitation or performance take their cues from the communication context for how they receive the message, for how the message resonates in them as it references their cultural tradition. When we go to a funeral we expect to hear messages about the deceased and to mourn the deceased and feel sympathy for the family. Attendance at a wedding sets up

very different cues for how to listen and what to expect. Some larger communication contexts have several subcontexts. A play performed in a theater has
changes of scene that affect how the dialogue is heard. A church service moves
from one communication subcontext to another, signaled by phrases such as
"Let us pray," "In the night in which he was betrayed," or musical signals by
the organ. The same phrase or statement would be heard differently in the
context of a pastoral prayer from that of a sermon. In a university classroom
the context might shift from lecture to open class discussion. The Mosaic
covenant given by God to Israel on Mount Sinai resonated differently when
invoked by the "founding fathers" in New England legislatures debating the
ratification of the recently drafted Constitution of the United States than it
did in pietistic Methodist congregations concerned with individual moral
purity (Ten Commandments).

As suggested in chapter 2 above and subsequent chapters below, the larger
communication context of the performance of Mark must have been communities of a first-century social-political movement that had spread beyond
Galilee into villages and towns of the eastern Mediterranean. "Churches" and
"synagogues" have too narrow and too "religious" a connotation. The Greek
terms *ekklēsia* and *synagōgē* both referred to the city or village assembly that
dealt with all sorts of community social and political issues as well as carried
out certain "civil-religious" ceremonies. Meetings of the communities of
Jesus' followers were more like those of chapters of a labor movement or civil
rights movement than they were like church worship services. Such community or "chapter" meetings would have dealt with relations with the broader
political-economic-religious structure as well as internal affairs and the
broader purpose of the movement. Such meetings would thus have dealt with
more than the hearing of Mark's Gospel. Besides discussion of how to deal
with political repression by the rulers, delegation of envoys to expand the
movement, and maintaining an egalitarian movement, they surely celebrated
the Lord's Supper together.

Not surprisingly, the Markan narrative deals with all of those matters
(see respectively: 8:34–38 and 13:9–13; 6:7–13 and 13:10; 10:35–45; and
14:22–25). Thus the subcontext of hearing the Gospel performed evoked,
touched upon, and in effect overlapped with other subcontexts within the
broader community meetings of the movement. The implication for modern
readers who want to appreciate Mark as oral performance is clear: they must
become as familiar as possible with the historical situation of the hearers of
Mark so that they can attend the performance of Mark in the proper context.
If the modern reader assumes or imagines the communication context of
Mark as narrowly religious, the "text" will be misunderstood, misconstrued,
distorted.

Register. The particular styles or configurations of speech associated with particular recurrent types of communication contexts are often called *registers* in sociolinguistics. Societies have many traditional registers devoted to various activities such as curing, puberty rites, weddings, political decision making in tribal assemblies, etc. In our own society, eulogies are appropriate register for funerals, toasts for wedding banquets, lecturing for large university classes, roasts for retirement parties. Sociolinguists think of a register as determined by three interrelated aspects of the recurrent type of context: the *field* of discourse pertains to what is being transacted, the subject; the *tenor* of discourse concerns who is involved, the relations among the participants; and the *mode* of discourse refers to the mode of communication, oral or written, etc.

For gaining an appreciation of Mark as performance, a sense of the register(s) involved is far more important than a determination of the literary genre. Even if we could reach consensus about how to label Mark's literary genre (biography, romance, history, etc.) we would still need to gain some sense of the particular registers in which the narrator and Jesus speak. When Jesus focuses on the ruling Temple and high priests, he speaks and acts symbolically in an Israelite prophetic register of indictment and condemnation. Jesus' disputes with the Pharisees over how Mosaic covenant traditions apply to everyday life shift into a controversy register. In developing a prolonged narrative, the Gospel of Mark has adapted the standard traditional registers familiar from Israelite tradition. Modern readers would benefit from far greater familiarity with those traditional registers in our attempt to appreciate how meaning "happened," as the particular language in particular episodes resonated with the hearers by referencing the cultural tradition out of which they were living.

While the rest of this chapter will focus on the "text" of Mark as performed, on its coherence and features as an oral narrative, it will be important to keep in mind the closely interrelated aspects of performance "context" and "register" in order to be as sensitive as possible to how the meaning resonated in the hearers as they heard the "text" performed.

Mark as Oral Performance: The "Text"

Since all literature in antiquity was heard by a group in performance, we must conclude that Mark was also originally performed before a group.[36] Since it was virtually impossible to follow undivided words on a papyrus roll, moreover, Mark must have been recited from memory, not literally read aloud from a text. Judging from comparative studies of oral performances, each new performance would not have been identical in wording with the preceding one. Yet the overall structure of the narrative and most of the wording would have been the same from one recitation to another,[37] as we know from our own experience of performing and/or listening to music. It makes sense therefore for modern readers attempting to appreciate Mark as oral performance to focus on the story as a whole, and not on the precise meaning of particular words and phrases. By no means should we suspend critical consideration of details. But those details, unimportant in themselves, will become significant only in the context of the whole sequence of episodes that comprises Mark's story.

Although we are not focusing on the question of the original oral composition of Mark, it is easily imaginable how it emerged as a sustained narrative of Jesus' mission and martyrdom. The Gospel of Mark would appear to have built on an ongoing storytelling tradition within one of the Jesus movements.[38] It seems unlikely that one composer-performer, in an unprecedented act of creativity—following some generic model of biography—suddenly strung together a selection of individually circulating stories (healings, exorcisms, controversies, parables, etc.). Mark's narrative rather would have made use of and/or developed out of earlier "connected" narratives comprised of shorter component stories. Even when working on the assumptions of print culture and written composition, Gospel scholars have concluded that "Mark" presupposed and worked with a collection of parables (behind and in some way incorporated into Mark 4:1–34), "chains" of miracle stories (behind the two parallel sets of five miracle stories in Mark 4:35–8:26), combinations of healing and pronouncement stories (behind the set of five stories in Mark 2:1–3:6), a prophetic discourse (behind Mark 13), and perhaps a narrative of the arrest, trial, crucifixion, and resurrection.

Sequence and Coherence of the Overall Oral Narrative

The first step in beginning to hear Mark as an oral narrative is to gain a sense of the "text" of this oral-derived text, the structure, patterns, contents of the Gospel, with sensitivity to the performer-and-audience. Although we must work from the written text of Mark, the mere "libretto" of the performance, which is all we have available, we must use our informed imagination to appreciate important extratextual features of performance such as varying volume, pauses, emphases, pace, etc.[39] Cross-cultural studies may stimulate our sensitivity.

Nowhere is cross-cultural study of oral performance more helpful than with regard to the overall dramatic flow and the particular patterning in the "text" of Mark. Bosnian and Serbian epic singers insisted that the "word" they sang was alternatively a set of lines, a speech, a scene, even a whole epic song. The minimal unit was at least the ten-syllable poetic line, not a single word, as in the printed texts we are accustomed to reading. Especially suggestive for a performed Gospel of Mark is recent imaginative analysis of

Native American storytelling. Particular performances and even textual transcripts of them can be discerned to have certain sequential patterns that we might call "lines," "verses," "stanzas," "scenes," and "acts."[40]

Partly with the aid of such comparative perspectives, we can easily discern that the fundamental units of narrative communication in Mark are the episodes, which correspond roughly to the stanzas or scenes of Serbian or ancient Greek epic singers or Native American storytellers. The episodes often include dialogues, proverbs, and recitations of "scripture" or allusions to Israelite traditions, but the lines and verses do not comprise separate units of communication; they take on contextual meaning only as parts of the episodes. Cross-cultural comparisons also confirm our sense, from considering Mark as a story (chapter 1) that the episodes do not stand on their own as independent units of narrative communication. They were rather "plotted" in a particular sequential arrangement to tell a whole story. The longer story that is Mark's Gospel has a dramatic flow in certain steps or "acts" as the overall drama unfolds. To begin to appreciate these aspects of Mark as oral performance, we will deal first with some distinctive features of Mark's oral style within and between episodes, then with the overall flow and coherence of the story in a sequence of "acts," and finally with some of the patterns within the "acts" of the narrative, before reflecting on the difference it makes for our appropriation of Mark's story to come to "hear" it as oral performance.

"Just one thing after another" and Repetition of Words and Sounds

To the modern reader Mark's story often seems like just one thing after another, with no rhyme or reason to connect the episodes. Modern writers make sophisticated connections of temporal, causative, and other subordinative relations between clauses. But traditional oral narrators simply told one episode after another and, within episodes, spoke one clause after another. The Greek philosopher Plato complained that orally delivered poetry and stories consisted simply of multiple "happenings," many things with no connections of cause and effect.[41] In such "additive" (or "paratactic") oral narrative the normal way of connecting sentences within an episode and the episodes with one another is with the simple connective "and." Virtually all episodes in Mark begin with "and" (kai). Even the parables, which do not seem like consecutive episodes, are connected by means of "and." This stacking up of one clause after another within episodes is not evident in most English translations (e.g., the NRSV) because the translators have replaced nearly all of them with subordinate, temporal, or causal clauses in order to render the Gospel into better English prose style ("when . . . ," "now . . . ," "as . . . ," etc.).

Another feature of Mark that seems awkward to the modern reader is its seemingly obsessive repetition of phrases and terms from sentence to sentence, verse to verse. This would be far more striking if it could be heard in Greek, for repetition of ideas, phrases, terms, even of sounds is perhaps the most salient characteristic of oral performance of all kinds. Cross-cultural studies have shown that in oral culture, people retain and retrieve memorable thoughts in mnemonic patterns, shaped for ready oral recurrence. Thought which is thus intertwined with patterns of memory comes into expression in "repetitions or antitheses, in alliterations and assonances, in epithetic and other formulary expressions, in standard thematic settings (the assemblies, the meal, etc.), in proverbs that . . . come to mind readily."[42] In most oral performance simply the repetition of sounds is remarkable. (See Appendix 1 for an illustrative example from Mark 1:21–28.)

Sometimes the repetition of (sequences of) words and sounds not only aids the communication between performer and audience, but also emphasizes the power of Jesus' speech and confirms the trust that petitioners have in his power. Sometimes this repetition of words and sequences of words can be appreciated even in English translation. For example, imagine the sequential repetition of words and sounds when the leper petitions and Jesus responds in 1:41–45:

> "If you will (it),
>   you can make me clean."
> "I do will (it).
>   Be made clean."
> . . . the leprosy left, and he was made clean.[43]

Less obvious but still evident is the repetition of sounds, words (and synonyms) after the Syrophoenician woman has bested Jesus in debate, embarrassing him into exorcizing the demon from her "little daughter" in 7:24–31. Jesus says to the woman,

> "For that saying, you may go, for has gone out of your daughter the
>   demon."
> And going home, she found the child lying on the bed and the demon
>   gone out.[44]

The Overall Flow and Coherence of the Narrative

Although Mark may not have a suspenseful plot like some modern novels, it does exhibit a dramatically escalating conflict that builds to a climax in a sequence of steps (see the outline in chapter 1, p 14 above). Similar to some

Native American narratives, Mark's overall story seems to develop in several (five) major "acts," with two long speeches between the first and second and the fourth and fifth. After a brief prologue introducing Jesus as the fulfillment of prophecy (1:1–13), he engages in a campaign of healing, exorcizing, and preaching in Galilee (1:14–3:35), whereupon the action pauses for teaching in parables (4:1–34). Action resumes with a second campaign in Galilee that expands into the surrounding regions of Tyre, Caesarea Philippi, and the Decapolis (4:35–8:26). In an overlapping third "act," Jesus announces three times that he must be killed and rise again and delivers important teaching to his followers in response to the disciples' persistent misunderstanding, as he begins his ominous journey to Jerusalem (8:22–10:52). Once in Jerusalem Jesus prophetically confronts the ruling circles of priests and scribes and the Temple in which they are based (11:1–13:2), after which he teaches about the future (13:3–37). In the final "act," as Jesus predicts at the "last supper," the intensely dramatic climatic events unfold: his betrayal, arrest, trial, abandonment, and crucifixion—followed by the open ending of the empty tomb and the direction of the disciples and the hearers back to Galilee (14:1–16:8).

As noted in chapter 1, moreover, these five main steps or "acts" in the narrative, interspersed twice by longer speeches, are closely linked by overlapping episodes and by repetition of types of episodes and key themes. Indeed as in Greek poetry and drama, so in Mark, oral narrative "operates on the acoustic principle of the echo."[45] Like other oral narratives, Mark's story is repeatedly both retrospective and prophetic. As the audience hears "one episode after another" ("and then . . . ," "and immediately . . .") the narrative is not linear but turns back on itself in order to assist the memory to reach the end by having it anticipated somehow in the beginning."[46] Mark seems almost to avoid surprises and novelties, both within particular sections and in the story as a whole. In a narrative style that assists memory the earlier episodes suggest or forecast later episodes which in turn recall the earlier ones while carrying the story further and adding to the drama and conflict. The narrative thus establishes numerous interconnections that resonate with each other as they resonate with the hearers of the Gospel.

In one of the most striking cases of echo and repetition, the story of Peter's declaration that Jesus is "the Messiah" (8:27–30) is set up in exactly the same way as the earlier story of John's execution by Herod Antipas (6:14–29), reciting popular views of Jesus. It is also immediately followed by Jesus' first announcement that he must suffer rejection by the Jerusalem rulers and be killed, and his sharp rebuff of Peter's objection (8:31–33). Not only does the story of John's execution prefigure that of Jesus' crucifixion, but Jesus' announcement of his own execution following Peter's declaration, along with its repetition twice in 9:30 and 10:32–34, anticipates the long story of arrest, trial, and crucifixion, one component of which is Peter's and the other disciples' misunderstanding and denial.[47]

Including such "echoes," Mark's narrative makes numerous connections across the sections or "acts" that tie the story as a whole together. The first campaign in Galilee begins with Jesus' announcing that the kingdom of God is at hand (1:14–15), which also announces the theme of the whole story. The general episode in 3:7–12 functions as a "wide-angle" summary of what has preceded, but also looks forward to subsequent healings and exorcisms and provides a general statement of all the other cases and of the Jesus movement in general (for which Mark was performed) that are not narrated in the Gospel. The two episodes of healing blind men, 8:22–26 and 10:46–52, not only frame the section they enclose, but they also link that middle section with the preceding and succeeding sections.[48] The narrator who has just followed one sequence of five miracle stories (sea crossing, exorcism, healing, healing, feeding in the wilderness) with a sequence of four miracle stories (sea crossing, exorcism, healing, feeding in the wilderness) makes the transition to the new "act" with the second healing story out of the second sequence—and the listeners sense that something to do with healing of blindness is about to happen. Besides completing the section on the disciples' difficulties in "seeing," the story of Bartimaeus's healing forms the transition to the following section on Jesus' confrontation with the rulers in Jerusalem by introducing the healer Jesus as "son of David."

Thus, with these and many other episodes and summary statements that look backward and/or forward in the narrative (as discussed further in chapter 1 above), Mark's oral story is far more than "just one thing after another." It is a dramatic story in which the dominant conflict between Jesus and the rulers, and the subordinate conflicts between Jesus and the disciples and Jesus and the demons, develop and escalate from "act" to "act" until they come to a climax in the final events in Jerusalem.

Patterns in the Narrative

Within, as well as among, the various "acts" of the narrative are echoes, repetitions, and other patterns that aid the memory of the performer and the hearing of the audience. In the first episode of the first campaign in Galilee Jesus calls disciples (1:16–20), then toward the end of this section he appoints the twelve (3:13–19). The sequence of episodes that begins with the first exorcism also sets Jesus, who has "authority," in opposition to the scribes, who do not (1:21–28), then closes with a healing of leprosy set pointedly against the dominant authority, the Temple and priests (1:40–45). The campaign that then extends beyond Galilee, in section 4:35–8:26, is structured according to two parallel sequences of five miracle stories (sea crossing—exorcism—healing—healing—feeding), with additional material being interjected between the healings and the feeding in the first sequence, and between the sea crossing and the exorcism in the second. Besides being strikingly framed by episodes of healing blind men (8:22–26 and 10:46–52), the middle section is organized around three announcements of the trial, killing, and resurrection in 8:31; 9:31; and 10:33–34, followed by the disciples' misunderstanding, in 8:27–33; 9:30–37; and 10:35–40.

When the narrator gets to the last "act" the audience already knows the sequence of events to expect from the announcements in 8:31; 9:31; and 10:32–34: rejection by and suffering under chief priests and elders, handing over to Romans to be killed, and resurrection. Besides that, it is highly likely that the narrative here follows a well-known pattern already deeply embedded in Jewish culture, that of the suffering righteous one who is martyred for the cause. The sequence of episodes is also interwoven with predictions and fulfillments: of various disciples' betrayal, denial, and flight, but also of Jesus going before them into Galilee. Finally, of course, the disciples' fear and failure are juxtaposed with the courage and faithfulness of the women, whose actions frame and hold together the final act of the Gospel (14:3–8; 16:1–8).

Within the various sections of the Gospel are yet other techniques of oral narrative that aid the performer's memory and audience's hearing. The already long-acknowledged Markan "sandwiches" juxtapose two episodes, one framed within the other. The raising back to life of Jairus's "twelve-year-old" daughter frames the healing of the woman who had been hemorrhaging for "twelve" years (5:21–43). The cursing of the fig tree frames the demonstration in the Temple (11:12–25). And Peter's denial of Jesus (15:54, 66–72) is juxtaposed with Jesus' trial before the Jerusalem high-priestly court (15:52, 55–65).

Other such techniques of "ring" or "chiastic" composition (inclusio), characteristic of oral narrative generally,[49] are prevalent in Mark, both marking the boundaries of individual episodes and connecting several episodes. In addition to inserting one story into another (the Markan "sandwiches"), the narrative arranges episodes in chiastic or concentric patterns of A–B–A or A–B–C–B–A or even more complexly (e.g., sequences of seven in 1:21–45; five in 4:1–34; six in 8:34–9:1).[50] Even within such chiastic patterning of episodes the parallel stories often display considerable similarities. Such patterns help both the performer and hearers remember and create relations of significance between the episodes. Ironically we modern silent readers, who can no longer hear the chiastic patterns and the similar language and motifs between two parallel episodes, must often visualize the patterns and parallels.

The most striking example comes in the five episodes from 2:1 to 3:6. Perhaps by seeing the pattern in diagram we can better imagine hearing the pattern and parallels in this sequence of episodes.

A. 2:1–12 HEALING STORY (LEG; 2:3–5, 11–12) WITH CONTROVERSY
(2:6–10)
    Jesus speaks twice to healed man (2:5, 10)
    Scribes' objection unspoken but discerned by Jesus
    (son of man = "I" saying, 2:10)
    Reaction by amazed people: never seen anything like this! (2:12)

    B. 2:13–17 EATING (WITH SINNERS) IN CONTROVERSY STORY
        Touched off by incident of Jesus' action (2:15)
        Pharisees voice objection to disciples (2:16)
        Proverb (2:17)
        "I" saying (2:17)

        C. 2:18-22 FASTING (NOT EATING) IN CONTROVERSY STORY
            Contrast of old and new
            Proverb

    B. 2:23–28 EATING (ON SABBATH) IN CONTROVERSY STORY
        Touched off by incident of disciples' action (2:23)
        Pharisees voice objection to Jesus (2:24)
        Proverb (2:27)
        "son of man" (= "I") saying

A. 3:1–6 HEALING STORY (HAND; 3:1, 3, 5) WITH CONTROVERSY (3:2, 4–5)
    Jesus speaks twice to healed man (3:3, 5)
    (Pharisees') objection unspoken but discerned by Jesus
    Reaction by Pharisees and Herodians: conspire to destroy Jesus (3:6)

The first and the fifth stories have similar subjects and parallel structure: healing-controversy-healing. The characters are the same or similar: Jesus, a man with a paralyzed/withered leg/hand, and the scribes/Pharisees ("they" in 3:2 = the Pharisees in the previous story, 2:24). The controversy part in both is set off by Jesus' direct address to the healed man. And in both the objection of the scribes or Pharisees is unspoken but discerned by Jesus. Both stories have dual reactions, but they are diametrically opposed: the amazed people have never seen anything like this, but the threatened Pharisees immediately conspire with the Herodians to destroy Jesus.

The second and fourth stories display similar subject (eating) and parallel structure as controversy stories. The characters are the same: Jesus, the disciples, and the Pharisees. The parallel structures do have some variation. The Pharisees object to Jesus' action to the disciples in the one, and to the disciples' action to Jesus in the other. They object to the company with whom Jesus eats in the one case, to the grain plucked in the field in the other. The stories conclude with parallel proverbs followed by parallel "I"/"son of man" sayings.

The central episode in the sequence begins with the flip-side of eating, i.e., not eating, or fasting. That issue leads into the real question of the episode: What time is it? Something unusual is happening with Jesus, a time of celebration, like a wedding. And what is now fermenting (wine) will simply burst through the old vessels (wineskins). In the overall sequence, healing the paralyzed and eating with sinners leads to the recognition that something new is happening, which is then exemplified in additional eating and healing that breaks through the standard old social-religious forms that the Pharisees defend.

Further parallels bind these stories together. The first two are about sin and sinners, the last two about actions on the Sabbath. Three of the four have "son of man" or "I" sayings. Moreover, the combination of themes and characters in this set of stories exemplifies and has many connections with the contents and principal themes of the rest of the Gospel. Two of Jesus' principal actions throughout the Gospel are healing (including exorcisms, from 1:20 through 10:52) and eating (especially the feedings and the last supper). Both kinds of actions manifest as well as anticipate the coming of the kingdom of God. And this set of episodes dramatizes the ways in which Jesus challenges, and is threatening to, the established order, represented here by the (scribes and) Pharisees, who represent the Jerusalem rulers in Galilee. This theme persists throughout the rest of the Gospel until the rulers manage to arrest and kill him. One could even say that this coordinated set of five episodes is paradigmatic for the rest of the Gospel—but then so also are several other sets of episodes, as is typical of oral narrative.

The Difference That Hearing Makes

Breaking the Grip of Theological Interpretation

Appreciating Mark as oral performance should move us further away from the reductionist and abstracting theological interpretation that has persisted in theological educational circles. Mark can come alive as a story. It need not continue to be merely a set of theological ideas that happens to take narrative form.

One of the dominant interpretations of Mark's Gospel in the last generation or two is that the author refutes a "christology" that emphasizes Jesus' miraculous powers by framing it within a "christology" that emphasizes the crucifixion and resurrection. Mark's is a theology of suffering and his Gospel summons readers into a discipleship of suffering. This agenda is supposedly found in the structure of the Gospel. Jesus' deeds of power, healings and exorcisms, dominate at the outset, then fade in importance after 8:22–26 and end with 10:46–52. Persecution and suffering, exemplified in Jesus' passion, are predicted in chapters 8–10 and then dominate the Gospel in its climactic events of Jesus' arrest, trial, and crucifixion in Jerusalem. This interpretation results from a theological interpretation that abstracts from the narrative and treats the episodes narrated as mere windows onto the really important world of theology.

People hearing the Gospel as an oral narrative, however, would never come up with such an abstract and schematic interpretation. Oral narrative does not refute one narrative portrayal of Jesus with another. Additive and aggregative oral narrative rather adds further episodes to those already narrated in a both-and presentation. Jesus performed healings and exorcisms and also confronted the rulers and their representatives and then also was arrested and tried and killed by them. Oral-aural "logic" (perhaps an oxymoron) is both-and. Both miracles and martyrdom. Both power and persecution. And if we allow any subtlety to the additive narrative that links episodes merely with one "and" after another, the power leads to the persecution. Jesus suffers martyrdom because he performs the miracles, which are a challenge and threat to the Jerusalem rulers. Whereas theology tends to abstract us into a strictly religious or spiritual level, oral narrative keeps us busily engaged in the real world of political conflict, between the people and their rulers and, in Mark's world, also between God and the "unclean spirits." The chapters below will explore further how an appreciation of Mark as a live story can cut through and overcome abstracting and reductionist interpretations of Mark as a particular christology or "apocalyptic" theology or a story of "discipleship."

Participation

In contrast with modern readers, who read to gather information, hearers of oral performance participate in the narrative. "Public verbal performance in an oral culture is participatory and essentially integrative. Speaker and audience and subject matter are raveled together."[51] Listeners are performance-oriented rather than information-oriented. Hearers do not listen to take away new information, but together with the performer experience the performed narrative.

The experience the original hearers of the Gospel of Mark performed in a group would thus have been very different from that of a modern, individual silent reader of a book. The original hearers would have been members of a community of a relatively new movement, people who had recently come to common commitments in similar life circumstances. The story focused on

Jesus, but was about far more than one heroic martyr figure. Thus the experience of hearing was not the individual cathartic identification that Aristotle observed in Greek drama, of the spectator drawn to identify with the suffering of hero in order to undergo an inner catharsis by way of a tragic emotional upheaval or a comic release. In performances where the ending of the Gospel story is still performed as tragic suffering, such as passion plays and Good Friday services of "the Seven Last Words of Christ"—and perhaps in certain individual silent reading of the Gospel—the individual hearer or reader may indeed still experience that part of the story as cathartic identification with the sufferings of Jesus. But Mark's Gospel as a whole is about more than Jesus' suffering. The oral narrative and the group experience of the hearers are "both-and." New life-giving and "empowering" forces are at work through Jesus. Oppressive rulers and institutions stand under God's condemnation. "The kingdom of God is at hand." Suffering and death are not the end of life.

This can perhaps be best illustrated by considering the implications of Mark's open ending. The last episode, where the women find the tomb empty and say nothing to anyone because they are afraid, does not stand by itself, nor is it the end of the story, in the sense of terminating the Gospel. In contrast to the Gospels of Matthew and Luke, the ending of the narrative itself in Mark is unresolved. As the narrator finishes speaking Mark's story lacks closure. We must hear again the whole story. Throughout most of the Gospel we hear episode after interrelated episode of the ways in which "the time is fulfilled and the kingdom of God is at hand." After Jesus announces the upcoming betrayal, denial, and disappearance of the disciples, he also says "but after I am raised up, I will go before you into Galilee" (14:28). Then at the empty tomb the youth in the white robe says that the risen Jesus "is going ahead of you to Galilee," i.e., where Jesus had started the movement and where it was based and continuing, after the face-off in Jerusalem.

The Gospel not only continues to be performed again and again, but it continues in the experience of the hearers past the end of any given performance. This lack of closure invites the hearers, already drawn into the story, to continue the Gospel. The open, unresolved ending of Mark's narrative, moreover, calls for a communal response. In contrast to a modern individualistic reader finding a call to "discipleship" in response to the disciples' failure after the story itself has ended, the participatory hearing in a community evokes a collective cooperative response by that community. Mark's open ending calls for a continuation of the Gospel story by a community of hearers, challenges them to continue building the movement inaugurated by Jesus. Not only are the boundaries between the performed story and everyday reality blurred; the Gospel story (and history) continues in the ongoing work of the movement, which in turn is motivated by the continuing performance of the story.

Modern Readers Becoming also Historical Hearers (If Not Doers) of the Word

To appreciate Mark's story as oral performance, modern readers would have to "identify" themselves with the historical audience in context, probably a step few are willing to take. Short of such a serious step, however, modern readers could at least become as knowledgeable as possible about the historical context of the communities in which the story was performed and the people whom the story is about, in order to be able to "empathize" with them at least in part. Acquiring such historical knowledge is necessary for us even to begin to share the common meanings and nuances of words, cultural conventions, historical experiences, and historical world views that are different from our own in ways we do not even begin to imagine. We require such historical knowledge to even begin to "get it." Recognition that Mark's story was performed in communal situations should lead biblical interpreters to begin joining oral-literary and historical analysis.

This effort to become more historically knowledgeable and sensitive hearers, however, will require self-criticism and abandonment both of some of our most habitual interpretive assumptions and practices and of a great deal of theologically based historical "knowledge." Several facets of the requisite changes in assumptions, focus, approach, and interpretive conceptual apparatus will form the subjects of the ensuing chapters in this book.

Perhaps the most obvious point to start with is the peculiar modern Western individualism focused on the persistent (usually silent individual) reading of Mark as a story of discipleship. Such an interpretation of Mark tends to ignore and even to obscure the oppressive political-economic situation and the broader political struggle in which Jesus, the disciples, and the broader movement they are leading is engaged. As noted in chapter 2, it seems likely that the hearers with whom the story resonated were also involved in such a situation and struggle. What if Mark's story is, among other things, an indictment of the disciples? Is it possible that Mark's story presses a criticism, within the broader Jesus movement, of what the twelve disciples had become in the course of the first generation, as it summoned the movement back to its roots in the social revolutionary practice and preaching of Jesus? The characters in Mark's story who might qualify as paradigmatic are not the disciples but the women, both those who experience healing when they are almost dead and those who appear prominently toward the end of the story in faithfully attending to Jesus. (See further chapters 4 and 9.)

The dominant conflict and "plot" of Mark's story focuses, not on the disciples, but on the struggle between Jesus and his program of renewing the people of Israel (plus other peoples) in their village communities over against the Roman and the high-priestly rulers. This requires us to scuttle any number of historical assumptions and interrelated items of false "knowledge." The main opposition in the Gospel is not between Jews and Gentiles, much less between Jewish and Christian, but between peasants (including fisher-folk) living in villages and Roman and Rome-appointed rulers and their representatives in Jerusalem. The latter may well be "religious" insofar as their power and privilege are mystified and ostensibly legitimated by their position as the priestly aristocracy in charge of the Temple. But Mark's story, far from portraying them as "Jewish leaders," consistently represents them as opponents and oppressors of the people. To "get" such a story, we must as much as possible "identify with" those third-world peasants in Galilee and the Israelite popular tradition that they cultivated orally in their village communities (see further chapter 5).

One more illustration of the serious shifts of assumptions and approaches required and the implications of Mark as an orally performed story: In all those debates with the Pharisees, Mark does not portray Jesus as attacking or breaking the "Law" of "Judaism." Mark rather has Jesus defend Israelite traditions and covenantal customs that had been cultivated orally in village communities over against the Pharisaic representatives of the Judean "great" tradition written on scrolls (see further chapter 7). And of course part of what the Pharisees represent in Mark's story is their "tradition of the elders," which was also oral. Moreover, if we have ears to hear, strange as it may sound to Protestant theological assumptions, Mark's Jesus advocates a renewed Mosaic covenant as part of his broader program of the renewal of Israel that has extended well beyond Israelite villages to the village communities among other peoples (see further chapter 8).

Any number of challenges to our previous understanding await as we attempt to become historically informed listeners in order to hear Mark's whole story as a narrative about a movement of renewal among a subjected people.

4

Disciples Become Deserters

Mark presents a dramatic portrayal of the twelve disciples. Jesus calls them to follow him in his first act after announcing that the kingdom of God is at hand (1:16–20). Soon he appoints the twelve to be with him and to proclaim the kingdom and exorcize demons, and then sends them out two by two on that mission (3:13–19; 6:7–13). Meanwhile, they receive the secret of the kingdom of God and explanation of everything in private (4:11, 34). Yet they become fearful and faithless when crossing the Sea of Galilee (4:35–41). And they do not understand what is happening in the feedings of the crowds in the wilderness, which begins to exasperate Jesus (6:35–37, 47–52; 8:1–21). By the middle of the Gospel they stubbornly fail to understand what Jesus pointedly declares to them—three times—about his having to be killed (8:31–33; 9:31–32; 10:32–40). After Peter rebukes Jesus, Jesus rebukes Peter: "Get behind me, Satan" (8:32–33). Jesus has to correct the disciples' misunderstanding after every announcement of his impending death. At the celebration of the Passover feast, when Jesus announces that one will betray, another deny, and all desert him, they all protest their loyalty (14:17–21, 26–31). But sure enough, they cannot remain awake while he prays in agony. And after Judas betrays him, the rest flee at his arrest and Peter denies him three times precisely while he is on trial (14:32–42, 43–50, 66–72). They all have disappeared from the story before the crucifixion and the empty tomb scene, with which the story ends.

With a closer look, the story of the twelve disciples opens up in greater detail. After the announcement of the general theme of the Gospel (the kingdom of God is at hand) Jesus calls Simon and Andrew and James and John to follow him and to "fish" for people in the very first episode of the story (1:16–20). Those four are then mentioned as being with him in the next few episodes and he takes them along when he heals the girl who appears to have died (1:19, 36; 5:37). Those who are eating with Jesus in three successive episodes are "the disciples" (2:15, 18, 23; 3:7, 9), although no indication is given about whether the four had expanded into more. As an outgrowth of a summary of how multitudes are flocking to Jesus from far beyond Galilee, he pointedly appoints the twelve "to be with him and [sends] them out to preach and exorcize demons" (3:13–17). In the listing of the twelve, Jesus nicknames Simon "Rock" (*Petros* in Greek) and Judas is explicitly designated as the one "who betrayed him." After Jesus tells the first parable, the narrator frames the rest with the explanations that "those who were around him along with the twelve" were "given the mystery of the kingdom of God" (4:10–11) and that he "explained everything in private to his disciples" (4:33–34). This framing clearly suggests that the twelve are closely associated with, apparently as a smaller group within, the disciples.

The disciples continue to accompany and, apparently, assist Jesus in the next sequence of his actions (5:31; 6:1, 35–44; 7:2, 17; 8:10). The disciples fear for their lives, however, in the very first episode of the new sequence, the first sea crossing (4:35–41). Indeed, in the second sea crossing they again panic (6:47–51). Compounding their lack of faith, they exhibit a remarkable density, a stubborn lack of understanding, at what is happening in Jesus' feeding of the multitudes in the wilderness. Their "hearts were hardened" (6:37, 52; 8:4, 14–21).

A whole section in the middle of the Gospel appears to be focused on the disciples' misunderstanding both of what Jesus' program of the kingdom of God is all about and of what is about to happen to Jesus. This section of the overall story, focused on the disciples' inability to "see" and to "follow" Jesus, is framed by two stories of Jesus healing blind men, the second of whom "immediately followed him on the way" (8:22–26; 10:46–52). Three successive times in this section of the Gospel Jesus announces that "the son of man" must be rejected and killed and rise again (8:31; 9:31; 10:33–34). Immediately following each announcement, Peter or the twelve or James and John, respectively, say something that indicates that they have not grasped either that Jesus must be killed or what the kingdom of God now at hand means for their own roles and behavior. It is then necessary for Jesus to explain in explicit terms that they must be ready to assume the role of servants, not rulers, of the movement, and to "take up their cross," even becoming martyrs like Jesus if it comes to that (8:32–9:1; 9:32–37; 10:35–45). Jesus must explain a second and third time despite the fact that Peter, James, and John all experienced the transfiguration of Jesus on the mountain with Moses and Elijah and heard Jesus' explanation that "Elijah has come, and they did to him whatever they pleased" (9:2–8, 11–13). Despite the commissioning of the twelve to preach and exorcize, moreover, the disciples prove incapable of exorcizing the demon that made the boy unable to speak (9:14–18). Considering what Jesus has clearly announced about what will soon happen to "the son of man," the disciples, the twelve, and Peter and James and John all appear utterly incapable of providing leadership for the movement Jesus has inaugurated by the time he approaches his anticipated martyrdom in Jerusalem.

Although the disciples accompany Jesus into Jerusalem and into the Temple for his prophetic demonstration, they play no role in his confrontation with the Jerusalem rulers (Mark 11–12). Peter, James, John, and Andrew, the pair of brothers called at the beginning of the story, do appear as the recipients of Jesus' instructions about the future beyond his own death and resurrection (13:3–37). Jesus mentions pointedly the perils of arrest and trials they should anticipate in their role of proclaiming the gospel to all peoples and repeatedly exhorts them to stay alert and keep awake through times of distress and confusion (13:9–13, 33–37).

The twelve disciples, however, prove incapable of meeting the challenge in the ensuing climax of the story. Judas arranges his betrayal with the high priests, which Jesus then predicts at the Passover meal (14:10–11, 18). Jesus also predicts that they will all become deserters and that Peter will deny him three times. Sure enough, after the disciples and particularly Peter, James, and John cannot "keep awake" while Jesus prays in agony, Judas carries out his betrayal and "all of them deserted him" (14:27–50). And precisely at the time Jesus is on trial for his life, Peter denies him three times (14:53, 66–72). The disciples thus disappear from the story before the crucifixion and do not witness the empty tomb. In the open ending of the story (16:7–8), the women who find the tomb empty are told to "go tell his disciples and Peter that he is going ahead of you to Galilee." But they do not say anything to anyone because they are afraid. We are left with no reason to believe that the twelve disciples ever "got the message" and went back to Galilee. Indeed, other New Testament literature feeds our doubts about this. Paul's letter to the Galatians and the book of Acts portray Peter and the other disciples as heading a community of Jesus-believers in Jerusalem.

Is the Gospel of Mark about Discipleship?

For over a century the disciples in Mark have been causing a lot of trouble for interpreters. Many devout Christian readers believe that the Gospel of Mark is primarily about *discipleship*. Most theological interpreters also assume that Mark is focused on discipleship.[1] Recent literary criticism of the Gospel works with the same assumption. And the literary critics have theories to explain how the disciples function in the interaction between the individual (modern) reader and the author to communicate a message of discipleship.[2]

In one influential theory, readers of Mark supposedly assume that a character role in the story to which they are attracted becomes a possibility for their own individual lives. Noting the similarity between aspects of their own lives and negative aspects of story characters leads them to change their own self-understanding and behavior. Christian (and presumably most modern) readers relate most readily to the disciples, the primary continuing characters who initially respond positively to Jesus. Toward the beginning of the story Mark gives the twelve a "special status and a special task, . . . with a special emphasis on the close relation of the disciples with Jesus and the similarity of their role to his." But he then portrays the disciples in conflict with Jesus on important issues, and finally shows the disciples as disastrous failures. The negative behavior of the disciples forces the reader into critical distancing from their failure. But that also leads to the reader's "self-criticism and repentance," because of the initial identification with the disciples. The story's negation of the originally expected encourages the reader "to ponder how those called by Jesus could go so far astray and what is required if [s]he is to escape similar failure."

One variation on this individual "discipleship" reading of Mark emphasizes the reader's emotions and decision. The reader sympathizes with the disciples and learns from their (negative) example. Mark "depicts the disciples as afraid, with little faith or understanding, concerned to save their own lives, . . . but leaving all and persevering in following Jesus." Yet they are unprepared to face persecution and death. Nevertheless the reader can learn from their failure. "If the disciples can fail again and again and Jesus still promises to go ahead of them, the reader can do the same." Mark leads the reader to face the question of what she or he "will do when faced with death for Jesus and the good news. Can you remain faithful? And if you fail, can you begin again?[3]

Another variation on this individual "discipleship" reading of Mark emphasizes the reader's knowledge, dispensing with the repentance factor. By having a better understanding than the disciples, the reader is able to become a *better disciple*. The reader also searches for the disciples' fatal character flaws that lead them to fail as disciples. "Because the typology the disciples illustrate is a universal truth (in Aristotle's *Poetics*) those same weaknesses [of character] may plague the reader as well." By a "catharsis," that is, "a process of clarification, an action of the will or mind," the reader can achieve clarity regarding her or his own discipleship.[4] Plato thought that if one could simply know the good or the right, then one could do it. Some "discipleship" theorists of Mark's story apparently believe that if only readers can recognize the disciples' character flaws, they can avoid them.

For the vast majority of modern (individual Christian as well as non-believing) readers, however, the whole scenario of this "discipleship" reading must seem unreal—and/or an expression of a distinctive kind of Christian piety. Of course, the discipleship reading did resonate realistically with many American activist Christians from the 1960s through the 1980s when certain branches of the United States government maintained surveillance on many citizens and infiltrated and invaded groups organized to oppose certain government activities. And reading Mark as a call to follow Jesus along the way of suffering and death in repentant reaction against the failure of the disciples may well resonate among readers living under repressive governments and/or the threat of violence from paramilitary forces tacitly supported by governments. But repentance in order to follow Jesus' way of political persecution and execution, in reaction against the disciples' failure, would not be an option for the vast majority of contemporary Western readers of Mark since they are not faced with persecution for their political or political-religious activities.

The modern reading of Mark as focused on individual discipleship "works" only insofar as the individual reader internalizes and spiritualizes what in Mark's story is concrete political struggle. Such an individualized spiritualized reading of the Gospel originated in a certain kind of Christian piety. It persists in scholarly interpretation because it is deeply rooted in a corresponding tradition of Christian theology.[5] Through the other Gospels, particularly Matthew, and the general development of Christian piety, Christians came to regard the original disciples of Jesus with a special reverence. They were the original witnesses of Christ's resurrection (1 Cor. 15:3–8). In the Gospel of Matthew (16:18) Jesus himself declared that Peter was the "rock" on which he was founding his church. Having been displaced mainly by the Gospels of Matthew and John, the Gospel of Mark was not widely used until the nineteenth century. Like any other book of the Bible, moreover, Mark was usually read in separate verses or "pericopes" lifted out of the overall story, and rarely if ever as a whole story. So it simply went unnoticed how badly the twelve disciples behave in Mark. When individualistic modern Western believers and theologians began reading Mark, therefore, they did so with discipleship in mind. They easily focused on the disciples and on terms such as "following" Jesus and "the way" that Jesus is traveling toward Jerusalem in what seemed like a whole section in the middle of Mark devoted to "discipleship" (8:27–10:52). They either did not notice or downplayed the severity of the treatment of the twelve disciples in most of Mark's story.

The new wave of literary (and rhetorical) criticism of Mark serves to reinforce the reading of the Gospel as primarily a story about discipleship. Literary critics simply begin with the standard Christian theological assumption that Mark was about discipleship. Most influential in reinforcing the discipleship reading is literary critics' emphasis on "character" and "characterization" in Mark. Almost by definition, attempts to characterize an author's characterization of characters involve abstraction from the rhetorically plotted action and teaching of the story. Recent literary critics of Mark borrow their concept of "character" and their theory of "characterization" from literary criticism of modern novels, which feature the inner psychological development of individual characters. They then tend to dissolve Mark's *story* into categorizations of its characters, such as "round" and "flat," "major" and "minor."[6] Jesus and the disciples turn out to be, like good scouts, characterized by a list of character traits: Jesus is "authoritative," "whole," "faithful," "compassionate," and "self-giving"; the disciples are "loyal," "committed," "observant," "obedient," "enlightened," "supportive," and "vulnerable" (etc.).[7] Despite their apparent awareness that characterization is not particularly important in ancient literature, in contrast to the modern novel, literary critics of Mark persist in applying categories derived from study of modern novels.[8]

In the course of their discussion of characterization, however, some critics offer many indications that character is relatively unimportant in Mark. "Mark does not develop full-blown characters as we find in modern literature." Mark's portrayal of characters reflects the ancient society from which it arose. People get their identity "from the social group to which they belonged." "Their place in the society shapes . . . the way characters interact with other characters."[9] Characters in Mark are mere types. Like the characters in other ancient literature, their character does not develop or change much, their portrayal coheres from one scene to the next. "They may, of course, change state, from good fortune to bad, . . . or from insider to outsider, for example, but such shifts are always implicit in the actions" of the characters.[10] In short, characterization is not important in Mark and other ancient literature because ancient characters were "subordinate to the overall plot or action."[11] They were agents in a plot.[12] In Mark the characters are basically components of the plot (and subplots). So it makes sense to refocus investigation of the Gospel on the overall story.

The discipleship reading of Mark has also been reinforced by recent "sociological" analysis of Synoptic Gospel materials. Jesus is represented as having inspired his followers to become "wandering charismatics" who abandon home, family, and possessions to pursue a "radical lifestyle" as vagabond beggars.[13] That construction of the "first followers of Jesus" then reinforces the individualistic reading of key Markan portrayals of the disciples, such as their call, their sending out on mission, and their claim to have left everything to follow Jesus. This ostensibly sociological construction, however, borrows an approach developed on the basis of modern industrial society that sociologists themselves abandoned as indefensible about thirty years ago. This construction of "wandering charismatics" is also based on "data" generated by a literalistic reading of certain sayings of Jesus lifted out of literary and historical social contexts. It has been severely criticized in several significant respects. Yet it persists in interpretation of Jesus and the Gospels, apparently primarily because it resonates with modern Western individualism.[14]

The discipleship reading, rooted in Christian theology and reinforced by recent literary critical treatments and sociological analysis, does not square with Mark's story as a whole. It mistakes a part for the whole, a subplot for the overall plot, a secondary conflict for the dominant conflict. Mark's Jesus is engaged in far more than merely gathering and teaching disciples.[15] In fact, Jesus does not even do much teaching in Mark, in comparison with Matthew, Luke, and John. When Mark does present Jesus as teaching, it is far more often "in an assembly/synagogue," or "among the villages," or to a "(large) crowd," or "in the Temple" (1:21–22; 2:13; 4:1–2; 6:2, 6, 34; 10:1; 11:17–18; 12:14, 35; 14:49) than it is teaching the disciples (8:31; 9:31; cf. 10:32). Jesus' call and commissioning of the twelve is only one aspect of a broader agenda of the kingdom of God, including the proclamation and practice of the kingdom in which they share. The principal conflict in Mark's story is not between Jesus and the disciples, but between Jesus and the Jerusalem rulers and their representatives. The twelve figure most prominently in the narrative between the last supper and Jesus' trial. But it is hardly appropriate to pretend that the last supper, the prayer in Gethsemane, the arrest, and the trial are all placed into the narrative mainly as settings for a story of how the disciples betray, desert, and deny Jesus. In these climactic events Mark focuses on the principal conflict, between Jesus and the rulers. The disciples' behavior is the focus not of the main plot of Mark's story, but of a subplot.

Besides constituting only a subplot, Mark's portrayal of the twelve disciples does not appear to serve some sort of didactic theme of "discipleship." Mark uses no such concept or term. Nor can any term such as "the way" be construed metaphorically to mean something like "discipleship." As used in interpretive discourse, the latter is a Christian and usually an individualistic concept. However, not just the disciples but also the crowds "follow" Jesus (e.g., 3:7; 5:24). Repentance in the sense assumed by the discipleship reading appears nowhere in Mark's story. The Greek term translated "repent" occurs only in connection with Jesus' (and the twelve's) proclamation that the kingdom of God is at hand and in connection with the "baptism of repentance" proclaimed by John, apparently a rite of renewal of the Mosaic covenant, a recommitment to covenantal Israel (to be discussed further in chapter 9). It is difficult to discern any suggestion in Mark that the twelve disciples' failure is somehow an illustration of the failure to "repent." The Gospel of Mark is not primarily a story about the disciples, and it is not a treatise on individual discipleship. At best, the disciples figure in one of the principal subplots of Mark. Our energies should be devoted to understanding that subplot and the narrative function of the secondary conflict between Jesus and the twelve.

Hearing Historically

In its focus on how the author portrays and the reader reacts to the disciples as characters, recent literary critical analysis of Mark seems uninterested in the contents of the story, i.e., what the twelve represent and are doing in the story. In the first part of the Gospel it seems sufficient that the reader recognize that the disciples have a "special relationship and responsibility . . . a special status and a special task." What matters is merely Mark's "special emphasis on the close relation of the disciples with Jesus and the similarity of their role to his," which seems no more precise than "sharing in [his] work of preaching and exorcism."[16] Their subsequent misunderstanding at the feedings of the crowds merely "suggests a perverse blindness that must disturb the reader." In this reading, Jesus' reply to their worry about their own supply of bread (e.g., in 8:13–21) appears to remain on the same mundane level, "reminding them of the abundant supply of food left over from the feedings." Only when we come to Mark's presentation of "Jesus' suffering as a model for Jesus followers" (8:34–35; 10:45) and Jesus' instruction about the future (13:9–13) is the story related to concrete "problems of the early church . . . the possibility of persecution and martyrdom." Except for the somewhat vague situation of persecution by anonymous people for no evident reason, the story has no setting and no content, no background, no historical and cultural context in which it could mean something to someone. What are the disciples preaching about? Why are they doing exorcisms? The discipleship reading leaves modern readers as confused as Mark's disciples about what they and Jesus were doing.

Attempts have been made recently to read Mark in the context of ancient Hellenistic-Roman culture rather than modern Western culture. While helpful in transcending the reading handicaps of the latter, however, they provide little illumination of the content of Mark's portrayal of the disciples. Mark is supposedly similar in style to ancient "novels" or "romances." But those "novels" were neither "popular" literature comparable to Mark nor examples of a genre similar to Mark.[17] Such comparisons simply pull the hypothetical ancient readers of Mark into the general stream of upper-class culture in which the heroes and heroines are rooted. Similarly, comparisons with rhetorical patterns in a range of "biographical" works focused on philosophers and their students place the readers of Mark in a relatively sophisticated Hellenistic philosophical culture.[18] It may well be that later generations of Greek and Roman Christians read Mark's story of Jesus and the disciples as that of a philosopher and his students, according to patterns made familiar by Xenophon's portrayal of Socrates or Philostratus's portrayal of Apollonius of Tyana. Like reading with the assumptions of modern Western culture, however, reading with the assumptions of the ancient elite culture represented in romances and philosophical literature tends to assimilate Mark's story to the thought patterns of the reader. In either case, Mark is absorbed into the culturally dominant patterns and not allowed to stand over against them. Once we recognize that Mark is a story about and for peoples subject to an ancient empire, however, then it seems incumbent on modern interpreters situated in the imperial metropolis not immediately to absorb this literature of subjected peoples into the dominant culture, ancient or modern.

One of the "spin-off" effects of finally facing the reality of illiteracy and oral performance of stories such as the Gospel of Mark in the ancient Roman imperial world is that we also realize that the performer and the listeners shared a common cultural tradition. In chapter 2 above, further, we recognized that, far from having assimilated into the general Hellenistic culture under the Roman imperial order, Mark and its audience identified strongly with Israelite cultural tradition and set themselves in opposition to the Roman imperial order. If we want to begin to understand what the twelve disciples are doing in Mark's story and what Mark's story is doing with the disciples, therefore, then we must begin to appropriate Israelite cultural tradition.

When in Mark's story Jesus appoints twelve to share his work preaching and exorcism it obviously has something to do with the people of Israel having consisted of twelve tribes. The twelve are not simply handy helpers but representative of the twelve tribes of Israel that are undergoing renewal as a people in the proclamation of the kingdom of God and the healing and exorcism. This hearing is confirmed again and again in the subsequent episodes of the story when Jesus does miraculous sea crossings and wilderness feedings as well as healings and then appears to Peter, James, and John on the mountain with Moses and Elijah. For Moses had led the twelve tribes across the sea into the wilderness, where he mediated miraculous feedings, and Elijah had performed miraculous healings and multiplication of food in circumstances of political-economic oppression and had built an altar of twelve stones representative of a renewed Israel. Whatever their apprehensions and misunderstandings, the twelve remain the representatives of Israel being renewed throughout the story, as in the meal of covenant renewal when they all drink of the cup as the "blood of the covenant, which is poured out for many." The leaders among them, Peter, James, John, and Andrew, are the representative figures who receive Jesus' instructions about what the movement should expect after his death and rising. Mark is presenting the twelve, the core of the disciples, as the representative figures of Israel undergoing renewal.

Literature from Judean scribal circles roughly contemporary with Mark confirms this hearing of Mark's portrayal of the twelve. The very composition of "the Testaments of the Twelve" patriarchs indicates that the tradition of Israel consisting of twelve tribes was very much alive. In one of those "testaments" the patriarch Judah has twelve as the "chiefs wielding the scepter in Israel" (*Testament of Judah* 25:1). In earlier scribal literature Elijah was expected to come and "restore the tribes of Jacob" (= Israel; Sir. 36:13; 48:10). The Dead Sea Scrolls anticipate the restoration of Israel in terms of twelve chiefs of the twelve tribes, along with the supplementary priestly leadership that might be expected from a priestly group (1QS 8:1–3; 1QM 2:2–3; 5:1–3; 11QT 18:14–16). The restoration of the twelve tribes had clearly become one of the principal images of the future renewal of Israel, an image which early Christian groups continued as they expanded among the other peoples of the eastern Mediterranean (e.g., Rev. 21:10–14; Acts 26:7; etc.). Jesus sayings identified as relatively early (in the "Q" source of Jesus speeches, Luke/Q 22:28–30// Matt. 19:30) also speak of representative figures among Jesus' followers doing justice for the "twelve" tribes of Israel in an image of renewal parallel to Mark's portrayal of the twelve.

Once we recognize that the twelve are representatives of Israel in renewal through the new Moses-Elijah, another disciples episode's allusion to Israelite tradition comes into view. Mark has John the Baptist, sent to "prepare the way of the Lord," introduce Jesus as the prophetic leader of a new exodus. Then Jesus spends forty days in the wilderness being tested and attended by God's messengers. Hearers acquainted with Israelite tradition cannot help but think of the prophet Elijah who spent forty days in the wilderness being tested and attended by God's messenger (Mark 1:12–13; 1 Kings 19:4–9). When Jesus then moves immediately from his testing into his prophetic proclamation and demonstration of the kingdom of God, the first act of which is to call disciples who immediately leave home to follow him, the hearer continues to resonate with the Elijah story. For Elijah moved immediately from his wilderness testing into his prophetic agenda, the first act of which was to call Elisha as his follower, who immediately left home to follow Elijah. The Elijah-Elisha narratives, moreover, speak of many other "sons of the prophets" who are engaged in the revival of Israel, just as Jesus' disciples are engaged in the renewal of Israel in Mark.

The disciples pointedly misunderstand what is happening in the wilderness feedings of the crowds. But what is it that they do not understand? These episodes in Mark are rich in overtones and metonymic references to Israelite tradition. After a woman who had been hemorrhaging for twelve years was healed by her faith and Jesus healed a twelve-year-old young woman who was virtually dead, the disciples take up twelve baskets of leftover fragments in the first feeding (6:30–44), which Jesus has to remind them of in his exasperation at their density (8:15–21). We are obviously still in the midst of the renewal of Israel, who appear "like sheep without a shepherd." And the feeding in the wilderness episode is clearly patterned after Moses' feeding of Israel in the wilderness, one of the key incidents in the foundational legends of Israel. The renewal of Israel in Mark has expanded beyond Israel itself to other peoples, included in the second wilderness feeding, from which seven baskets of the overabundant bread is gathered. Even while they assist Jesus in the miraculous feedings, the disciples misunderstand what is happening. The people of Israel, who "were like sheep without a shepherd," are now undergoing a renewal like their original formation in the exodus and wilderness under Moses' leadership, *and* the kingdom of God is now being expanded to include other peoples as well in the renewal led by the new Moses-Elijah, God's prophetic agent in miraculously multiplying food.

The disciples in Mark thus have an integral role in Jesus' program of renewal. Jesus' commissioning of the twelve articulates this clearly and unambiguously.[19] In the ongoing narrative Mark places this episode in the middle of the section in which Jesus performs miracles of wilderness feedings and healings and exorcisms as the new Moses-Elijah, that is, actions that effect the renewal of Israel (as symbolized by the healings of the woman hemorrhaging for "twelve" years and the "twelve"-year-old young woman who is virtually dead). The close parallel to this "mission discourse" in the "mission discourse" of "Q" (the speeches of Jesus shared by Matthew and Luke but not found in Mark) indicates that Mark is following common early tradition of the Jesus movement(s). A closer look at these parallel discourses as a whole (Mark 6:7–13; Luke/Q 10:2–16) indicates that the mission had a particular pattern or strategy. Following the sending and a list of what (not) to take come instructions for staying in households (Mark 6:10), and on eating (Luke/Q 10:5–7), and instructions on how to respond to places that reject them (Mark 6:11) and places that welcome (Luke/Q 10:8–11). Mark put into a narrative (6:12–13) what Q has as instructions for healing and preaching in the receptive towns.

These are instructions for mission, a systematic expansion of the movement, not teaching about an itinerant "lifestyle" of which the twelve are the models to be imitated. The program focuses on proclamation and exorcism and healing. Jesus gives them the same "authority over the unclean spirits" he demonstrated in 1:21–28. They proclaim that all should repent, clearly continuing Jesus' own proclamation that people should repent since the kingdom is at hand in 1:14–15. And Mark reports the success of their mission of exorcism and healing. The sites of their mission are "places," presumably small villages. The envoys who work in pairs are to stay in local households while working in village communities. Whether Mark's (and Q's) mission discourse reflects the time of the original disciples' mission or practice at the time of Mark or both, the preaching and healing activities focus apparently on small rural communities.

This is confirmed by a previously unrecognized factor in Mark's presentation of Jesus' activities. It is usually assumed, not only that Mark's Jesus belongs in the sphere of religion, but also that Mark portrays Jesus as preaching and healing/exorcizing in religious *buildings*, or "synagogues." The Greek term *synagōgē*, however, like the Hebrew term *knesset*, referred to an assembly, sometimes the assembly of all Israel, but most often the local village assembly that met regularly to deal with community affairs. Thus Mark portrays Jesus as carrying out his teaching and healing activities in the local village assemblies (1:21, 39; 3:1; etc.). When the mission discourse directs the disciples to work in "places," it appears to be continuing the program of renewal of Israel village by village. And, after all, the village was the fundamental social form of an agrarian society, whether in Galilee and Judea or in the surrounding areas subject to Tyre, Caesarea Philippi, or the Decapolis. That Mark's story portrays Jesus and the disciples working on the renewal of local community in the villages and their assemblies/synagogues also fits with and explains Mark's complete lack of the term *ekklēsia* (= church) and an incipient picture of church office, which is so striking when compared with Matthew (16:18; 18:17) and Luke (Acts 1:26; 2:42; 4:37; 8:1; 9:31).[20]

It is significant, finally, that the envoys are instructed to "shake off the dust that is on your feet as a testimony against them," that is, a curse against the "place" as a whole that does not welcome them. Mark portrays a mission focused on villages as whole communities, not directed to recruit individual "followers" who will pursue an "unconventional" itinerant "lifestyle." Mark presents the twelve not just as the representatives of an Israel undergoing renewal, but as envoys commissioned to expand Jesus' program of renewal in village communities.

Hearing Politically

Recognition that the twelve in Mark's story resonate with the audience in metonymically referencing a prominent aspect of Israelite tradition enables us to sense more clearly the rhetorical function of the disciples' persistent misunderstanding and failure to "follow." As illustrated in the cases of the wilderness feedings, the disciples serve as a foil for what Jesus is doing and saying in the story. But they are foils not for philosophical teaching "on the nature of discipleship." Plato repeatedly portrays a dim-witted or disputatious disciple as a foil for Socrates' discussion of a particular doctrine.[21] Nevertheless, the disciples of Socrates and other ancient teachers, however slow at first, usually came around and generally agreed with and faithfully followed their teachers, even attending to their every reflection at the moment of death. In Mark's story, by contrast, Jesus becomes exasperated at the disciples after their willful misunderstanding of the feedings. Their willful misunderstanding intensifies thereafter, becoming persistent and programmatic, until, at the end, they betray, deny, and disappear.[22]

The twelve disciples in Mark serve as foils for Jesus in a far more pervasive and programmatic sense than the disciples of famous Greek and Hellenistic teachers. Mark's story not only references Israelite tradition, but evidently portrays Jesus' disciples as the virtual opposites of those typical of the dominant Hellenistic culture. The twelve in Mark persistently and consistently act in ways counter to Jesus' actions or instructions. He announces he must die; Peter objects. He announces he must die; the twelve discuss which one is greatest. He insists that they welcome children; they send them away. He announces he must be killed by the rulers; they ask him to appoint them as rulers. He instructs them to watch while he prays in agony; they fall asleep. He instructs them to take up their cross and follow; they abandon him. He is arrested and condemned to a gruesomely agonizing death; they deny and desert him. The disciples' function as foils becomes all the more poignant because they insist on their unwavering commitment. James and John then declare they are prepared to share his martyrdom but then abandon Jesus at his arrest. Peter insists that he will remain faithful to the death, but then denies Jesus three times. The impact of the twelve as foils is all the more powerful because they are the representatives of the renewed Israel and include the three or four who were closest to Jesus. For it is precisely the specially chosen figures who provide the negative examples of how not to respond to the good news of the kingdom of God, highlighting that the movement is to embody egalitarian social-economic relations and disciplined commitment in the face of possible political repression.

Even once we recognize that the twelve in Mark are negative examples, not paradigms of discipleship, we still may not have grasped the severity with which Mark portrays them. The issues on which the twelve's behavior displays a foil for Jesus' teachings suggest that Mark is using them to dramatize a political struggle. Our suspicion that Mark's representation of the disciples is politically "loaded" is confirmed by how both Matthew and Luke frequently omit, tone down, or reverse the criticism by Mark's Jesus, the most poignant being Matthew having Jesus declare that Peter is the rock on which he is founding the church (16:18).[23] A closer review of Mark's disciples subplot, including a closer examination of particular points of portrayal, may enable us to probe more critically the politics of the Gospel story in its historical context.

In the early stages of his story Mark presents the twelve straightforwardly as the hand-picked representatives of Israel undergoing renewal, whom Jesus commissions to expand his program of proclamation and exorcism (3:13–19; 6:7–13). Among the disciples, Peter, James, John, and Andrew have prominence by their calling and priority with the twelve as well as privileged access and intimacy with Jesus (1:16–20; 5:37; 9:2–9; 13:3). Mark even indicates that the twelve were effective in their mission (6:13). No sooner do the twelve receive the secret of the kingdom and have everything explained to them in private, however, than they begin to manifest both lack of faith in and serious misunderstanding of Jesus and his program (4:35–8:21). By the middle of the story, Jesus's exasperation has already reached in a fever pitch a series of rhetorical questions (8:17–21). Are their "hearts hardened," like those of the Pharisees who had attacked him for healing on the Sabbath (3:5)? Their failure to "remember," using the standard term for consistent observance of the Mosaic covenant from Israelite tradition, means that they have become unfaithful. Their having eyes but failing to see and having ears but failing to hear places the disciples to whom had been given the secret of the kingdom of God suddenly among the outsiders (cf. 4:10–12).

In the following section of the Gospel, it very quickly becomes evident that the disciples not only do not understand Jesus' program, but they have a very different understanding of what the movement is about and their own roles in it. This happens most dramatically in the exchange between Jesus and Peter, but also in that between Jesus and James and John.

The episode of "Peter's Confession" in 8:27–33 is often understood as one of the high points in the overall story. Peter finally declares boldly that Jesus is the "Messiah." It is just that he does not fully understand what kind of messiah. At first the hearer might think that Peter's response, "You are the Messiah," is correct. But the story continues immediately not just to qualify but to correct or even to reject Peter's "confession." Jesus uses stern language in immediate reply to Peter, the same language he uses in sharply "rebuking" the demons (1:25; 3:12; 9:25). Jesus immediately "rebuked" Peter, and sternly forbade Peter to speak to anyone concerning him. But is this merely a "messianic secret"? Is he forbidden to speak of Jesus as the Messiah because it is true and his messianic identity needs to be kept hidden? Or because it is a false understanding of Jesus, based on wrong assumptions or expectations?

The story then moves directly to Jesus' first of three announcements that he must be rejected by the rulers and killed and rise again, adding that Jesus said this pointedly, in bold speech, publicly. But Peter now rebukes Jesus, and Jesus, firing right back, rebukes Peter and even addresses him as "Satan." This is no little difference of opinion. After Jesus rebukes Peter for believing he is the "messiah," Peter rebukes Jesus for saying he has to die, which lead Jesus to rebuke Peter as "Satan," the demonic force with which God and his own program are engaged in struggle. Mark may well be skillfully manipulating the hearers into immediate identification with Peter and his confession that Jesus is the "Messiah" only to then turn the tables on the hearers' false initial response. But this exchange here at the middle point in the overall story portrays Peter not only as utterly misunderstanding—after being given special instruction in the secret of the kingdom of God—but as a demonic opponent of God's kingdom and Jesus' agenda in renewal of Israel plus. Mark 8:27–33 is thus Peter's *confrontation* with Jesus more than Peter's "confession," which is only the opening salvo in the intensifying confrontation. But if we have ears to hear, this narrative sequence is rather the sharp rebuke of "Peter" for his willful opposition to Jesus' program, the "things of God." And indeed, if we survey all the other references to Peter in Mark, after the initial call and appointment of the twelve, every one portrays him as speaking stupidly or behaving faithlessly.

After this low point in the story, in which Peter provokes a confrontation with Jesus, the rest of the section supposedly devoted to discussion of "the true nature of discipleship" has the disciples, led by James and John, giving indications that their agenda is the virtual opposite of Jesus' agenda. They are expecting that Jesus will somehow lead them into a glorious messianic reign, in which they will not only be prominent figures, but possess political power ("sitting at his right hand and left hand" as "rulers" and "great ones," 9:34; 10:35–45). And they are already presuming to operate as if they were in charge of things, stopping an allied exorcist and limiting access to Jesus (9:38–41; 10:13). In portraying their persistent "misunderstanding" of what Jesus and his movement are all about in three successive series of oppositions between Jesus and the disciples, Mark's story offers no signal that they are likely to change their view of the movement and behavior that are so contrary to Jesus' agenda.

At the climax of the story in Jerusalem, the twelve persist in their unwillingness or inability to follow Jesus in a portrayal that has one negative representation of them after another. In both the episode of the betrayal arrangements and the betrayal itself Mark insists on reminding the hearers of his story that Judas was "one of the twelve" (3:13–19; 14:10–11, 43). At the Passover meal, when Jesus announces that one of the twelve will betray him, their response ("Surely, not I," 14:19) indicates that every one is uneasy that he may be under suspicion. At Gethsemane, of course, comes another sequence of three times that the disciples fail Jesus. It is surely significant that at Gethsemane, where Peter and others cannot "keep awake" as ordered, even "in the hour of crisis," Jesus, who had given Simon the nickname Rock at the appointment of the twelve, reverts to his original name, Simon. (Surely by the time Mark was composed, Simon was known as Rock/Peter; so Mark is here pointedly having Jesus strip him of the name with the connotations of the solid head of the movement.) And of course after Jesus declares they will and the disciples insist they will not, the disciples do indeed betray, abandon, and (three times!) deny Jesus.

The sequence from just after the meal to the end of the story, finally, is decisive with regard to the twelve. Jesus announces that he will go before them, but they abandon and deny him. They have all disappeared before the crucifixion, their absence made all the more conspicuous by the presence of the women who look on, at least from a distance. Again at the burial of Jesus the twelve are conspicuous by their absence. Mark pointedly indicated that after John was executed by Herod Antipas, "his disciples came and took his body, and laid it in a tomb" (6:29). But Jesus' disciples do not come for his body. Again at the empty tomb, by contrast with the presence of the women, the twelve are conspicuously absent. When the women are told to tell the disciples that he is leading the way back up to Galilee, the story ends with the explicit statement that the women "said nothing to anyone, for they were afraid" (16:8). Thus in Mark's story the twelve (and Peter) never find out about Jesus' rising. They have already parted company with Jesus, gone a different way, after his arrest. They are no longer part of the unfolding Gospel story of the kingdom of God.

Those who, uncomfortable at Mark's portrayal of the twelve as faithless deserters, want to use the "open ending" of Mark's story to rehabilitate them—suggesting, e.g., that Peter's breakdown means he must have repented and followed Jesus' call for service—have a serious problem with the evidence outside of Mark. Nothing suggests that Peter followed Jesus back up to Galilee. All evidence points to his having remained in Jerusalem to assume the leadership of a community of Jesus-believers based there. The traditions behind the early chapters of Acts have Peter located in Jerusalem. Paul confirms these traditions in his account of his own calling as an apostle about three or four years after the crucifixion: he did not go up to Jerusalem to confer with those who were already apostles (Gal. 1:17). If we are honest about Mark's portrayal of the disciples and follow the implications, it would appear that Mark's story and the movement it addresses defined the continuation of the Gospel story over against the twelve.[24]

It seems fairly clear from other early literature produced by Jesus movements that after Jesus' death (and resurrection), Simon Peter and others of the twelve became the leaders of the loose network of movements and apostles centered in Jerusalem. Referring to events that happened less than twenty years after Jesus' crucifixion, Paul writes of Peter and John, along with Jesus' brother James, as the "acknowledged pillars" (Gal. 2:9) who commanded respect and deferential treatment as authority figures of the movement(s) as a whole. Matthew, who is believed to have known and used Mark's Gospel in composing his own, appears to reverse Mark's portrayal of Peter, presenting him as the "rock" on which Jesus founded the movement in general (which, like Paul, he calls the *ekklēsia* or "assembly"; Matt. 16:18).

It is also clear from other early literature of the Jesus movements that Peter and the rest of the twelve had been the original witnesses on which faith in the resurrected and exalted Lord (Jesus Christ) was based. When he wants to establish common ground with the Corinthians who are expressing doubts about the resurrection of the dead, Paul appeals to the standard "creed" that he and apparently other apostles had been teaching among the communities they had started: "he was raised on the third day in accordance with the scriptures, and that he appeared to Cephas [Peter], then to the twelve" (1 Cor. 15:4–5). Peter and the twelve were the authorities who emphasized the resurrection and whose authority, in turn, rested on their role as the original witnesses. Earlier treatments of the twelve in Mark emphasized their role as the authorizing mediators between Jesus and the developing "church" for authenticating the truth of the gospel. But they simply explained away rather than came to grips with Mark's story's portrayal of and attitude toward them.[25]

The strikingly abrupt but also "open ended" ending of Mark's story should be heard with this role of the twelve and particularly the inner circle of Jesus' disciples in mind. Compared to the later Gospels of Matthew, Luke, and John, Mark deemphasizes the resurrection at the end of the Gospel.[26] Earlier in the story, Mark suggests that resurrection is important. The raising of the virtually dead twelve-year-old woman suggests resurrection (Mark 5:35–43). And Mark's Jesus both presupposes and defends the reality of the anticipated resurrection in the debate with the Sadducees, who had no use for it (12:18–27). At the end of the Gospel story where Paul, Matthew, Luke, and John all assume and portray Jesus' resurrection, however, Mark presents merely an empty tomb, with no resurrection appearances to anyone (16:1–8). Mark's reticence almost pointedly contradicts the early "creed" quoted by Paul, that "according to the scriptures" Jesus was raised on the third day and "appeared to Cephas and then to the twelve" (1 Cor. 15:4–5). The figure at the empty tomb tells the women to tell the disciples and Peter that "he is going ahead of you to Galilee; there you will see him, just as he told you." But the women, in their terror, "said nothing to anyone"! End of story!—without Peter and the disciples hearing the words and going to Galilee where they would "see him." Mark had earlier given a clue to the in-group's "density" when, after witnessing Jesus transfigured on the mountain together with Israel's founding and renewing prophets, Moses and Elijah, they "questioned what this raising from the dead could mean" (9:2–10). And at the ending, Mark does not rehabilitate the twelve disciples. In Mark's story—in utter contrast to the assumption attested by Paul in the early creed he cites and the consistent portrayals in the other Gospels—the disciples have no authority based on their having witnessed the resurrection. With Peter and the rest of the twelve having disappeared from the story before its open ending, Mark has transformed Jesus' "resurrection" into an instruction to continue the movement back up in Galilee without them.

At the time Mark was being performed, however, the disciples had long since become the heads of the community in Jerusalem and of the wider movement in general, i.e., revered and prestigious "pillars." It thus may not be historically surprising that Mark's story deploys the disciples as foils for Jesus' insistence that his movement be egalitarian, with no heads who enjoy veneration, power, and privilege. Jesus' apparent rejection of his family in Mark 3:31–35 could well be a related passage, a rejection of Jesus' brother James's prestigious role in Jerusalem. In its historical situation, Mark's story may well be calling a particular Jesus movement or set of communities back to the egalitarian ideal with which it began, over against the inner circle of the twelve who became the revered heads of the movement(s). The story accepts that they were with Jesus and indeed the representatives of the renewed Israel. But it has historical grounds for using them as foils for recalling the movement to its more egalitarian origins represented in Jesus' exasperated responses to and repeated instructions to the disciples, particularly in Mark 8:13–10:52.

When we think back through Mark's story with this irreconcilable conflict between Jesus and the twelve in mind, a number of episodes come to mind that suggest attempts to authorize a movement that stands over against the disciples as prestigous leaders of the broader movement headquartered now in Jerusalem. The episode about the exorcist that the twelve attempt to suppress suggests that Mark is having Jesus authorize exorcism that is not approved by the apostolic "pillars" in Jerusalem (9:38–41). Jesus' explanation that their inability to exorcize a demonic spirit because "this kind can come out only through prayer" suggests that perhaps the branch of the movement Mark addresses practiced exorcism through prayer in a way divergent from the practice of the Jerusalem-based heads of the wider movement. Perhaps Mark's persistent focus on women and insistence on the acceptance of "children," including the declaration that "whoever does not receive the kingdom of God as a little child will never enter it" indicates that the humble, egalitarian-spirited village-based movement Mark addresses is defending itself against "apostolic" authority figures who, it feels, look down on them. The ideal of disciple leadership as servants articulated in 10:42–45, where Jesus explicitly rejects the claims to primacy of the inner circle and the twelve. Mark's story may well be attempting to console the communities it addresses and call the larger movement back to what it considers the original base and ideal of the movement Jesus launched as a program of village community renewal, over against any "leadership" (let alone oppressive rule) exercised from Jerusalem.

Devout modern Western Christians have been reading, and established biblical scholars have been expounding, the Gospel of Mark as focused on discipleship. If we take the Gospel whole, however, attending to the story of the twelve disciples as they are actually portrayed, it is difficult to find anything but unmitigated faithlessness and failure from the middle of the story to the end. Mark's Gospel must be about something other than discipleship.

5

Getting the Whole Story

As we attempt to discern what Mark's story is mainly about, we would do well to recognize that we approach the Gospel as relatively uninformed readers/hearers. We know too little partly because we know too much. Our over-familiarity with the story as filtered through—and overlaid by—centuries of Christian and Western cultural interpretation has blocked our ability to hear Mark in a historical setting that was different from our own in most respects. It is particularly important to free ourselves from the deeply entrenched Christian theological interpretation. As noted above, nothing in Mark's story itself suggests that it is about the origin of the supposedly universalist religion "Christianity" as it breaks away from the particularist religion "Judaism." To abstract a christology from the story, namely, that Mark is primarily a presentation of Jesus as the "suffering Messiah," ignores the story itself in favor of ideas abstracted from it. That Mark focuses mainly on discipleship, a reading that persists in suggestive recent literary analysis of Mark's narrative, has more to do with the individualistic faith of modern Western readers than with Mark's story itself.

In attempting to hear Mark's story more sensitively, carefully, and completely, perhaps it would help to begin at the end with the climax of the story and work backward through its unfolding in hopes of discerning its dominant plot(ting). Once we begin to discern what appears to be the main plotting of the story, we can then take steps to become more informed hearers by reexamining and relearning the historical context in and for which Mark was performed.

Discerning the Dominant Plot

Mark's story climaxes in Jesus' execution as "the king of the Judeans" by order of Pilate, the Roman governor (15:1–32, esp. 15:2, 16–20, 25–32).

That he was executed by crucifixion, a gruesome form of execution used for slaves and provincial rebels, on the charge of being "the king of the Judeans," indicates that the Roman governor viewed him as a leader of a popular insurrection against the Roman imperial order. Jesus was handed over to Pilate by the chief priests after they had seized him surreptitiously at night outside the city of Jerusalem and condemned him at a nighttime trial for threatening to destroy the Temple and for blasphemy in referring to "the coming of the son of man, seated at the right hand of Power" (14:1–2, 10–11, 43–65; 15:1). The chief priests, scribes, and elders had been attempting for some time to arrest and kill Jesus because of his disruptive prophetic demonstration against the Temple and his prophetic condemnation of their oppression and exploitation of the people as rulers of the temple-state (11:15–19; 12:1–12, 38–40; 13:1–2). The disciples' betrayal, abandonment, and denial are connected and interwoven with the episodes of the Jerusalem rulers' arrest and condemnation of Jesus. But they are clearly secondary to the dominant conflict between Jesus and the Roman and Jerusalem rulers that comes to a climax once Jesus arrives in Jerusalem and aggressively attacks the rulers and ruling institutions.

If we then review the rest of Mark's story from the perspective of how it climaxes, we can discern any number of clear indications that the dominant plot, focused in the dominant conflict, has Jesus attacking the Jerusalem and Roman rulers, who plot to destroy him and finally succeed—except of course that, his tomb being empty, he goes ahead of his followers back to Galilee where the movement presumably continues. Most obvious perhaps are Jesus' three explicit announcements in the middle of the story that "the son of man will be handed over to the chief priests and the scribes, and they will condemn him to death; then they will hand him over to the nations; they will . . . flog him and kill him; and after three days he will rise again" (8:31; 9:31; 10:33–34). And virtually from the beginning of the story, we know that the Pharisees who, like the scribes, come down from Jerusalem, "conspired with the Herodians against him, how to destroy him" and charge him with working in cahoots with Satan (3:6, 22). More subtly, perhaps, in Jesus' first act of healing or exorcism for the beleaguered people, and again in the rulers' first challenge to Jesus in Jerusalem, the conflict is framed in terms of power-authority (1:21–28; 11:27–33). Indeed, if we attend closely to the first several episodes of the story, Jesus' exorcisms, healings, and pronouncements at several points are simultaneously actions against the prerogatives and authority of the Temple and its priestly aristocracy (e.g., 1:21–28, 41–45; 2:1–12; cf. 7:1–13; 8:15; 10:2–9, later in the story). In direct reaction or in direct provocation of such actions and pronouncements, the representatives of Jerusalem rule oppose and conspire against Jesus (2:1–12; 3:1–6; 7:1–13; 10:2–9).

Integrally related and interwoven with this conflict that runs throughout the story, Mark emplots other indicators. The sequence of settings is broadly schematic: Jesus' proclamation and manifestation of the kingdom of God begins and becomes well known in the villages of Galilee and surrounding areas, then he enters Jerusalem and the Temple for the climactic face-off with the rulers, before the story finally directs the audience back to Galilee. In the middle of the story, he begins a journey from the northernmost area he reaches in his campaign, Caesarea Philippi, back through Galilee and other areas he had previously reached, through Judea and beyond the Jordan, to Jerusalem and the Temple (8:27–11:1). Jesus is accused of blasphemy by the scribes toward the beginning in Galilee and then at his trial before the chief priests, scribes, and elders toward the end, the charge for which they condemn him to death (2:1–12; 14:61–64). In both his symbolic condemnation of the Romans in the demon identified as "Legion" and in his condemnation of the Temple, Mark portrays them as destroyed in the Sea (5:1–20; 11:15–24).

More prominently in the broader sequence of episodes, the story makes parallels and connections between what happens with John the Baptist, Jesus, and the disciples. John proclaims a baptism of repentance, is arrested, and killed by Herod Antipas (1:2–4, 14; 6:16–29); Jesus' "followers" are to maintain steadfast loyalty when standing trial before governors and kings for proclaiming the gospel, all the while prepared to "take up their cross" (8:34–38; 13:9–13); and Jesus proclaims and manifests the kingdom of God, is finally handed over, tried, and condemned to take up his cross. These many indicators in the sequence and interconnections of the episodes make abundantly clear that the dominant plot focuses on the conflict between Jesus, his program and movement, and the Jerusalem rulers and their representatives backed up by Roman rule.

Jesus Is Leading a Renewal of Israel . . .

Being such uninformed readers/hearers, however, we still may not "get it." Why, more precisely, are Jesus' healings and exorcisms so threatening to the scribes and Pharisees? Aren't they simple acts of mercy? After John the Baptist is arrested and executed by Herod, why does Jesus, who stays clear of Herod's capital cities in Galilee, march directly up to Jerusalem where he knows he will be arrested and killed? Why is it "necessary" that Jesus suffer and be killed?

For many modern readers such questions do not even arise because they still read Mark in terms of standardized Christian theology. After all, as we have learned in our religious training and practice, Christ died for our sins. It is easier to find that articulated in the Gospels of Matthew or John or in the

letters of Paul. But in Mark? Only two phrases in Mark might fit such a doctrine; "the son of man came to . . . give his life as a ransom for many" (10:45)
and "my blood of the covenant which is poured out for many" (14:24). But
these statements, heard in Markan context, do not exactly refer to Jesus dying
for people's sins. Far from simply accepting his role in the divine economy of
salvation in passive resignation, Mark's Jesus is on the offensive throughout
the story, especially in his confrontation with the rulers and ruling institutions
in Jerusalem. By starting from its climax in Jerusalem and then picking up
many other indicators, we have discerned that the dominant conflict in Mark's
story lies between Jesus and the rulers, but we must now strive to sense more
precisely what Jesus is doing that is so threatening to the rulers and begin to
understand the substance of the confrontation that escalates to the climax in
Jerusalem.

Again we must work at cutting through inappropriate previous assumptions
and we must strive to become more informed readers in order to understand
what that conflict is all about. In earlier chapters we have already recognized
that Mark's story is not primarily about individual discipleship. Nor is Mark
about Jesus as an individual person, or focused narrowly on his title(s) or role(s).
Reading/hearing a story requires holding together its interrelated aspects, such
as setting, characterization, and plotting, etc. Thus, for example, Jesus heals
and teaches people in village assemblies and households in Galilee and nearby
areas; the disciples are called and commissioned both as representatives of
Israel and to help in extending Jesus' program of healing and teaching in those
village communities. From the massive response to his activities in households
and villages, Mark makes clear that Jesus is building a movement with wide
extension into Galilean and other villages. Having observed this briefly in chapter 2 above, we must now explore more fully and carefully how Mark tells a
story about Jesus leading a renewal of Israel in village communities over against
its rulers. Even as relatively uninformed readers we can detect some of the signals and symbols that help us understand this more precisely.

Mark's story opens with a recitation of a prophecy that presents John the
Baptist as the messenger crying in the wilderness: "Prepare the way of the
Lord." "The Lord" in Mark refers to Jesus, not God as in Isaiah 40:3. But "the
way of the Lord" is (still) the new exodus. Jesus is leading a new exodus, that
is, a liberation of the people of Israel from foreign domination, just as Moses
had led the liberation from bondage in Egypt. The messenger, moreover, if we
pick up the allusion to the source of the phrase in Malachi 3:1, is the messenger of the Israelite/Mosaic covenant. And sure enough John, in "proclaiming
a baptism of *repentance* for the forgiveness of sins," is announcing and enact-
ing a renewal of the Mosaic covenant. The "baptism with the Holy Spirit" that
Jesus will perform, further, is the empowering divine presence that will inspire

the new exodus and covenant renewal, i.e., the renewal of the people of Israel. Jesus as the prophet of renewal then undergoes forty days' testing in the wilderness, just as the prophet Elijah had undergone forty days of testing in preparation for leading the renewal of Israel (1 Kings 19; and as Moses was tested in the wilderness before being sent to lead the exodus).

Mark's first episodes, therefore, indicate clearly what Jesus is about when he comes to Galilee proclaiming the time fulfilled and the kingdom of God at hand. Prepared by the preceding prologue, we sense immediately that "the time is fulfilled" for the new exodus and renewed covenant led by the Lord who now takes charge, and that "the kingdom of God" being at hand, the theme of the Gospel, refers to the renewal of Israel as God's direct rule becomes a reality in society.[1] Jesus' call to the first disciples evokes memories of Elijah's call of Elisha as his assistant and successor, with the overtones of the larger bands of (sons of the) prophets active in the renewal of Israel spearheaded by Elijah (1 Kings 18–19). When, further along in Jesus' campaign in Galilee, he "went *up the mountain*," like Moses and Elijah, and "appointed *twelve*" to be sent out to proclaim the message and to have authority/power to cast out demons, i.e., to extend Jesus' own activities of personal and social restoration in village communities, it is abundantly clear that a renewal of Israel in its twelve tribes is underway, symbolized in the twelve as representatives of Israel. Other renewal movements in Israel and contemporary Judean renewal literature exhibit significant parallels, as noted in chapter 4. The distinctively priestly-scribal Qumran community that left the Dead Sea Scrolls was led by a community council consisting of twelve laymen along with three priests, and the scribal *Psalms of Solomon* anticipated that the coming Davidic "messiah" would establish Israel in its twelve tribes on its land in justice. These variations in parallel building on Israelite tradition confirms our hearing of Mark's Jesus as carrying out a renewal of the people of Israel.

Mark also gives indications toward the beginning of the story that, as a central aspect of the renewal of Israel, Jesus is carrying out a covenant renewal. In healing the paralytic (2:1–12) Jesus says "your sins are forgiven," which, he then explains, against his scribal accusers, is equivalent to a declaration of healing. The common assumption of Israelite society, of all parties in this episode, was that the paralysis had been caused by the paralytic's or his parents' sins, i.e., breaking of the covenant laws. As in John's baptism of repentance for forgiveness of sins, Jesus in voiding the punishment for sins is giving the people a new lease on life, empowering them to renew personal and community life (note the larger community present, particularly the four who had carried the paralytic). In the next episode at the toll collector Levi's house, in response to a challenge by the Pharisees, caricatured guardians of covenantal righteousness, Jesus declares that he came "to call not the righteous but sinners." The implication is that over against the official designation of people as sinners, he again is including them in (the table fellowship of) the renewed community. In the last episode before the parables speech, which brings the initial Galilean campaign to completion (3:31–35), Jesus then declares that the criterion of membership in the renewed familial community or movement is "doing the will of God," which in Israelite tradition is a synonym for covenant keeping as well as for the "kingdom of God." In other teaching of Jesus perhaps the first petition in Matthew's version of the Lord's Prayer illustrates this most vividly: "Your kingdom come, your will be done" (Matt. 6:10).

The parables speech clearly emphasizes the amazingly abundant harvest despite the extreme difficulties and obstacles to the seed germinating, growing, and reaching maturity (4:1–34). The last parable, however, grounds the interrelated analogies in what was a standard political image. As evident in late Judean prophetic literature such as Ezekiel, the tree that towers high above other trees of the forest and provides shelter for all the birds' nests is a symbol of empire (e.g., Ezek. 31:4–6). Mark's Jesus rather compares the kingdom of God to a tiny mustard seed that grows into the greatest of *shrubs* in whose branches the birds can nest. This pointedly anti-imperial image fits the renewal of a society based in village communities that Jesus is spearheading in his village-by-village building of a movement.

The continuation of Jesus' village-by-village activity in the next step of the story is the clearest section of the story in its allusion to the formative traditions of Israel. As noted in chapter 1 above, the sequence of episodes follows two parallel sets of five miracle stories with a few other episodes fitted in.[2] The first set consists of a sea crossing, an exorcism, two healing stories, and a feeding in the wilderness. The episodes of Jesus in his hometown, the mission of the twelve, and Herod's execution of John the Baptist are inserted before the feeding (4:35–6:44). The second set consists again of a sea crossing, an exorcism, a healing, a feeding in the wilderness, and a second healing, placed after the wilderness feeding so that it forms a transition to the next step of the story. The dispute with the Pharisees over Korban is inserted right after the (second) sea crossing (6:45–8:26). This suggests that both in Mark and in the Jesus traditions on which he drew, the miracle stories were recited and understood not in isolation but in sets that signified some broader agenda and activity.

The first wilderness feeding has several unmistakable allusions to Israelite stories of Moses feeding the people of Israel in the wilderness following the exodus from bondage in Egypt, i.e., allusions to the very formation of Israel as a people (see especially Exod. 16, a tradition repeated at numerous points in Israelite traditions). Most obvious perhaps, the twelve baskets of leftover pieces symbolize Israel in its twelve tribes. That the people "sat down in groups of hundreds and of fifties" refers clearly to the traditional organization of the people beginning with the exodus-wilderness narratives (see Exod. 18:21, 25; as a military formation, Num. 31:14). Since the discovery of the Dead Sea Scrolls we have been aware that precisely such symbolism of the organization of Israel as a people was current at the time of Jesus and Mark, in the community "Rules" and organization of the scribal-priestly community at Qumran (1QS 2:21; 1QSa 1:14–15, 27–2:1; 1QM 4:1–5:16). That the crowd "were sheep without a shepherd" not only alludes to Israel's exodus-wilderness origins as a people under Moses' leadership, it bluntly criticizes the high priests in Jerusalem and/or "king" Herod Antipas (who has just executed John the Baptist in the previous episode) as "shepherds" (i.e., rulers, in the traditional image of prophetic indictment, e.g., Zech. 11:5, 17; Ezek. 34).

The first wilderness feeding thus presents Jesus as the new Moses providing food for the hungry people in the wilderness as part of the renewal of Israel, which was a crucial step in the overall exodus story of the people's liberation from bondage and movement into a new life on their land. By implication, the second wilderness healing also alludes to the formation of the people of Israel in the exodus-wilderness narratives, only the provision of food for the hungry folks now being molded as a people is extended beyond Galilee, insofar as this feeding takes place in the "region of the Decapolis" and the seven loaves and seven baskets of leftover pieces apparently symbolize peoples other than the Israelites proper. The wilderness feedings may also allude to stories of the great (northern Israelite!) prophet of renewal of Israel (and resistance to oppressive rulers) Elijah and his protégé Elisha, who both multiplied food in times of need with plenty left over (1 Kings 17:8–26; 2 Kings 4:42–44).

Less clear in their allusion are the sea crossings that begin each set of miracle stories. In recent decades they have been taken as symbolic of Jesus moving back and forth from the "Jewish" side of the lake to the "Gentile" side of the lake to "bridge the racial divide" or create a unity or universalism in "Christianity" among Jews and Gentiles.[3] But there is no indication whatever in the story that the one side is "Jewish" (and the only occurrence of the term *ioudaioi* before the crucifixion episodes is a regional reference to the Pharisees and all the "Judeans," 7:3). It seems a bit of a stretch, moreover, to take the windstorm on the sea as a symbol of primordial chaos—as if Mark and the people he addressed shared the elite ancient Near Eastern myths of the king of the gods defeating the forces of chaos to create the established order of which the dominant imperial kingship was the earthly representative.[4] The mere fact that Mark represents the lake as the Sea, like the great Mediterranean Sea, suggests an allusion to the Red (Reed) Sea. That Jesus commands and the "wind and sea obey him" in the first episode seems an even clearer allusion to Moses' (God's) command of the sea in the exodus (Exod. 14:21–28; 15:1–18). Elijah and Elisha were also known for water crossings, of the Jordan

River, in obvious allusions to Moses' earlier leadership of the exodus (2 Kings 2:8–10, 12–14). These episodes in Mark involve more than allusions to the exodus sea crossing (and/or Elijah's miraculous crossings), but that is the underlying reference, particularly in connection with the wilderness feedings.

Given the allusions to the exodus in the sea crossing episodes, it seems likely that the exorcism episode in the first set of miracle stories alludes to the destruction of the armies of the foreign ruler Pharaoh. After casting out the demon, Jesus ascertained that the demon's name was "Legion," i.e., "Roman army." Once "Legion" was "dismissed" to go into the swine, the "company/herd" (note further military imagery, and pigs do not group in "herds") of swine "charged" down the bank into the sea and were drowned. Jesus' exorcism is, like the exodus of old, a liberation from alien forces.

Jesus' healings in these two parallel sets of episodes allude to, indeed could even be roughly patterned after, the healings of the prophets Elijah and Elisha. Most strikingly, both Elijah and his successor, who received a double portion of the Spirit, brought back to life young people who appeared to have died, parallel to Jesus' healing of the seemingly dead daughter of Jairus and the possessed daughter of the Syrophoenician woman. It is also very noteworthy that these most famous northern Israelite prophets extended their activities to nearby peoples in areas beyond Israel proper. The Elijah-Elisha cycle of stories in 1 Kings 17–21 and 2 Kings 1–9 suggest that in popular northern Israelite tradition, Israelite prophets had readily reached out to other peoples.

The two interwoven healings in the first set of miracles (5:21–43), moreover, make further unmistakable allusions to Israel. The hemorrhaging woman who boldly touches Jesus had been afflicted for twelve years and the daughter of a leader of a local village synagogue (= assembly),[5] turns out to be twelve years old. These women remain two individual persons in these episodes. But they also represent Israel. Israel, which has by implication been "hemorrhaging" due to its exploitation, is in the one woman's initiative represented as being restored to wholeness by reaching out to touch Jesus in faith. And as represented by the twelve-year-old woman who appears to be virtually dead just as she is coming to childbearing age, Israel is brought to life again by Jesus, prepared to give birth to a new generation.

In these many allusions in the two sets of miracle stories that form the nucleus of this step of his story, therefore, Mark is presenting Jesus as the new Moses and Elijah engaged in a systematic program of (again) renewing Israel and nearby peoples. Just as in the original liberation and formation of Israel, Moses had led the Israelites and exercised command over the storm in crossing the sea and fed the people in the wilderness, so now Jesus exercises command over the storm in sea crossings and feeds the people in the wilderness. And just as in a time of resistance to oppressive rule by Ahab and Jezebel,

Elijah performed healings and multiplied food for people, so now Jesus is performing healings and multiplying food.[6]

The other episodes in this section of Mark's reinforce the message that Jesus is engaged in a renewal of Israel in adaptation of a traditional pattern. After the healings in the first set of miracles, followed by the episode in his hometown in which he is pointedly identified as a prophet, he commissions the disciples to extend his program of proclamation and exorcism (6:1–6, 6–13). In the preface to the episode of Herod Antipas's killing of John, it is clear that people have recognized Jesus as one of the prophets, even Elijah himself, and that in Herod's mind, at least, Jesus' activity is similar to John's, by implication a renewal of the covenant, including the insistence that the rulers adhere to it. After the second sea crossing, moreover, as Jesus continues his healings in the villages, Mark presents him insisting on the "basic [covenantal] commandment of God" over against the scribes and Pharisees. Here is yet another case of an episode in which Jesus takes action to restore or defend the people's interests against the Jerusalem Temple and its representatives. Against the Pharisees who were encouraging people to "devote" their land or the produce of it as a "sacred" offering to God (*korban*, 7:1–13), Jesus insists that those resources are needed to support the basic economic subsistence of families, as in the covenantal commandment to "honor your father and mother." The restoration of covenantal life in local communities is part and parcel of the renewal of Israel that Jesus is leading as the new Moses and Elijah.

If we had any doubts about Mark's portrayal of Jesus as the new Moses and Elijah engaged in the renewal of Israel, Mark erases them in the next step of his story. Following Jesus' rebuke of Peter for his stubborn resistance to Jesus' impending martyrdom—and, by implication, his misunderstanding of Jesus as the "messiah"—Jesus appears on a "high mountain" together with Moses and Elijah (9:2–8). In ascending a "high mountain" Jesus and the intimate disciples, Peter, James, and John, are moving dramatically closer to the heavens for divine revelation, just as Moses had received revelation on Sinai and Elijah on Horeb (Exod. 24:15–18; 1 Kings 19:11–18). And indeed the prophetic founder and the prophetic renewer of Israel appear with Jesus on the mountain. In contrast to the tendency of some interpretation to elevate and glorify Jesus, the founder of Christianity, into a more exalted divine essence above Moses and Elijah, who are taken as figures parallel to the disciples in this scene, Mark pointedly has Moses and Elijah "talking with Jesus," not parallel with the disciples. Similarly, Peter's impulse is to build three booths, "one for you, one for Moses, and one for Elijah," suggesting that Jesus is being compared and ranked with the great prophetic founder and renewer of Israel. This explicitly revelatory experience confirms the many allusive indications earlier in the

story that Jesus is a prophet heading the renewal of Israel in the present, just
as Moses and Elijah had led the people in the past.

As in many other episodes of Mark's story, the transfiguration of Jesus with
Moses and Elijah carries a far more complex message than simply the confirmation of Jesus' role as the new Moses-Elijah. The divine voice emanating
from the cloud (again a standard Israelite tradition for God's revelatory
speech) confirms in the disciples' hearing (and for the audience) the revelation
that only Jesus saw and heard at his baptism, that "This is my Son, the
Beloved," instructing them to "listen to him!" (which they are having trouble
doing in recent episodes of the story). And in the actual transfiguration, Jesus
appears on the mountain in dazzlingly white clothes. The dazzling whiteness
of the garment reminds one immediately of the throne scene in apocalyptic
literature where martyrs are vindicated as well as empires judged and the
people restored to independence (Dan. 7:9–14; cf. the white garments of the
martyrs vindicated in heaven in Rev. 3:5, 18; 4:4; 6:11; 7:9, 13; and cf. the figure in the empty tomb, Mark 16:5). That is, Jesus appears to the intimate disciples as a vindicated martyr (virtually in heaven, as it were, there on the high
mountain), in accordance with what he had just announced, after which he
declared that if they wanted to become his followers, they too must be prepared for martyrdom. In this episode, however, Mark is not setting the beloved
sonship of Jesus and his impending martyrdom against or above his role as the
prophet of renewal, but is fusing them. Indeed, the rest of this middle section
of the Gospel confirms this when Jesus lays out what can only be called a
renewal of Mosaic covenantal social-economic-political order in direct explanation of the further announcements of his impending arrest, execution, and
rising (10:2–45; to be discussed in chapter 8 below).

Throughout Mark's story prior to the confrontation in Jerusalem, therefore, Jesus is expanding a systematic campaign of the renewal of Israel patterned after and evoking memories of the events of Israel's founding led by
Moses and the renewal of Israel in resistance to oppressive rulers led by
Elijah. As with the activities of Elijah and his successor Elisha, Jesus' activities reach beyond the frontiers of Israel to include other peoples. The
movement he spearheads village by village, moreover, is not simply a religious revival focused on prayer and other rituals. Following up on John's
baptism of repentance, Jesus is pressing a renewal of village life according
to the Mosaic covenant, the time-honored "constitution" and guide for
social-economic-political relations in village communities, the fundamental social form of the society (and presumably the guide for relations
between village and Jerusalem as well). Particularly striking is his adamant
insistence on covenantal commandments for marital and family relations
and for economic relations (7:9–13; 10:2–12, 16–31).

. . . in Opposition to the Rulers

From the outset of Jesus' campaign in Galilee his movement quickly gathers momentum and expands rapidly into surrounding areas, even into Judea and Idumea. Such a widespread movement would understandably be threatening to the established rulers even if it did not directly challenge them. In several episodes, however, Mark also presents Jesus' actions or pronouncements as a direct alternative or challenge to the ruling institutions, rulers, or their interests and procedures. Besides the explicit contrast between Jesus' "authority" and the chief priests' and scribes' (lack of) authority, mentioned above, Jesus provides the people with healing of leprosy or forgiveness of sins that makes it unnecessary for them to obtain these from the ruling institutions, which would cost them some of their precious economic resources (1:41–44; 2:1–12). In the Korban discussion and his final harangue against the scribes (7:9–13; 12:38–40) he sharply condemns the scribal-Pharisaic representatives of the Temple for predatory practices whereby they induce the poor to render up their scarce economic resources for maintenance of the Temple establishment.

When Jesus marches up into Jerusalem for his dramatic confrontation with the rulers, it is a continuation of his village-by-village renewal of Israel over against the rulers. But he now dramatically escalates the renewal of Israel in his prophetic demonstration and pronouncement of God's condemnation of the Temple, the high-priestly rulers, and their scribal representatives, and declares the people's rightful freedom from Roman rule. We must be aware of the timing of Jesus' entry into the capital city in order not to miss that his aggressive attack on the rulers and their institutions is a continuation of the new exodus with which Mark opened the whole story in the introduction of John. We do not hear explicitly until 14:1–2 that Jesus and his followers entered Jerusalem during the week before Passover, the most important Israelite festival that celebrated the origins of the people in its exodus liberation from Pharaoh's oppression in Egypt. Indeed, the people in Jerusalem for the Passover festival would be unusually edgy because of what they were celebrating, only under the watchful eye of the Roman governor and his troops, who turn out to be already in Jerusalem, as we learn from the episode of Jesus' trial before Pilate.

Were we sufficiently informed about ancient Israelite society, however, we would have picked up already in the episode of Jesus' entry into the ruling city and its Temple that it was Passover time (11:1–10). In their cry of "Hosanna! (Save!) Blessed is the one who comes in the name of the Lord," those accompanying Jesus—who is mounted on a donkey, as a peasant messiah?—are reciting Psalm 118, part of the Hallel psalms (113–18) sung at Passover time (which begin with a recounting of the exodus and entry into the land in Ps. 113!).

Remembering that the exodus celebrated in the Passover was a liberation from oppressive foreign rule enhances our appreciation of Mark's plotting of Jesus' confrontation with the Roman-sponsored Jerusalem rulers in a way reminiscent of the exodus. And Mark gives clear signals of just how tense the conflict between rulers and people was in Jerusalem as Jesus directly attacked the rulers and was in turn challenged by them. Three times during the sustained confrontation Mark mentions explicitly that the chief priests and scribes were afraid of him because of the crowds (11:18, 32; 12:12). And when they finally resolve to proceed against him, Mark makes explicit the connection with the Passover celebration of the exodus liberation: "Not during the festival, or there may be a riot among the people" (14:1–2).

Besides being a continuation and escalation of the new exodus, however, Jesus' confrontation with the rulers in Jerusalem is also a continuation and climax of his insistent restatement of covenant commandments and renewal of the covenant. His dramatic prophetic demonstration in the Temple is patterned after Jeremiah's condemnation of Solomon's Temple and cites part of Jeremiah's indictment that "you have made it a bandits' stronghold/cave" (Mark 11:15–17; cf. Jer. 7, esp. 7:11). Mark's Jesus would thus appear similarly to be pronouncing God's condemnation of the Temple because the high priests in charge have been exploiting the people in violation of the Mosaic covenant while seeking refuge and protection in their sacrosanct positions as heads of the Temple like bandits seeking refuge in their mountain strongholds/caves.

The parable of the violent tenants in the vineyard similarly presupposes Mosaic covenantal criteria as the basis of its indictment of the chief priests, scribes, and elders (12:1–12). The parable draws upon a traditional image of Israel as God's vineyard, in apparent allusion to the prophet Isaiah's famous prophecy that begins like a love song but indicts the rulers for predatory oppression of the peasants in violation of the covenant (Isa. 5:1–7). Jesus' parable draws an analogy between the violent tenants responsible for the vineyard and the priestly rulers responsible for tending Israel as God's vineyard. The application of the analogy in the parable—which summarizes Mark's whole story and the history of Israel it presupposes leading up to Jesus' campaign—pronounces God's imminent destruction of the violent tenants, i.e., the high-priestly and other rulers, themselves the great landlords of the society, who have been utterly unfaithful, even predatory, in not only failing to render up the desired produce of justice but also in beating and killing God's servants (the prophets) and now his son (Jesus). In Isaiah's lament over the rulers' failure to observe covenantal principles as they expropriated people's land and became large landowners, "he expected justice, but saw bloodshed; righteousness, but heard a cry" (Isa. 5:7–10).

Later on in Jesus' sustained confrontation with the Temple rulers and retainers, a scribe admits that Jesus' prophetic indictment on the basis of the Mosaic covenant is justified (12:28–33). To Jesus' summary of the Mosaic covenant by adding "love your neighbor" to the usual Deuteronomic summary of "love the Lord your God with all your heart," etc., the scribe admits that "to love one's neighbor . . . is more important than all whole burnt offerings and sacrifices," i.e. more important than all the operations conducted in the Temple—which also sustain it in power. Shortly thereafter, finally, Jesus condemns the scribes generally for "devouring widows' households," i.e., for preying on the poor by urging them to give their scarce resources to the Temple, thus leaving themselves destitute of even the usual subsistence livelihood (12:38–40). The confrontation that began and persisted with Jesus' prophetic condemnation of the Temple, the high-priestly rulers, and their scribal representatives, concludes with Jesus' declaration that the Temple will be destroyed (13:1–2).

Over against indictment of the Temple and Jerusalem rulers on the basis of the Mosaic covenant, Jesus, precisely in the setting of a Passover meal with his disciples celebrating the exodus liberation, performs a covenant renewal that becomes the central communal ritual of the movement he has built (14:12, 22–25). His words over the cup that so clearly refer to the original covenant ceremony make this explicit. Just as the blood of the covenant in the original ceremony (in Ex. 24:3–8) represented a bond between God and the people, who had just vowed to keep the covenant commandments, so the cup Jesus offers represents "my blood of the covenant which is poured out for many." This ceremony of covenant renewal at the Passover meal celebrating the exodus, however, is instituted directly over against the Jerusalem and Roman rulers who, just at that point in Mark's story, are about to capture, condemn, and execute Jesus—presumably with the effect of decapitating the new exodus, the renewed covenant movement of renewal of Israel that Jesus has been heading.

Confirming the Dominant Plot

A review of important factors in the historical context of Mark will confirm and elucidate how Mark's story is focused on Jesus' renewal of Israel in its village communities over against and in condemnation of its rulers. Such a review of the historical background of the Gospel, particularly in Israelite history and cultural tradition, should also make us more "informed" readers of a story that does not mesh with modern Western social experience and certain standard assumptions about the world of the New Testament. In the rest of this chapter we can deal with three particular factors in the historical context and their implications for understanding particular aspects of Mark's story, leaving others for subsequent chapters.

The Fundamental Conflict between Rulers
and Ruled in Roman Palestine

The fundamental and seemingly irreconcilable opposition in Mark's story between Jesus and his village followers and the Jerusalem and Roman rulers may be the most difficult for modern Westerners and Western Christians to comprehend. Interpreters of Mark persistently refer to the chief priests as "Jewish leaders," as if they had some legitimacy and following among the people.[7] But Mark states explicitly right at the outset that not even their scribal representatives have any "authority" among the people (1:21–28). Pilate is assumed to have condemned Jesus to death either on trumped-up charges or in order to please the crowd of "Jews" that had been stirred up by the chief priests. But it was standard Roman practice to summarily slaughter or crucify any agitators who in any way disturbed the pax Romana—such as the "Robin Hoods" who were crucified on either side of Jesus. In New Testament studies it is assumed that the principal division in Palestine at the time of Jesus was between "Jews" and "Gentiles" or between "Jewish" religious practices or "Judaism" and the "Hellenistic" culture that dominated the eastern Roman empire. Historical sources, however, give clear and explicit indications that the dominant division throughout the ancient "Hellenistic" and "Jewish" and Roman world was between rulers and ruled. Under the early Roman empire the gulf was expanding between the wealthy and powerful who lived lavishly in the cities on the taxes, rents, and interest payments they collected, on the one hand, and the peasant agricultural producers living in village communities who rendered up considerable portion of their produce in tithes, taxes, tribute, and interest on debts, on the other.[8]

The overarching level of domination, of course, was the Roman empire. People such as Galileans and Judeans were subjected to imperial rule and forced to render up tribute to Caesar (as discussed in chapter 2). Jerusalem rulers and their scribal representatives were also subject to imperial rule. But in return they were maintained in their positions of power and privilege as instrumental to the overall imperial system of domination. During the lifetime of Jesus, for example, the high priests, to whom the Romans entrusted the rule of Judea, Samaria, and Idumea, were responsible for collecting the tribute from the peasantry. As illustrated by the "Fourth Philosophy," the tax-resistance movement led by Pharisees and "teachers," the payment of tribute to Caesar violated the covenantal commandment that the people were to have no god (or king) other than the God of Israel.[9]

This was the most crucial and delicate issue on which the Pharisees and Herodians, representatives of the Jerusalem and Herodian rulers, could have "tested" Jesus on. Their question that aimed to entrap Jesus reveals as no other question could the fundamental political-economic-religious structure of the life situation of the people that Mark's story is about. Payment of the tribute was a direct violation of the Israelite people's traditional way of life, as commanded to them in the covenant given on Mount Sinai. The Jerusalem high priests and their Pharisaic representatives were responsible for enforcing and collecting the tribute, knowing full well both that it was against the covenant and that the Romans would treat failure to pay it as tantamount to rebellion and take punitive military action against them as well as the people. Mark's Jesus skillfully and subtly avoids making a direct statement against the tribute. But he leaves no doubt in anyone's mind, including a well-informed reader's, that the people owe Caesar nothing, since according to the covenant everything belongs to God—who of course graciously gives it to the people for their use.

For such purposes as collection of the tribute and maintenance of local social control the Romans maintained the high priests in power in Jerusalem and Herodian rulers such as Antipas in Galilee. In these positions of political power they could command revenues from the peasant producers to support their own lavish lifestyle. Herod the Great must have taxed the people rigorously, on top of the tithes and other Temple dues they were paying, to fund his many huge gifts to the imperial family and Hellenistic cities and his many massive building projects such as whole cities named for the emperor and his complete rebuilding of the Temple in grand Hellenistic style. His son Antipas, ruler of Galilee, built two capital cities in the first two decades of his reign, which must have placed a considerable economic burden on the Galilean villagers. Besides the economic strain, Galileans must have felt the imposition of suddenly having their rulers residing in Galilee itself, one or the other capital city being within view of nearly every village in "lower" (southern) Galilee, including Nazareth, Jesus "hometown," and Capernaum, the village "headquarters" of his Galilean mission. Given the hostility that existed between Galileans and the alien Roman-style, and Greek-speaking, capital cities suddenly imposed on their landscape and subsistence economy, it is not surprising that Jesus steers clear of Antipas and his cities in Mark's story. The sharp opposition between Antipas's rule and the people he ruled and taxed is vividly illustrated in Mark's episode of his execution of John the Baptist at a mere whim during a drunken banquet, a story that mocks the decadent lifestyle of the wealthy and powerful rulers. The Galileans' hostility to the cities of Sepphoris and Tiberias apparently persisted and erupted dramatically in the great revolt of 66–67, according to the accounts of the Judean historian Josephus, who was sent there by the provisional government to maintain control of the area.[10]

While Herod Antipas ruled Galilee, the rulers of Judea during the lifetime of Jesus were the high priests in Jerusalem (under the watchful eye of the Roman governor, of course).[11] Modern Western readers, who presuppose the separation of church and state, of religion and politics, may have difficulty understanding that the high-priestly families who controlled the Temple were actually the wealthy and powerful rulers of Judea. Professional biblical interpreters, for example, persist in calling them "religious leaders." Potentially their political-economic rule might have been all the more effective by virtue of their position as their sacred status as mediators between God and the people. The wealth that they controlled consisted of tithes commanded by God and offerings given to God, according to the official (scriptural) ideology of the Jerusalem temple-state. And indeed the Temple itself and the office of High Priest and the position of chief priests, like those of ordinary priests, surely commanded a certain degree of respect and reverence among the Judean populace, who had been centered in these sacred institutions for centuries. Judging from the hymn of adoration composed by the earlier Jerusalem scribe Jesus ben Sira, some of the scribal circles who served the priestly aristocracy in various capacities held the High Priest in great awe.

The sacredness of the office, however, did not effectively prevent rejection of, or resistance to, the institution among the people or opposition to the incumbents even among scribal and rival priestly circles. The temple-state had been created by and remained an instrument of empire. Rival priestly factions had previously usurped the high-priestly rulership. The Qumran community that left the Dead Sea Scrolls adamantly rejected the incumbent high priest as "wicked." Some apocalyptic literature envisioned a future for Judea/Israel without a temple or high priesthood (a "house" for the sheep and other creatures, but no "tower" = temple, in *1 Enoch* 90:28–39). The high priestly officers controlled the vast Temple revenues, including tithes for the priests. The four high-priestly families that Herod left in power as the priestly aristocracy steadily expanded their own wealth at the expense of the people. Archaeologists have discovered that they built themselves lavish mansions in the New (Upper) City on a hill looking out over the Temple. Far from cultivating the goodwill of the people and the ordinary priestly families, the rival high-priestly families became downright predatory. For example they sent gangs of thugs to seize the tithes from the village threshing floors, leaving the ordinary priests to starve (compare the "posse" armed "with swords and clubs from the chief priests" that captures Jesus, Mark 14:43).

A few decades after Jesus' crucifixion a scribal terrorist group called "Dagger Men" became so disillusioned with their own high-priestly patrons that they began assassinating them in the crowds at (Passover) festival time.[12] Meanwhile prophets such as Theudas led popular movements out into the wilderness to experience a new exodus from oppression and/or new entry into a liberated land. Like Jesus and his movement in Mark's portrayal, these popular prophets and their movements aimed at a renewal of Israel patterned after

Moses and Joshua leading the exodus and entry into the land of old. An "Egyptian" (Jewish) prophet even led a popular movement up to the Mount of Olives opposite the Temple, where they would see the walls of Jerusalem collapse and the Roman forces disappear, as Joshua had led the "battle" of Jericho in the formative history of Israel. In the last years before the outbreak of widespread popular revolt in 66, a peasant prophet named Jesus ben Hananiah began pronouncing a lament over the ruling city: the divine voice was pronouncing woes against the capital. Finally in the summer of 66, the people began sustained attacks against the high-priestly families and their mansions. As Josephus, the wealthy priest who later wrote a history of the revolt, makes clear, for most of its prolonged course the great revolt consisted of peasant movements from the countryside attacking the priestly rulers and their allies in Jerusalem and then holding out against the inevitable reconquest by the Roman armies.

Although its protagonist engages in nothing any more violent than obstruction of Temple business at festival time, Mark's story of Jesus' aggressive confrontation with the high priests and prophetic condemnation of the Temple parallels the action of other popular leaders and movements at the time. The opposition between rulers and ruled, between the wealthy and powerful living in comfort in the cities and the producer-peasants living on subsistence in villages, was the standard political-economic structure and fundamental condition of life in ancient Palestine under the Roman empire. The advent of the kingdom of God in Mark's story does not initiate conflict.[13] Mark's story presupposes that the situation into which Jesus enters is beset by conflict. The demons and Satan, the scribes and high priests, the Legions and Roman governor are already realities in Mark's world. The direct presence of God's rule in Israel as manifested in Jesus' actions does intensify the conflict. And the conflict, including the possibility that Jesus' followers may have to "take up the cross," continues in the open ending of the story.

Galilean Regional Differences
Compounding the Fundamental Conflict

Unlike other popular renewal movements against the rulers who were based in Judea, which had been under Jerusalem rule for centuries, Jesus' movement as portrayed by Mark originated in Galilee, which had (again) come under Jerusalem rule only about a century before Jesus' birth.[14] The considerable differences in regional historical experiences between Galilee and Judea must have been a significant factor in Jesus' program that Mark narrates. As discussed in chapter 2, the northern Israelite ancestors of the Galileans had rebelled against the Davidic monarchy in Jerusalem over eight centuries earlier. Only in 104 B.C.E. did Galilee again come under Jerusalem rule. Although it was during an extremely turbulent time of civil war and Roman conquest, the Jerusalem high priesthood imposed "the laws of the Judeans" (presumably the official Torah and other Judean laws) on the Galileans, at least with regard to anything that affected the relations of the villages with the Jerusalem rulers, such as tithes and taxes. During that century the Temple government would presumably have delegated "scribes and Pharisees" to represent their interests and to advocate "the laws of the Judeans" in the village communities of Galilee. Although the Romans had removed Galilee from their direct jurisdiction after 4 B.C.E. (setting Antipas and his Herodian successors over Galilee), the high-priestly aristocracy in Jerusalem had not given up their claims to influence and control the area. As soon as the great revolt erupted in 66 C.E., the Jerusalem priestly provisional government sent Josephus and other ranking priests and Pharisees to take and maintain control of Galilee.

Certain aspects of Mark's story suddenly become puzzling once we recognize this different regional historical experience of Galilee with regard to the Temple and high priesthood in Jerusalem. Yet we must now rethink how to hear those aspects of Mark's story precisely in the context of this different regional history. There is little historical basis for believing that the Pharisees were based in Galilee. Like the scribes who, says Mark, came "down from Jerusalem," the Pharisees were representatives of the Temple and high priesthood. We lack any references outside of Mark and other Christian Gospel sources that place them in Galilee during the lifetime of Jesus. Jerusalem rule of Galilee during the first century B.C.E., however, provides a historical context in which they may well have been actively representing Jerusalem's interests in Galilee (see further chapter 7 below.)

The different regional historical experience of Galilee should also help explain another aspect of Mark's story that suddenly becomes puzzling. Since Antipas was the direct ruler of Galilee, why does Mark's Jesus march up to Jerusalem to confront the high priests and scribes who no longer had direct jurisdiction over Galilee and wind up crucified as "the king of the Judeans"? For the Galileans, a century of being again in a common situation under Jerusalem rule with other Israelites such as the Judeans may have heightened their awareness of belonging to a larger Israel with common covenantal traditions. Yet Galileans probably harbored a good deal of ambivalence about Jerusalem rule. After his appointment as king by the Romans, Herod faced sustained resistance to his rule in Galilee. And at his death, rebellion erupted immediately in villages such as Nazareth. A generation after Jesus' mission in Galilee, Galileans resisted attempts by Josephus and other priestly Pharisees delegated by Jerusalem to control them. Mark's story of Jesus' pursuing a program that attempts a renewal of Israel while attacking Jerusalem rule fits precisely that combination of Galilean response to having been under Jerusalem rule during the previous generation. For the kingdom of God to come, i.e., for God to rule Israel directly in its village communities, not only would the Romans have to go back into the sea from whence they came, but Israel would have to come directly under the rule of God, as under the traditional Mosaic covenant, freed of oppressive ruling institutions and rulers in its capital.

Village Communities: Threatened with Disintegration But the Basis of a Movement

The peasant producers of Galilee and surrounding areas lived in larger or smaller village communities comprised of many patriarchal households.[15] Each family was basically self-sufficient economically, raising or making nearly all that they ate or used and producing sufficient surplus beyond their own subsistence needs to pay the tithes, taxes, tribute, and interest on debts that they owed to the various layers of rulers. Some peasants may have lost their land to their wealthy creditors, becoming sharecroppers or day laborers. Archaeological explorations and historical sources evidence many large landed estates in the hill country of Judea. Landless laborers and sharecroppers would probably not have been very responsive to social movements because they were so directly dependent on their landlords and employers. Most peasants in Galilee, however, appear to have been living on their ancestral inheritance of land.[16] The heavy demands for taxes placed on the peasants by Herod's and his son Antipas's building projects—and the prominence of debts in the teachings of Jesus—suggests fairly clearly that these peasants were coming increasingly into debt during the time of Jesus. Threats to the viability of peasant households meant that the village communities were probably beginning to disintegrate, with increased tensions, malnutrition, and illness. There was need and reason for a renewal movement to emerge. Moreover, peasants laboring under heavy indebtedness, hunger, and malnutrition are precisely the ones who respond to leaders' visions and form popular movements of protest and revolt or renewal. We thus have reason to believe that Galilean villagers would have proven responsive to prophets such as Jesus who offered a hopeful vision of renewed social life along with healings in the power of the Spirit. There are thus good historical reasons why Jesus and his movement emerged when and where they did. Mark's narrative is a highly credible account of the emergence and expansion of just such a movement.

Villages, moreover, are semiautonomous communities that run their own affairs without interference from their rulers as long as they render up the required taxes, tribute, and interest on debts. Local family and community life operates on the basis of cultural traditions and local customs. Anthropologists who study peasant communities point out that the cultural tradition and customs operative at the local level are usually different from those cultivated by the ruling elite and the cultural specialists who aid them, who are often literate, i.e., "scribes." The "little tradition" cultivated among the peasantry and the "great tradition" maintained by scribal circles often have common historical roots, parallel versions of common stories and laws, and have influenced each other. Not surprisingly, regional differences make for greater variations between the popular tradition and the central official tradition. The Galilean villages in Mark's story where Jesus operates, versus his Pharisee and scribe critics who "come down from Jerusalem," fit exactly such a difference of popular and official traditions.[17]

This is of such importance for understanding Mark's story that we will devote a chapter to it. At this point, however, we should take note of the basis in the Galilean version of the popular Israelite tradition for Jesus' mission and movement, as represented in Mark. Because peasants do not write and thus leave texts for later generations to read (except perhaps in Mark's story!), the only access we have to the Galilean popular tradition may be the official Jerusalem tradition that eventually became the Hebrew Scriptures and the Christian Old Testament. But we must acknowledge the existence of the Galilean popular Israelite tradition and take into account that it provided the basis for Jesus' mission and Mark's story about it. And that popular tradition would have articulated the interests of Galilean peasants, not the Jerusalem high priests or their Pharisaic representatives. Mark's Jesus and his followers did not only draw upon traditions of Moses and Elijah, covenantal laws, Sabbath observance, and Passover celebrations that would have been at variance with the official traditions represented by the Pharisees. They also had numerous other popular traditions of popular messiahs and popular northern Israelite prophets, such as Ahijah the Shilonite, as well as traditions they may have learned through representatives of the Judean-Jerusalemite "great tradition," e.g., of Jeremiah, who led rebellion against or condemned oppressive Jerusalem rulers and their institutions.

In addition to their indigenous popular tradition, villagers have already existing networks of communication and cooperation, along with local squabbles and quarrels. Particularly important are the local village assemblies, called *synagōgai* in Greek and long misunderstood as religious buildings. Archaeologists have failed to find public buildings in Galilean villages until late antiquity. The synagogues in the Gospel of Mark are thus apparently local assemblies where the villagers would gather for community business, discussion, and prayers. In episode after episode in Mark's story it is clear that Jesus is dealing not with isolated individuals who leave family and fields to follow

Jesus, but with people embedded in households and village communities. Mark represents Jesus repeatedly as working in the village assemblies and households. The paralytic is brought to Jesus by several (literally) supportive friends (2:1–12). In other healings and exorcisms, Jesus leaves or sends the healed persons (back) in(to) their homes and villages (5:18–19, 34, 42–43; 7:29–30; 8:26). Only the disciples temporarily and Bartimaeus, with newly regained "sight," and in a pointedly symbolic way, "follow" Jesus "on the way" (1:16–20; 10:29–31, 52). The disciples on mission are to stay in households and villages for a while, apparently in effect cultivating a movement through their healing/exorcizing and preaching (6:6–13). In Mark's story, Jesus and his disciples operated in the key social forms of peasant life, the household and village, and particularly in the principal social form of community communication and governance, the assembly.

In order to gain a firm grasp of how the overall plotting of Mark's story focuses on Jesus' renewal of Israel in opposition to the rulers, we have oversimplified a far more complex narrative. With the dominant conflict between Jesus and the rulers more clearly in mind, however, we can now move into other subplots that, like the subplot of the conflict between Jesus and the twelve disciples, complicate the overall story. Thus in the first half of Mark's story, the dominant conflict between Jesus and the rulers is framed within a higher-level conflict between Jesus as God's agent in the coming of the kingdom of God and Satan and his demons, one that becomes resolved into the overarching conflict with Roman imperial domination (chapter 6). Because of its distorted reading in more traditional Christian interpretation, the conflict between Jesus and the Pharisees, which can now be seen as the part of the dominant plot most visible in the first half of the story, can be reexamined against a more precisely understood historical context of contested Israelite traditions (chapter 7). The results of that exploration then lead directly to the recognition that Jesus' program of renewal of (an extended) Israel involves a renewal of the Mosaic covenant as integral to the presence of God's kingdom among the people (chapter 8). Finally, among the subplots of Mark's Gospel, just as the twelve function as negative examples of how not to respond to the coming of the kingdom of God and the renewal of Israel, so the women in the story function not only as representative figures of renewal for the people but as paradigms of following and serving for the communities that hear the story (chapter 9). All of these further explorations then set up a concluding examination of how the story arose out of and resonated with certain "scripts" of leaders and movements that were alive among Galilean and Judean villagers at the time of Jesus and Mark (chapter 10).

6

The Struggle against Roman Rule

Mark's story of Jesus' renewal of Israel in opposition to the rulers seems to be caught up in a broader conflict between divine and demonic spirits. After John the Baptist declares that the "stronger one who is coming" will "baptize you with the Holy Spirit," the Spirit descends upon Jesus as he emerges from his baptism. Immediately thereafter, as Jesus is undergoing his wilderness preparation for his prophetic mission, the struggle is engaged between Jesus, endowed with the Spirit and served by the divine messengers, on the one hand, and Satan, later called the "ruler of demons," on the other. In his first public action, Jesus then casts an "unclean spirit" out of a possessed man in the assembly at Capernaum, which manifests to the assembly that, in contrast to the scribes, he teaches "with power/authority." In appointing the twelve to expand his mission, he commissions them with "power/authority to cast out demons" as well as to proclaim the message of the kingdom of God. In the final (double) episode of his inaugural campaign in Galilee, in response to the scribes' charge that he himself is possessed by Beelzebul the ruler of demons, Jesus asserts that, contrary to that inherent absurdity, the plundering of Satan's "house" evident in his exorcisms indicates that Satan has been bound. Throughout this initial section of the story, moreover, Jesus' battle against the demons is featured in the several summaries of his mission (1:32–34, 39; 3:7–12).

Exorcism continues as a prominent component in Jesus' program through the next two main steps in the story. In the most dramatic exorcism of all, he casts out a demon whose name turns out to be "Legion" from a man in the country of the Gerasenes. "Legion" then enters a herd of swine who charge down the bank to their death in the Sea (5:1–20). In commissioning the twelve for mission Jesus (again) gives them "power/authority over the unclean spirits" and they "cast out many demons" (6:7, 13). Jesus himself thereafter performs two more exorcisms in the story, for the Syrophoenician woman's daughter and for the deaf and dumb (and epileptic) boy (7:24–30; 9:14–29). Finally, Jesus accepts exorcisms done in his name even by nonmembers of the movement he is building (9:38–40). Thereafter, however, both exorcisms and the struggle between Jesus and Satan disappear from the story.

While Jesus may have driven Satan and the demons from the scene by the middle of the story, another superhuman figure in the heavens takes up an increasingly prominent role. In response to whether the followers of Jesus, when brought into trial, will "take up their cross" for the sake of Jesus (and his cause) or be ashamed of him, a heavenly figure called "the son of man" "will also be ashamed when he comes in the glory of his Father with the holy angels" (8:34–38). Again when Jesus delivers his long speech to the four closest disciples regarding what they may expect in the near future, he warns that they must expect to be brought to trial, but that after all the suffering inflicted by the imperial armies "they will see the son of man coming in clouds with great power and glory . . . to gather his elect" (13:9–13, 14–27). Analogously, when Jesus is brought to trial he appeals, apparently, for divine vindication: "You will see the son of man seated at the right hand of Power, and coming with the clouds of heaven" (14:62). At three crucial points in Mark's story, therefore, the disciples and Jesus have a heavenly adversary/advocate and/or a heavenly deliverer.

Mark's Story Compared with Judean Apocalyptic Literature

Both the conflict between Jesus and Satan and "the Son of Man" have been interpreted as key elements of the "apocalypticism" that supposedly permeates or dominates Mark's Gospel. In fact, interpreters commonly declare that Mark is an "apocalyptic" Gospel. When they read Jesus' long speech toward the end of the Gospel (chap. 13), they even detect a veritable "apocalypse": "Wars and rumors of wars, . . . the end . . . , the beginnings of the birth pangs . . . the sun will be darkened, . . . the stars will be falling from heaven, . . . then the Son of Man coming in the clouds with great power and glory."

The concept of "apocalyptic," however, is another one of those modern scholarly constructs that may obscure Mark's story rather than illuminate it. Indeed, the more we hear Mark as a story addressed to subordinated people, the less "apocalyptic" it sounds. And the less Mark is assimilated to the modern scholarly concept of "apocalypticism" as somehow "alienated" from history, the clearer it becomes that Mark's story is concerned with opposition to Roman imperial rule.

Mark's Story vs. the
Modern Concept of Apocalypticism

The judgment that Mark is "apocalyptic" or contains an "apocalypse"[1] is based on the story's inclusion of a number of motifs that scholars have labeled "apocalyptic," such as the resurrection, the "son of man," "mysteries," Satan and his demons, the doctrine of "two ages," etc. There are two insuperable problems with such a categorization, however. Mark's story lacks more of the features usually deemed key to apocalyptic literature than it contains. And it de-emphasizes or seriously adapts the ones it does include.

The story is not received by divine "revelation" (*apokalypsis* in Greek). No angel-interpreter appears to explain mysteries, much less to aid a hapless humanity. The Gospel knows nothing of concepts such as the "end time," the "eschaton," or a new world portrayed in fantastic terms. Although Mark is full of judgment in the form of Jesus' prophetic pronouncements against the rulers, it is difficult to find even a "last judgment" in the story (8:38?). Although some have claimed otherwise, it is extremely difficult to find any indications in Mark of pessimism, historical determinism, cosmic disorder, or impending "cosmic catastrophe."

Even the handful of "apocalyptic" motifs present are relatively insignificant or seriously adapted in the story. "Mysteries" appears once, almost in passing reference to Jesus' parables (4:11). "This age" and "the age to come" appear in passing (10:30), but oddly enough the restoration of houses and fields is to occur in "this age," not the next. Although Jesus includes the rising again of the "son of man" in his three announcements of the suffering, trial, and execution, Mark's story lacks any real resurrection episode or appearance, in striking contrast with other Gospels. Mark is permeated with fulfillment of prophecy and its "theme" announced by Jesus at the outset appears to be the "kingdom of God." But those features are not distinctive to apocalyptic literature. As noted above, the so-called "future" or "apocalyptic Son of man" appears once in the middle and twice toward the end of the story. In striking contrast to Paul's letters and Matthew's Gospel, however, Mark contains nothing that could be called the *parousia* of the Son of Man (i.e., identified as Jesus returning in judgment). As we shall see below, finally, many of the features of Mark 13 that have been labeled "apocalyptic" are not distinctive to apocalyptic literature. As Mark's Jesus says at the beginning of his supposedly "apocalyptic" discourse (Mark 13:5), "beware that no one leads you astray." A more attentive hearing of Mark's story in its historical context suggests that "apocalyptic" features are not determinative in Mark's Gospel.[2]

The concept "apocalypticism" thus obscures rather than illuminates Mark's story. "Apocalyptic" is a highly problematic modern interpretive category. European scholars constructed the concept about a century ago, when many previously unknown documents of Judean apocalyptic literature were just being discovered. They developed "apocalypticism" as a synthetic construct composed of what they deemed typical elements abstracted from a variety of Jewish "revelatory" literature from different historical situations ranging from the third century B.C.E. to late antiquity. These texts were read somewhat literally, without taking into account the ways in which symbols and images may have been used rhetorically. Thus ancient Jewish apocalypticism supposedly entailed expectations of the imminent "end" of the world in a "cosmic catastrophe." With historical life determined by evil cosmic forces, apocalyptically minded people were "alienated from history," oriented instead to otherworldly existence. Having identified certain terms, motifs, and themes as typical of "apocalypticism," scholars then tended to assume that the appearance of some of those terms and motifs in a particular piece of literature indicated a whole worldview, "apocalypticism." Accordingly, the mere appearance of some of those elements in Mark's Gospel meant that it was "apocalyptic."

Given this assumption that a few motifs carried a whole "end-of-the-world" mentality and an overly literal understanding of such "apocalyptic" language, it is not difficult to imagine how some of Jesus' statements in Mark were taken. "There are some standing here who will not taste death until they see that the kingdom of God has come with power" (9:1) meant that Mark expected the "end" to come imminently. "The sun will be darkened, . . . and the stars will be falling from heaven, . . . and the Son of Man coming in clouds with great power and glory" (13:24–26) was taken as a reference to the "cosmic catastrophe." To the modern liberal scientific way of thinking, however, that also meant that Mark (and possibly Jesus) was deluded, because obviously the world did not come to an end.

To save Jesus from being implicated in such "fanaticism" and delusion, scholars contrasted his sober preaching of the presence of God's rule mainly in terms of individual "authenticity" and ethics with the "apocalyptic" Judaism, in which John the Baptist was supposedly still rooted. Insofar as New Testament literature displays a Christian version of apocalypticism, however, they also had to attribute that to the resurrection faith of the early Christians that Jesus was the apocalyptic "Son of Man" who at the *parousia* (= coming) would soon return in judgment at the *eschaton* (= end, hence the term "eschatological," i.e., "end-time" events). But now the problem was how to save Mark from appearing deluded. The principal solution was to identify Mark 13, where most of the "apocalyptic" elements were concentrated, as a "Jewish" or "Jewish-Christian" "fly-leaf" that was utilized but significantly edited by Mark.

The problem for interpretation (of Mark or Jesus) lies not in Mark, however, but in the modern construct of "apocalypticism." There is simply no point in perpetuating debate about "apocalypticism" in Mark on the basis of the old synthetic construct. More critical analysis of Judean apocalyptic literature during the last three decades has enabled us to appreciate the considerable differences between particular documents and to discern much more precisely the historical contexts they addressed.[3] This makes possible a much more defensible procedure of making comparisons between particular documents in their respective historical contexts—in this case between particular passages in Mark and particular passages in a given Judean apocalypse, both understood in their respective specific historical context.

Differences in Social Location,
Similarities in Imperial Situation

Before examining certain features of Mark's story against the background of their appearance in particular Judean prophetic and apocalyptic literature, however, we should address a seldom-raised question. Ordinarily it is simply assumed that Judean apocalyptic literature from around the time of Jesus addressed and gave expression to a common Jewish culture or "Judaism." That assumption, however, does not take into account clear differences in social location and in interests between the vast majority of people, who were peasants, and the scribal circles, who produced literature such as the apocalypses.[4] Apocalyptic literature was a new development among scribal circles in late Second Temple Judea. We have no direct evidence for similar themes or views among the ordinary people. For example, nothing warrants labeling the popular prophets who led their followers out into the wilderness to experience new divine acts of deliverance as "apocalyptic." Their movements, rather, were informed by older and more deeply rooted Israelite traditions of popular prophets such as Moses, Joshua, and Elijah.

Under what circumstances and in what regard, then, might apocalyptic literature composed in scribal circles be possible sources for what ordinary people were thinking and doing? The crises in the structural dynamics of the imperial order that apparently led to the composition of apocalyptic literature may provide the answer. Scribes ordinarily worked under the authority of the high priests in cultivating the "great tradition," including the "laws" according to which the temple-state was governed. When the governing high priests, collaborating with the imperial rulers, compromised or even abandoned the indigenous Judean way of life, scribal circles were inevitably "caught in the middle." Remaining loyal to the traditional Judean culture and laws of which they were the very guardians could lead to breaking with, even opposing, their high-priestly patrons. That is precisely what is evident in early apocalyptic literature such as the dream-visions of Daniel 7–12 and sections of *1 Enoch*.[5] Thus in the very circumstances that evoked apocalyptic literature, certain scribal circles came to experience not only a subjection to foreign rulers but also opposition from and to their own rulers in ways similar to what the peasantry experienced most of the time. These similar experiences may well have evoked similar responses from those rooted in the same cultural tradition.

A Common Agenda, Different Modes of Articulation

Thus it may not be surprising that the common agenda of the principal apocalyptic literature prior to the time of Jesus bears a broad resemblance to the agenda evident in Mark's story.[6] Literature such as Daniel 7–12 and sections of *1 Enoch* and the *Testament of Moses* (esp. chap. 10) portray God as resolving the crisis of oppressive imperial (and/or domestic) rule both by judging the oppressive rulers and by restoring the people to independence or sovereignty. If, in the course of oppression and persecution, some of the faithful have been martyred for the cause, then God will also vindicate the martyrs (often by resurrection!). That same agenda, of course, is evident in Mark, as Jesus pronounces that God's kingdom is at hand, soon to come "with power." Jesus himself renews the people in village communities through healings, exorcisms, and teaching, and Jesus the martyr is vindicated in the empty tomb. But God's judgment of oppressive empires and restoration of the people had also been the agenda of the later Israelite prophetic literature. Sharing this agenda thus does not make Mark apocalyptic. It simply places Mark and apocalyptic literature in the Israelite prophetic tradition of seeking and proclaiming the judgment of unjust rulers and the restoration of the people, while sharing the relatively new ("apocalyptic") motif of vindication of martyrs.

Comparing Mark's handling of this agenda with its treatment in Judean apocalyptic literature, however, reveals a significant difference between them.[7] The "wise" who composed Daniel 10–12 (see 11:33) understood themselves to be living midway through the last "week" of years before God would intervene in judgment against the oppressive rulers and restoration of the people. The Qumran community that wrote the Dead Sea Scrolls was so convinced that God's decisive "visitation" was imminent that they went out into the wilderness of Judea to "prepare the way of the Lord" (1QS 8:14; 9:19). Yet in all these cases, the decisive action of God was clearly in the future. Mark's story displays a greater urgency and intensity about deliverance that is already happening. In Mark the long-awaited renewal of Israel is already happening. Mark's story is thus more focused on fulfillment and kingdom already underway, already present, and far less on the future, however imminent.

Common Themes, Different Articulation: Kingdom of God and Son of Man

Mark's focus on the present fulfillment and the Judean apocalypses' focus on future fulfillment can be seen in their respective presentation of the kingdom of God. Daniel 7 and the *Testament of Moses* 10 both looked to God to implement his and the people's kingdom in the imminent future. In Mark, on the other hand, Jesus declares at the outset that the kingdom of God is at hand, and then proceeds to manifest the power of God's kingdom in exorcism, healing, and teaching. In the parables that disclose the mysteries of the kingdom to the disciples and others, the seeds that will grow to produce an amazingly abundant harvest or large sheltering bush are already planted and growing (4:11, 26–32). Imminently, the kingdom will finally come "with power" (9:1). And Jesus will again, imminently, "drink the fruit of the vine . . . new in the kingdom of God" (14:25). Meanwhile it is present to be received or to enter: one must receive it as a child. It will be impossible for rich people (who have gained their wealth by defrauding others) to enter (10:15, 17–25).

That the martyr Jesus is already vindicated by God, as evident in the empty tomb in Mark's story further intensifies the sense of fulfillment in the present and excitement over the renewal already underway. Mark significantly makes no reference to a vindicated Jesus "shining like the stars of heaven" (cf. Dan. 12:3 and *T. Mos.* 10:9) or to Jesus' enthronement in glory (cf. Phil. 2:9–11; 3:20–21; and Matt. 25). Mark rather directs Jesus' followers and his own audience back to Galilee, where Jesus has gone before them, to continue the project of Israel's renewal. Thus, while Judean apocalyptic scribes looked for eventual vindication in the future, Mark portrays vindication as already accomplished in Jesus. That confirms and reinforces both the conviction that God's judgment on the rulers is certain and the sense that renewal of Israel is already in process.

The appearance in Mark of the so-called "future" or "apocalyptic son of man" is one of the principal reasons the Gospel has been called "apocalyptic." Most of the "son of man" sayings in Mark, however, are evidently not derived from the influence of visionary imagery from Daniel 7 and have nothing to do with judgment or the gathering of the elect. Debate continues about the origin and meanings of the term "son of man."[8] Mark's story uses the term in at least three different ways, all of them indefinite. In its first two occurrences the term appears to signify "humankind" or people generally in their authority "to forgive sins" and over "the sabbath" (2:10, 27–28). In those passages Jesus may also be using the term in reference to himself as representative of "humankind." And the connotation of "humankind" seems to carry over into the second usage, evidently a mode of self-reference. The three announcements of the "son of man's" suffering, condemnation, execution, and rising (8:31; 9:31; 10:33–34) are central in Mark's story. Four or five related references to the "son of man's" death or rising are closely related (9:9, 12; 14:21, 41; 10:45).

In the third usage, the three "future son of man" sayings that have figured prominently in Mark's "apocalyptic" career are puzzlingly different, with no consistent scenario or consistent role for the figure. The "son of man" figure appears as more of an accuser than a judge in 8:38, although the scenario is clearly one of divine judgment, with the attending company of angels. This reference to the "son of man" in the heavenly court functions as a sanction on the followers of Jesus remaining faithful to the cause if handed over to a tribunal. Both Mark 13:26–27 and 14:62 allude, if not to Daniel 7:13, then to the same figure appearing there, the "humanlike one" who is "coming in/with the clouds." Compared with the figure in Daniel 7:13, however, the "humanlike one" in these Markan passages is less a symbolic representative of the people and more of an eschatological judge or deliverer, as in the contemporary *Similitudes of Enoch* (*1 Enoch* 62). The "son of man" in Mark 13:26–27 presides over the gathering of the elect from the four winds. In Mark 14:62 the "son of man" may still have connotation of the restored people, but is "coming" as in judgment to vindicate Jesus and/or condemn the high priests who have just condemned him.

Curiously in none of these cases is the "son of man" clearly identified with Jesus. Indeed, in 14:62 he is apparently coming to vindicate Jesus. By using the same term "son of man" both for Jesus as the martyr and for the future accuser/judge/deliverer, Mark may have been the first in the Synoptic Gospel tradition to suggest (intentionally or unintentionally) that the two were the same person. Thus, although Mark's story has no *parousia*, it has taken a decisive step toward the more elaborate Christian apocalyptic scenario of the *parousia* (second coming) of Jesus as heavenly Lord, such as we find in Matthew and later Christian doctrine. Yet, as indicated in its open ending of the empty tomb scene with Jesus "gone before them into Galilee," Mark's story emphasized not the resurrected and exalted Lord who was coming again but the continuation of Jesus' mission of renewing the people of Israel.

In sum, to continue to debate whether Mark's Gospel fits the modern synthetic concept of apocalypticism would simply divert attention from the agenda of both Mark and ancient Judean apocalyptic literature. Comparisons between Mark's story and particular Judean apocalypses, however, may well illuminate the similarities and differences between their respective agendas and their different emphases on present and future fulfillment. Most important, of course, will be to discern the function of certain themes and motifs at key points in Mark's story.

Jesus' Prophetic Speech in Mark 13

Jesus' speech to the disciples about the future (Mark 13) is the main basis on which Mark has been deemed "apocalyptic." Ironically, the principal motive for Christian interpretation of Mark 13 as a "little apocalypse" or an apocalyptic "flyleaf" was the concern to rescue not just Jesus but Mark as well from seeming to be caught up in an apocalyptic fanaticism that proved wrongheaded historically. Because of the confusion generated by so much debate we must devote special critical attention to Mark 13 and its function in Mark's overall story in its own historical context.

Just as Jesus delivered his first long speech after beginning his campaign to renew Israel in Galilee, so now he delivers his second long speech after completing his campaign against the rulers of Israel in Jerusalem. Jesus' declaration that the Temple will be destroyed evokes the disciples' questions (when? and what sign? 13:1–2, 3–4). Jesus then addresses their questions in four steps, alternating between narrative of future events and exhortation to the disciples—and through them to the audience (13:5–8, 9–13, 14–27, 28–37). In the parables speech he declared the prospect of an abundant harvest resulting from the preaching and manifestation of the kingdom despite inconspicuous origins and overwhelming obstacles. In the speech about the future, he explains that his followers should expect unprecedented political conflict and brutally violent imperial repression followed by the final deliverance, and he exhorts them not to be deterred from aggressively witnessing to repressive rulers and faithfully developing their movement.

On Not Being Misled by Apocalyptic Motifs as Historical Allusions: The Date of Mark's Story

More than other sections of Mark's story, Jesus' prophetic speech to the disciples about the future features some terms and motifs typically found in Judean apocalyptic literature.[9] In responding to the disciples' questions ("When will this be?" and "What will be the sign?") Jesus' prophetic speech about what to expect moves from "the beginning of the birth pangs" (13:5–8) through the "sufferings" (violent military repression) the disciples and other must expect (13:14–23), to the cosmic disorders and the "son of man's" ingathering of the elect (13:24–27). The list of wars, nation against nation, earthquakes, and famines (13:7–8) draws upon traditional prophetic rhetoric (Isa. 8:21; 13:13; 14:30; 19:2; Ezek. 5:12). This rhetoric apparently became elaborated and stereotyped in apocalyptic literature only after the time of Mark (*4 Ezra* 9:3; 13:31; *2 Bar.* 27; 70:8).[10] Besides many possible allusions elsewhere, Mark makes two explicit references: in 13:14 to the symbol of the "desolating sacrilege" known from the apocalyptic visions of Daniel 9:27; 11:31; 12:11, as well as from the historical account in 1 Maccabees 1:54; and in 13:19 to the suffering unprecedented since creation, known from Daniel 12:1.

The most apocalyptic-sounding part of the speech focuses on the climactic restoration of the people (13:24–27). As with many other motifs in Mark 13, the references to certain cosmic disturbances derive from prophetic tradition (see esp. Isa. 13:10; 34:4), which was continued in apocalyptic literature. These standardized prophetic symbols of disruptions in the divinely created natural order that accompany "the day of the Lord" usually referred to God's "military" action against foreign rulers as he acted in deliverance of his people (see also Ezek. 32:7–8; Joel 2:10). Mark's prophecy here focuses solely on the gathering of "his elect," with no apparent allusion to judgment against Rome.[11] Moreover, not God but "the son of man coming in clouds with great power and glory" effects the ingathering by sending out his angels.

As noted above, however, we may wonder just how directly and explicitly this scenario may be alluding to or drawing on the apocalyptic vision in Daniel 7:13. In Daniel 7 the "humanlike one" symbolized the people (Israel!) who were about to be delivered and returned to sovereignty, whereas in Mark 13:26–27 "the son of man coming in clouds" is the deliverer of the people. The angels' "gathering the elect from the four winds, from the ends of the earth to the ends of heaven" refers to the dispersed in the restoration of Israel, a standard prophetic image (see Zech. 2:10 [= 3:6 in NRSV]; 8:7–8; Isa. 43:5–7; 56:8; Jer. 29:14; 31:8; 32:37; Deut. 30:4; Ps. 107:2–3; *Ps. Sol.* 11:2–3).[12]

Ironically, in the history of Markan interpretation, Mark 13, which is supposedly "apocalyptic," hence supposedly "alienated from history," is also understood as referring to great historical events which are in turn the key for both dating and interpreting the Gospel as a whole. Most ominously, the "desolating sacrilege" ("the abomination that makes desolate") along with the parenthetical admonition "let the reader understand" are taken as references to the Roman destruction of the Jerusalem Temple. That provides a basis for dating the Gospel after the Roman devastation of Jerusalem. But it has also led to the Christian interpretation, not only that Jesus' prophecy of the Temple's destruction was right, but also that in destroying the Temple God was therefore punishing "the Jews" and "Judaism" for killing the Messiah. More recently this reading of Mark 13 has led to a devastating critique of Mark's sup-posedly "apocalyptic" Gospel as the presumed source of such historically omi-nous interpretations.[13]

Mark, however, does not suggest that the Temple had already been destroyed in this speech. In their rewriting of Mark's account, both Luke and Matthew indicate clearly that the Jerusalem Temple has been destroyed by their time. Luke (21:20) simply wiped out Mark's reference to the "desolat-ing sacrilege" as part of his historicizing transformation that looks back on the Roman siege of Jerusalem. Matthew (24:15) not only mentions explicitly that the prophecy about the "desolating sacrilege" comes from Daniel, but indicates that it was fulfilled in the Roman conquest of Jerusalem, "standing in the holy place." These rewritings make the vague and indefinite simplicity of Jesus' statement in Mark 13:14 all the more striking. Nothing in the say-ing or its immediate context suggests Jerusalem or the Temple. The whole speech, of course, addresses the disciples' question "when will this be" in response to Jesus' prediction that the Temple would be destroyed (13:1–2, 3–4). But in its hyperbole, Jesus' prophecy of destruction is so different from what the Romans actually did in their conquest that it cannot be taken as a prophecy after the fact. Jesus' prophecy in Mark 13:2, for example, does not correspond very closely with the description of Titus's destruction of the Jerusalem Temple and city wall in Josephus (*War* 7.1–4). If Mark presupposed the destruction of the Temple, moreover, there would have been little reason to include the warning against false messiahs and false prophets (13:22), since the outcome of events would have been unmistakably clear. We must con-clude that Mark's story must have been composed prior to the destruction of the Temple.[14]

Repressive Imperial Military Violence and Popular Resistance

We are left then with the problem of how to hear the relatively indefinite prophetic language and allusive images in Jesus' speech. The historical back-ground of Jesus' speech in Mark 13, as of Mark's story as a whole, was the sharp political-economic-religious conflict prevailing throughout early Roman times in Palestine.[15] After widespread revolt at the time of Herod's death (and Jesus' birth) in 4 B.C.E., conflict was escalating again throughout the middle of the first century C.E. and finally erupted again in the great revolt of 66–70. The Synoptic Gospel traditions included in Mark thus developed during decades of extensive popular discontent, periodic protests, numerous resis-tance and renewal movements, and recurrent repression by Roman military action. The turmoil of the great revolt and the Roman reconquest, including war, slaughter of people, desperate flight, famine, prophets, and messianic pretenders, is best known among scholarly interpreters. Hence the tendency of those who do not date the Gospel after the Roman destruction of Jerusalem is to place it sometime during the great revolt. All of those same phenomena, however, occurred repeatedly throughout the mid-first century and were vivid in the people's memory of earlier Roman conquests (especially the popular resistance and punitive Roman devastation in 4 B.C.E.). Thus the numerous movements and conflicts of the 40s, 50s, and early 60s offer other possibilities for the events and figures to which particular motifs in Mark 13 may be referring. It may simply be impossible to reach any degree of precision regarding particular allusions or references—to "wars and rumors of wars," "famines," attacks so vicious that it was too dangerous to "turn back to get a coat," "false messiahs and false prophets."

Wars. Within a decade after Jesus was crucified, several wars raged through the Middle East in general and Palestine in particular. Besides the war between the Romans and the Parthians along the frontier of their empires, a war erupted between Herod Antipas in Galilee and Perea (east of the Jordan River) and Aretas, the Arab king, after the former rejected the daughter of the latter, whom he had previously married. When Antipas was defeated, Roman troops came to his defense. Of course, the Roman governors of Judea regularly sent out their military to suppress popular movements and bands of brigands, sometimes destroying whole villages as well as slaughtering people in these punitive and terrorizing expeditions.

By far the most serious of these "wars and rumors of wars" was the extreme crisis in 39–40 when the emperor Gaius (Caligula) ordered that a statue of himself as the god Jupiter be installed in the Jerusalem Temple and sent a large Roman army to implement the order. Galilean peasants mounted a massive strike, refusing to plant their crops, on which the Roman, Herodian, and high-priestly rulers depended for their revenues. Everyone fully expected a full-scale war, which clearly would have ensued if Gaius had not been assassinated (accounts in Philo, *Legat.* 197–337; Josephus, *War* 2.184–203; *Ant.* 18.256–309; Tacitus, *Hist.* 5.9.2). This is almost certainly the (expected) event of desecration (not destruction) of the Temple that would have evoked memories of and allusions to the "desolating sacrilege" placed in the Temple two centuries before by the Seleucid emperor Antiochus Epiphanes (mentioned in 1 Maccabees 1:54 and Daniel 9:27; 11:31; 12:11). This must have occasioned the allusion in Mark 13:14—although that does not mean that the speech in Mark 13 originated at the time of the war threatened by Gaius's order.

Famines. Famine was one of the results of war for the peasantry. The widespread strike in protest over Gaius's plan, the peasants' refusing to plant the ground, would have resulted in famine—with the ensuing "harvest of banditry," as the local ruling elite pointed out to the Roman officials (*Ant.* 18.273–75). A prolonged drought during the late 40s in Palestine resulted in serious famine throughout Palestine (Josephus, *Ant.* 3.320–21). Long before the great revolt the people were suffering from famine, which was a factor leading to the revolt, not just one of its eventual results.

Brutal Roman Devastations. Galileans and Judeans, further, had prolonged experience and memories (especially from the vicious reconquest of Galilee and Judea by Varus in 4 B.C.E.) of the "scorched earth" and "search and destroy" practices of Roman armies in suppressing a revolt or a movement. Anytime after Pilate's brutal treatment of popular resistance, and especially after the broad resistance touched off by Gaius's order, no clairvoyance was necessary to prophesy a scenario so devastating for the people that "one in the field must not turn back to get a coat." The people would hardly have forgotten how the Roman soldiers treated people such as pregnant or nursing women who remained in their villages during their reconquest in 4 B.C.E.[16] Thus a prophet or evangelist would not need to have heard about the brutal Roman reconquest of Galilee or northwestern Judea in 67–68 to have articulated the admonitions in Mark 13:14b–18.

False Messiahs and False Prophets. The false messiahs and the false prophets of 13:6 and especially of 13:21–22 could well be the ones who appeared during the course of the great revolt in 66–69. Popular prophets and prophetic movements, however, were more prominent a few decades earlier, and the memories of the popular messiahs who arose after Herod's death in 4 B.C.E. were still alive among the people. Nor should we imagine that the Jewish historian Josephus mentions all of the popular messiahs and prophets who were active.

Listening Carefully for What Jesus Is Speaking About: Persistence under Roman Imperial Repression

A helpful, although not sufficient, key to understanding what events some of these motifs may be referring to is the point in the speech where "Jesus" shifts from references to the past and present events and begins to prophesy about the future. References to past events known to the hearers serve to lend authority and credibility to the prophecies about future deliverance. This shift most likely comes in 13:24 rather than in 13:14. All of the motifs mentioned in 13:5–7 and 14–23 could easily refer to events and figures of the great revolt of 66–70. But they all can equally well refer to events and figures regularly experienced by people in Palestine during the three previous decades, particularly the crisis touched off by Gaius and its aftermath.[17] Also the comment that "if the Lord had not cut short those days, no one would be saved" suggests that the motifs in 13:14–23 are references to well-known past experiences. Many of the terms and phrases used in 13:5–8 and 14–23 are vague, stereotypical, and/or traditional prophetic images. But only with the prophecy in 13:24–27 does Jesus' speech finally shift into vague language derived from prophetic traditions that cannot refer to already known historical events. Thus, when we read Jesus' speech with this in mind, 13:5–8 seems like a vague general summary of "future" events, while 13:14–23 refers somewhat more specifically to several related aspects of Roman treatment of Judeans and Galileans and the latter's responses during the middle of the first century.

If anything, the extensive debate about historical references encoded in the prophetic (and some apocalyptic) imagery of Mark 13 and about using these to date (and locate) Mark's Gospel threatens to obscure the real concern addressed in this speech. Most if not all of the images and motifs used in the narrative parts of the speech—war, kingdom against kingdom, famines, "desolating sacrilege," fleeing to the mountains without taking time to get a cloak or provisions, brutal military violence against women and infants, popular messiahs and prophets—pertain to the Roman imperial military practices in the conquest and terrorizing intimidation of subject peoples, or the response of the subject peoples in popular resistance and renewal movements. The narrative parts of Jesus' speech in Mark 13 are thus concerned about the severe repression and suffering of the Judean, Galilean, and other peoples under Roman rule that escalated in repeated crises during the middle of the first century. This was precisely the time during which the movement represented and addressed by Mark's story was spreading and becoming established in Galilee and the surrounding areas.

A close look at the exhortative parts of the speech reveals that they also focus on that same Roman imperial repression and the Jesus movement's conflict with it. The prophecies of "future" events in Jesus speech are both framed and interpreted by the exhortations in 13:5–6, 9–13, and 28–37. Along with the important assurance about the final gathering of the elect, these admonitions constitute the speech's principal message. Warnings to "watch" (13:5, 9, 23, 33) and "keep awake" (13:35, 37) are carefully positioned and repeated throughout. The main concern of the admonitions, as of the prophecies framed by them, is to exhort the hearers not to be deterred from the struggle by its attendant difficulties. The first section (13:9–13) warns that repression and persecution should be expected. Far from being discouraged, however, they must use trials before "governors and kings" as opportunities to boldly bear witness to them, for he promises the guiding presence of the Holy Spirit in these situations of direct confrontation with the rulers. The climactic prophecy of final ingathering (13:24–27) reassures the hearers that God is ultimately in control.

The second section of exhortation (13:28–37) follows up this prophecy of deliverance in two ways. First comes assurance of both the imminence of divine deliverance and the veracity of Jesus' words (13:28–31). This has the same function as the saying about the kingdom coming soon with power, i.e., as a reassurance to Jesus' followers to remain focused on their cause in similar circumstances of persecution ("take up their cross . . . and confess" 8:34–9:1). Then, as the concluding point in the speech, comes the insistence that, since no one knows precisely when deliverance will come, the hearers are to "keep awake" while pursuing their respective responsibilities in building the movement.

"Beware That No One Leads You Astray"— What Jesus Did and Did Not Say

This survey of Jesus' "apocalyptic" speech in Mark 13 suggests that it is almost antiapocalyptic in function. If we listen carefully to the speech it becomes evident by the end that Jesus never really answers, indeed never really directly addresses, the questions asked by the four disciples in 13:4. "When" God's judgment and deliverance would come and "what would be the signs" may have been questions often addressed in Judean apocalyptic literature. Perhaps we should have been forewarned by Jesus' exasperated rejection of the Pharisees' request for a sign ("I tell you, no sign will be given to this generation!" 8:11–12) to realize that the disciples are asking an inappropriate question.

Instead of explaining when the Temple would be destroyed, Jesus focuses on the extreme difficulties that his followers will experience at the hands of the Roman imperial military rulers and the final deliverance of a dispersed Israel. Far from giving a "sign" that all these things are about to happen, Jesus insists that his followers not take the events they are about to undergo, no matter how extreme, as signs of impending judgment or deliverance. As he explains explicitly toward the end of the speech, "about that day or hour no one knows, . . . only the Father" (13:32–33). Mark thus utilizes a few stereotyped "apocalyptic" images along with a number of rather vague standard prophetic traditions to caution the listeners against an "apocalyptic" interpretation of their own situations of crisis. The speech insists that whatever current difficulties the hearers are facing will not last forever and must not be allowed to divert them from the struggle to establish a renewed society in opposition to the Roman imperial order and its repressive violence. Far from being interested in speculating about the "end," Mark is concerned with the struggles of the present time.

Finally, considering the ominous role that Mark 13 has played in Christian anti-Judaism and biblical interpretation, it is important to summarize what Jesus does not say in the speech in Mark 13. Following his prophetic condemnation of the Temple and the high-priestly rulers in the previous section of the story (Mark 11–12), Jesus declares that the Temple will be destroyed. The disciples' questions about "when . . . and what will be the sign?" then link the prophecies that ensue with that prediction of the Temple's destruction. Nothing in the ensuing prophecies of Mark 13, however, has anything to do with the destruction of Jerusalem or the Temple. The "desolating sacrilege" (13:14) refers to a desecration of the Temple, but not to its destruction by the Romans in 70 C.E. In fact, judging from the phrase "those in Judea" these imperatives and warnings are delivered from a perspective outside of (or far wider if inclusive of) Judea and Jerusalem. The concerns of the movement Mark represents are the renewal of Israel—including here the ingathering of the dispersed "from the four winds" (13:27)—over against its rulers and their Temple as exploitative and unfaithful stewards. That dominant conflict in Mark's story is deeply rooted in and mirrors the long-standing historical conflict between rulers and ruled in Second Temple Judean-Israelite society. Jesus' pronouncement that the Temple will be destroyed provides the occasion for his speech about the future. But the speech itself pays little attention to Jerusalem or its rulers. Thus Mark is clearly not proclaiming God's judgment of "the Jews" and their Temple because they had killed Jesus. Jesus' speech in Mark 13 rather focuses on his movement's struggle against the repressive violence of Roman rule.

The Battle with Beelzebul

The prominence of exorcisms, along with healings, in the first half of the story, and then their sudden disappearance in the rest, has led to much speculation and several theories about the "theology" of the Gospel. The question to be explored here, however, is how Jesus' struggle with Satan and the demons in the first half of the story may fit with or be integral to the overall story and its dominant plot of the renewal of Israel over against its rulers. We noted in the previous chapters that the two sets of five miracle episodes with their allusions to the actions of Moses and Elijah clearly signify that Jesus is engaged in the renewal of Israel. Jesus' general struggle against the demonic forces therefore must be a significant aspect of that same renewal. The overarching theme of the story, moreover, as Jesus announces at the very outset, is that the kingdom of God is at hand now in the fulfillment of time. Jesus' exorcisms therefore must be manifestations of the kingdom of God.

Jesus Did Not Just "Rebuke" the Demons, He Subjected Them to God's Rule

The exorcism that Jesus performs as his first public action confirms both of these points. In chapter 3 above we recognized that Mark's story probably developed in repeated performance before communities of a Jesus movement as it expanded into Greek-speaking areas beyond Galilee. The story and its hearers, moreover, whether or not they were themselves of Israelite heritage, identified with Israelite tradition. In our own hearing of the story, therefore, we must strive to become aware of the ways in which terms, motifs, names, and whole episodes refer or allude (metonymically) to aspects of Israelite tradition such that they resonate with hearers by evoking wider meanings from that tradition. Then, continuing to hear episodes in the context of the overall story, we can be more fully aware how those meanings continue to resonate as subsequent episodes remind the listeners of the references and allusions in similar earlier ones, in this case the exorcisms and related episodes.[18]

The term used for Jesus' overcoming the "unclean spirit" in both this episode and that about the deaf and dumb boy is *epitiman* in Greek. This term is distinctive to Jesus' exorcism stories in the Gospels, and is not used in Hellenistic exorcism stories.[19] Nor is it the term for exorcism in Mark's story, which uses mostly *ekballein*, "cast out" (1:34, 39; 3:15, 22; 6:13; 9:18). *Epitiman* is translated "rebuke" in NRSV. But far more than "rebuke" is involved, as becomes evident from examination of how *epitiman* and the Hebrew term *ga'ar* translated by it are used in both Hebrew biblical passages and in texts from the Qumran community found among the Dead Sea Scrolls. This literature provides windows onto how *epitiman* and the Hebrew or Aramaic terms behind it would have been used and how they would have resonated with the hearers of episodes about Jesus struggle with demons. In many psalms, for example, *ga'ar/epitiman* is used parallel to such strong language as "destroy, blot out, root out, vanquish, trample, stun, make perish," in appeals to God as a Warrior coming in judgment against foreign nations or imperial regimes who conquer and take spoil from Israel (e.g., Pss. 9:6; 68:31; 78:6; 80:16). The meaning is more like "conquer" or "subject" than "rebuke." Interestingly enough, the term is used for Satan in one late prophetic passage where the LORD declares: "The LORD subject (*ga'ar/epitiman*) you, O Satan!" (Zech. 3:2).

Most significant for Mark's story surely is the near-contemporary usage in the Qumran community, a parallel, scribal movement of renewal. Not only is the term used for Abram's or God's subjection of evil spirits (1QGA), but it occurs in a context of the struggle between God and Belial (= Prince of Darkness,

Satan). Most significant is a passage from the *War Scroll* (1QM 14:9–11, as supplemented from 4Q491):

> During all the mysteries of his [Belial's] Malevolence he has not made us stray from Thy Covenant; Thou hast driven his spirits [of destruction] far from [us] (*ga'ar*), Thou hast preserved the soul of Thy redeemed [when the men] of his dominion [acted wickedly].[20]

That is, *ga'ar* and its Aramaic or Greek equivalent in such contexts must be understood as the decisive act of God or his representative by which evil powers are brought into submission and the rule/kingdom of God (re-)established and God's people delivered.[21]

In Jesus' first public act in Mark's story, the "unclean spirit" indicates precisely what is happening: "Have you come to destroy us?" (1:24).[22] Note the plural pronoun. The demon knows that Jesus has appeared as God's agent whose "kingdom of God" program of casting out demons is about to bring defeat for all the demonic forces. The rest of the episode, showing no interest in the thaumaturgic techniques used by Jesus (simply the brief command: "Be silent, come out of him"), instead elaborates on the severity, the violence of the struggle engaged: "And the unclean spirit, convulsing him and crying with a loud voice, came out of him!" (1:26).[23] The Hellenistic and rabbinic exorcism stories and those of Jewish exorcists in Josephus, which do not use the term *epitiman* or its equivalent, are all told mainly to glorify the wonder-worker.[24] Only in the first exorcism episode does Mark's story make much of Jesus' "fame" spreading as the result, and that is clearly part of establishing at the beginning of the story that he acts with (divine) "power/authority" on behalf of the people, in contrast with the scribes and high priests with whom he is in conflict throughout the story (cf. 11:27–33). Otherwise, the narrative makes no fuss over Jesus' glory, draws no "christological" point from these episodes. In fact, after his exorcism in Gerasene territory, the people ask him to leave! (5:17). In Mark's story Jesus' (and the disciples'?) casting out of demons manifests the general defeat of the demonic forces in the wider program of the establishment of God's rule, the kingdom of God.[25]

This understanding of the significance of Jesus' exorcisms in Mark's story is confirmed by the "stilling of the windstorm" episode (4:35–41). There the same term occurs as in Jesus' first and last exorcisms: "Jesus subdued/subjected (*epitiman*) the windstorm." It would not be quite right to conclude that the stilling of the storm is really an exorcism, at least not in the sense that the windstorm is another demon under Satan the ruler of demons.[26] Rather, the same term is used for two parallel ways in which Jesus exercises divine power over dangerous and destructive forces to bring about God's rule.

The End of Satan's Kingdom Has Come

In Jesus' response to the scribes' accusation that Jesus is himself possessed by Beelzebul, casting out demons by the Prince of Demons, Mark presents an almost programmatic statement that in Jesus' exorcisms the rule of Satan is being ended as the kingdom of God is being established (3:22–27).[27] Having come "down from Jerusalem," the scribes accuse Jesus as representatives of the Jerusalem high-priestly aristocracy, who in turn of course were client rulers appointed by the Romans. The name "Beelzebul" used by the scribes is of Semitic derivation, meaning something like Baal the Prince.[28] Baal ("Lord Storm"), as the king of the gods in ancient Canaanite societies, had long been vilified by Israelite prophets and then demonized by spokespersons of the Jerusalem temple.[29] Like other representatives of the "orthodox" establishment, the scribes from Jerusalem looked upon country people, particularly Galileans, who lived in "Galilee of the Gentiles" (see Isa. 9:1–2; Matt. 4:15), as half pagan. Thus insofar as Jesus was drawing on remarkable powers that were obviously not derived from or approved by the Temple authorities in Jerusalem, they viewed his powers as derived from the demonic opposition forces, headed by Beelzebul. This is exactly parallel to how Christian theologians and church authorities, both Catholic and Protestant, viewed peasant midwives and healers in early modern Europe during the witch-hunts: if their unusual powers and practices were not derived from and approved by the church, then they were by definition derived from Satan.

Jesus' response also presupposes that life circumstances involve a struggle between God and demonic forces headed by Satan. In the parables or analogies of his logical (*reductio ad absurdum*) argument he uses what were already standard political terms for rulers. "Kingdom" is the same term as in "the kingdom of God," and "house" was a standing metaphor for the ruling family or dynasty (see 2 Sam. 7). It would be absurd, argues Jesus, to imagine that Satan would "cast out" himself. Even so, his kingdom or house would fall. Having demonstrated the absurdity of the scribes' accusation, he states what is, obviously, really happening in another parable or metaphor. One cannot plunder a strong man's goods or property without first tying up the strong man. In the exorcisms Jesus is obviously "plundering the strong man's goods/vessels," i.e., Satan's demons.[30] Obviously Satan must have been bound first (by God or by Jesus, who by implication is a stronger one, as John announced at his baptism). The point is that in Jesus' exorcisms Satan and his demons are being overpowered, defeated. The further implication set up by the starting assumption of the struggle between God and Satan is stated at the climax of the parallel version of the Beelzebul controversy in the Synoptic Sayings Source Q: "Since it is by the finger of God I cast out demons, the kingdom of God has come upon you" (Luke/Q 11:20).

The Battle with Beelzebul
Is a Political Struggle

The second and most dramatic, riveting, and violent exorcism in Mark's story brings the political-military dimension of Jesus' struggle against the demonic forces vividly to the fore (5:1–20). No sooner does Jesus step out of the boat in which he has just crossed the "sea" than he is confronted by a demoniac, whose desperate condition the narrator describes in horrifying, violent terms. He is possessed by an "unclean spirit" so violent that he had to be "restrained with shackles and chains. But the chains he wrenched apart, and the shackles he broke in pieces, and no one had the strength to subdue him. Night and day among the tombs and on the mountain he was always howling and bruising himself with stones." Besides being a threat to the community, he was directing the violence against himself. The community had tried desperately to control the behavior driven by the demon that had taken possession of the man, with the most severe means of restraint available. But the demonic force that has taken possession of the man has driven him utterly berserk, completely beyond control.

Immediately as he commands the unclean spirit to "come out of the man," however, Jesus is able to elicit its *name:* "Legion." The Greek-speaking/hearing audience would immediately recognize what that Latin term meant: a legion (division) of Roman troops which, in their recent experience, would more than once have attacked their villages unmercifully, burning their houses, slaughtering or enslaving the people, plundering their goods, either in their own or nearby areas (see the discussion in the previous section above). The identity of the demon is *Roman army.* The violent attacks of the Roman army are what has been driving this man into such violent behavior, in which he does repeated injury to himself and utterly disrupts the community and is totally beyond their ability to control.[31] This means, however, not only that the demon's name is symbolic, indicating that the Roman army is the cause of the possessed man's violent and destructive behavior, but that the man also is symbolic of the whole society that is possessed by the demonic imperial violence to their persons and communities.

The narrative in this exorcism episode then turns the tables on "Legion"— at least symbolically. First, the hearers, who have themselves suffered under Roman conquest and continuing imperial violence, are treated to the picture of (the Roman) Legion "bowing down before" Jesus and "desperately begging him not to send him/them out of the country" that they had taken possession of! More ominous politically and empowering for the audience, however, Jesus "dismisses" Legion to enter the great "herd" of swine there on the hillside, who then suddenly "charge" down the steep bank "into the Sea" and "were drowned in the Sea." We must think of the concrete circumstances in connection with both the special terms used here and the connotations of some of those terms in Israelite tradition. The Roman legion becomes identified with swine. Military imagery abounds:[32] the term behind "herd," while inappropriate for a bunch of pigs in Greek, was often used for a troop of military recruits. "Dismissed" is a military command given to the troop by the officer in command. And "charging" suggests troops rushing headlong into battle. But in this case they charge into the Sea to their own destruction. "Sea" is hardly a term for the large inland lake between Galilee and the Decapolis ("ten cities") in which this episode is set (there is some confusion in the manuscripts as to whether it is in the countryside of Gerasa, further away from the lake to the south, or Gadara, much closer to the east side of the lake). "Sea" rather suggests the Mediterranean Sea, across which the Roman legions had come to conquer the countries of Syria and Palestine. Finally, "into the Sea" and "drowned in the Sea" would evoke memories of the exodus of Israel, when the Pharaoh's armies pursuing the fleeing Israelites had been cast "into the Sea" and "drowned in the Sea" (esp. Exod. 15:1–10).

This episode thus tells of the people's liberation from the Roman legions and the destruction of those legions, as it evokes memories of God's original deliverance of Israel from Egyptian bondage in the exodus. Symbolically in this episode, as in the first exorcism of Mark's story, Jesus is taking control of, even destroying, the demonic forces that possess the people, and establishing God's rule. Now, however, the alien demonic forces that are wreaking such violence among the people are clearly identified as the instruments and effects of Roman imperial rule.

"My Name Is Legion"

That the struggle between transcendent *spiritual* forces, between God and Satan, between Jesus and the demons is also a this-worldly *political* struggle has been difficult for modern biblical interpreters to grasp, given the standard assumption of a separation between religion and politics. That Jesus' exorcisms of "unclean spirits" constituted battles in the struggle against Roman imperialism can be better understood perhaps through analogy with modern peoples' experience of colonialism. In the famous book *The Wretched of the Earth*, Frantz Fanon, who received his training in psychiatry in Paris and then became head of a mental hospital in colonial Algiers, makes a number of striking observations about life in colonial Algeria just as the anticolonial struggle was beginning there. His combination of social-psychological and political-historical analysis enables certain connections to emerge that are usually missed by those who analyze religion and politics separately.[33]

It is not possible, of course, to draw a precise analogy between colonial Algeria and Roman-dominated Judea and Galilee. Modern Algeria was not simply subject to France; it was a French colony with over a million French living there at the middle of the twentieth century. The principal cities such as Algiers were heavily populated by French people generally, not just the military and other government officials. Ancient Judea and Galilee, on the other hand, were not Roman colonies, with large numbers of Romans settled there. The Judean priestly and Herodian aristocracy still governed Jerusalem and Judea. Nevertheless other cities in Palestine were to a considerable degree settled and dominated by Hellenized non-Israelite peoples. Thanks to Herod's massive building program, moreover, statues, temples, and whole cities dedicated to Rome and Roman emperors were prominently placed throughout Palestine. And Antipas had built two new, Roman-style capital cities even in the tiny area of Galilee. Most important for possible illumination of demon possession and the opposition between God and Satan in ancient Palestine and Mark's story is the analogy with the "Manichean" structure of life in Algeria and its effect on the subjected people.

The "Manicheism" of the Colonial/Imperial Situation

On the basis of his experience in Algeria and elsewhere, it seemed to Fanon that "the colonial world is a world divided into compartments . . . cut in two, . . . inhabited by two different species." The settler's town is "a strongly built town, all made of stone and steel, . . . well-fed, easy-going, its belly is always full of good things. The settlers' town is a town of white people, of foreigners. . . . The native town is a hungry town, starved of bread, . . . on its knees, . . . a town of dirty Arabs" (38–40). This is a "Manichean world," created by violent colonial military conquest and maintained by police violence. "The agents of government speak the language of pure force." The colonial power and its intermediaries bring violence "into the home and into the mind of the native" (38). This violence destroys native social forms, including even customs of dress and external life (40). The colonizers, however, are not content with overt physical and social violence, which they never attempt to hide (84). "As if to show the totalitarian character of colonial exploitation the settler paints the native as a sort of quintessence of evil" (41). The native is not simply lacking in values, but is the very enemy of values, the absolute evil. "He is the corrosive element, the deforming element, he is the depository of maleficent powers, the unconscious and irretrievable instrument of blind forces" [Fanon knew this as the standard view of the French psychiatrists who practiced in Algeria]. Thus the colonizers constructed the colonial situation as a "Manichean world" (41).

For their part, the colonized know that "colonialism is not a thinking machine, nor a body endowed with reasoning faculties. It is violence in its natural state, and it will only yield when confronted with greater violence" (61). Having the sense that their liberation can only be achieved by force, the natives are convinced that here and now their fate is in the balance. They live in the atmosphere of doomsday. Since their situation seems so impervious to any action they might take, many believe that everything is going to be decided elsewhere, for everybody, at the same time (73, 81). "The natives' challenge to the colonial world is not a rational confrontation of points of view" (41). "The violence with which the supremacy of white values is affirmed and the aggressiveness which has permeated the victory of these values over the ways of life and of thought of the native mean that, in revenge, the native laughs in mockery when Western values are mentioned in front of him" (43). "To the theory of the 'absolute evil of the native' the theory of the 'absoute evil of the settler' replies. The Manicheism of the settler [thus] produces a Manicheism of the native" (93).

Similarly in ancient Roman Palestine, the "Manicheism of the native" may be understood as a response to the "Manicheism" of Roman conquest and domination. Roman military conquest and reconquest, including techniques of terrorizing the populace such as slaughter and crucifixion, made a profound impact on subject peoples. The people of ancient Israelite heritage must have had particular difficulty reconciling imperial domination with their own faith and cultural tradition. Their God was supposed to be in charge of history. Foreign empires, the Romans being only the latest and most brutal to rule the people, however, were obviously not under God's effective control. They developed a "Manicheism" that provided an explanation, as we can see in scribal apocalyptic literature and some of the Dead Sea Scrolls: The problem was not simply the Roman armies. Superhuman evil forces—Belial or The Spirit of Darkness in the Dead Sea Scrolls, Satan in the Gospels—had seized control of history. But God was ultimately in control and would finally at a certain time intervene (even with heavenly armies) to defeat the oppressive empire and restore the people to sovereignty and life under God's own rule. Understanding their own conquest and subjection as part of Satan's or Belial's transcendent struggle against God and the divine purposes brought both reason for and significance to their otherwise inexplicable and meaningless fate. Belief that God would ultimately reassert control over history also gave the people reason to continue in their traditional way of life in resistance to the encroachments of the imperial order.

Demon Possession and Imperial Rule

By comparison with the basic Manicheism of colonial and imperial situations, the belief in demons and demon possession is more complicated and difficult to grasp. Fanon's reflections on what he observed among Algerians, partly based on his clinical notes, may illuminate demon possession as well.

The colonial situation keeps the natives "hemmed in." They quickly learn to "stay in their place, and not to go beyond certain limits," even though they dream of freedom (52). They are overpowered, perhaps, but not tamed. Obsessed with his own security, the settler reminds the native with repeated exhibitions of his power, that he alone is master. Thus, "the settler keeps alive in the native an anger which he deprives of outlet; the native is trapped in the tight links of the chains of colonialism" (53–54). Full of anger but hemmed in, the native finds himself in a permanent tension.

A particularly important means of social control in a colonial or imperial order is the belief in fate or in demons as a way of ignoring the worst features of concrete domination and avoiding direct confrontation with the colonizers or rulers. Developing a belief in Fate or in God as Fate, who is responsible for poverty and misfortunes, "removes all blame from the oppressor" (54). Belief in demons and demon possession, however, enables the oppressed people not to blame their own God. In this way "the native will strengthen the inhibitions which contain his aggressiveness by drawing on the terrifying myths which are so frequently found in underdeveloped communities. There are maleficent spirits which . . . create around the native a world of prohibitions, of barriers and of inhibitions far more terrifying than the world of the settler. . . . The atmosphere of myth and magic frightens me and so takes on an undoubted reality. . . . Believe me, the zombies are more terrifying than the settlers. . . . The supernatural, magical powers reveal themselves as essentially personal. . . . We no longer really need to fight against [the settlers] since what counts is the frightening enemy created by myths. We perceive that all is settled by a permanent confrontation on the phantasmic plane" (55–56).

In more social-psychological terms, Fanon suggests that this way of avoiding direct conflict with the French by living in fear of the demons is "at the same time a symptom and a cure." The person "resolves the conflict by unsatisfactory, but on the whole economical means. The organism in fact chooses the lesser evil in order to avoid catastrophe" (290). In a "regression in service of the self," the oppressed deal with situations in a way that does not threaten the social position of the dominators.

Belief in demons and demon possession in ancient Palestine had similar causes and functions in the context of Roman domination. Ironic as it may seem, belief in demons helped enable the people to persist in the Israelite faith and way of life. By blaming superhuman evil forces for their sufferings Galileans and Judeans could avoid blaming themselves as well as God. This was particularly important given their traditional covenantal way of life, in which misfortune would have been understood as due to the people's sins and God's wrath in appropriate punishment for violation of the covenantal law. The healing of the paralytic episode makes clear that this was a serious problem. There the paralysis is understood as due to the man's (or his parents') sins. Attributing illnesses to demons, on the other hand, was an appropriate ascription of responsibility to outside forces that were invading people's lives, even if it diverted attention from the "real" political-economic forces affecting them.

Precisely that diversion of attention from the real, political forces that had invaded their life, however, kept the people from taking suicidal actions, individually and collectively. The Judeans' and Galileans' frequent insurrections to reassert their independence, followed by brutal Roman retaliation, destruction of villages and slaughter of the people, indicate that this was a serious problem. Demon possession, for example, of the manically violent man among the Gerasenes, can be understood as a combination of the effect of Roman imperial violence, a displaced protest against it, and a self-protection against a suicidal counterattack against the Romans. In becoming possessed and violently crazy, the man sacrificed his sanity, but at least he was still alive. We should probably understand the Gerasene demoniac's violence, in close connection with the people's reaction in sending Jesus away, in social-psychological, even political-psychological terms, not in terms of individual psychology. The demoniac became the repository of the community's resentment of the violent effects of Roman domination. The demon's possession of the man functioned as the diversion of the whole community from blaming and striking out against the Roman order. But the combination of internalized effects of Roman violence and anti-Roman resentment embodied in the possessed man are extremely difficult to control. Far from feeling liberated by the exorcism of the demon and the revelation of Roman "Legion" as the real, political-military cause of their distress, they found Jesus' exorcisms a threat to their delicately balanced adjustment to the Roman order.

For ancient Galileans, Judeans, and other peoples, understanding their life under Roman domination as being caught up in a struggle between God and superhuman demonic forces was thus both an enabling revelation and a diversionary mystification. On the one hand, convinced that their oppression was part of a larger world-historical struggle and that God was ultimately in control, it enabled them to avoid suicidal rebellion against the Romans and to persist in their traditional way of life. On the other hand, it diverted attention from the concrete political-economic realities of Roman imperial rule and channeled resistance into a battle against the "unclean spirits" that were taken as responsible for their worst troubles—a diversionary solution that proved very "functional" for the imperial order.

The Battles against Demon Possession as Struggles against Roman Imperial Rule

Against this background it is possible to discern more clearly the importance of Jesus' exorcisms in Mark's story. For the peoples of ancient Galilee and the surrounding peoples, imperial domination was caught up in a conflict of a higher order, between superhuman spiritual forces, God versus Satan, Holy Spirit versus unclean spirits. The effects of Roman military violence and economic exploitation were often attributed to demon possession. Indeed a subject people so possessed, precisely to avoid provocative rebellion that would evoke imperial annihilation, cannot even discern the real, political forces to which they are subject until their demons are exorcized, brought under God's control. Only then can they even recognize and face that it is "Legion," Roman military violence, that holds them in subjection.

Something like this appears to be operative in the exorcisms in Mark's story, which stand out so prominently toward the beginning, but then disappear from the narrative. The sequence of exorcisms and Jesus' reply to the scribes' accusation of having Beelzebul in Mark seem to push the story *through* the climax of the struggle against the demonic forces *toward* an explicit focus on continuing political conflict with the Jerusalem and Roman rulers.

Almost from the beginning of Mark's story the struggle against the demons looms prominently. The Spirit's descent upon Jesus, and then Satan's testing in the wilderness at the beginning, frame the story of Jesus' proclamation of the kingdom and renewal of Israel within the higher spiritual struggle between God and the demonic forces. Jesus' programmatic renewal of the people begins dramatically with the concrete experiences of the people who believe in and are possessed by "unclean spirits." He casts out the demons and in exercising control over them establishes the kingdom of God. The people immediately recognize that in his command over the alien forces that plague them he exercises a power/authority (among and for them) that the scribal "authority figures" do not have.[34] Already in the first exorcism, which is Jesus' inaugural public action, the struggle against the demonic forces is also a conflict with the representatives of the Jerusalem rulers. Mark's narrator then makes clear that such exorcisms are one of the two or three key activities in which Jesus is engaged in his renewal of Israel, emphasizing how many he performs and his appointment of the twelve to expand this struggle against the demons (1:34, 39; 3:15).

Jesus' response to the accusation that he is casting out demons by the ruler of the demons provides an overview of what is happening in his exorcisms generally. Again Jesus begins from what is happening concretely among the people in his mission: In his command over and casting out of the demons, it is obvious that "the strong man's" house has been entered and his goods/vessels are being plundered. That can only mean that Satan has been bound, that his rule has been ended and the rule of God established. That is, the people's liberation from the alien possessing forces at the concrete level of interpersonal experience implies that God is defeating or has defeated Satan at the transcendent level. Again the political conflict between Jesus and the rulers is evident in the episode insofar as his explanation of what is happening is framed as a response to an accusation of being a combination traitor and witch by the scribal representatives of the Jerusalem rulers.

Mark then pushes the story toward a more explicit focus on political conflict in the episode of the Gerasene demoniac. When Jesus casts out "Legion," which is then destroyed by charging into the Sea, he brings the political conflict to the fore, at least in a symbolic way. Once Jesus has ordered the demon to come out of the man and elicits its name, it is evident that the struggle is really against Roman imperial rule—and by implication when Legion enters the swine who charge to their death in the Sea, that the struggle promises to result in the people's liberation from Legion. Mark's story includes another exorcism, partly to dramatize the intensifying debility of the twelve. Yet then the struggle against the demonic forces disappears as a theme.

Nevertheless, since Mark is a narrative, not a christological treatise, we should seek an explanation, but not in a "correction" of a "wonder-worker" christology by a "death-and-resurrection" christology. Mark is the story of Jesus' spearheading a movement of renewal among subject peoples over against their rulers. We should listen to the sequence of events or episodes in the story. If God or Jesus has already "bound" the "strong man," Satan, then the demons he rules must be in disarray. Once Jesus has forced out the identification of the demonic forces as (the surrogates of) the Roman political and military forces in the exorcism of the Gerasene demoniac, the veil of mystification has been pulled back. The casting out and naming of "Legion" is a demystification of (the belief in) demons and demon possession. It is now evident to Jesus' followers and to the hearers of Mark's story that the struggle is really against the rulers, ultimately the Romans. And the story now focuses accordingly on Jesus' confrontation of the Roman client rulers of Israel and eventually with the Romans themselves in his trial and crucifixion. This is why the dramatic battles against demons leave off just as the explicit political conflict comes to a head in Mark's story.

Significantly, even as the story moves into a sharp political confrontation, the narrator includes a few verbal echoes of the exorcism episodes in Jesus' confrontation with the rulers in Jerusalem. He "casts out" those who were buying and selling in the Temple, just as he and the disciples "cast out" the demons (11:15; cf. 1:34, 39; 3:15; etc.). He would not allow anyone to carry any "vessel" through the Temple, just as the "vessels" of the strong man were plundered (11:16; cf. 3:27). Most ominously, immediately after his prophetic demonstration against the Temple, in the framing of that episode with his cursing of the fig tree, he declares that through intense faith his followers can, in effect, cause the Temple mount to be thrown "into the sea," just as the swine possessed by "Legion" charged "into the sea" (11:23; cf. 5:13). And the immediately ensuing episode in his confrontation with the Jerusalem rulers focuses on the issue of "power/authority" from God, which by implication he exercizes and they lack. This certainly does not make the Temple demonstration into another exorcism like that of "Legion." And it certainly does not suggest that the Temple and the high-priestly aristocracy are demonic or Satanic (although, in their association with the Romans, they may be implicated as under the influence of the demonic forces).[35] But the same struggle that focused on casting out demonic forces in the first half of the story continues in Jerusalem, only now as an explicitly political struggle and focused on concrete human institutions and rulers.

Exploration of the "apocalyptic" elements and the struggle with demonic forces in Mark's story has brought us full circle to where we started in chapter 2 with the historical context that the story addresses. And it confirms what we identified as the dominant plot of the story in chapter 5. The story is directed to people subjected by imperial rule, and it is about a renewal movement among those people. That renewal also entails continuing opposition to and from the local and imperial rulers.

7

Jesus vs. the Pharisees:
Contesting the Tradition

Western Christian culture has made the Pharisees into the stereotypical hypocrites. They always receive "bad press" in biblical studies. In standard interpretations of Jesus, they are always the "bad guys" who persistently harass him
for not keeping the Law. Although it is Matthew who has Jesus scream
"hypocrites" at the Pharisees, Mark has also contributed heavily to the caricature of "the scribes and Pharisees." No characters in Mark's story have been
more distorted in standard interpretation than the (scribes and) Pharisees. That
distortion of the Pharisees, moreover, continues to limit Mark's Gospel to a
chapter in the story of "Christianity's" break with "Judaism" over the issue of
the Law.

Recent critical studies of the ancient Judean historian Josephus, rabbinic literature, and certain Dead Sea Scrolls, however, are dramatically challenging
the standard Christian picture of the Pharisees. A reexamination of the role of
the scribes and Pharisees in Mark's story therefore has special importance. It
will also provide occasion to review a number of related revisions in our historical picture of the ancient Judean and Galilean context of Jesus and his
movement, revisions that are requiring us to hear Mark' story with new ears.

Mark's Plotting of the Scribes and Pharisees

Mark's story presents Jesus' first public act, his exorcism of an "unclean
spirit,"as "teaching with authority," in contrast with the scribes. A few episodes
later the scribes turn up "sitting there" at Jesus' house in Capernaum accusing
him (in their hearts) of "blasphemy" for declaring to the paralytic, "Son, your
sins are forgiven." Jesus fires right back at them that "the son of man (the
human one, humanity) has authority on earth to forgive sins." In the next four

episodes the Pharisees exercise surveillance over Jesus' or his disciples' every move. The scribes and the Pharisees question why Jesus "eats with toll collectors and sinners," to which he retorts "I have come to call not the righteous but sinners." The Pharisees, whose disciples' practice fasting, challenge Jesus' disciples' not fasting, to which he replies that in his mission something new and special is happening. When the Pharisees accuse Jesus' disciples of unlawful practices on the sabbath, he declares that "the sabbath was made for humankind, not humankind for the sabbath." Finally, when Jesus pointedly heals a man on the sabbath directly under their disapproving surveillance, "the Pharisees went out and immediately conspired with the Herodians against [Jesus], how to destroy him." As if that were not enough, the scribes "who [come] down from Jerusalem" reappear, accusing Jesus of being possessed by Beelzebul, of casting out demons by the ruler of demons. Jesus seizes upon the accusation to pronounce that his exorcisms demonstrate rather that Satan must have been "bound," hence by implication, God's rule is now being established. Not only does Jesus carry out his mission in contrast and opposition to the scribes and Pharisees, but they actively oppose him at every turn and seek to destroy him from the time of his initial campaign in Galilee.

In the next main step of the story, the scribes and Pharisees disappear from the narrative while Jesus performs the Moses- and Elijah-like series of sea crossing, exorcism, healings, and wilderness feeding. But "the Pharisees and some of the scribes who had come from Jerusalem" reappear to challenge Jesus because his disciples do not observe "the traditions of the elders." Jesus seemingly escalates the conflict by accusing them of violating the basic covenantal commandment of God by encouraging people to "devote" as an "offering to God" resources that are needed to support elderly parents (7:1–13). Then, like the first step of the story, this section of the story closes with the Pharisees' request for and with Jesus' refusal to provide "a sign" and his warning about "the yeast of the Pharisees" (complicated now by Jesus' frustration at the disciples' stubborn misunderstanding of Jesus' wilderness feedings and other actions, 8:11–15).

In the middle section of the story, "some Pharisees" appear again to "test" Jesus with the question "whether it is lawful for a man to divorce his wife." Jesus' response is the affirmation of marriage, in the first episode of his reconstitution of Israelite covenantal relations (10:2–9, 10–12). After Jesus goes up to Jerusalem, the "chief priests, scribes, and elders" move to the center of the stage. In the midst of Jesus' confrontation with the rulers in the Temple courtyard, however, they send some Pharisees along with some Herodians to entrap him with the question about whether it is lawful to pay tribute to Caesar (12:13–17). Skillfully eluding the trap by avoiding a direct answer, he declares that one should give to God the things that are God's (i.e., everything) and to

Caesar the things that are Caesar's (i.e., nothing). At the end of the confrontation in the Temple, Jesus not only refutes the scribes teaching about the messiah; he both warns that they devour widows' houses and then illustrates how it happens in the poor widow's giving all she had (12:35–44).

Mark's story makes clear at several points that the scribes and Pharisees are representatives of the Jerusalem high-priestly rulers. Not only do "the scribes" come (down) from Jerusalem (3:22; 7:1) but they are closely linked with the high priests in the Jerusalem confrontation. The Pharisees are also directly linked with and subordinated to the chief-priestly rulers. Their "accusation" and "plot" against Jesus early in the story is couched in the same terms as the chief priests' "plot" and "accusation" against Jesus after arresting and trying him in Jerusalem (3:6; 15:1, 3–4). Mark states explicitly that the rulers "sent" the Pharisees along with the Herodians to entrap him (12:13). By implication, in their surveillance of Jesus in Galilee as well, the Pharisees operate all along as representatives of the Jerusalem rulers.

A Quest for the Historical Pharisees

Even to begin to listen with "ears to hear" how the Pharisees function in Mark's story is unusually difficult because our preconceptions about them are so tied up with the standard older Christian picture of "Judaism" that has determined much New Testament interpretation. As noted at the outset in chapter 1, Mark's Gospel was read as both a reflection of and documentation of the separation of "Christianity" (a supposedly more spiritual universal religion consisting increasingly of Gentiles) from "Judaism" (which was ostensibly parochial and particularistic). "Judaism" was understood as a unitary religion practiced by all Palestinian "Jews" generally, whether in Jerusalem, Judea, or Galilee. Central to Judaism was the Law or Torah, the authoritative word of God revealed to Moses on Mount Sinai, which all Jews looked to as God's law code which must be observed in order to achieve righteousness and salvation. The authoritative interpreters of the Torah were the Pharisees, the leaders of Judaism who determined what was normative Judaism. Besides the Temple in Jerusalem, where the priests offered sacrifices, "Judaism" had synagogues in the cities and towns in which the Law was read and interpreted in services on the Sabbath and in which the Pharisees were the authorities and leaders.

Not only is this whole picture of Judaism a modern construction, but none of the principal components of the picture is warranted by historical evidence, as is now apparent from recent studies of ancient texts and archaeological sites. As noted above, there was no definable entity that could be called "Christianity" as distinct from "Judaism" until many decades after the ministry of Jesus.

Not only did diverse movements or communities of Jesus-believers emerge in the decades after his ministry, but they all considered themselves renewals or expansions of the people of Israel. Paul still understood his "assemblies" comprised largely of Gentiles as branches "grafted into" the main trunk of the olive tree of Israel (Rom. 11:17). Even the Gospel of Matthew, believed to have been composed several decades after Mark's Gospel, is increasingly recognized as representative of a community that understands itself as a movement within the wider community or communities of Israel. Indeed, Matthew's sharp polemic against the scribes and Pharisees (Matt. 23) is taken as evidence of a struggle for authority among groups, both of which claim to represent the proper understanding of the Mosaic covenantal tradition.[1]

As implied in the previous paragraph, there was also no unitary "Judaism." The very concept of "Judaism" in late Second Temple times is an abstraction from—and an anachronism projected onto—a complex society in Palestine under Roman rule in the first century B.C.E. and the first century C.E. The diversity among Jewish groups in late Second Temple (early Roman) times has long been recognized at least with regard to the differences between the Pharisees, the Sadducees, and the Essenes. The discovery of the Dead Sea Scrolls provided dramatic textual evidence for the sharp disagreements between the Pharisees and the priestly-scribal community at Qumran, now often identified with the Essenes.

To accommodate the diversity of these groups, some interpreters now refer to "Judaisms" or "sectarian Judaism." Both these alternatives to monolithic unitary "Judaism," however, still tend to reduce these historical groups and their concerns to religion. And the term "sectarian" imposes a sociological concept designed to understand the relationship between modern European dissident or "breakaway" churches and the mainline established church (Catholic, Anglican, Lutheran, depending on the country). Moreover, in focusing on the Sadducees, Pharisees, and Essenes, and whatever texts they left to posterity, we are considering only the priestly and scribal elite, a tiny fraction of the society, and are left with no sense of the concerns of the other 90–95 percent, the villagers and the ordinary people of Jerusalem.

Insofar as the religious dimension of life in traditional societies was inseparable from the political-economic aspects of life—and therefore cannot be understood apart from them—it is necessary to consider the religious features of institutions, groups, and movements as they were embedded with the political-economic structure and dynamics of life in the overall society. Indeed, given the diversity among the various geographical areas of Palestine and the diversity of groups, communities, and movements in those areas, even the concept "society" seems like an abstraction from the shifting social configurations and Roman-dictated political arrangements. To understand the (scribes and)

Pharisees and their relationship with the Jesus movement behind the Gospel of Mark, we must come to grips with the several interrelated factors.

1. Our sources of information on the Pharisees are extremely limited and have been used for different modern historical reconstructions. It can no longer be assumed that the rabbis simply continued Pharisaic teachings and that therefore the rabbinic literature can be read back into the Pharisees contemporary with Jesus and Mark. The Judean historian Josephus presents the Pharisees as a political party that was very active at the center of Judean political affairs under the Hasmonean kings–high priests but less prominent under Herod the Great and the Roman governors. Early rabbinic literature contains occasional references to traditions of opinions or rulings of various Pharisees and of debates between the Hillelite and the Shammaite factions, most of which refer to issues of eating and tithing. The Synoptic Gospels are the only sources that portray the Pharisees as active in Galilee, keeping Jesus and his followers under surveillance and (in Luke's Gospel) occasionally eating with Jesus. In comparison with the other sources of information, the Synoptic Gospels make the Pharisees appear much more important and influential than they would have been historically during the time of Jesus. The Dead Sea Scrolls, the fourth source of references to the Pharisees, criticize them as "smooth interpreters" of the traditional laws. That is, their rulings were lax and liberal in comparison with the rigorous interpretation of the Qumran community itself—quite a different picture from the traditional Christian stereotype of strict legalists.

2. Although the Pharisees can no longer be understood as the representatives of a "normative Judaism," and were nowhere near as important and influential as previously imagined, they did play an important role in the Jerusalem temple-state just prior to and during early Roman rule. A few decades after the Maccabean Revolt they appear as experts in the laws who propound rulings for the society beyond those in the (written) Law of Moses, rulings known as "the traditions of the elders." In a dispute with the Pharisees the Hasmonean high priest John Hyrcanus rescinded their rulings as part of official state law (*Ant.* 13.296–97). They then apparently provided leadership for a virtual civil war against the next high priest, Alexander Jannai (13.372–83). His wife and successor as head of state, Alexandra Salome, however, placed the Pharisees in charge of the government (13.400–410). The Pharisees then suffered a serious diminution of power and influence when Herod superimposed his own regime above that of the temple-state.

In reaction to the previous overestimation of their central importance for "Judaism," a close critical analysis of rabbinic traditions about the Pharisees has been used as the basis for viewing them as little more than a society of table fellowship after they had ostensibly withdrawn from politics under Herod.[2] Yet as the Judean historian Josephus attests, they remained active at court, while also refusing to sign a loyalty oath to Herod and agitating court intrigue against Herod. They apparently remained centrally active in the political affairs of the temple-state under the Roman governors as well, since they figured prominently in the delegation sent by the high-priestly government to take charge of Galilee after the outbreak of the great revolt in 66 C.E. Throughout his accounts, Josephus presents the Pharisees as "the most accurate interpreters of the laws."[3] It seems clear, then, that the Pharisees must have been an important faction among the priestly-scribal circles in Jerusalem, politically active particularly prior to the time of Herod. While less powerful thereafter, they remained active participants in and representatives of the high priestly government of the temple-state.

3. The most serious problem for considering the Pharisees' relation to Jesus is locating them in Galilee. Mark's story, especially toward the beginning, presents them as in Galilee actively challenging the actions of Jesus and his disciples. If they were participants in and representatives of the Jerusalem temple-state, however, that should seem problematic. Throughout the lifetime of Jesus, Galilee was under the political-economic jurisdiction of Herod Antipas, not under the Jerusalem temple-state. We might surmise that the Pharisees might have been present in Galilee representing the interests of the temple-state. If so, their activities must have been narrowly confined; for it is difficult imagining that Antipas would have been happy about their urging Galileans to continue paying tithes to the priests and sending offerings to the Temple or dedicating resources to the Temple (see, e.g., the discussion of *Korban* below), which would have siphoned off the very produce of the peasants upon which his own taxes depended.

Nor can we imagine that the Pharisees, having been relatively inactive in Galilee during the first half of the first century C.E. suddenly established their presence in the decades immediately prior to the great revolt, the very time that Mark's story was taking shape. Such a hypothesis is based on the unwarranted historical assumptions that immediately after the Roman destruction of Jerusalem and the Temple, the Romans recognized the surviving Pharisees, supposedly the proto-rabbis, as the authorities in charge of the Jewish communities in Palestine.[4] That older assumption is now challenged by many Jewish historians, who point out that the early rabbis did not establish a presence in Galilee until after the Roman devastation of Judea in suppressing the Bar Kokhba Revolt of 132–35 C.E. Thus there is no basis for imagining that the Pharisees had already expanded their activities from Judea to Galilee in the middle of the first century. The temple-state still held no political jurisdiction over Galilee.

Pharisaic presence and influence in Galilee becomes even more problematic when we consider that, after Galilee had been independent of Jerusalem rule for eight hundred years, it finally came under the Jerusalem temple-state only in 104 B.C.E. and remained so for only a century. That was a time of extreme turbulence in Jerusalem itself, moreover, when the Pharisees were at first engaged in civil war against the high priest and then in effect demoted under Herod's regime. Yet this is the time during which the Pharisees would presumably have become active in Galilee, as they were already in Judea, as representatives of the temple-state. As experts in the law, they would presumably have been the officials who pressed Jerusalem's interests in Galilee after the Hasmoneans took over Galilee and forced the inhabitants to live "according to the laws of the Judeans" (Josephus's phrase).[5] That means, of course, that at the time of Jesus' mission and Mark's Gospel, the Pharisees would have been a memory more than a current presence in Galilee.

4. Not only were the Pharisees not the leaders or authorities in synagogues, they were not even members.[6] As mentioned in several connections previously, "synagogues" in Mark refer not to religious buildings but to village assemblies. Archaeologists date the public buildings they have found in Galilean villages much later than the time of Jesus and Mark. And the term *synagōgē* in Greek refers not to a building, but to an assembly anyhow. It has been argued that the disputes between Jesus and the Pharisees in Mark's story take place in and around the synagogues.[7] But that is a misreading of Mark. In one episode only do the Pharisees appear watching Jesus when he takes action in a synagogue (3:1–6). Mark's Jesus later warns that the scribes like "to have the best seats in assemblies and places of honor at banquets." Jewish historians now insist, however, that the Pharisees and the rabbis were not members, let alone leaders of and authorities in the village assemblies. Not until much later, even the seventh century, did the rabbis come to have authority in Jewish synagogues.[8] At the time of Mark and in Mark's story, therefore, the Pharisees have little or nothing to do with the village synagogues in Galilee.

In sum, the Pharisees appear to have comprised a political faction among the broader range of scribes functioning in connection with the Jerusalem temple-state. The fragments of information available indicate that, while their influence was diminished under Herod's regime, they remained active in connection with the Jerusalem Temple government and that they served as representatives of the high-priestly rulers in dealing with villages and outlying districts such as Galilee. They were known especially as "accurate interpreters" of the Law and as having promulgated additional rulings, "the traditions of the elders," that held the authority of state law at points under the Hasmoneans. The more rigorous scribal-priestly community at Qumran, however, considered them "smooth interpreters." Their legal rulings and opinions in later rabbinic literature are concentrated on issues such as eating and tithing of agricultural produce. There is no information outside of the Synoptic Gospels, however, that they were active in Galilee during the mission of Jesus and the development of Jesus movements in Galilee. So we must exercise caution in attempting to understand the function of the many episodes in Mark's story of conflict between Jesus and the scribes and Pharisees.

Jerusalem-Based Torah
vs. Popular Israelite Tradition

Integrally related to the Pharisees in Mark's story is the question of the "scripture," particularly the Torah or Law. It is often simply taken for granted that all "Jews" or "Judaism" shared a common Torah or Law, which was widely known and of which the Pharisees were the authoritative interpreters. It is increasingly evident from recent studies that we must come to grips with several interrelated historical variations and distinctions in the cultivation of Israelite tradition.

1. As discussed in chapter 3 in connection with the dominant oral communication environment in ancient Palestine, however, *no standardized text of the Torah* had yet become authoritative. In fact, even the dominant high-priestly families and the different factions and groups in priestly-scribal circles who cultivated Israelite traditions had different versions and interpretation of those traditions, only some of which were written on scrolls. Indeed, the Torah (the five books of Moses known in the Hebrew Bible and the Christian Old Testament), may not have been the only or even the central authority for some groups and areas. The Temple presumably dominated life in Jerusalem and exerted great influence on Judean villagers as well. The priests had their own traditions (Deut. 33:8–11), probably including their own version of Torah orally transmitted that varied from what is now known as the Torah. The Dead Sea Scrolls indicate the variety of legal positions even among the high-priestly families themselves and their client scribal circles. Moreover, the scriptural Torah did not become central and determinative in rabbinic circles. The Mishnah, completed around 200 C.E., which actually cites the biblical Torah relatively infrequently, is not concerned mainly with interpretation of the Law. Since there was no standardized authoritative Law or Torah accepted in all social strata, all areas, and among all scribal circles and priestly groups, therefore, the Pharisees could not have been accepted as the authoritative interpreters of the Law accepted by the whole society.[9]

Besides having variant scriptural and oral legal traditions, moreover, Jewish scribal groups such as the Pharisees and Essenes (Qumran community) disagreed and argued over many points of interpretation of Judean-Israelite tradition, such as tithing obligations, oaths and vows, the conditions for divorce, keeping of the Sabbath, dietary laws, and priestly purity codes—some of the very topics at issue in Mark's story.[10] It is hardly possible, therefore, to continue discussing the disputes between Jesus and the Pharisees in Mark in terms of a supposed standard Jewish interpretation of the Law as determined by the Pharisees. For the Pharisees themselves were engaged in a struggle with other scribal and priestly groups over authoritative interpretation of legal traditions.

2. We must take into account *when and how the Torah was introduced into Galilee.* The role of the Torah in Galilee before and during the time of Jesus involves extremely difficult questions of *regional historical differences* and influences between Jerusalem and Galilee. After eight centuries of separation, Galilee again came under Jerusalem rule only about a hundred years prior to Jesus' birth (as noted in chapter 2). During the previous centuries, Galilee and Judea had been under different imperial administrative arrangements or districts. What we know as Hebrew biblical literature, including the Torah, was being developed and cultivated during that time in Jerusalem. Since the discovery of the Dead Sea Scrolls, we now even have manuscripts of the evolving text of the Hebrew scriptures. We may assume that central to those scriptures was "the book of the covenant of the Most High God, the Law that Moses commanded us," referred to by the late-third-century B.C.E. scribe Jesus ben Sira (Sir. 24:23). Presumably Josephus is referring to this same Law when he mentions the written "laws of Moses" that the Pharisees supplemented with the rulings from their "tradition of the ancestors," both of which were functioning as officially authorized temple-state law (*Ant.* 13.296–97).

When the Hasmonean regime took over Galilee, they allowed the inhabitants to remain in the area on the condition that they live "according to the laws of the Judeans" (*Ant.* 13.318). Assuming that, whatever else they may have included, "the laws of the Judeans" included "the laws of Moses" (the Torah), this means that the Torah was introduced to Galilee only about a hundred years before Jesus' birth, clearly from the top down. It is difficult, however, to discern whether Josephus's account implies simply that the Galileans were henceforth to live under the polity of the Judeans, i.e., under the Jerusalem temple-state (which seems more likely), or whether the temple-state was pressing the Galileans to conform their village community life to "the laws of the Judeans" (which would have required an ambitious major program of re-socialization). In either case, the Pharisees as the legal-policy experts in the Jerusalem high-priestly government would have been the obvious functionaries to have been mediating "the laws of the Judeans" to the Galileans.

3. The *distinction* that anthropologists and others make *between the "great tradition" and the "little tradition"* in agrarian societies may help us understand the relation that would have developed between "the laws of the Judeans" and

the Galilean villagers during the century of Jerusalem rule just prior to the lifetime of Jesus. This distinction is rooted in the broader structural division
between rulers and their representatives who live in cities and the peasants
who live in semi-autonomous village communities in which life is governed
largely by local custom.[11] The little tradition is "the distinctive patterns of
belief and behavior which are valued by the peasantry." The great tradition is
the corresponding patterns among the ruling circles, often partially in written
documents. Neither the great tradition nor the little tradition was unitary. We
noted just above that there was variation of both content (including textual
transmission) and interpretation in the Torah or Law among Jerusalem high-
priestly and scribal circles. The little tradition is even more likely to vary considerably, given the relative isolation of its carriers from one another in various
village communities. Nevertheless, given the common circumstances of peasant cultivators subject to the political-economic demands of the state,
centripetal tendencies partly compensate for the fragmentation into separate
villages.[12]

The great and little traditions are usually parallel, interrelated, and interactive in many ways. The great tradition may derive at some point from or
adapt or transform the previous popular tradition. For example, Hebrew biblical literature produced by the scribal-priestly elite took over the traditions of
early Israel's liberation from bondage in Egypt and victories over the kings of
Canaan, but framed them in a larger story that led to the establishment of a
monarchy and temple in Jerusalem. The deuteronomistic history of the kings
based in Jerusalem even adapted stories of Elijah's leadership of popular resistance to the oppressive king Ahab, a case of the official Jerusalem history using
for its own purposes what originated as popular northern Israelite stories. In
cases such as the deuteronomic "reform" carried out under king Josiah in the
late seventh century B.C.E. and the "holiness code" in the book of Leviticus,
Mosaic covenantal law that had been cultivated among Israelite villagers for
centuries was adapted into monarchic or temple-state law. Isaiah's or Jeremiah's prophetic oracles, originating in Jerusalem and preserved in Jerusalem
circles or on written scrolls, on the other hand, would have become known
among Galilean villagers only through direct or indirect contacts with representatives of the Jerusalem-based great tradition. In all these cases the result
was parallel traditions existing respectively in Jerusalem ruling circles, including in written form on scrolls kept in the Temple, and in village community
life, cultivated orally from generation to generation.

For all their parallels and interaction, however, the great and little traditions are not simply variations on the same cultural tradition. Rather "each
represents a *distinct* pattern of belief and practice." In the absence of integrat-
ing factors such as mass media in modern industrial societies, the popular tra-

ditions(s) of an agrarian society such as Galilee at the time of Jesus would have differed considerably from the Jerusalem great tradition.[13] The cultural distance that separated the two can be discerned, for example, in matters such as residence, income, consumption, language, religious practice, education, juridical status, and ethnicity.[14] At the time of Herod, the high-priestly and Herodian elite were building increasingly luxurious mansions in Jerusalem, financed presumably by the revenues they derived from the peasantry, while the peasants themselves fell increasingly into debt under multiple layers of taxes, tithes, and interest payments. A social-religious gulf, moreover, separated the peasantry from the concentric circles of priestly aristocracy and high ranking scribes and Pharisees in Jerusalem. Galileans suffered the further social stigma of being viewed as provincial, as detected in their speech and their laxity with regard to the Torah. This is "audible" in Mark's episode of Peter's denial, where the High Priest's servant girl recognizes from his speech that he is a Galilean (Mark 14:66–70). A much later rabbinic legend has Yohanan ben Zakkai, who supposedly spent some of his early years in Galilee, lamenting, "O Galilee, Galilee, You hate the Torah!" (y. Šabb. 16:8). Differences of language and education further reinforced the gulf between Jerusalem elite and Galilean villagers. The former apparently still used "biblical" Hebrew in cultivating their great tradition, while ordinary Galileans and Judeans presumably spoke some variant (local dialect) of Aramaic. Whereas scribal circles operated formal instruction in scriptural and other traditions, popular traditions would have been cultivated and transmitted in the course of local communication and practice. Such differences point to a considerable gulf between the great tradition based in Jerusalem, such as that cultivated and interpreted by scribes and Pharisees, and the popular tradition(s) cultivated in Galilean villages.

The Galilean regional differences in historical experience would have further exacerbated the difference between the great and little Israelite traditions. "The closeness of an elite's culture to that of its peasantry depends, in large part, on how its great tradition developed" and its historical relation to the peasantry and its tradition.[15] As noted just above, the great tradition in Jerusalem developed during the many centuries that Galilee was under separate imperial arrangements. Then suddenly it was introduced by the Jerusalem temple-state around 100 B.C.E. Meanwhile, the Galilean villagers, assuming that the Assyrians left most of the northern Israelite peasants on the land when they deported the ruling elite from the city of Samaria in the late eighth century B.C.E., would have continued to cultivate their indigenous Israelite covenantal traditions, stories about the great prophets of the north such as Elijah, and their customary observances such as Sabbath and Passover.[16]

Rabbinic literature actually provides revealing windows onto significant examples of the variations in local customs. Modern scholars who deal with rabbinic literature and related materials have discussed these variations in terms of whether Galileans had a distinctive "halakhah," i.e., a tradition of legal interpretation different from the normative Judean one presumably cultivated by the Pharisees.[17] Many of these regional variations are in local customs of village-level practice, not in scribal-scholarly legal interpretation. Besides the many variations in weights, measures, and agricultural practices dependent on different climatic conditions, the rabbis noted variations in marriage customs, vows, tithes, and festivals. Some of these are very revealing about Galileans' relation to the Temple. For example, certain vows taken in comparison with tithes or offerings due to the priesthood or Temple that were not allowed in Judea are allowed in Galilee because "the people of Galilee are not familiar with the contribution to the sanctuary . . . [and] consecration offerings which are set apart for the priests" (*m. Ned.* 2:4). That, in contrast to the Judeans, the Galileans could not be trusted to observe purity rules in removing the priests' share and other dues from their crops fairly clearly suggests that tithing was not a standard customary part of Galilean life as it was in Judea, which had been subject to the temple-state for centuries.[18] The Galileans also had customary celebrations of Passover and the Day of Atonement different from (and stricter than) those of the Judeans.

In sum, no standardized Jewish Torah or Law would have been known in Galilean villages at the time of Jesus' mission and the development of early Jesus movements. Community affairs in the semi-autonomous village communities would have been guided by local customs and culture. Those local customs, insofar as we can reason through the fragmentary evidence, would presumably have included age-old Israelite traditions. Particularly important would likely have been the Mosaic covenantal tradition, including observance of the Sabbath, the rest of the covenantal commandments, and law codes that had grown up around the covenantal commandments. The Galilean popular Israelite tradition would likely have also included stories of premonarchic Israel such as the exodus, stories of northern Israelite heroes and heroines such as Deborah (Judges 5), and, during the monarchic period, stories of rebellion against Jerusalem rule and of resistance to oppressive rulers, such as those of Elijah and Elisha. Of course, since (illiterate) peasants leave no literary records, we have no direct access to Israelite popular tradition in Galilee— only indirect access through Israelite traditions taken up into the nascent Hebrew Bible of the great tradition in Jerusalem. The Torah of the Jerusalem great tradition was introduced into Galilee only about a hundred years before Jesus, probably primarily as the general guidelines for the relations of Galilean villagers to the Jerusalem temple-state, i.e., matters such as tithes and offerings. It seems unlikely that the temple-state, given its own civil wars at the time, would have been able to mount a major program of imposing "the laws of the Judeans" onto internal local community relations. Whatever limited role "the laws of the Judeans" played for a hundred years in Galilee, the Pharisees and other scribes are the obvious functionaries who would have been responsible for mediating the relations between the villagers and the temple-state by way of application and interpretation of the Law.

Jesus Renewing Popular Israelite Tradition

We may now return to the conflicts between Jesus and the Pharisees in Mark's story with new perspective from which to understand what is at issue and some distinctions more appropriate to the historical situation. Mark's story, focused on events of Jesus' heading a movement of Israel's renewal in Galilean villages, must be understood squarely in the interaction between Galilean popular Israelite tradition and the great tradition of Jerusalem that had been imposed roughly a century and a half before. It seems likely that coming again under Jerusalem rule after centuries of separation would have revived among Galileans a sense of their Israelite heritage. Given the content of the popular tradition, however, it would also have revived a sense of common popular Israelite heritage shared with Judeans over against the Jerusalem rulers, their scribal and Pharisaic representatives, and particular features of Jerusalem tradition. Cross-cultural comparisons indicate that "the material and symbolic hegemony normally exercised by ruling institutions does not preclude, but rather engenders, a set of contrary values which represent in their entirety a kind of 'shadow society.'"[19] In Galilean villages, as among the peasantry in other agrarian societies, the little tradition would have been "not simply a crude version of" the great tradition of Jerusalem. It would also have been, in effect, a symbolic criticism of elite values and beliefs . . . for the most part muted within a context of subordination. . . . Under certain circumstances, however, . . . forms of symbolic conflict may become manifest and amount to a political or religious mobilization of the little tradition."[20]

We catch brief glimpses of the mobilization of the Israelite little tradition in the popular messianic and prophetic movements that erupted in Judea and Galilee around the time Jesus was born and in the decades following Jesus' mission. In the emergence of Jesus movements, particularly in the movement that generated Mark's story, we can see more fully yet another mobilization of the Israelite popular tradition. More particularly, in the conflicts between Jesus and the scribes and Pharisees included in Mark's story, we can hear ways in which a popular movement defended its own little tradition against the parallel great tradition that it was determined to resist. By listening closely to several of the particular conflicts Jesus has with the Pharisees and scribes in Mark's story it will become evident that they were not simply about seemingly minor matters of keeping purity laws or a strict code of sabbath observance, but about fundamental political-economic matters such as adequate food, the disintegration of marriage and the family, and the siphoning off of economic resources needed locally to support the Temple and the empire.

The episodes of conflict between Jesus and the Pharisees take a distinctive form of challenge or question by the Pharisees (and/or scribes) and response by Jesus.[21] In the first several episodes, the scribes/Pharisees challenge such actions as Jesus' healings and the disciples' eating or not eating. In later episodes they raise questions regarding the lawfulness of divorce and the tribute to Rome, central issues of common concern in Judean and Galilean society. Jesus responds with a clever saying that decides the issue and "puts down" the Pharisees/scribes and the basis of their challenge. In most of these episodes, Jesus' decisive saying appeals either to popular Israelite tradition or to common Israelite tradition over against the Pharisees' basis in their own great tradition. Mark's story presents the Pharisees and scribes as physically present to challenge Jesus, mainly in Galilee. It seems likely at least that they had been active in Galilee during the century of Jerusalem rule there (104–4 B.C.E.). But whether or not they were still active in Galilee in the middle of the first century C.E., when Jerusalem no longer held political jurisdiction over Galilee, does not matter for the function of these episodes. It suffices that historically the scribes and Pharisees were known to the Galileans, among whom the Jesus movement developed, as the advocates of the great tradition that was being pressed upon them in previous generations. For these episodes function in advancing the overall agenda and plot of Mark's story, that is, that Jesus is carrying out a renewal of Israel in Galilean villages and beyond over against the Jerusalem rulers of Israel.

Plucking Grain on the Sabbath (Mark 2:23–28)

Contrary to much Christian interpretation, this episode does not address the issue of whether Gentile Christians should observe the "Jewish Sabbath." Jesus' declaration toward the end that "the sabbath was made for humankind, and not humankind for the sabbath" takes a strong, entirely positive view of observing the sabbath—presumably as commanded in the Mosaic covenant (Exod. 20:8–11; Deut. 5:12–15). At issue is rather what is lawful to do on the sabbath, as indicated by the parallelism between the Pharisees' accusation "what is not lawful on the sabbath" and the first step in Jesus' retort about David's having eaten the bread of the Presence "which is not lawful for any but the priests."[22]

To obtain a better feeling for the issue, it would be helpful to review some of the Israelite customary "common law," as well as related scribal discussion regarding plucking and harvesting of grain and the kind of work prohibited on the sabbath. Deuteronomy 23:24–25 gives us a window onto what was probably standard Israelite "common law" that one could snack on one's neighbor's grapes or grain when walking through the fields, but not harvest and carry away grapes or grain, which would presumably have come under the decalogue principle of "you shall not steal." The standard rules on "gleaning rights" for the poor may also be relevant. "When reaping the harvest of your land, you shall not reap to the very edges of your field, . . . you shall leave them for the poor and the alien" (Lev. 19:9). A fragmentary text in the Dead Sea Scrolls contains a Judean scribal ruling on the same matters contemporary with Jesus and Mark's Gospel: "Any destitute [Israelite] who goes into a threshing floor may eat there and gather for himself and for [his] hou[sehold. But should he walk among grain standing in] the field, he may eat but may not bring it to his house to store it" (4Q159; later rabbinic rulings in *m. Pe'ah* 1:3; *t. Pe'ah* 1.6). The disciples, particularly insofar as they may have been hungry, would have been following customary practice of plucking (but not harvesting) standing grain and if they were poor would have been exercising gleaning rights. And those customary practices and rights were confirmed by scribal rulings.

The Pharisees' accusation, however, is that such plucking was not lawful *on the sabbath*. And that is what Jesus responds to in his retort. While we lack information on popular customs on this matter, we do have texts of elite scribal discussion of work prohibited on the sabbath. In a whole section on observance of the sabbath following the creation story, in which the sabbath was grounded, the second-century B.C.E. book of *Jubilees* (from Jerusalem?) mentions twenty-two kinds of labor proscribed on the sabbath (*Jub.* 2:17–33). In rabbinic discussion over three centuries later, thirty-nine kinds of labor are prohibited (*m. Šabb.* 7:2, where the rabbis see no need to cite a Torah text such as Exod. 34:21). But plucking grain or fruit is not mentioned along with sowing, ploughing, reaping, binding sheaves, threshing, winnowing, selecting (fit from unfit crops), grinding, sifting, kneading, and baking among the items related to raising and preparation of food. (The Hellenistic urban Jewish philosopher Philo does mention plucking any kind of fruit, *Mos.* 2.22.) Would the distinction in Deuteronomy 23:25 between plucking a few ears by hand and cutting the grain with a sickle suggest that in contrast to reaping, plucking grain would not have been viewed as work prohibited on the sabbath? Scribal rulings certainly did prohibit preparation of food of any sort on the sabbath; all such preparation was to be done the previous day (*Jub.* 2:29–30 is a text well prior to Jesus' time). So plucking grain may well have been excluded by implication in some scribal discussion. Although walking a thousand yards or so was generally allowed, the relatively rigorous "Damascus Rule" among the Dead Sea Scrolls does have an interesting ruling among the sabbath laws: "No man shall walk in the field to do business on the sabbath" (CD 10:19–20)—yet another scribal ruling suggesting restrictive application of the commandment to rest on the sabbath. Yet these scribal discussions from different groups and different times provide no clear indication that the Pharisees, much less the more rigorous Qumran community, would have included plucking grain for a passing snack as work prohibited on the sabbath. It may well be that this episode in Mark presents a caricature of the Pharisees prohibiting even passing snacks on the sabbath as a foil for Jesus' statement on sabbath observance.[23]

In the first step of his retort Jesus pointedly opposes the Pharisees as advocates of a super-sacred aura around the sabbath, which he then mocks. His mockery begins immediately in his challenge to them as the presumably knowledgeable authorities on the scriptures, the sacred written texts of the Jerusalem great tradition: "Have you never read . . ." Mark's Jesus and Mark's listeners, who were almost certainly illiterate and not wealthy enough to possess written scrolls, had themselves never read. But they knew of the Pharisees and other scribes as ostensibly authoritative interpreters who appealed to sacred texts as the basis of their own authority. What better strategy than to throw back in their face one of the scriptural stories that would surely carry the day on the issue at hand? (especially insofar as the audience listening was a community of Jesus' followers, not the Pharisees).[24]

We who possess not only hindsight but critical texts of those scriptures, however, recognize that Mark's Jesus is drawing on a distinctive version of the story about David, i.e., not the version we know and, probably, also not the one the scripturally informed Pharisees would have known. The biblical text of 1 Samuel, in which this story occurs (1 Sam. 21:1–6), was notoriously "unstable" in antiquity. For example, the received Hebrew text and the standard Greek translation (the "Septuagint") exhibit many variations from one another.[25] As measured by the standard biblical texts even in their variations, however, Jesus' version of the story is peculiar. Most strikingly, Mark's Jesus mentions not Ahimelech as the priest at Nob when David was a fugitive outlaw, but his son Abiathar, who was one of the head priests after David had established a monarchy in Jerusalem. (Cf. 1 Sam. 21:1–2; 2 Sam. 15:35; 20:25. 1 Sam. 23:6–11 may help explain the confusion of the father and the son.) Mark's Jesus adds several details that do not appear in the biblical story (as we know it from texts of 1 Sam. 21:1–6): David has companions with him; they have need and are hungry, David enters the house of God rather than simply asking for bread, and David actually eats the bread. Even if we allow for variant versions of written texts at the time of Mark, Jesus is not here quoting from scripture. Given the predominantly oral communications context of Mark as well as Jesus, Mark's Jesus in this episode must be reciting what he needed of this story about David from the popular Israelite tradition (i.e., the popular oral tradition that Jesus, the performer of the story, and the audience would all have been rooted in).

Jesus uses his version of story from Israelite tradition with great skill in his rejoinder to the Pharisees' accusation that his disciples were violating the sacred sabbath. He assumes and implies fairly clearly that "the house of God" was the Temple in Jerusalem, which is further confirmed by the identification of Abiathar as "high priest." Appealing to David's behavior as a parallel that justifies that of his disciples,[26] he boldly presents David as boldly entering "the house of God" (= the Temple) and helping himself to "the bread of the Presence." That would have been an egregious violation of the purity regulations that surrounded access to the sanctuary within the Temple and of laws protecting the holiness of the bread of the Presence. According to the latter, the twelve loaves of the bread of the Presence, freshly placed upon the altar every sabbath, were reserved for the high priests: "They shall be for Aaron and his descendants, who shall eat them in a holy place, for they are most holy portions for him from the offerings by fire to the LORD, a perpetual due" (Lev. 24:9). Jesus' version of the story also emphasizes that David and his companions "were hungry and in need of food." That is what motivates them to violate so egregiously the sacred precincts and to eat the bread of the Presence which, he states boldly ("in their face," as it were), "is not lawful for any but the priests to eat."

Jesus thus throws directly into the face of the Pharisees this incident from the scriptures. We can imagine the delight of the popular audience that would have been familiar with this and other stories of the brash young David as an outlaw leader on the run from the king (stories accessible to us in 1 Samuel 19–26). He appeals to David's scandalous behavior that violated the most sacred space and the most sacred bread to satisfy his and his companion's hunger as a precedent that justified his disciples' violation of the Pharisees' overly restrictive regulations for their supersacred sabbath.[27] We should not imagine, however, that Mark's Jesus is giving a fair picture of the Pharisees, let alone of the standard practice of "Judaism" at the time.

In the second step of his response to the Pharisees' accusation, Jesus builds on the common Israelite tradition not only that the sabbath was grounded in the creation but that the sabbath was instituted for the sake of humankind as well. Indeed, the very formulation of his declaration, that "the sabbath was created for humankind, not humankind for the sabbath," built on the sequence of the creation of humankind prior to the institution of the sabbath (Gen.

1:26–31; 2:1–3). That humans were given dominion over the rest of creation (Gen. 1:28–29; Ps. 8:6–9) carried over to the idea that the sabbath also was made for humans. Jesus' saying here about the sabbath closely parallels what was probably a common understanding that "humankind was not created for the world, but the world for humankind" (*2 Bar.* 14:18). It should not be surprising therefore to find in later rabbinic literature a saying strikingly similar to Jesus' declaration about the sabbath: "the sabbath is delivered unto you, and you are not delivered to the sabbath" (*Mekilta* 109b on Exod. 31:14).

The parallel second saying, "so the human one is lord also of the sabbath," draws the conclusion implicit in the first. Because of its parallelism with "humankind" in the first saying, the phrase "son of man" here appears to refer to "the human one," as in Mark 2:10. Because of the implication in the whole episode that Mark's Jesus is restoring the priority of humankind over the sabbath intended by God, "the human one" might also have the same connotations as it has in the apocalyptic vision of Daniel 7:14, i.e., the restoration of sovereignty to the people. In any case, Jesus' sayings about the sabbath are not "Christian" declarations over against the sabbath of "Judaism" or christological declarations (although that is the direction in which Matthew takes Mark 2:28).[28] They are rather renewals of common Israelite tradition.[29]

In the context of the episode as a whole, Jesus is saying, over against the Pharisees as representatives of the great tradition's emphasis on sacrality of the sabbath, that people can violate restrictive rules for the sake of human needs such as hunger. Subsistence needs trump the elite's concerns for holiness. As the people's prophet speaking from the popular tradition, Jesus defends their right to satisfy their most basic needs such as hunger on the sabbath, which was created for their rest and recuperation in the first place. That was a matter of fundamental importance for peasant producers in Israel and beyond.

Korban (Dedicated to the Temple) vs. "Honor your Father and Mother" (Mark 7:1–23)

The opening of the episode sets the conflict directly into the broader religious-political-economic opposition between the Jerusalem rulers and the Galilean villagers: "the Pharisees and some of the scribes *who had come from Jerusalem*" (7:1; cf. 3:22). That the surveillance officers (as in the episode of plucking grain) challenge the practice of Jesus' disciples suggests that in this episode Jesus again functions as spokesperson for Galilean practices and interests in opposition to the representatives of Jerusalem's practices and interests. The accusers notice that some of the disciples were eating with "common, that is, unwashed hands." They seize upon this as an occasion for a more general challenge: "Why do your disciples not conduct their life according to 'the tradition of the elders'"—which becomes the object of Jesus' counterattack.

First, however, Mark's narrator, addressing Greek-speaking communities who have joined the Israelite renewal movement but require explanations for the particulars of Jerusalemite-Judean practices which they would not have learned in the movement itself, provides some "parenthetical" background to the impending Pharisaic charge and Jesus' counterattack. The Greek term *hoi ioudaioi* cannot be translated simply as "the Jews," as previously done without critical questioning. Roman and Greek outsiders probably thought that all the peoples living in Palestine, which had come under the rulers of the Judeans such as Herod, were Judeans. Ancient Judean writers such as Josephus, however, fairly consistently distinguish between Judeans and other peoples who had lived at points under Jerusalem rule, such as "the Idumeans" to the south and "the Galileans" in the north. "Israel" or "Israelites" was the inclusive term for the whole people.[30] Significantly, in the narrative of the crucifixion of Jesus, it is the Roman governor and soldiers who name and mock Jesus as "the king of the Judeans" (15:2, 9, 18, 25), while the Judean chief priests and scribes mock him as "the king of Israel" (15:32). Almost certainly the phrase *pantes hoi ioudaioi,* linked with "the Pharisees" and in the context of "some of the scribes who had come from Jerusalem," is a geographical reference: "the Pharisees, and all the Judeans." Thus the conflict here is not between Jesus and his movement and "all the Jews" or "Judaism" generally, but only between the Jesus movement and the Pharisees and other Judeans, probably Jerusalemites, given the practices in the ensuing explanation.

The narrator's explanation focuses on the purity practices of "the Pharisees and all the Judeans," with reference to the washing of hands, food brought from the market, and cups, pots, and bronze kettles—all in observing the tradition of the elders. Recent critical analysis of rabbinic references to the Pharisees prior to the Roman destruction of the Temple has considerably clarified our picture of their likely practices and how they compare with the practices of the priests, on the one side, and those of ordinary people on the other, around the time of Jesus and Mark. The maintenance of purity, with regard to food, its handling, and its eating, was a concern for priests with responsibility for serving in the Temple. Ordinary Judeans as well as other Israelites would not have been concerned about their own purity, except temporarily when they were headed into the Temple for one of the pilgrimage festivals such as Passover. No evidence suggests that ordinary Israelites other than Pharisees and Essenes (Qumranites) wanted to be cultically pure in their eating practices or in other respects.[31] The early rabbinic discussion in *m. Hag.* 2:7 portrays the hierarchy of purity with regard to washings of hands, foods, and utensils.[32] The

Pharisees are indeed concerned with cultic cleanness, but are lower in the purity hierarchy than priests and their families who eat the priestly rations or heave-offerings. The officiating priests who are going to eat holy things from the Temple altar must maintain yet stricter purity regulations. In this hierarchical list the Pharisees appear to have been concerned about purity in a way that lifted them above ordinary people who had no regular concern about it.

The Pharisees thus appear to have been nonpriestly people who ate ordinary food, yet strove to maintain priestly purity regulations in their own eating.[33] Contrary to older Christian stereotypes they were not rigorists, but even somewhat lax in this and other regards, at least from the viewpoint of stricter groups such as the Essenes and the priests; and they did not attempt to impose their own practices on the people in general.[34] No sources, however, suggest that Judean, much less Galilean, peasants were concerned about purity or that the Pharisees were urging others to maintain purity codes in their own eating practices. In his parenthetical explanation Mark's narrator may well be pointing to typical Pharisaic practices of the time. But he is almost certainly caricaturing the scribes and Pharisees' purity practices,[35] and he is surely exaggerating for rhetorical effect in suggesting that "all the Judeans" also observed such "traditions" of purity.

All these practices are entailed in conducting life according to "the traditions of the elders." This was apparently a virtual technical term for the distinctive legal rulings which they had promulgated over a period of several generations, regulations that were not written in the Law of Moses (hence rejected by the Sadducees).[36] The term used here in Mark is virtually synonymous with Josephus's reference to "the tradition of the ancestors (fathers)" (*Ant.* 13.296–97, 408; cf. his projection back into the time of king Josiah of "the tradition of the elders," *Ant.* 10.51; and cf. the apostle Paul, who claimed to have been a Pharisee, on his zeal for "the tradition of my ancestors," Gal. 1:14; Phil. 3:5–6). The Pharisees may have emphasized that these regulations were derived from ancestral tradition precisely to lend them the authority of hoary antiquity, which was revered in traditional societies in general and in Greco-Roman antiquity in particular (cf. Sir. 44:12; *War* 2.417; *C. Ap.* 1.36). As noted above, as recently as the early first century B.C.E. under the last Hasmoneans these regulations of the Pharisees had functioned as part of the state law of the Jerusalem temple-state.[37] We cannot say for certain the degree to which the Pharisees' unwritten regulations in "the tradition of the elders" were observed in Jerusalem and Judea during the first century C.E. Presumably Mark's narrator in this parenthetical explanation is exaggerating in saying that "all the Judeans" were observing them. Yet they must have had some prominence, even in Galileans' memory, or they would not have been threatening to the Jesus movement Mark emerges from.

In response to the Pharisees' and scribes' question, Jesus immediately attacks the "tradition of the elders." He is definitely not attacking the "Jewish Law"—in fact, he is about to appeal to the Mosaic covenantal "commandment of God." He launches his assault with a recitation of a version of a prophetic lament known to us from Isaiah 29:13. Although the text of Mark 7:6–7 in the ancient manuscripts of Mark is far closer to the Septuagint (the Jewish Bible in Greek) than to the Hebrew text of Isaiah 29:13, it still displays some significant differences.[38] This suggests that the recitation of the prophetic lament in Mark 7:6–7 was from oral memory. In the same interaction by which leaders and spokespersons in the Jesus movement became familiar with the practices of the Pharisees and other Judeans, they would have become familiar with prophecies that originated in Judea and had been carried in the great tradition, particularly prophecies that appealed to or resonated with them. Mark's Jesus applies "this people" of the prophetic lament to the Pharisees and scribes (and certainly not to "all the Jews"). The first lines lend prophetic authority to Jesus' accusation that they are "hypocrites." Only the juxtaposition of "human precepts" with "teaching" in the last line sets up the point of his accusation, alluding to their "tradition of the elders," that they "abandon the commandment of God and hold to human tradition." Mark's Jesus has also just taken the first step in changing the subject from purity regulations, with which the conflict began, to the Pharisees' "tradition" itself.

Jesus then repeats and intensifies his charge against the scribes and Pharisees, concentrating on an illustration from the most sacred and fundamental of duties in any society, people's care for their aging parents. This effectively refocuses the conflict on the use of economic resources. His intensification of the charge begins with a sarcastic tone: "(How) beautifully [i.e., with admirable piety!] you reject the commandment of God in order to hold to your tradition." His immediate illustration indicates that he is indeed referring to the most basic "commandment," in the ten commandments of the Mosaic covenant that supposedly provided the principles of social policy for all political-economic relations and in Israel. Moses, who received the covenant commandments from God on Sinai, said: "Honor your father and mother," and, in the ensuing covenant law code, the oldest, most venerable law code in Israelite tradition, "Whoever speaks evil of father or mother must surely die" (Exod. 20:13; 21:17). The verbs in the next two sentences indicate that Jesus clearly understands this to mean economic support of (apparently aging) parents. The Pharisees are not allowing people "*to do anything for*" a father and mother, they are siphoning off "whatever support [the parents] might have had from [their children]." And the Pharisees are thus "making void" the fundamental "commandment of God" precisely through their "tradition of the elders" that they are handing on.

The particular device in their "tradition" by which they are denying fathers and mothers any economic support from their children is *korban*. Mark's narrator, addressing Greek-speaking communities who identified with Israelite tradition but required help with technical terms, explains that *korban*, as used in an oath formula, meant a dedication to God. In a discussion of various obligations to God, the priests, and the Temple, such as first fruits and tithes, Josephus mentions people who had been so dedicated, who then had to pay a large sum (thirty to fifty shekels) to the priests to be relieved of their obligatory service (*Ant.* 4.73; cf. Lev. 27:1–8; and *C. Ap.* 1.167). That suggests that the practice of dedicating people or an animal or other resources to the service of God, i.e., to the Temple and the priests, was current at the time.[39] A report by the early Christian writer Origen illustrates the binding economic implications of "dedicating" something to God/the Temple," even if the details of the report may not be trustworthy. His Jewish informant mentioned that in revenge against debtors who could not or would not repay their loans, creditors would declare that what was owed was *korban*—thus foregoing repayment themselves but leaving the debtors still obligated to pay their debts.[40]

For *korban* to have had the effect of depriving parents of needed support from their children, it must have involved the dedication of part of the family land or rather its produce to the Temple. That is, for Jesus' charge to be a credible example of the "many things like this" that the Pharisees were doing, the latter must have been encouraging the people to devote or dedicate to support of the Temple resources (produce of their land) that were needed locally for such purposes as support of aging parents. This would fit both the historical context and the larger context of the story. No longer having direct jurisdiction over Galilee, the Jerusalem temple-state and its representatives could no longer be very aggressive in demanding payment of tithes and offerings, given Herod Antipas's expectation of the tax revenues from the area. The Pharisees' pressing Galilean peasants to devote a portion of their land's produce to the Temple as a sacred dedication would have provided an alternative way of deriving revenue from that area. Moreover, such a reconstruction of how *korban* as Pharisaic/scribal "tradition"would match a similar charge against the scribes later in Mark's story, e.g., that they "devour widows' houses," inducing them to give away their "whole living" to the Temple (12:38–44).

Mark's Jesus has turned an ostensible Pharisaic and scribal challenge to his disciples' not living according to their "traditions of the elders," in reference to the trivial matter of hand-washing, into a devastating indictment of their whole program of regulations as exploitative of the people: They are in fact blocking obedience to the basic Mosaic covenantal commandment(s) of God! We can imagine that in the formulation of this particular conflict, positioned centrally in the overall story, the "cases" were carefully selected for maximum rhetorical effect, juxtaposing "washing of hands" and "honoring father and mother." That is, the audience of villagers in the Jesus movement would have taken the Pharisees' and scribes' focus on hand-washing as an elite concern appropriate only for Jerusalem priests and their scribal allies. Their focus on hand-washing here served to belittle and denigrate their "tradition of the elders" in general. Jesus' own choice of "honoring father and mother" as the exemplary case was just that, appealing to the most fundamental filial concern of village families. By focusing attention on their encouraging people to "dedicate" part of their land or produce to God/the Temple, which removed scarce economic resources from families so they could no longer care adequately for their aging parents, Jesus illustrated how their representation of and advocacy for the Jerusalem temple-state meant draining away to the Temple the economic resources needed for continuing local economic viability of peasant families who were already in desperate straits.

Only after Mark's narrator has moved the scribes and Pharisees off the stage again does he return ostensibly to the issue of purity they raised at the outset of this conflict. Yet the focus has changed from defiled hands to the foods being eaten (note how Matthew attempts to make the link back to the issue of hand washing, 15:11, 20). The tone is still one of mocking the elite representatives of the great tradition whom Jesus has just attacked. Jesus now addresses the crowd, in an allusion that is almost scatological in its mockery of the elite's concerns about purity: "There is nothing outside a person that by going in can defile; but the things that come out are what defile a person." Alluding back to the Pharisees' and scribes' question about the disciples eating with defiled hands, the first part refers to what goes in through the mouth. The second part presumably refers to what later goes out the "other end."

Jesus' "humor" becomes earthier yet when he enters the house to instruct the (perpetually misunderstanding) disciples further on this matter—as if the audience didn't "get it" yet. But he now focuses only on why what goes in cannot defile: "since it enters not the heart but the stomach and comes out into the shithole—decontaminating all foods!" That last participial verb is the word for "catharsis!" The person has just been "purged" of any contamination. Although surely not in the modern West, in some societies it was simply a truism that once food was digested and defecated it was no longer clean or unclean. This reading of Mark's text at 7:19 follows one of the later manuscript traditions. Another manuscript tradition of Mark's text has provided the somewhat flimsy basis for the usual modern reading: "Thus he [Jesus] declared all foods clean." But that reading has serious problems, not the least of which are its obvious relevance to a later situation in the history of the movement when Gentile "Christians" wanted to be relieved of any obligation to observe Jewish food laws.[41] Moreover, if Mark's Jesus had declared so clearly that all foods were clean, then why was so much debate devoted to the issue elsewhere in Jesus movements without referring to this saying? Another possibility is that the last phrase is a later addition to Mark, for example, because the term here for "food" does not occur elsewhere in Mark and the whole phrase is missing in Matthew 15:1–20 where Matthew is otherwise reproducing Mark's episode.[42] In any case, Jesus' scatological statement here, with or without the last phrase, is a humorous declaration, still mocking the Pharisees as straw men, that purity codes are simply not a matter of concern for his movement. (In effect, Jesus is denying that defilement is even a problem—not to worry!)

Returning finally to "what comes out," Jesus changes the focus completely to social relations generally. Following up on the basic commandment(s) of God in the Mosaic covenant, moreover, he twists "defile" into a metaphor for how destructive the behavior forbidden in the Mosaic covenant would be for the common life of the community. The terms are mostly those typical of lists of vices more familiar from Hellenistic culture. But most of these "vices" refer explicitly to behavior explicitly prohibited by the Covenant commandments: murder (do not kill), fornication, adultery, licentiousness (do not commit adultery), theft (do not steal), envy, slander (do not bear false witness), coveting (do not defraud; with "honor father and mother" already mentioned in 7:10–12 above). Mark's story, of course, will return to the Mosaic covenant both explicitly (10:17–22; cf. 12:28–34) and programmatically (Mark 10, on which see the next chapter).

The conflict between Jesus and the scribes and Pharisees over "the tradition of the elders" and the basic "commandment(s) of God," occurring close to the center of the story, directly engages a central issue in the story as a whole. The scribes and Pharisees, as representatives of the Jerusalem rulers, attempt through their "traditions" to channel resources as well as loyalty to the central institutions of the Temple and high priesthood. Jesus, as the representative of the Galilean villagers, declares that their "traditions" in effect violate and void the fundamental Mosaic covenant and its principles of justice and mutual caring. Again he defends the Israelite popular tradition, particularly the Mosaic covenant that guided common life in the village communities, against the great tradition that had been developed in and for the interests of the ruling circles in Jerusalem, in this case the Pharisaic "traditions of the elders" designed to devote resources to the support of the Temple and high priesthood that were needed to sustain life in local families and communities.

Divorce and Marriage (Mark 10:2–9)

In what way could the Pharisees have been "testing" Jesus? We do not have to remember very far back into the story to imagine at least one possibility. The prophet John the Baptist, who announced that Jesus was the "stronger one" coming to baptize with the Holy Spirit, had been arrested and then executed for pronouncing that "it was not lawful" for Herod Antipas "to have his brother's wife." That is, he made this pronouncement on the assumption that remarriage after divorce was adultery—precisely what Jesus is about to pronounce in this episode. Why was divorce such a "loaded" issue, such that prophets were killed for condemning it and tested about whether it was lawful? Divorce would not have been very frequent among peasant families because it would break up the fundamental family unit of production, which was barely viable under normal circumstances. Among the elite families, on the other hand, marriage, divorce, and remarriage were common as instruments of securing, rearranging, and consolidating political-economic power. John the Baptist was condemning Antipas for far more than simply his personal morality. Besides his divorce of the Arab king Aretas's daughter having international political fallout, his remarriage to Herodias, the last remaining member of the Hasmonean family, presumably had ominous implications for further Herodian consolidation of power in Palestine.

Liberal divorce laws were important in enabling the ruling families and their ambitious underlings to maneuver for position and power via marriage and remarriage. This maneuvering under liberal divorce laws, moreover, had implications for the peasantry in at least two respects. Peasants indebted to a Herodian officer in one of the capital cities, for example, could be caught in the middle of such manipulations. And such maneuvering via divorce and remarriage provided a paradigm for ambitious villagers who might attempt to take advantage of the disintegration of other families resulting from the severe economic pressures of multiple layers of rulers and tax demands on their limited productive capacity.

This dispute between Jesus and the Pharisees revolves completely around references to key parts of Israelite tradition. We must attend carefully to the twists and nuances to detect how Jesus takes his stand on what was common Israelite tradition (common to the great and little traditions) in order to reject the great tradition represented by the Pharisees.

The Pharisees again function as a foil for Jesus' pronouncement(s)—this time in "the region of Judea," closer to their Jerusalem base. In this episode they do not challenge his or the disciples' behavior but ask a fundamental question of social policy and social order: "It is lawful for a man to divorce his wife?" The wording of Jesus' counterquestion in response is significant: "What *to you* did Moses *command*?" If he were establishing common ground with the Pharisees on Israelite tradition at this point he would have said simply, "What did Moses command" (i.e., "to us"). The Pharisees' response that "Moses *allowed* a man . . . to divorce" and Jesus' subsequent reference to that again as a "command" make clear that Jesus is making far more of what Moses said to *them* than they are. It is commonly recognized that what they say Moses "allowed" alludes with a few terms to the discussion of divorce and remarriage in Deuteronomy 24:1–4. That the text of Deuteronomy 24:1 in either Hebrew or Greek does not lend itself to description as a command[43] suggests fairly clearly that Mark's formulation makes this allusion on the basis of oral popular tradition, not by tinkering with the text of scripture.

But why would Jesus be separating himself from "them" with regard to a legal tradition in Deuteronomy? As discussed above in connection with the differences between the great tradition based in Jerusalem and the popular tradition in the outlying region of Galilee, what we know as the Torah, the five books of Moses, was produced in Jerusalem during the many centuries of divergent history between Judea and Galilee. There is no evidence that Galilean villagers would have known of the law codes in Deuteronomy and Leviticus prior to the time that the Jerusalem high priesthood took control over Galilee in about 100 B.C.E. And it seems likely that the Pharisees, from whom the Galileans may have gained familiarity with "the traditions of the elders," would have been the only viable candidates to have mediated the Torah law codes to Galileans. Meanwhile, Galileans such as those initially involved in Jesus' movement had their own version of the Mosaic covenantal tradition, certainly the covenantal commandments such as "You shall not commit adultery" and "Honor your father and mother," and related local customs that governed marital and family relations.

Indeed, there is fragmentary textual evidence in later rabbinic discussions not only that Galilee had local regional customs different from those in Judea and Jerusalem, but that those Galilean customs and practices were far more conservative than those in Judea. From their discussions of marriage contracts it is clear that once the rabbis migrated north to Galilee they found that, in contrast to Judea where laxer moral standards prevailed, Galilean brides and grooms relied on each other's upstanding character and lack of problematic previous behavior. The Galileans had no need to develop legal rulings for such contingencies as surrounded marriage in Judea (see, e.g., *m. Ketub.* 1:4, 5; 4:12; *m. Yevam.* 4:10).[44] Thus there is no reason to imagine that Jesus and his movement viewed Deuteronomy as authoritative law. To Galileans the Deuteronomic provision for a man being allowed to simply "write a certificate of dismissal, put it in her hand, and send her out of the house" (Deut. 24:1) would probably have appeared as liberal laxity stemming from the urban elite.

Jesus' immediate retort to the Pharisees' reference to the permissiveness of "Moses" both mocks the Pharisees' attribution of authority to *their* Law of Moses and, in effect, attacks their (written!) law as the virtual opposite of the will of God. "To incite your hardness of heart he [Moses] wrote you this command."[45] Contrary to the usual interpretation, Mark's Jesus is saying not that the command was given as an antidote to humanity's hardness of heart in general; that would weaken the contrast with God's will that immediately follows in Jesus' argument ("But from the beginning of creation—"). Rather, Moses "wrote" it to exacerbate the Pharisees hardness of heart. Presumably he has in mind the deleterious effects on the common people of the Pharisees' advocating such permissive laws and traditions that allow license to the wealthy and powerful (e.g., probably in manipulating property arrangements, as implied in the dispute with the Sadducees about levirate marriage in 12:18–27).

Over against the Pharisees' written law of Moses from the Jerusalem great tradition, Jesus looks to and defends the popular and, in this case, common Israelite tradition of God's creation of humanity. Moses had written such a permissive command for the Pharisees. "But from the beginning of creation 'male and female he [God] made them.'" Immediately following this recitation of a brief portion of the creation account known to us in Genesis 1:27, Jesus jumps to the further account of God's creation of humankind known to us in Genesis 2:24: "'For this reason a man shall . . . be joined to his wife, and the two shall become one flesh.'" In reciting from the creation account of common Israelite tradition, Jesus has also shifted the focus from divorce to marriage. And since marriage is founded in God's very creation of human beings, "male and female," who therefore become "one flesh," the marriage bond is not to be dissolved!

In his final declaration—"Therefore, what God has joined together, let no one separate"—Jesus makes a formal pronouncement as a prophetic lawgiver, a new Moses. This whole conflict with the Pharisees is no debate about the interpretation of the Law. Rather Mark's Jesus sharply attacks the law of the lax and permissive Jerusalem great tradition that the Pharisees apply and appeals instead to the common Israelite tradition (as understood in the popular tradition in which he is rooted): marriage, the most fundamental social relationship on which the rest of the social order is dependent, is founded in God's very creation.

In his follow-up teaching to the disciples, he clarifies the thrust of his declaration. Again Jesus speaks as a lawgiver declaring covenantal law (in the standard form of case law, "whoever . . ."): To divorce for the sake of remarriage is, in violation of the Mosaic covenant, to commit adultery. As noted at the outset on this controversy, given the importance of the marriage bond as the basis of the fundamental productive unit of an agrarian society, it is easy to imagine how lax divorce laws allowed the powerful families or ambitious aggressive local "big men" to expand and consolidate control of land and production precisely through divorce and remarriage, further exacerbating the disintegration of the family and village community in the tightening political-economic situation of Galilee and surrounding areas.

It is surely significant that the Qumran community that left the Dead Sea Scrolls objected to the Pharisees' permissive stance on divorce and remarriage and, like Mark's Jesus, understood marriage as grounded in creation, although from a completely different social location and perspective. In a context of a renewed covenantal community, the priestly-scribal authors of the Damascus Rule accused the "builders of the wall," who appear to be identical with the "smooth interpreters" (i.e., the Pharisees), of being "caught in fornication twice by taking a second wife while the first is alive, whereas the principle of creation is, 'male and female created He them'" (Gen. 1:27; CD 4:19–21). A similar stance against divorce and remarriage appears in another law code from Qumran, significantly directed to the prospective new king (an expansion on Deut. 17:14–17): "he shall not take another wife in addition to her, for she alone shall be with him all the time of her life. But if she dies, he may marry another" (11QTemple 57:17–19).

Like Mark's Jesus, these priestly-scribal statements in the Dead Sea Scrolls attack the Pharisees and are apparently concerned particularly about divorce and remarriage among the powerful. In contrast to Mark's Jesus and in common with the Pharisees, however, the priestly-scribal community at Qumran includes Deuteronomy among its authoritative scriptures. But that highlights all the more that Mark's Jesus has limited acquaintance with and sharply attacks the Deuteronomic law code, along with its Pharisaic interpreters. Jesus rather works from the common Israelite tradition of God's creation in which marriage was grounded as fundamental and inviolable, protecting the integrity of the basic social-economic unit of society.

In summary, as can be seen in all of these conflicts with the scribes and/or the Pharisees, far from abandoning or breaking with the "Jewish Law," Jesus is insisting upon the most fundamental commandments in the Israelite tradition as the basis of societal life. He is doing this, however, in direct rejection of the great tradition of Jerusalem represented by the scribes and Pharisees, whether in their "tradition of the elders" or the written law codes that they hold authoritative. In every one of the cases we have examined, Jesus appeals to the most fundamental "commandments of God" in the Mosaic covenant, the decalogue: "remember the sabbath," "honor your father and mother," "you shall not commit adultery," and the integral relation of the commandments of exclusive loyalty to God with the commandments of justice among fellow Israelites. It is necessary next to examine the other ways in which Mark's story portrays Jesus as renewing the Mosaic covenant as part of his renewal of Israel.

8

Renewing Covenantal Community

In a standard Christian understanding of God's grand scheme of salvation, Jesus and Paul brought the Gospel, the good news of the kingdom of God, to replace the Law with which "Judaism" was supposedly obsessed. Almost by definition, therefore, one of the Gospels cannot emphasize the covenant that formed the core of the Law. That was replaced, after all, at the Last Supper when Jesus, in the words of institution, presented the cup as "the new covenant in my blood" (1 Cor. 11:25). And in the beginning of the Gospel of Mark, Jesus proclaims that "the kingdom of God it at hand," which is the gospel in which the hearers are to have faith. It is not surprising, therefore, that Christian biblical interpreters have not found much covenant and covenantal teaching in Mark.

When we hear the Gospel as a whole, however, with sensitivity to rich references to Israelite tradition, then the Mosaic covenant appears as a prominent theme. In contrast to the standard earlier reading of the Gospel that had Jesus virtually breaking with the Law in sharp disputes with its Pharisaic defenders, we realize that Jesus himself appeals to the basic "commandment of God" against the Pharisaic "traditions of the elders" (Mark 7:8–13), as discussed in the previous chapter. Jesus is the one insisting on the fundamental authority and validity of the covenant law, as illustrated in the case of "Honor your father and mother." When asked by the man, "What must I do to inherit eternal life?" Jesus responds by reciting the covenantal commandments: "You shall not murder; . . . commit adultery; . . . steal; . . . bear false witness; . . . Honor your father and mother" (10:17–22). Then, in response to the scribe's question about which commandment is the greatest, Jesus attaches "love your neighbor as yourself" inseparably to "you shall love the Lord your God with all your heart" (12:28–31)—a concise summary of the covenantal commandments. When we then look more closely at Mark's "last supper" passage, it turns out that the best ancient manuscripts of the Gospel lack the term "new" in the word about the cup: "This is my blood of the covenant, which is poured out for many" (14:24). That is, Jesus is not instituting a *new* covenant but solemnizing a *renewal* of the Mosaic covenant.

This conclusion is confirmed by several other references to the covenant in Mark's story (as noted in chapter 5). We might miss these if we were not sensitive to the referencing of Israelite traditions that enabled the hearers of the Gospel to resonate with its performance. These briefer references to the Mosaic covenant work on the assumption, shared with the hearers, that the covenant is the basis of social-economic-political life. That the gospel of the kingdom of God as a renewal of the covenant is prominently signaled in two significant ways at the very beginning of Mark. It is often recognized that the reference to Isaiah's prophecy "prepare the way of the LORD" indicates that the "way" of Jesus is a new exodus. But the recitation of that "Isaiah" prophecy includes a reference to a prophecy in Malachi (3:1) as well, which indicates that the "messenger" is "the messenger of the covenant." Moreover, John's proclamation of the "baptism of repentance for the remission of sins" (1:4), with which the Gospel opens, presupposes that the covenant is the measure of what constitute sins (against its commandments) and that it provides the traditional guideposts for societal life to which the people recommit themselves as they undergo the ritual of baptism, entering the renewed *covenantal* society. References to various aspects and principles of the covenant then occur periodically throughout the Gospel. The juxtaposition of healing with the forgiveness of sins, with discussion of illness as due to sinning (2:1–12), presupposes an understanding of social life in terms of the Mosaic covenant. The disputes with the Pharisees over what is allowed on the Sabbath (2:23–28) and about divorce and remarriage in terms of "committing adultery" (10:10–12) similarly assume the covenant as the basis of societal life.

The Community/Movement That Mark Addresses

In contrast to the predominantly individualistic reading of Mark as a story about discipleship,[1] some interpreters have noticed that Mark exhibits considerable concern for community.[2] That people "enter" the kingdom of God (9:47; 10:23–25) suggests that the kingdom has a social-community dimension.[3] Mark emphasizes several key corporate images, such as the family. It was even discerned that Mark includes covenant themes, indeed that Mark's community may be a covenant community.

Those who finally discerned that Mark is indeed addressed to and concerned with the life of community, however, were still reading Mark as addressing a new religion, Christianity, that was different from Judaism from which it broke away. If Mark is concerned about community, therefore, it must have been a new community, one that was formed over against the old society in response to Jesus' ministry. Jesus "inaugurates a new people." In the wilderness feedings God is calling together a new people (8:19–20). Those who abandoned their households and families would be compensated "in the new pattern of relationships and identity that would develop in the Christian community" (10:28–30).[4] As can be seen in that last image, this reading also perpetuates the prevailing individualism of modern interpretation. Mark's Jesus was supposedly addressing individuals who, in responding, left their previous communities and formed or joined a new community.

Indeed, the picture becomes more grandiose. "As the process of community formation takes place," with its "strong sense of social displacement" and "relativizing of existing social norms," Mark's story describes nothing less than "a new social world in the making"[5] This "new community" reading also projects the model of the church in modern North American society back into the time of Mark. "The covenant community in Mark is a voluntary association from the standpoint of human response to the gospel."[6] "Jesus brought into being a new community based, not on ties of blood and heredity, but a voluntary association, open to anyone who repents and does the will of God."[7] The new community reading, finally, also continues the Christian theological interpretation of Mark, with Jesus cast in the role of the founder of a new covenant.[8] The "new community" reading of Mark, like the "discipleship" reading, is thus rooted in modern assumptions, not on a hearing of the whole Gospel in its historical context.

In order to get a clearer sense of Mark's concern for community and how a renewal of Mosaic covenant fits that concern it is important to cut through two fundamental misconceptions underlying the "new community/covenant" interpretation: (1) the Christian notion that Mark was addressed to "Gentiles," in a break with or departure from "Judaism," and (2) the common impression that Jesus called his followers generally to leave their homes, with the implication that they formed a new community of some sort.

1. The view that Mark addresses a "Gentile" community that formed as the result of a mission to the "Gentiles" or a "universal" community combining "Jews" and "Gentiles" is rooted in a Christian theological scheme.[9] The Gospel of Mark itself, however, does not suggest that a new religion or religious community is being created, whether comprised mainly of "Gentiles" or uniting "Gentiles" and "Jews." In order to cut through this misconception we must recapitulate some of the discussion from chapter 2 regarding the movement that Mark addresses.

It seems clear that the movement Mark addresses included people beyond the villages of Galilee who were not ethnically Israelite. After all, Mark is composed in Greek, whereas most Galilean villagers presumably spoke Aramaic. The story includes episodes of Jesus himself spreading the movement beyond Galilee to the villages of Tyre, Caesarea Philippi, and the Decapolis, and the Greek(-speaking) Syrophoenician woman forces Jesus to agree that the "children's" bread should be shared with the "dogs" (7:24–30). And Jesus mentions twice in passing that the "gospel must be proclaimed to all peoples/in the whole world" (13:10; 14:9).

But there is no justification for taking the parable of the tenants to mean that "the Jews" generally reject Jesus so that the "vineyard" is taken away from them and given to the "Gentiles" (12:1–12). Contrary to such standard Christian readings, this parable implicated the chief priestly rulers in Jerusalem, not the Judeans and other Israelites in general. And it is unwarranted to take the direction of the women, disciples, and readers to "Galilee" at the end of the Gospel as meaning "the Gentiles" on the basis of the reference to "Galilee of the peoples" in Matthew (4:15; citing Isa. 9:1). The view that the Markan movement embodied a universalism in combining "Jews" and "Gentiles" rests on the assumption that one side of the Sea of Galilee was "Jewish" and the other "Gentile" which Jesus united in his boat trips back and forth across the lake. But Mark gives no indication that the one side was "Jewish" and no other sources suggest that the people living around the western shore of the Sea of Galilee were primarily Judeans.

Far from indicating some sort of break with "Judaism" toward a mission to Gentiles and/or a newly formed community, Mark's story as a whole emphasizes the continuity between Jesus' ministry and the history and tradition of Israel, as discussed in chapters 2, 5, and 7. The dominant conflict is between the Roman-appointed rulers in Galilee and Jerusalem, on the one side, and the peoples among whom Jesus works, on the other. Jesus enacts the fulfillment of Israel's history and expectations as the new Moses-Elijah catalyzing the renewal of Israel. In so doing, he is portrayed as easily moving across the frontiers of Galilee into ostensibly "foreign" territories. But Jesus carries the same message and program of exorcism and healing into Syrian villages that he had taken into Galilean villages earlier. Mark observes no well-demarcated borders or boundaries around "Israel." The kingdom of God in fulfillment of historical longings is apparently "at hand" also for the villagers of Tyre and Caesarea Philippi and the Decapolis. For Mark's story, however, no issue emerges of whether or how other peoples might join Israel by undergoing circumcision, as the people from James insisted upon in Galatia (Gal. 2). And Mark has nothing at all like Matthew's separation of the disciples being sent "only to the lost sheep of the house of Israel" during Jesus' ministry from the resurrected Son of Man's charge to "preach the gospel to all nations" at the very end. Mark addresses communities that stand in continuity with Israelite tradition, perhaps that understand themselves as part of the fulfillment of Israel's history.

2. The standard picture of Jesus' followers leaving their homes and families is grossly exaggerated. Virtually the only episode in the story where disciples leave their homes and make a long-term break with their families is the call of those members of the twelve who were Jesus' intimates (1:16–20). And it is not at all clear that the story holds them up as models to be imitated, as explored in chapter 4 above. If anything, Mark deploys them as negative examples, of how not to respond to the good news of the kingdom and the "way" of Jesus. They and the rest of the twelve have a special role in the story as the representative heads of Israel and the leaders of the movement who share the mission of Jesus to preach and heal. The purpose of their sending (6:7–13) is to pursue that mission in village communities, not to establish a particular itinerant lifestyle or to found new communities. The people Jesus heals, with the exception of the Gadarene demoniac and Bartimaeus, used as a counter-example to the disciples, are supported by and are integrated back into their communities of origin (e.g., 2:1–12; 5:21–43; 5:1–20; 7:24–30; 8:22–26; 10:46–52). The crowds "follow," but nothing in the story suggests that they have abandoned their homes to join a new community. The open ending of the Gospel, finally, sends the hearers as well as the women back to Galilee, evidently to continue the movement in the villages where Jesus had gotten it started.[10]

Rather than portraying Jesus and the twelve as pulling people out of their homes and village communities, Mark's story pictures them as remaining in or returning to their homes and villages, only with a "new lease on life," healed, forgiven, and acclaiming what is happening. As noted in chapter 2, Jesus himself carries out his preaching and healing in the village assemblies. He sends the twelve two by two to broaden the same program village by village. The people healed remain in or return to their communities. Even those disciples who left everything to "follow" Jesus are to be restored to their traditional family/household and village life in a remarkably renewed form (10:28–30). We cannot, of course, simply read the situation that Mark addresses as a mirror image of the effects of Jesus' ministry reflected in the Gospel episodes. Yet we have no alternative but to take our cues from Mark's story itself. And Mark's story appears fairly clearly to address people living in (village) communities similar to those Galilean and other village communities portrayed in Mark's episodes, that is, people who remained in their communities of origin rather than join some new "voluntary association" (presumably in a city).

New Testament scholars usually picture "early Christianity" as an urban phenomenon. That picture, however, depends heavily on the mission of the apostle Paul. The vast majority of people in the Roman empire generally lived in villages or towns, not cities. In most traditional agrarian societies, nine or ten people working the land were needed to support those who lived in urban areas. Some of our sources indicate that movements of Jesus followers spread in rural areas as well as in the cities. Pliny the Younger, Roman governor of Pontus-Bithynia, writing to the emperor Trajan three generations after Jesus' ministry, gives vivid evidence that Jesus-believers were active in villages as far away from Palestine as northwestern Asia Minor (*Epistles* 10.96–97). The general circumstances of the spread of Jesus movements thus corresponds to the internal evidence from Mark's story, which portrays people remaining in their villages. It seems likely, therefore, that Mark was addressing people who, like the people portrayed in the Gospel, remained in their families and villages.

If Mark seems to be addressing people whose life situation was very similar to that portrayed in Markan episodes, therefore, we can gain at least some sense of their life situation by analogy with Mark's portrayal of village life in Galilee and the surrounding regions. The village community and its component units of households/families were the fundamental forms of social life throughout the ancient Mediterranean world in which Jesus movements spread. Personal life was embedded in these corporate social forms. The (ideally self-sufficient) household or family was the fundamental unit of production and consumption as well as the unit of social reproduction. The families of a village were also interrelated and interdependent, with many crisscrossing ties and tensions between them, whether because of mutual borrowing and lending or occasional misunderstandings.

Villagers were always subject to rulers and the economic obligations they imposed. Thus villagers elsewhere would have labored under multiple obligations somewhat parallel to the Galileans' taxes to Herod Antipas, tribute to Caesar, and (pressure to continue paying) tithes and other dues to the Temple in Jerusalem. Difficulties meeting these obligations while simultaneously attempting to feed their families resulted in increasing indebtedness to the people who controlled a "surplus," such as the officers of the Herodian regime in the newly built capital cities of Sepphoris and Tiberias. Such wealthy and powerful creditors demanded interest on loans. Through the debt mechanism they had the leverage to build up a handsome independent income of their own and could even come into control of villagers' lands, or at least dictate what the villagers raised in their fields. As long as the people rendered up the requisite taxes and tribute and interest payments, the various layers of rulers did not intervene in local affairs. Villages were thus semi-independent self-governing communities. But insofar as a significant number of village households fell seriously into debt and, under similar outside pressures, the usually manageable internal conflicts escalated, the village community might begin to disintegrate.

It is often observed that Mark gives no evidence of any organization of the community(ies) it addresses. But if Mark's movement was based in village communities, then the organization was already in place and is simply pre-supposed. Mark portrays Jesus as preaching and healing in the "synagogues" of Galilean villages. As discussed before, however, the "synagogues" in which Jesus and the disciples worked were not religious buildings, but village assemblies. These were the form of local self-government and other communal life in the villages of Galilee. Villages in other areas had similar forms of local community governance and social cohesion.[11] Such local assemblies probably served certain functions we would call religious, such as communal prayers. But they also served political and economic functions, such as delegating a committee to repair the local water supply or appointing a court to hear cases of local disputes. Mark is thus simply assuming that community organization is already in place in the village assemblies, i.e., the gatherings of villagers in which local community affairs were dealt with, prayers recited, stories told, and gossip spread.

One further observation may be important in enabling us to understand the communities Mark addresses and how a renewal of the Mosaic covenant would resonate with them. The older Christian interpretation understood Mark's Jesus as breaking free of the particularism of the "Jewish" law, as represented by the Pharisees, so that new religious community of his followers could attract Gentiles who might be put off by certain rituals and food laws. As discussed in the previous chapter, however, Mark's Jesus in fact does not break with but reaffirms the most fundamental Israelite traditions, the basic commandments of God. The audience of Mark, the communities to whom the story is addressed, are thus identifying and resonating with basic Israelite law. The Israelite law they are thus resonating with, however, derived from the Israelite popular tradition that had functioned for centuries as the fundamental "common law" of village life. The guidance of Israelite village life, of course, was the purpose of the Mosaic covenant and covenant law in the first place, insofar as the village community was the principal social form in which "Israel" was constituted. That basic covenantal law of Galilean village life dealt with fundamental principles pertinent to other village communities. Far from seeming alien or off-putting, fundamental principles of the Israelite popular tradition may well have been relevant to village and town communities in other areas.

Covenant Forms and Covenant Renewals

Thanks to the discovery of the Dead Sea Scrolls we know of a parallel movement of Mosaic covenant renewal, albeit a priestly-scribal movement. Moreover, it has been easier for biblical scholars to discern forms of covenant renewal elsewhere in Jesus' so-called sermon (on the mount/plain) in Matthew and Luke, rather than in Mark. But an exploration of covenant renewal and covenant traditions in the Qumran community and in a parallel Jesus movement may help set the stage for consideration of Jesus' covenantal teaching in Mark.

Mark presents the scribes and Pharisees as based in the Jerusalem Temple. They press upon the Galilean and Judean peasants the importance of declaring (some of) their property *korban,* that is "dedicated" to the support of the Temple (7:9–13) and they press even poor widows to give their limited resources to the Temple until they exhaust their "houses" or inheritance (12:38–44). Mark's representation in these episodes displays historical verisimilitude. The contemporary Judean historian Josephus reports that Pharisees were active in the provisional Jerusalem government's attempt to control the revolt that erupted in the summer of 66. Their inclusion in the highest councils of the priestly aristocracy did not "come out of nowhere" historically. It is understandable that the scribes and Pharisees, who worked for the temple-state, like the priests who presided at its sacred center in the Temple, were concerned to generate support for it among the villagers, the productive segment of the society. So long as priests and scribes served the central institution of the Temple they could be expected to emphasize the parts of the Torah that supported and legitimated the central institution such as tithing and offerings, with less concern for the exodus and Mosaic covenantal parts of Israelite tradition.

The community that produced the Dead Sea Scrolls, however, were dissident priests and scribes. Apparently because the Hasmonean family who had led the Maccabean Revolt against the oppressive Hellenistic empire was accommodating itself to the empire again, these dissidents went out into the wilderness "to prepare the way of the LORD." In breaking with the incumbent high-priestly regime and identifying with the more liberative parts of "the Law and the Prophets," they undertook a new exodus under their leadership of the Teacher of Righteousness as a new Moses, and set up a community in the wilderness of Judea as a renewed Mosaic covenant.[12] Although it consisted mainly of priests and scribes from Judea, the Qumran community understood itself as engaged in the renewal of Israel, as indicated in its council consisting symbolically of "twelve" representative men, along with three priests. One of the most important documents they left in the caves near their community facilities at Qumran by the Dead Sea was a *Community Rule* (referred to as 1QS).

The *Rule* reads like a handbook of key teachings, rituals, and rules and laws for their community life. The overall structure of the *Community Rule* displays many of the same kinds of material and structural components as the (Mosaic) covenant in Hebrew biblical texts such as Exodus 20–24, Deuteronomy, and

Joshua 24. While the Qumran *Rule* includes the same structural components as the traditional Mosaic covenant, however, it changes the emphasis from past to present and future deliverance and deploys one of the principal components in a significantly different way. The traditional Mosaic covenant set up God's commandments for the conduct of society life by recounting God's great act of deliverance in the exodus, then sanctioned the people's observance of the commandments by having the people call down blessings and curses upon themselves for observance or nonobservance. The Qumran covenant also sets up the principles and rules for communal life with a declaration of God's deliverance. But the deliverance declared is now happening in the present or imminent future (1QS 3–4). And instead of the blessings and curses functioning as a motivating sanction on observance of community rules by offering a reward or threatening a punishment in the future, the Qumran covenant ceremony declares that those who are in the community are already blessed and those outside are cursed (1QS 1–2). Another significant feature of the *Community Rule* is the anticipation that, at the "time of visitation" when God terminates the power of the Prince of Darkness, God would restore the human conditions that prevailed at the creation of humankind (Adam; 1QS 4:19–24).

In the principal non-Markan branch of the Synoptic Gospel tradition represented by "Q" (the "Source" of Jesus' teachings included in both Matthew and Luke, but not in Mark), Jesus enacts a renewal of the Mosaic covenant in his first and longest speech.[13] This consists of what is often labeled the "Sermon on the Plain" in Luke 6:20–49. Matthew used most of the same material and the overall framework of the speech in composing the "Sermon on the Mount." Readily recognizable as traditional covenant components are the blessings and woes in Luke/Q 6:20–26, teachings similar to traditional covenantal laws and teachings in Exodus and Deuteronomy in Luke/Q 6:27–42, and motivating sanctions on those teachings in the double parable about the houses built respectively on the rock and the sand in 6:46–49. Jesus' covenant renewal speech, however, like the *Community Rule* from Qumran, has changed the emphasis in the covenant structure from past to present-future deliverance and has redeployed the blessings and curses. Ordinary people of Jesus' day would likely have understood their oppression and suffering as the covenantal curses visited upon them because they had not kept the covenant laws. Apparently addressing just such a debilitating attitude, Jesus declares that they are blessed (rather than cursed) because God is now giving them the kingdom ("blessed are you poor, for yours is the kingdom of God"). Similar to the new pattern evident in the Qumran *Community Rule*, Jesus here transforms the blessings and curses component of the covenant into a declaration of new deliverance for the people and woes against their wealthy rulers (Luke/Q 6:20–26).

After declaring God's new act of deliverance in bringing the kingdom for the poor, Jesus' covenant renewal speech addresses covenantal teachings to the people: "Love your enemies, do good, and lend" (Luke/Q 6:27–42). Pacifists and others have found here generalized admonitions to nonviolence, even nonresistance. Recent academic interpreters see here mainly a collection of "wisdom sayings" and clever "aphorisms." These teachings, however, stand in a long tradition of covenantal teaching, as evident in Exodus 22:25–27; 23:4–5; Leviticus 19:2, 17–18; Deuteronomy 15:1–11; 22:1–4; 24:10–13. As evident in the context indicated by the content of Jesus' admonitions, he is addressing local community interactions in which people are borrowing and lending and caught in petty disputes rooted in their deteriorating economic circumstances. The "love your enemies" set of teachings first addresses local economic inter-action, the desperate need for mutual cooperation in borrowing and lending, as insisted upon in traditional Israelite covenantal teaching (Luke/Q 6:27–36; cf. Exod. 22:25–27). Then Jesus addresses the sort of petty local social con-flicts that can develop out of just such economic difficulties as the people were placed in by the multiple demands placed on their produce by the Herodian and Roman rulers (Luke/Q 6:37–42; cf. Lev. 19:17–18). The covenant renewal speech in "Q" thus deals with both economic and social-political relations among people in the communities of the Jesus movement it addresses. And it prepares us to discern a parallel covenant renewal section in Mark's story.

Renewed Covenant in Mark 10

The "middle" section of Mark (8:22/27–10:52) is a distinctive step in Mark's story. As often noted, two episodes of healing blind men frame this section and the three announcements of "the son of man's" killing and rising, followed by the disciples' misunderstandings, provide its internal structure. The narrative also slows down significantly. The term "immediately" (*euthys*), which occurs more than thirty times in the preceding narrative, crops up only three times in this section, all in one episode, the exorcism of the demonized boy. The slower pace gives a quality to Jesus' teachings that transcends the particular circumstances in which they narratively occur. Mark 10:1–45 is further distin-guished somewhat within Jesus' longer movement on the way from Caesarea Philippi to Jerusalem by being set "in the region of Judea and beyond the Jor-dan," traditional Israelite areas south and southeast of Galilee. Although the twelve continue to function as foils for Jesus' teaching, the crowds again gather around him for teaching. While some of the teachings in Mark 10:1–45 are directed to the disciples (as representative recipients), the wider movement represented by the crowds remain nearby, continuing with Jesus "on the way" (10:32, 46). It has long been noticed that the teachings in Mark 10 in particular appear to belong together, leading to suggestions of a pre-Markan collection of Jesus traditions.[14] Substantively, Mark 10 combines traditional materials dealing with social concerns also evident in other ancient communities and movements, inviting characterizations such as a "manual of discipleship" and a "community rule."[15]

Indeed, the teachings in the sequence of dialogues in Mark 10 comprise a certain covenantal "charter" for communities Mark addresses. Mark has skillfully interwoven these episodic dialogues with Jesus' announcements of his arrest, trial, and execution in the middle section of the Gospel, on the "way" to Jerusalem. It is surely significant that what have been called "statements of holy law," in the formulaic form beginning with "whoever" (*hos an*) figure prominently at several points in this sequence of teachings (10:10–11, 14, 29–30, 43–44; cf. 3:35; 8:34, 35; 9:37). These are general statements of law or principle on issues of grave importance to the community or movement. Most such "statements of holy law" have to do with social relations within the community. In this section Mark's Jesus delivers general principles on the four successive issues of marriage, membership, economic relations, and political relations. These sayings are, in effect, statements of (renewed) covenantal principles designed to govern social relations in the communities of the movement.[16]

While not in the same handbook form as the Qumran *Community Rule*, Mark's sequence of covenantal dialogues presents analogous materials and plays a similar function for its hearers. It does not take the same form as the sustained covenant renewal discourse in Luke/Q 6:20–49 or Matthew's Sermon on the Mount (Matt. 5–7). But the sequence of episodic dialogues in Mark 10 has the same function as a restatement of covenantal teachings within Mark's broader story about the kingdom of God and the renewal of Israel. Jesus' teaching in Mark 10 covers less of a range of community issues and problems than the *Community Rule* from Qumran. But while it deals with both economic and political interaction in the communities of the movement in a way parallel to the Q covenantal discourse, it also covers the integrity of marriage and the family, as does the original Mosaic covenant.

Marriage and Family

Jesus' controversies with the Pharisees in Mark set up and focus his definitive teaching on covenantal subjects such as the sabbath and honoring father and mother (as noted in the previous chapter). The Pharisees' question here thus immediately signals to the hearers that covenantal teaching is coming. The controversy with the Pharisees in Mark 10:2–9 deals with the integrity of the marriage bond and family units of the society. This was a key issue for a traditional agrarian society insofar as the family was the fundamental unit of production and consumption as well as reproduction. In the original Mosaic covenant, two out of six of the principles of social policy governing social-economic relations focus on the family: "You shall not commit adultery," and "Honor your father and mother." As can be seen in later rabbinic discussions, marriage and divorce were not simply matters of "marital relations," but of economic rights (especially for the wife who left her father's family to join a strange family) and of inheritance (in the male lineage) of the family land, the basis of the transgenerational family livelihood.

Christian interpreters have tended to picture the Pharisees as strict legalists. As we now know from the Dead Sea Scrolls, however, the priests and scribes at Qumran, themselves extremely rigorous in their understanding and application of Mosaic covenant law, considered the Pharisees "smooth interpreters." They were known for loosening the requirements of covenant law to accommodate the "contingencies" of social-economic life, in this case apparently the possibility of consolidating economic power at others' expense, as discussed in the previous chapter. In response to the Pharisees' attempt to entrap Jesus with the question about whether "it is lawful for a man to divorce his wife," his counterquestion forces the "smooth interpreters" to show their hand first. Sure, Moses was very flexible, permitting a man to simply "write a certificate of dismissal." Jesus dismisses the Pharisees' overly flexible "great tradition" as given by Moses "to stimulate your hardness of heart," suggesting that those who appeal to this tradition are greedy and/or cruel to the women who would be so summarily "put away."

Jesus then, without any transitional comment, abruptly changes the subject—or at least refocuses the debate—from divorce to marriage. His appeal to the creation story in Israelite tradition is remarkable for its implications. Like the Qumran *Community Rule*, Mark's Jesus here appeals to the original situation of creation. Apparently, since the kingdom of God is at hand, the conditions of creation are valid, including God's original creation of humanity in gendered polarity as embodied socially in marriage. "From the beginning of creation, 'God made them male and female.'" Appealing then to the concluding statement in the creation of humanity story, "the two shall become one flesh," Jesus declares, "what God has joined let not mankind separate!" Marriage is inviolable since grounded in God's gendered creation.

Jesus' follow-up reply to the disciples' question in the house (10:10–12) declares that divorce for the purpose of remarriage, on the initiative of either the husband or the wife, is tantamount to adultery, i.e., a violation of God's covenantal commandment. Jesus' declaration takes the form of two covenantal/legal principles beginning with the formulaic "whoever . . ." (*hos an*), a form often used in Gospel and other New Testament literature when Jesus (or the exalted Christ) is giving instructions for the life of the community. The use of this form at key points in this sequence of episodes in Mark 10 is a key indication that Mark is presenting a covenantal charter for the communities of the movement.

Membership in the Covenantal Community

The next episode addresses the issue of membership in the kingdom community or movement. Jesus' teaching is framed by the twelve disciples' continuing their exclusionary action in the preceding episodes of this section and picks up the theme of "children" from Jesus' criticism of their concern with their own greatness (9:33–41). Both the disciples' words and Jesus' reaction have a hostile edge. The former "rebuke" the people bringing children to Jesus, just as Jesus had previously "rebuked" demons and Peter (1:25; 8:33), and Jesus is "indignant" at them, signaling that the issue engaged here is a very important one. Jesus had already declared that "whoever *receives* a child, *receives* me . . . and the one who sent me" (9:37). The disciples, moreover, should understand about being received or not, because in the commission for their mission they were instructed in effect to curse any place that would not "receive" them (6:11). But the twelve now turn around and rebuke rather than receive the children. Their failure to receive the children sets up Jesus' declaration that it is to such as the children that "the kingdom of God belongs" and that one must "*receive* the kingdom of God as a little child" (10:13–16).[17]

Interpretation of these sayings must surely take its cue from the contrasts within this section of the story between the children, on the one hand, and greatness and positions of political power desired by the disciples and the rich, who cannot possibly enter the kingdom of God. Modern interpreters tend toward the sentimental in exploring what receiving the kingdom of God "as a little child" might mean—e.g., innocent childlike trust. "Childhood" is an invention of modern Western society. Childhood had no social reality before. Childhood should therefore not be idealized or romanticized. In ancient Palestine, as in most any traditional agrarian society, children were the human beings with the lowest status. They were, in effect, not-yet-people. The "the kingdom of God belongs" to *children* sharpens the agenda of the whole Gospel story that the kingdom of God is present for the people, the peasant villagers, as opposed to people of standing, wealth, and power. This statement is parallel to the opening declaration of "blessings" in the covenant discourse in Q (the "Source" of Jesus speeches used in Matthew and Luke): "Blessed are you poor, for yours is the kingdom of God."

Jesus' second saying then drives home the implication for ongoing participation or "membership" in the renewed covenantal community. The saying is pointedly prefaced by the signal of unusual significance, "Truly I tell you," to evoke the hearers' special attention. The form of the saying, "Whoever does not (*hos an mē*) . . . will not . . . ," is a prime example of the general statements of "holy law" or covenant principles that appear prominently in these episodes. One must not receive and enter the kingdom of God out of desire to gain status or power. This is a difficult saying. The usual poverty and power-lessness of being a peasant was not pleasant. The only alternative with which peasants were acquainted was the luxurious lifestyle of their wealthy and pow-erful rulers in their mansions in Tiberias or Tyre or Caesarea Philippi or Jeru-salem (where archaeologists have indeed found spacious mansions in the "New City" built during the time of Jesus and "Mark").

Covenantal Economics

The most sustained discussion in Mark 10 concerns covenantal economics. What are often separated into three paragraphs in English Bibles—Mark 10:17–22, 23–27, 28–31—should all be read together to understand how these three brief dialogues fit together as a statement of egalitarian economics for the Markan movement. Because biblical interpreters focus on its religious aspect, they tend to miss the importance of economics in the Mosaic covenant. Most of the principles of social policy stated in the commandments focus on or include concern for people's economic rights: "You shall not covet," "you shall not steal," and "you shall not bear false witness" all protect people's eco-nomic resources and rights in the interactions of community members. The other three—no murder, no adultery, and honoring father and mother—also include economic aspects. If this is not clear from the principles themselves, then it becomes clear in examination of the covenant law codes such as Exo-dus 21–23, which apply the principles to the contingencies of social interac-tion (e.g., Exod. 22:1–6, 14, 25–27). For example, economic restitution is made for debilitating injuries (Exod. 21:26–36). Even observance of the sab-bath day, to be used in honor of and loyalty to God, has economic implica-tions, which are expanded symbolically in the sabbatical cancellation of debts, release of debt-slaves, and rest for the land whose produce serves as welfare aid to the poor (Exod. 21:2; 23:10–13; Lev. 25).

Like the Pharisees in the discussion of divorce and marriage in 10:2–9, the "man" who asks Jesus how he can "inherit eternal life" serves as a foil to set up both the recitation of the covenant commandments and Jesus' supplementary teaching based upon it. If we are sensitive to peasants' economic situation, which is always subsistence and marginal, we will recognize that the man's question, like his obsequious flattery of Jesus, is a dead giveaway. Only some-one who is wealthy would be inquiring about "eternal life." Peasants such as

Jesus' followers would rather have been wondering how they could support their families, or even where their next meal was coming from.

In reply, Jesus pointedly recites God's commandments. This also functions to set the pompous fellow up for a fall. The audience knows that these principles govern social-economic-political relations in the society. They are the stipulations for loyalty to and blessing by God in concrete social relations. We may wonder whether "You shall not defraud" is a pointed addition in a list that just happens to omit "You shall not covet" or a pointed substitution for the latter that gives it a telling concrete application. For coveting someone else's goods, desiring to gain control of them, would lead the coveter to defraud a vulnerable person desperate for wage labor or for a loan to feed his children or heavily in debt from previous loans (see, e.g., Deut. 24:14–15). Sensitive listeners would hear immediately that the man's insistence that he has observed them was phony. Of course he cannot respond to Jesus' command to sell his goods and give to the poor because he not only has great possessions but is deeply attached to them. The hearers, of course, understand what Jesus has been talking about all along. The only way someone became wealthy in Israelite society (as in any traditional agrarian society) was to take advantage of someone else who was vulnerable, to defraud others by charging interest on loans, which was forbidden in covenant law, and eventually gaining control of others' possessions (labor, fields, households). This first episode in the sequence of three concerning covenantal economics thus provides the hearers with a negative example of a man who has gained great wealth by defrauding others, by breaking the covenantal commandments not to covet and steal (and, probably, not to bear false witness).

With this negative example in mind, Jesus reflects on the implications in dialogue with the uncomprehending disciples (10:23–27). He moves from the particular case of how extremely difficult it will be for the wealthy to enter the kingdom of God (10:23), to the more general situation of anyone and everyone (10:24), then back to the case of the wealthy (10:25). The proverb about the camel going through the eye of a needle, meaning that it is impossible for a rich man to enter the kingdom of God, is a piece of peasant humor. As often in biblical materials that derive from the popular tradition, Israelite peasant hostility against their wealthy rulers and exploiters is not even veiled. In all of these sayings that follow up on the negative example of the wealthy man in search of eternal life, the criteria for "entering the kingdom" are the simple and straightforward covenantal economic principles.

The density of the disciples in 10:23–27 in turn sets up Peter's desperate plea in the last of the three dialogues concerning covenantal economics. Throughout the previous dialogue they represent the viewpoint that one's current state of economic welfare is a mark of God's blessing, which involves forgetting the covenantal criteria for future blessing. Typically concerned for his own reward, Peter exclaims that he and other disciples have "left every-thing" to follow Jesus. Jesus' answer is remarkable. Readers in modern middle-class industrial society usually lack "ears to hear" because of our very different life circumstances. The import of the saying is signaled by its prefacing with "Truly, I tell you." The form is similar to the covenantal or legal principles elsewhere in this covenantal section and elsewhere in Mark, only with the shift from "whoever" to "no one who . . . will not . . ."

The subject of the dialogue in 10:28–31 is *restored* households, not new communities or "voluntary associations" in the process of social formation after the disciples have abandoned their original households. Peter's appeal recalls the episode of his and the other intimates' call to "leave" and "follow." But far from being a repetition of the call to leave household and property, this is a reassurance of an astounding "this-worldly" compensation. The restora-tion is to occur "now in this age." The last clause, "and in the age to come eter-nal life," is a "throwaway" line that refers back to the "unreal" question of the rich man with which the economic issue was opened. Mark gives no indica-tion anywhere else in the Gospel of interest in "eternal life." Only wealthy people who defraud the poor are interested in that. Mark's reference here to "in this age" is made all the more real and concrete by the addition at the end of "with persecutions." Jesus is not talking about "never-never-land." He is talking, with wondrous exaggeration, about a restoration of the traditional peasant household and village life *in this age*, with all the trials and tests that the members of the movement may experience at the hands of the rulers who are still intact—not yet eliminated by the kingdom of God "coming with power" (cf. Mark 9:1). Both before and later in the story, Mark makes clear that participation in the movement will almost certainly evoke persecution and trials (4:17; 8:34–38; 13:9–11).

Jesus' declaration about restoration of households may be the most signifi-cant indication in the whole of Mark's story that the movement's program is the renewal of Israel (along with or including other peoples) in village com-munities, which were the fundamental social forms of life in the first place. The third dialogue completes the instruction in covenant economics begun in the first with the recitation of the commandments and the negative example of the rich man. Observance of egalitarian economic principles, where no one seeks to become wealthy by taking advantage of others' vulnerability, will result in abundance for all in the community, albeit with no illusions about political realities in the larger world.[18]

The effect of the triad of dialogues in Mark 10:17–31 is like that of the covenant discourse in Q (Luke 6:20–49) as supplemented with the Q discourse about anxiety (Luke 12:2–31). In Q's covenant speech, after announcing that the kingdom of God is being given to the poor, Jesus insists that the poor now engage in mutual sharing of limited resources and social cooperation. Indeed, if they single-mindedly pursue the kingdom of God in that spirit of cooperation, then there will be sufficient food, clothing, and shelter for destitute people. In Mark, after announcing that the kingdom of God is at hand and manifesting its presence in healings and exorcisms, Jesus insists upon observance of egalitarian covenantal economic principles. And that will result in an amazing restoration of households in their village communities.

The egalitarian economic principles Jesus enunciates here, and the Israelite covenantal tradition in which it is rooted, bear a distinct resemblance to what has been called the "moral economy of the peasant," as evident in cross-cultural studies of other peasant societies.[19] "First-world" directors of "development" programs in the "third world" have been baffled that the peasants whom they attempted to motivate to produce higher-yield crops for sale in the world market would decline to cooperate. What was important to them was that each household, each family in their village have at least a subsistence income so that the family could remain a viable member of the village community. Anthropologists studying such peasants found that they held dear certain traditional values and principles apparently designed to promote certain cooperative efforts among the villagers and to protect the viability of each family. The mechanisms designed to make possible the survival of families in ancient Israel, laid out in Leviticus 25 and shorter passages in Exodus and Deuteronomy, would appear to be the ancient Israelite equivalent. Mark 10:17–31 articulates a similar value on the basis of that Israelite tradition of a covenantal "moral economy."

Covenantal Politics

Jesus' third announcement that "the son of man" must be tried and killed serves as preface and foil for his pointed teaching about social-political relations in the community (10:32–34, 35–45). Until now in the episodes in Mark 10, Jesus has been teaching the crowds directly or indirectly through the disciples. The instruction on political relations in the movement is also intended for a broader audience. Mark now has Jesus take the twelve aside and has Jesus' intimates, James and John, pointedly display their contrary political values to highlight his point. Their outrageous request to be seated in positions of rulership and highest honor at Jesus' right and left hands when he comes into his glory borrow the image of imperial rule, as if that is what Jesus' program of the kingdom of God is about. Of course that is not Jesus' agenda, nor does he possess the power to elevate disciples to positions of political preeminence and power. As we learn later in the story, the two who are at Jesus' right and left hands will be the two brigands between whom he is ignominiously crucified. Here the "baptism" and "cup" point precisely to the martyrdom of Jesus for the cause of the kingdom.

Jesus gets to specific instructions about political relations in the movement in 10:42–44. That the point of this passage is the internal politics of the movement is often missed because the sanction on the teaching stated in 10:45 has been so important to Christian faith in Christ's death as a "ransom for many." In Mark's story, however, the saying about "the son of man" giving his life as a ransom is not the point of the episode but functions as a motive clause for the preceding teaching. Substantively, moreover, this motivating sanction on the previous teaching reminds the hearer that the discourse is still squarely within the covenantal tradition. That "the son of man" is to give his life as a "ransom" for many refers to the covenantal mechanisms by which Israelites who had fallen into debt-slavery could be ransomed and their land which had been taken because of indebtedness could be redeemed by the next of kin (Lev. 25:25–28, 47–55).

Jesus presents his political principle for the covenantal community in two steps. He first draws a contrast with the peoples or nations (mentioned as those who will kill him in 10:33–34!). In biblical history and the ancient Near East the rulers and "great ones" of the nations were the high and exalted kings and emperors (cf., e.g., how God will make David into an imperial "great one," 2 Sam. 7:9). Such terms could also refer to the highest royal officers or imperial officials charged with rule over a given area (1 Chron. 27:33; 2 Macc. 8:9). Mark uses unusually strong verbs to draw the contrast. Those "great ones" of the nations lord it over them, tyrannically exercising absolute domination over them (10:42).[20] Such, of course, is the very opposite of Jesus and his movement. The second step again utilizes the form of a covenantal legal principle: "Whoever . . . " "Servant" and "slave" were terms used for anyone who served at the orders of others, including rulers. While "slave" was a term used with reference to chattel slaves in the Greek-speaking area of the Roman empire, it did not necessarily have connotations of chattel slavery in Israelite tradition. The emphasis here in both terms is probably menial service. In these seemingly paradoxical principles Jesus is declaring that not only will there not be rulers, leaders with political-economic power in his movement, but that the leaders will play the role of servants (of others) in the movement. And, in pointed contrast to the faithless behavior of the twelve, Mark presents the women who "followed and served" Jesus as models of service (see 15:40–41; as discussed in chapter 9 below). This final episode in the covenantal charter calls for radically egalitarian political relations within the communities of the movement.

Covenant Renewal in the Rest of Mark's Story

That the sequence of teachings in Mark 10 presents a covenantal charter for the communities of the movement, finally, seems all the more convincing when placed in the context of Mark's overall story. With Jesus' appointment of the twelve, the series of sea crossings, healings, and wilderness feedings, and Jesus' appearance with Moses and Elijah, Mark is clearly portraying Jesus as engaged in a renewal of Israel, as laid out in chapter 5. The recitation of the prophecy of the new exodus at the very beginning of the Gospel indicates that this manifestation of the kingdom of God in the renewal of Israel constitutes that new exodus. Thus, just as covenant follows upon and completes the exodus deliverance in Israelite tradition, so in Mark's story Jesus completes the renewal of Israel in a renewed covenantal charter, with principles of social policy as guidelines for community life.

Once we discern that the sequence of teachings in Mark 10 constitute a covenantal charter, moreover, we become better attuned to its interrelationship with other episodes in Mark's story. Those two prophets, Moses and Elijah, who appear with Jesus on the high mountain just prior to his delivery of covenantal teachings, were in Israelite tradition, respectively, the original mediator of the "Mosaic" covenant and the restorer of Israel's covenantal life directly under the kingship of God in resistance against the oppressive and foreign monarchy of Ahab and Jezebel. Jesus' question to James and John, whether they can be baptized with his baptism, reminds us of John's baptism of repentance for the forgiveness of sins at the very beginning of the story. John's baptism, releasing the people from their sins, brought them a "new lease on life," parallel to Jesus' opening declaration of blessings at the beginning of the covenant discourse in Q (Luke 6:20–22), so that they were ready for renewed covenantal life. The episode of Jesus forgiving the paralytic's sins and his assertion that the son of man has authority to forgive sins, which comes early in the story (Mark 2:2–12), has the same effect of empowering people for entry into renewed covenantal life.

Most striking of all in their interrelation with the covenantal teachings in Mark 10 are the anticipation of covenant renewal in the episode about Jesus' familial community (those who do the will of God) with which Jesus completes his initial campaign of renewal in Galilee (3:19–21, 31–35), and the scribe's assent to the validity of Jesus' covenantal teaching at the end of his confrontation with the rulers (12:28–34). The covenantal character of these episodes merit fuller exploration. The climax of covenant renewal in Mark's story, finally, is its ceremonial renewal at the last supper (14:22–25).

The (Covenantal) Will of God in
Familial Communities (Mark 3:31–35)

Jesus' discussion of his "family" at the completion of his inaugural campaign in Galilee is an important anticipation of the presentation of the covenantal charter later in the story.[21] Mark opens Jesus' campaign for the renewal of Israel with his declaration that the kingdom of God is at hand. Just prior to the "family members" episode, Jesus appoints the twelve as representatives of Israel undergoing renewal and, in the "Beelzebul"episode, argues that the kingdom of God has already prevailed over the defeated kingdom/house of "the strong man." Since the kingdom of God is at hand, it is only appropriate to live the kingdom of God, i.e., to "do the will of God." That doing the will of God is synonymous with living the kingdom of God can be confirmed from the parallel in Matthew's version of the Lord's Prayer, where "Your kingdom come" stands parallel with "Your will be done" (Matt. 6:9–11).

The very formulation of Jesus' concluding pronouncement—"Whoever does the will of God, that one is my brother and sister and mother" (3:35)—indicates clearly that it is yet another statement of covenantal principle, like the similar statements in Mark 10:9, 15, 43–44. The formulation "whoever . . ." is generalized. The pronouncement pertains to anyone in the society who, presumably responding to Jesus' mission, does the will of God. "Doing the will of God" meant observing covenantal commands and teachings in the fundamental social relations and contexts of societal life, the family and village community.

Thus in anticipation of the covenantal "charter" later in the story (Mark 10), the episode that concludes with the covenantal pronouncement about "doing the will of God" also asserts the renewal of covenantal community as a central aspect of the renewal of Israel. Previous interpretations of this episode have often claimed that Jesus is here rejecting his family. But that is an overinterpretation of the rhetorical ploy of Jesus' "mother and brothers standing outside." Neither here nor elsewhere (e.g., 6:1–6) does Mark express hostility to or rejection of family. This episode is not a call to reject one's family in order to follow Jesus on his "way" or to join a new community. Nor is the motivation antisocial or counter-conventional. The emphasis is not individualistic, although the singular "brother," "sister," and "mother" make it personal. And the true family members are not spiritual, as opposed to this-worldly. The contrast between the crowd that "came together" and was "seated around him" and Jesus' own family, "his mother and his brothers standing outside," is simply a rhetorical ploy that sets up Jesus' pronouncement of the covenantal principle. Mark's Jesus is here calling people to do the will of God in ordinary social interaction in community life; that is the point.

Far from being anti-family or replacing the family, the principle of doing the will of God, which constitutes people "brothers and sisters and mothers," extends kinship relations to the whole community. Members of popular movements often use such kinship terms for each other, implying a mutual solidarity, attachment, and care similar to those of family—without necessarily implying that they have all left their families of origin and formed a new, replacement "family." Kinship relations provide the very foundation of traditional agrarian social relations. The loyalty and mutual care of kin traditionally provide social and economic protection for individuals and families. Under intense pressure from outside forces that caused disintegration in village communities, however, kin loyalty might both fail to protect and stand in the way of needed local cooperation. But if people in the communities of Jesus' movement understood themselves as brothers and sisters and mothers to each other, they might take care of each other with the same sense of responsibility that families traditionally exercised. And, of course, if some families had disintegrated to the point of leaving some people isolated, the larger community could function as the supportive "family"—precisely the sort of supportive functions that traditional Mosaic covenantal teaching advocates. The effect of the principle would have been to reinforce both inclusiveness in the movement and mutual cooperation in local community relations.

In the prominent pronouncement about "doing the will of God" by constituting his followers as his mother and sister and brother, Mark's Jesus is calling people to operate as familial communities in caring for those left vulnerable by the disintegration of families and village communities under increasing economic pressures from multiple layers of rulers. He is advocating mutually supportive relations among his followers as familial local communities that would provide family-like support for their vulnerable members. This concern can be seen again later in the story, in the repeated attention to children (9:36–37; 10:13–16). It is pertinent to note, insofar as Mark's story is addressed to an imperially subjected people, that mutually supporting familial community often emerges in movements among colonized and subjected peoples, such as African American communities in the rural southern United States, where orphans are taken into extended families.

A Scribe's Confirmation of Jesus' Covenantal Teaching (Mark 12:28–34)

In addition to flowing directly out of the narrative of Jesus' renewal of Israel, the Markan covenantal "charter" (Mark 10) stands in narrative as well as substantive opposition to the ostensible rulers of Israel in Jerusalem. Mark pointedly has Jesus present the covenantal charter for the village communities of renewed Israel during his journey through Judea, immediately before he enters Jerusalem, where he will pronounce God's condemnation of the Temple, its rulers, and scribal staff in prophetic demonstration and prophetic parable. Correspondingly, the central principles of Mark's renewed covenant stand in stark opposition to everything the Jerusalem Temple stands for: "smooth interpretation" of Israelite tradition on fundamental matters such as marriage, wealthy men who cannot possibly enter the kingdom of God, and "great ones" who lord it over the people.

Jesus' response to a scribe's question about which commandment is the greatest forms the climax of his extended confrontation with the rulers that begins with his prophetic demonstration in the Temple and proceeds through a whole series of conflict episodes. The scribe acknowledges that Jesus' statement of the greatest commandment as not only loving God but also loving neighbor "is much more important than all whole burnt offerings and sacrifices." That acknowledgment constitutes a confirmation by the hostile elite of the basis on which Jesus has been attacking the rulers and their scribal and Pharisaic representatives throughout the story.

Taken out of the context of Mark's overall story, this episode has been interpreted to imply that at least one scribe and Jesus have come to basic agreement. If heard in its narrative context, however, this episode makes no suggestion of rapprochement between Jesus and the scribes. The scribe's question to Jesus is no less antagonistic than that of the Sadducees in the previous episode or that of the Pharisees when they were "testing him," where the same verb is used (12:28; cf. 12:18 and 10:2). Indeed, the scribe does not approach him even with mock respect, as did the Pharisees and Herodians in their attempt to entrap him. Only after Jesus has answered "well" does the scribe address him with respect. The summary statement at the end, "after that no one dared to ask him any question," indicates that Jesus had decisively confuted this scribe just as he had the chief priests, the Pharisees and Herodians, and the Sadducees in the previous episodes. Immediately following this episode, moreover, Jesus turns from direct confrontation with the chief priests, scribes, etc., to address the crowd. And, in sequence, he confutes the scribes' understanding of the messiah, condemns the scribes for "devouring widows' houses," as exemplified in the widow's giving away her whole living to the Temple, and finally declares that the Temple, in which the scribes are based and which they support by exploiting such widows, is to be destroyed (by God).

The hearer of this episode must be struck by the asymmetry, the difference between the scribe's question and Jesus' reply. The scribe, serving as the foil for Jesus to score his final summary point in the whole series of disputes, asks, "Which commandment is the first of all?" Jesus begins his answer with what the scribe himself would surely answer, citing the *Shema*, the basic Israelite confession of faith in the one God and the fundamental commandment of intensive exclusive loyalty to the one God (known in our biblical text in Deut. 6:4–5). But Jesus immediately proceeds to a second commandment, "love your neighbor," and then binds them closely together so that they are inseparable as well as incomparable. Jesus is pointedly going beyond the scribe's question and expectation by adding "love your neighbor," on which he is thereby clearly placing the emphasis. Moreover, by adding the command "love your neighbor" (known in our biblical text in Lev. 19:18) to the fundamental Israelite confession of faith and commandment to "love God," Mark's Jesus is making a bold innovation by comparison with contemporary Judean literature. Hellenistic moral philosophy sometimes linked justice toward people with piety toward the gods in abstract ways. But not even Hellenistic Jewish literature attests this close attachment of "love God" and "love your neighbor."

As in the conflicts with the scribes and Pharisees earlier in the story, Jesus appears to be rooted in and defending the Israelite popular tradition, not "quoting" from the written texts of the great tradition. In both the first commandment about loving God and the second one about loving one's neighbor, Jesus' recitation differs from the texts known from biblical manuscripts. More significant substantively, Jesus is juxtaposing two different commandments that are widely separated in the scripture of the Jerusalem great tradition, Deuteronomy 6:4–5 and Leviticus 19:18. While the Mosaic covenant itself structurally holds the commandments pertaining to exclusive loyalty to God together with the commandments pertaining to social justice and equality (see, e.g., Exod. 20:3–11, 12–17 and Deut. 5:7–15, 16–21), it is curious that the subsequent layers of covenantal teachings edited by earlier generations of Jerusalem priests and scribes do not appear to hold these two together explicitly in the structure of the literature they produced (e.g., the books of Leviticus and Deuteronomy).

Given their own political-economic interests, however, as illustrated in previous prophetic oracles that clearly defend the covenantal rights of the peasantry against rulers' exploitation, villagers rooted in the Israelite popular tradition would almost certainly have known the traditional direct application and fundamental meaning of "love your neighbor." It pertained to the protection of the peasants' fundamental economic needs and rights. This is evident even in the scriptures of the Jerusalem great tradition, as indicated in the literary context where the principle "love your enemy as yourself" occurs. It functions there as the summary of a whole series of Mosaic covenantal injunctions to leave crops in the field for the poor to glean at harvest time, not to steal or deal falsely, not to oppress the neighbor, not to do injustice, and not to slander or witness against the neighbor (Lev. 19:9–18).

But these injustices in violation of the Mosaic covenantal commandments are precisely what Jesus accuses the Temple rulers and their representatives of practicing almost systematically. So Jesus' addition of the second commandment inseparably linked with the first is "loaded." It pronounces again the standard by which the Temple and its representatives are being found wanting in Jesus' prophetic indictments and condemnation. The scribe's response then functions as the confirmation of Jesus' prophetic condemnation by a member of the establishment. "You are right. To love God . . . and to love one's neighbor . . . is much more important than all whole burnt offerings and sacrifices!" That is, loving God *and* loving neighbor is more important than the operations of the Temple system! Jesus had him. The scribe had to acknowledge he was right. This episode in which a scribe confirms the validity of Jesus' covenantal teaching thus summarizes the whole sequence of disputes in Jesus' confrontation with the rulers in the Temple and sets up his subsequent pronouncement that the Temple would be destroyed.

Ceremonial Renewal of the Covenant in the Last Supper (Mark 14:22–25)

Jesus' question whether James and John can drink the cup he drinks, finally, leads forward in the Gospel to the "last supper." Just as Moses, after leading the original liberation from oppressive rule in Egypt, officiated at the original covenant-making ceremony, so Jesus, after spearheading a new exodus, presides over the ceremony of the renewed covenant. After building an altar with twelve pillars and dashing half of the blood of the sacrificed oxen against it, Moses read the book of the covenant to the people and, after they vowed obedience, threw the other half of the blood over the people: "See the blood of the covenant that the LORD has made with you" (Exod. 24:3–8). Similarly, at a Passover meal with the twelve, previously appointed as representatives of the renewed Israel, having already declared the covenant charter, Jesus presents the cup to them as "my blood of the covenant which is poured out for many."

In summary, Mark's Gospel tells the story of a renewed Mosaic covenant as well as a new exodus. If we have ears to hear, the story includes repeated references and allusions to the Mosaic covenant as the basis of the people's life. In his conflicts with the scribes and Pharisees in particular, Jesus repeatedly insists upon the basic covenantal commandments of God as the basis for the people's common life. Most programmatically in the sequence of teachings just before he marches up to Jerusalem to confront the ruling circles, Jesus delivers what is in effect a renewed covenantal "charter" that lays down teaching on the fundamental matters of marriage and family, economic relations, and the political relations in his movement. In anticipation of that more elaborate covenantal teaching Jesus insisted that his followers constitute supportive familial communities. And at the end of his confrontation with the ruling circles in Jerusalem, a scribe confirms the validity of Jesus' covenantal teaching, which is the basis of his condemnation of the Temple and its incumbent rulers. In a final affirmation, Jesus solemnizes the renewed covenant in the Passover meal that constitutes his last supper with the twelve, representatives of Israel: "This is my blood of the covenant, which is poured out for many."

9

Women as Representative
and Exemplary

We still have not managed to get the whole story—even after we have gained a clear sense of the dominant conflict in Mark's Gospel. We must still come to grips with a subplot of the overall story that stands pointedly juxtaposed with the subplot focused on the twelve disciples. Just as Mark portrays the twelve, particularly the three intimates of Jesus, as negative examples of "following" Jesus, so Mark portrays women in the story as both representatives of renewal and positive paradigms of faithfully responding to and "following" Jesus. These juxtaposed subplots, moreover, unfold in dramatically opposite ways. Peter, James, John, and the rest of the twelve start out at the head of the renewal movement Jesus is building—called to "follow," explicitly appointed as representatives of Israel-in-renewal, and commissioned for mission by Jesus himself—then misunderstand and resist Jesus' agenda and, after finally betraying, abandoning, and denying Jesus, disappear from the story. Women, on the other hand, almost completely absent at the beginning, suddenly appear as representatives of Israel undergoing renewal, then take initiative in relation to Jesus—forcing expansion of his agenda and prophetically "anointing" him— and at the climax of the story appear prominently as the only figures who have faithfully persisted in "following" and "serving."

Until recently, interpreters (mainly males) tended to downplay and even to denigrate women in Mark and other New Testament literature. It required the emergence of women in scholarly interpretive communities to call attention to what went unnoticed and unchallenged: Not only were women among the crowds and wider circles of disciples following Jesus in Mark's story (14:41), but they played significant roles in the leadership of the community behind the Gospel (e.g., the woman who anointed Jesus, 14:3–9).[1] The importance of that breakthrough, of recognizing that women were important in the Gospel and the Jesus movement(s), however, may have been somewhat blunted by a continuing tendency to absorb the women in Mark's story into the dominant "discipleship" reading.

At first glance, Mark seems to portray women as subordinate and inferior. Typical of literature produced by and focused on men and presupposing men as the primary agents in social life, Mark even renders women and their roles invisible at points, such as the meal that Jesus and his (male) disciples have with "toll-collectors and sinners" (2:13–17). Mark confines women to the private domestic sphere of the home, having both the synagogue leader's and the Syrophoenician woman's daughters healed in their houses.[2] To be more precise, in a story that reflects a traditional agrarian society, in which the fundamental social form was the patrilineal male-headed household, women appear as wives and daughters subordinate to the dominant husbands and fathers. The synagogue leader, who also heads a family, takes the initiative in seeking help for his helpless daughter (5:21–24). Women are identified not by their own name, but by their relationship to males, whether father, husband, son, or son-in-law.

Yet Mark's story seems to break with the traditional patriarchal, androcentric pattern at significant points. The hemorrhaging woman not only appears in the public sphere but boldly approaches and even touches Jesus. The Syrophoenician woman, like the head-of-household leader of the assembly, not only takes initiative vis-à-vis the male protagonist of the story, but takes initiative on behalf of her helpless daughter. Several other women also appear in the story without association with or identification by male head of household (e.g., the hemorrhaging woman, the woman who anoints Jesus, Mary Magdalene). It may seem a significant androcentric feature in Mark at first glance that most women appearing in the story are nameless figures. Yet except for the twelve, the same is true of men in the story (e.g., eight of nine male figures in healings and exorcisms, except Bartimaeus).[3] Especially striking in contrast to patriarchal patterns typical of traditional narratives is that Jesus' own family, used as a paradigm or analogy for the Jesus movement in Mark (3:31–35; 6:1–3), pointedly lacks a patriarch.

That Mark's story both exemplifies and yet breaks with patterns typical of traditional patriarchal narratives must be considered in connection with its representation of and address to subordinated "third-world" people (discussed in chapter 2) in devising an appropriate feminist approach. A simple contrast of the abstraction "woman" with the modern Western abstraction "man" will likely fail to come to grips with the "colonial" or "imperial" differences as well as the historical differences between Mark's story and its modern Western readers. (Mark's story, moreover, does not directly address modern Western women any more than it directly addresses modern Western men.) Gender must be considered together with imperial-colonial (and racial and class) power relations as interrelated analytical categories.[4] The notion of gender and analysis of the interaction of men and women must be historicized in relation to Mark's context and particularized with regard to Mark's story.[5]

With regard to Mark and other early New Testament literature in particular, analysis of the gender roles and relations must free itself from the distorting residue of Christian anti-Judaism that persists even in recent feminist interpretation. The desire to construct a Jesus (or a Mark) who is liberative of women has resulted in uncritical perpetuation of an older Christian construction of "Judaism" or "Jewish society" obsessed with purity codes that were supposedly restrictive and even punitive of women. That construction, however, is an unhistorical essentialist generalization on the basis of decontextualized texts. Recent critical investigations of ancient Jewish texts are now available to counter previous anti-Jewish readings.

Most analysis of women in Mark's Gospel to date has focused on particular women and individual episodes. The individualistic orientation implicit in such treatments misses both the corporate context and implications of the episodes and their narrative function in the overall story. In keeping with our attempt to deal with the story as a whole it seems more appropriate to discern how all of those episodes form a subplot focused on women and to analyze how that subplot functions in relation to the dominant plot and the subplot focused on the twelve. It may help first to take an overview of the women subplot before then delving more deeply into particular episodes. Then in relation to the results of that analysis we can examine how other episodes that deal with the relations of women and men fit with the women subplot and the dominant plot.

The Plotting of Women in Mark's Story

That the plotting of women in Mark's narrative is crucial in the overall story does not become clear until the climax of the story. Only at the end of the crucifixion scene does the narrator finally state explicitly that "Mary Magdalene, and Mary the mother of James the younger and of Joses, and Salome used to follow him and serve him when he was in Galilee; and there were many other women who had come up with him to Jerusalem" (15:40–41). If not before, then surely after that statement, the hearers would realize that Mark includes the women among Jesus' followers or disciples. Now, moreover, the hearers would recognize that Mark is presenting these women as the paradigms of "following" and witnessing to Jesus—in pointed contrast to the twelve, who by this time in the story have proven utterly incapable of following. Modern readers may still be missing the narrative signals simply because some standard translations submerge the prominent roles of women in the story, suggesting that the women's service was merely the typical domestic "women's" role of "waiting on" or "providing for" Jesus.

In the first main step of the story, women seem insignificant and subservient to Jesus and his male disciples. After Jesus announces that "the kingdom of God is at hand"—the theme of the story—he calls the four most important figures among the twelve in the first action. Then he performs his first exorcism, highlighting how he works with power/authority, in contrast to the scribes. His first healing, of Simon's nameless mother-in-law (1:29–31), is almost inconspicuous, overshadowed by that dramatic first exorcism. Indeed the scene of her healing is almost immediately overwhelmed by the townspeople bringing the sick and demon-possessed to Jesus for healing and exorcism at the door of the house. Only later might hearers/readers realize how significant it is that as soon as she was healed, "she began to serve/minister to them," just as the "messengers/angels" had "served/ministered to" Jesus in the wilderness (1:13, 31). Thereafter Jesus heals four more men before Mark narrates another healing of a woman. Meanwhile, the apparently all-male disciples have accompanied Jesus in his conflicts with the scribes and Pharisees and Jesus has appointed the twelve to be with him and to assist in his program of preaching and exorcism and disclosed to them the "mystery of the kingdom" (2:1–3:6; 3:13–19; 4:10–11).

The next woman in the story appears almost indirectly, as the "little daughter" of a male head of household who appeals to Jesus to make her well. The listeners, however, have been alerted by the first sea crossing and the dramatic exorcism and destruction of the demonic forces of "Legion," in addition to the appointment of the twelve, that a Moses-Elijah-like renewal of Israel is underway in Jesus' actions. Thus when the hemorrhaging woman is said to have been suffering "for twelve years" and the synagogue leader's daughter is noted to be "twelve years of age," it could not be clearer that these women, while individual women, have greater significance in the story: they symbolize Israel itself, the people who are experiencing restoration and renewal in just such acts of healing by Jesus. The episode of the hemorrhaging woman, moreover, is strikingly different from other healings in Mark's story because the woman herself takes the initiative throughout, with Jesus finding out only later what had just happened. In his closing pronouncement, "Daughter, your faith has made you well," he declares her to be the paradigm of faith, of trust in Jesus' manifestation of the kingdom and of taking aggressive action to effect the restoration of Israel now underway.

Just as intertwined episodes of the two women's healing appear in the first series of miracle episodes, so an exorcism of a girl appears in the second series. Her mother, however, a "Greek of Syrophoenician origin," must insist that

Jesus reach out to her daughter. Her argument in reply to his insulting statement that "it is not fair to take the children's [Israelites'] food and throw it to
the dogs [non-Israelite peoples]" persuades him to exorcize her daughter. The
Syrophoenician woman thus becomes the only person in Mark's story in which
someone bests Jesus in debate.

While the twelve-year-old woman and the hemorrhaging woman are thus
appearing as representatives of Israel undergoing renewal and the
Syrophoenician woman forces Jesus to expand the renewal to non-Israelites,
the twelve who had earlier been called and appointed are commissioned to
share in Jesus' program of renewal. But they also succumb to fear and misunderstand what Jesus is doing in the wilderness feeding, which flabbergasts
Jesus.

Women then disappear from the story during the middle section in which
Jesus explains that he must suffer, die, and be raised, while the twelve disciples
resist the implications in their stubborn misunderstanding of Jesus' overall
program of renewal. In this section, however, Jesus does give teaching on marriage and divorce, uses children as paradigms of "receiving the kingdom," and
declares that those who would be leaders must serve or minister to others, all
of which are pertinent to the relative relations of women in the renewal of the
social order.

Similarly, in Jesus' face-off with the rulers and ruling institutions in Jerusalem, women are absent from the story, except for the implications of his
debate with the Sadducees. Only in the final episode of this section of the story
does a woman appear, the widow who gives the last "coppers" of her "house"
or "living." Her giving away the last pittance of her resources to the Temple,
however, is not held up as a positive example. It functions rather as an illustration of how the scribes are so unrelenting and unscrupulous in their efforts
to maintain high levels of giving to the Temple that they "devour widows'
houses." In Israelite tradition, of course, widows were the very epitome of the
poor, helpless before the predatory wealthy and powerful. The episode of the
widow therefore becomes the final explanation of why the Temple, the high
priests, and the scribes all stand under God's judgment, as the story of Jesus'
renewal of Israel moves to its climax.

At the beginning of the climactic events in Jerusalem, as the high priests are
forming their plot to apprehend Jesus surreptitiously, a woman interrupts
Jesus at table and anoints his head with costly ointment of nard. "Some" in the
room object. But Jesus praises her action as "a good service for me, . . . she has
anointed my body beforehand for burial." The hearers of the story, who would
have been thoroughly familiar with Israelite tradition, recognize immediately
that this woman's action, which will be told "in remembrance of her," is that
of a prophet in anointing (literally "messiah-ing" or "christ-ing") the figure

designated by God to head/lead Israel. The immediate juxtaposition of this woman's action with Judas' betrayal of Jesus (for money) and its contrast with Jesus' announcement at his celebration of the Passover meal that the rest of the twelve will abandon and deny him could not be more pointed. And at the very end of the story, after the twelve do in fact betray, abandon, and deny Jesus, the three women come to the fore. They are the only ones who still follow Jesus, standing at a distance at the crucifixion, taking note of where Jesus' body was buried, and then coming to the tomb, where they are the only witnesses of the empty tomb and the only ones who hear the message that Jesus will meet them back in Galilee. In Mark's startlingly abrupt ending they "said nothing to anyone because they were afraid." The hearers, of course, know that they eventually did tell the story—or it could not be retold—including "to the disciples and Peter." But the latter had apparently remained in Jerusalem and not gone to Galilee. These three women, who "used to follow him and ministered to him when he was in Galilee," are the only figures in the story who remain faithful to the end and provide the bridge to the continuation of the movement in Galilee and beyond as well as constituting the paradigm of faithfulness in the continuing movement.

Women as Representative Figures

With the overall subplot of women in mind, we should take a much closer look at the episodes of individual women for the important functions they carry in Mark's story. This will help us discern just how centrally the women subplot operates in Mark's Gospel.

The Hemorrhaging Woman and the Daughter of the Assembly Leader (Mark 5:21–43)

The importance of the woman who had been hemorrhaging for twelve years and the twelve-year-old woman who was almost dead just as she reached the age of childbearing has been obscured in recent interpretation. Indeed, by setting Jesus in opposition to "Judaism," Christian theological interpretation has not only blocked recognition of important aspects of Mark's story; it has imposed some highly distorting false issues onto these episodes and the significance of these women. It is important to dispense with these distorting false issues in order to clear the way for a fresh hearing of these intertwined episodes.

The hemorrhaging woman is portrayed as severely stigmatized and ostracized in Jewish society. In a serious misunderstanding of the purity regulations of Leviticus 15:19–30, her bleeding, understood as menstrual discharge, is said to have "isolated her socially from friends and kin. . . . Her illness, then, has placed her outside the religious community and the honorable human community, . . . a social death [comparable to] the actual death of the twelve-year-old daughter of Jairus."[6] In "a Jewish context" the "permanent uncleanness" of her bleeding also supposedly "polluted" anything and anyone with whom she came in contact, "a violation of religious law." Since she had ostensibly died, the corpse of the twelve-year-old woman is also presumed to have been a source of pollution to anyone who touched her (cf. Num. 19:11–13). "Any physical contact with these women should render Jesus unclean." According to this line of interpretation, fearlessly risking pollution, Jesus restores the women to purity and reinstates them in the social and religious community that is now "whole, inclusive, and without boundaries."[7]

Far from being distinctive to ancient Jewish society, "purity codes" appear in most ancient societies. It is simply assumed that "people will contract impurity as a matter of course." But "impurity is not prohibited, and being impure implies no moral censure."[8] In ancient Jewish society impurity was a condition vis-à-vis the Temple and sacred rituals in which both men and women found themselves most of the time. Far from placing emphasis on women being specially stigmatized, "the biblical record as a whole shows much greater concern over the potential desecration of the sacred by an ejaculant than by a menstruant."[9] In the legislation of Leviticus 15:19–30 on women's menstrual discharge, a woman is neither inhumanly restricted nor socially ostracized. Indeed the rulings regarding her bedding and what she sits on suggest that her hands do not transmit impurity and indicate that she is not socially ostracized, not excluded from her home and most normal social interactions in household and village. Moreover, "there is no unambiguous evidence from the Mishna, Josephus, the Gospels, etc., that Jewish groups in Hellenistic and Early Roman times removed the menstruant or one suffering from abnormal vaginal or uterine bleeding from social contact."[10]

In fact, if we listen carefully, the intertwined episodes of the twelve-year-old woman and the hemorrhaging woman contain no suggestion whatever of impurity. The episode of the hemorrhaging woman gives no indication that the purity codes known through Leviticus 15 were in mind.[11] Nor does the episode of the twelve-year-old woman give any hint that corpse uncleanness was at issue. Thus Mark's intertwined episodes make no suggestion that in healing the two women Jesus overcame any purity codes or broke with Israelite tradition. "The ritual purity that would be lost by touching a corpse or touching a menstruant was required only for participation in the Temple in Jerusalem" and these episodes are faraway, in Galilee.[12] The scribes and Pharisees, usually understood as official guardians of the purity codes, moreover, are far from the scene, having been left behind after accusing Jesus of colluding with Beelzebul, and they are not to reappear again until they accuse Jesus' disciples of not washing their hands before eating (3:22–30; 7:1–4).

We can now listen again, without the false issue of the purity codes, to the interwoven episodes of the two women. Immediately audible is how different the hemorrhaging woman's healing sounds in comparison with other healings in Mark's story. These episodes all appear to unfold in three steps with some variation in standard motifs within each step: The person to be healed comes into the presence of Jesus and makes a request, and/or the illness is described; then with an utterance or a gesture Jesus heals the person; finally the onlookers display astonishment, the healed person is dismissed, and the healer's fame is spread.[13] First of all, the description of the prolonged severity of the woman's situation is by far the most elaborate among the healing episodes in Mark: . . . for twelve years, . . . many physicians, . . . spent all she had, . . . no better but grew worse! (in a long series of participial phrases, 5:25–27). Second, although in other episodes the person seeking to be healed, or her/his friends or relatives, take initiative (e.g., lowering the paralytic through the roof, 2:2–4), the hemorrhaging woman is the sole actor taking initiative in her healing. Although she "came up behind him in the crowd," she is neither hesitant nor secretive, but takes bold, deliberate action. Most striking is that her healing is attributed not to Jesus but to her own aggressive action. The narrator even comments explicitly how "the woman herself prescribes touching as the means of her healing":[14] "for she said, 'If I but touch his clothes, I will be made well.'" And sure enough: "Immediately her hemorrhage stopped; and she felt in her body that she was healed of her disease." That is, instead of the healing being confirmed by others, it is attested by her own experience. In all the other healing episodes, Jesus either utters some statement or makes some gesture of healing (and Matthew has Jesus speak before the woman is healed, Matt. 13:21–22). In this one he is utterly passive, while the initiative, action, and confirmation are all by the woman. Jesus himself, although aware that "power had gone forth from him," is not aware that the woman had been healed. It is by the woman's initiative, again, that he learns of it. And then, in the final motif of the episode, he simply confirms what she already knows: that it is her own faith that has made her well (cf. the difference in 2:5; the similarity in 10:52). The hemorrhaging woman's faith-driven action summons hearers "to take heart, to refuse despair, and to act," for themselves and for each other.[15]

In contrast to the way in which most interpreters represent Jesus the healer in the stance of benign paternal sovereignty—which might well be suggested by his addressing the woman as "Daughter"—the hemorrhaging woman's "courageous work" is solely responsible for the healing in this episode. Jesus participates in the unexpected new power, but it is not his alone. Restorative, healing power becomes operative in this episode by the initiative and aggressive action of one perceived as weak who reveals the divine way of power.[16] Indeed, without the trusting, faithful action of people such as the hemorrhaging woman, the power operative in Jesus is unable to become effective, as the episode in his hometown indicates (6:1–3). The episode of the hemorrhaging woman, more than any other, reveals that, while mediated through Jesus, divine healing power is relational in its operation. Healing is not produced by Jesus' action (alone), but through the woman's faith that divine power will work through Jesus.

The twelve-year-old woman is as passive as the hemorrhaging woman is active. Yet the two women, whose stories interpret each other, are similar. The younger is near death and later assumed to be dead and the older is also near death, not "socially dead" because of the supposed pollution of her discharge, but bleeding to death. They are also similar in social status. Both have been mistaken as wealthy or belonging to a powerful family. Nothing in the characterization of the older woman, however, indicates that she at one point had "money." The misapprehension about the father of the younger woman was simply the result of a misunderstanding by translators of both "synagogue" and what being "one of the heads of a synagogue" meant. As mentioned above, the term *synagōgē* in Mark's story refers to a local village assembly, not "the synagogue" as a synonym for "Judaism." And an *archisynagōgos* was thus not a Jewish "ruler" (cf. Matt. 9:18) but a leader of a local Galilean village assembly, a community leader, but not wealthy or powerful. The twelve-year-old's father is thus not a representative of the elite. Mark, in contrast to Matthew (9:18), does not portray a Jewish "ruler" falling at Jesus' feet. Thus Mark's story is not, "by juxtaposing the two extremes of the Jewish social scale," advocating a new social order in which a young noblewoman is snatched from death even as an lowly outcast is liberated.[17] Both women are villagers and, while the younger is still in the household of her father, both are in desperate condition, their life ebbing or having ebbed away.

The most striking similarity between the two women, of course, is the symbolic number twelve, the one being twelve years of age, which is mentioned pointedly at the close of the episode, and the other having been bleeding for the whole lifetime of the younger woman, which is now apparently ended. These women are surely representative figures—as suggested also in the hemorrhaging woman's demonstration that the operation of restorative healing power is relational—and that in a double sense. They represent other women whose life circumstances and illness are similar. They are typical of peasant women involved in the Jesus movement and addressed in the Gospel.[18] Insofar as they represent other women in similar circumstances, moreover, they represent the whole society, Israel. Just as the Twelve are appointed as representatives of Israel undergoing renewal and twelve baskets of leftover fragments are gathered from the great feeding of Israel in the wilderness (3:13–19; 6:30–44), the twelve-year-old woman now near death, whose father is "one of the leaders of the synagogue" (local assembly of Israelites), and the other woman's twelve years of bleeding represent (the twelve tribes of) Israel in desperate condition. And their respective healings by aggressive action out of faith and restoration to life by Jesus represent the new life of Israel.

We might even hear connotations of the hemorrhaging woman as representative of Israel being bled to death by the oppressive circumstances in which she is caught—particularly insofar as this episode follows immediately on the symbolic exorcism and destruction of the alien force named "Legion" (occupying Roman troops). Her trusting response to the powers working through Jesus, representative of the people's response in faith to Jesus' manifestation of the kingdom, is what effects her restoration. And we might even hear connotations of the twelve-year-old woman near death just as she was coming through puberty into childbearing age as representative of the people Israel near death. In being restored to life by Jesus she was representative of a dying Israel being restored to life and ready to bear the fruit of new life of, and in, Israel. It almost goes without saying that these two women can be representative and symbolic of Israel only *as women*. "The social aspect of the story can only make sense if the women are specifically understood in their femaleness under patriarchy. . . . The hemorrhaging woman regarded, not in some essential humanness, but in her historical particularity *as a woman*, represents the radical implications."[19]

The Syrophoenician Woman (Mark 7:24–30)

Like the hemorrhaging woman and the twelve-year-old woman, the Syrophoenician woman is a representative figure, only of non-Israelites who want to participate in the renewing power of the kingdom of God manifested in Jesus and in the renewal of Israel as well. She is pointedly described as a "Greek" as well as a Syrophoenician, indicating that she was culturally Greek (in language, etc.) as well as ethnically Syrian, as were most of the people living in areas around Galilee. If the village population in "the region of Tyre" were of mixed ethnic background, some possibly of Israelite extraction, the explicit identification of the woman makes all the more sense. The NRSV paraphrase (substitution of) "a Gentile" for "a Greek" is a misleading imposition of a (later) Christian and Jewish dichotomy between "Jew" and "Gentile" as essentialist markers of religious-ethnic identity.[20] In a frontier area of mixed cultural as well as ethnic background, the Greek text specifies both. For villagers in a mixed frontier area, ethnic differences were much less important than they were for the scribes and Pharisees, whose societal role it was to maintain the ethnic-religious-cultural traditions and boundaries of their people over against the dominant culture and political-economic pressures. In certain circumstances ethnic strife might erupt as the Roman rulers engaged in "divide and conquer" strategies, as with the ongoing conflicts between Judeans and Samaritans. Given the lack of pertinent source material, it is difficult to know whether and to what degree cultural (linguistic, etc.) differences would be the source of tensions and conflict among villagers in such ethnically and culturally mixed or frontier areas. We have the impression that many indigenous peoples in Syria had assimilated Greek language, hence might have been identified by others as "Greek" in culture generally.

From the viewpoint of the Jesus movement's origins in Israelite Galilee, the "Greek woman of Syrophoenician origin" is a double outsider, culturally and ethnically (with the religious dimension included in those categories, not a separate one).[21] In Mark's story, however, she may be a representative of the non-Israelite peoples who have become included in the movement. Thus she may well represent the insiders. The situation is complicated, however, and that is the important issue this episode deals with. For in joining the movement, the Markan "insiders" who were ethnically and culturally "outsiders" to Israel identified with Israelite history and cultural heritage. Their identity, like the identities of many "postcolonial" people today, is hybrid. So they know that, in Paul's terms, they have become grafted into the trunk of the Israelite historical-cultural tree. The "Greek Syrophoenician woman" is representative of them, their participation in the Markan Jesus movement, and their interests.[22]

The most important aspect of the "Greek Syrophoenician's" identity, however, is that she is a woman, in particular a "marginalized" woman. In that also she may be a representative figure. In a traditional patriarchal society, women are ordinarily connected with and identified not as individuals, but as family members under the authority of their fathers or husbands—or in the absence of both, the nearest male relative, such as a son or a son-in-law. There was no place, no role, for a woman outside of the patriarchal family, the fundamental social form of such a society. In Mark's story, however, only the twelve-year-old woman fits the dominant pattern, being identified in terms of her father, one of the leaders of a local assembly. The first woman Jesus healed was identified by her son-in-law, Simon. Other women, such as the hemorrhaging woman, in Mark's story are striking for being alone, not attached to any male head of household. The Syrophoenician woman, similarly, appears without husband or son. Is she a widow or divorced?[23] All she has is a "little daughter." And that the daughter is demon-possessed is yet another indication that hers is not a stable patriarchal family. In brief, the Syrophoenician woman has (to use a badly overused term) become "marginalized": she is a desperate, poor, widowed or divorced woman alone in the world with a possessed daughter. Precisely in those respects, however, she is a representative figure, representative of people who were in or threatened with such circumstances.

The Syrophoenician woman seems either boldly aggressive or humbly acquiescent, depending on how the episode is heard. Certainly she was viewed as overly bold (for a woman and/or a non-Israelite) by both Matthew and other transmitters of Mark' story. In the textual transmission of the story, some of the latter attempted to make her appear more submissive by inserting "Yes" into her reply to Jesus (this is the only occurrence of "yes" in Mark and it is missing from important early manuscripts such as papyrus 45).[24] Matthew blunts her boldness in Mark by having Jesus add, "I was sent only to the lost sheep of the house of Israel." Matthew also inserts the disciples' attempt to get rid of her, deepens Jesus' rejection, and stresses her faith rather than her persuasive argument.[25] Without those touches blunting her approach, the woman takes the initiative as an aggressive protagonist, first as a woman intruding upon and interrupting a popular male leader, but particularly in firing right back at his rejection of her request with an insulting put-down. On the other hand, her response, which seems aggressive in style, appears acquiescent in substance. Far from challenging Jesus' ethnic rejection or subordination, she settles for "crumbs" and "second-class citizenship" which she has internalized, "like a dog who is grateful even when kicked."[26]

Whether this woman appears as bold or submissive, therefore, depends on how we understand the substance of her challenge to Jesus and his response. Nearly all interpretations of this episode have been carried out from the retrospective viewpoint of equality of Jews and Gentiles in the church(es) and the eventual Gentile Christian cooptation of the Israelite heritage, including the Bible in Greek as the "Old Testament." It is informative, perhaps, to recall that the apostle to the Gentiles, Paul himself, thought of the peoples among whom he formed "assemblies" of the movement as "wild shoots" that had been grafted into the main trunk of Israel. No matter how independent the course he had taken in his mission to the non-Israelite peoples, he felt a need to get the approval of the "pillars" in Jerusalem and to deliver his collection for the saints in Jerusalem as an offering from the peoples. In modern times, other American nations looked to the United States as the leader and paradigm of "democracy" and "freedom" (for better or worse) and the socialist parties in some countries looked to the communist party of the Soviet Union or China as international leader (for better or worse). If the Jesus movement represented by Mark's story were comprised of communities of non-Israelite peoples who had joined a movement of renewal of Israel, which is what it purports to be throughout the Gospel, then perhaps their relationship was one of following and, in effect, subordination to the fulfillment of Israel. Israelites (Jews) first and then other peoples, to paraphrase Paul from a different but perhaps parallel branch of the movement.

Here then would be the point of this episode, or, more precisely, of how it ends. What Jesus says in rejecting the Syrophoenician woman's request is a statement of clear subordination, based in what appears to be an ethnic slur: "Let the children (Israelites) be fed first, for it is not fair to take the children's food and give it to the dogs (non-Israelites)." But the woman shoots right back at him, "Sir, even the little dogs (puppies) under the table eat the little children's crumbs." Not only does the woman "humor" Jesus to get what she wants, but she wins the debate and he acknowledges it: "For that retort, you may go—the demon has left your daughter." She "had him" and he knew it. She is vindicated because of, not in spite of, her assertive behavior.[27] And she is vindicated because of her argument insisting that societal renewal in the kingdom should include non-Israelites.

This episode, like others, must be understood in the context of the flow of Mark's story. Jesus has already expanded the movement to include non-Israelites, preaching and exorcizing in areas surrounding Galilee (e.g., where the Gerasene demoniac lived and "the region around Tyre and Sidon"). The healing that immediately follows takes place in the Decapolis, and the second wilderness feeding of non-Israelites takes place immediately afterward. Indeed, the wording of Jesus' parabolic image makes allusions to the wilderness feeding ("become satisfied," 6:42; 7:27; 8:4, 8) as symbols of the fulfillment now underway in the renewal of Israel (and others) he is spearheading. In the flow of Mark's story, therefore, the Syrophoenician woman, the utterly marginal, poor, single-parent mother of a demon-possessed daughter, is the representative non-Israelite who secures the participation and position of non-Israelite peoples, particularly Greek-speaking people, in the movement of the fulfillment of Israel, in the kingdom of God.

Again, as with the two intertwined episodes of healed women, there are implications in her having achieved this inclusion of other peoples in the movement, not just as a person but as a woman, although these may not become evident until the story is complete. As noted in chapter 4, the story as a whole is ambivalent about, and perhaps declares its independence of, the leadership of the twelve disciples based in Jerusalem. Thus the "Greek, Syrophoenician woman" may be taking her place along with other women in the story as paradigms of faith and leadership and service in Mark's story over against the Twelve, who are beginning to balk. And in this case, she is responsible for insisting on the inclusion of non-Israelites in the movement, in contrast to Jerusalem leaders such as Peter who were not so enthusiastic or at least were not so directly involved in their recruitment.

The Poor Widow (Mark 12:41–44)

The poor widow who gives "everything she had" to the Temple treasury has been domesticated into a paradigm of Christian piety and support of the church—she gave all that she had. Indeed in the dominant interpretation of Mark's Gospel, she has been "a model for discipleship," having given "her whole living," even as Jesus was about to give his life.[28] The assumption of such interpretation of the episode, taken out of its narrative context, is that Jesus is commending the widow's gift.

This episode, however, must be heard in the flow of the larger story with a sense of social realities in historical political-economic context. The widow's giving is indeed contrasted with that of rich people as well as with the caricature of the scribes in the preceding episode. And, as often noted, the widow's gift here and the woman's anointing of Jesus in 14:3–9 are pointedly juxtaposed with the male rulers' actions in the immediate narrative context of Mark 12 and 14. The widow's gift, however, must be understood primarily in the sequence of the narrative, in both the immediate and the broader context.[29]

In the broader narrative context, Jesus has been pronouncing condemnation of the Temple and high priesthood in demonstration and parable. The poor widow gives away to the Temple treasury all that she had to live on, becoming then totally destitute, at the end of the sequence of Jesus' prophetic campaign against the rulers and ruling institutions. It thus provides a vivid vignette of how the high-priestly rulers have made the Temple into a "den of brigands" and provides the reason why the owner of the vineyard will come and destroy the violent tenants. The rulers are using their control of the Temple to "rob" people of their livelihood. In the immediately preceding episode (12:38–40), at the end of his series of conflicts with the high-priestly ruling groups and their representatives, Jesus sounds the warning to "Beware of the scribes . . . who devour widows' houses." "House" means not simply a dwelling but a family's or person's resources for living generally, as evident in the covenantal commandments not to covet or steal others' houses (including draft animals, etc.). The widow's giving "all she had to live on" exemplifies and confirms Jesus' warning: Sure enough, a widow's "house" just got devoured, presumably because the scribes encouraged people to give to the Temple. In the immediately following episode (13:1–2), Jesus declares that the Temple, whose condemnation he had just prophetically demonstrated (in 11:15–17), is imminently to be destroyed. The high priests make the Temple into a brigands' stronghold from which they rob the people; the scribes based in the Temple "devour widows' houses"; a widow gives away the last coppers of her "house"; the Temple is about to be destroyed.

The widow, like the women earlier in the narrative, functions as a symbolically representative woman in the story. The point is lost if she is taken as a generic abstract human. The widow in biblical tradition, as in ancient agrarian society in general, was a typical figure, almost stereotypical. All peasant families were marginal economically, vulnerable to drought and famine and exploitation by rulers and/or creditors. In a traditional society in which women were members of a family under the authority of the male head of household, first their father and then their husband, widows were extremely vulnerable economically, both in the sense of being without the labor necessary to farm the family fields and in the sense of being vulnerable to predatory creditors or guardians. Israelite covenantal law included provisions to protect widows, along with mechanisms to protect the economic viability of peasant families in general (e.g., cancellation of debts and release of debt-slaves every seven years, as in Exod. 21:2; 22:25–27 and Lev. 25). The widow in this episode in Mark's story is thus a symbolic and representative figure. She illustrates the extremes to which the scribes (and the rulers generally) had gone in securing revenues for their Temple stronghold. Not only did they engineer the exploitation of the people generally, but they even preyed on helpless widows, inducing them to give away even their last coppers to the maintenance of the Temple.

The Woman Who Anointed Jesus (Mark 14:3–8)

The narrator could not state any more clearly the importance of the woman's act of anointing Jesus for the movement to which the Gospel is addressed: "Truly I tell you, wherever the good news is proclaimed in the whole world, what she has done will be told in remembrance of her." "Nowhere else in Mark is any person or action singled out for future remembrance."[30] Apparently the objection by "some" that the resources spent on the costly ointment should have been channeled to the poor, along with Jesus' answer that she was anointing his body "for burial," has led to an emphasis on the woman's act as "an example of loving compassion" or "private, personal acts of love for individuals in particular need," in contrast with "public acts of almsgiving."[31]

Given the thorough grounding of Mark's story in Israelite tradition and its theme of the fulfillment of Israel's history, the woman's act is far more. In anointing Jesus with costly ointment the woman is acting as an Israelite prophet who anoints God's chosen one as king.[32] The term "messiah," translated as *christos* in Greek, means "anointed." During the desperate struggle of Israel to free itself from domination by the Philistines, the great prophetic "judge" or "liberator" Samuel had anointed first Saul, and then David, as the one who would lead the people (1 Sam. 10:1; 16:1–13). In the same tradition, the prophet Ahijah from the Israelite center of Shiloh had "messiahed" Jeroboam to lead Israel's independence from Jerusalem rule, and Elijah was commissioned by God to "messiah" Jehu to lead the people's independence from Ahab and Jezebel's tyrannical, foreign-oriented rule (1 Kings 11:26–39; 19:15–16; the latter completed by Elisha, 2 Kings 9:1–10).

Again this episode of the subplot of the women must be heard in the context of the overall plotting of the story. Although John the Baptist was declared to be Elijah by Jesus after the transfiguration, John did not "messiah" Jesus at the beginning of the story. Rather the Spirit came down upon, in effect "anointed," Jesus and the divine voice declared him to be "My son, the Beloved." At the midpoint of the story Peter, in effect attempting to step into the prophetic role, declared Jesus to be "the anointed one." But his misunderstanding of Jesus' agenda was quickly exposed. In that context and twice more Jesus declared that "the son of man" must suffer and be executed. Now that the story is coming to its climax with the announcement of the Jerusalem rulers' plot "to arrest Jesus by stealth and kill him" (14:1–2), this woman assumes the prophetic role of anointing Jesus.[33] That term *messiah* = "anoint" is not used, but we cannot miss the significance of her action. And since Jesus is about to become a martyred messiah, the woman (as Jesus declares) "anoints" his body "beforehand for burial." The woman's prophetic act of service anticipates and prepares Jesus for his primary and paradigmatic act of service.[34]

As with the Syrophoenician woman, this episode shows Jesus as "receiving from a woman in ways he is never shown as receiving from men."[35] Moreover, "the anointing, as a foreshadowing of healing and resurrection, transferred the role of healer and healed. . . . Divine power, unleashed by the reversal, flows between the women and Jesus. This healing act buoys the coming trial with an undercurrent of connection. Divine power remained in the community of those who healed and ministered to each other"[36] (as in 15:41!). The woman's act of anointing was the prophetic act of empowerment that enabled the martyrdom to issue in renewed life for and of the people.

Marriage, Family, and Community in Mark

The role of women in Mark's story is closely interrelated with its treatment of marriage, family, and community. Liberal scholarly interpreters, especially in North America, have recently pictured Jesus as anti-family, calling individual followers to break with their families and live as ascetic wandering charismatic beggars.[37] The appearance in Mark of women outside of patriarchal family relations, such as Mary Magdalene, would presumably fit into such a scenario. This picture, however, is constructed by taking individual Jesus sayings out of both literary and historical social context, and by taking them as general instructions about life, literally understood. Most of the "proof texts" utilized are taken from early Christian documents later than Mark. The few proof texts taken out of Mark say something quite different when heard in the narrative and social context indicated in Mark's story. The episode in 1:16–20 is Jesus' call of the four leading figures among the Twelve to assist in his mission, not a generalized call to an "itinerant lifestyle." Jesus' declaration to the disciples who had left everything to follow him promises not a metaphoric family-equivalent but a remarkably concrete (if somewhat hyperbolic) restoration of houses, families, and fields, with persecutions (10:28–30). It is difficult to understand how the Nazareth villagers' "stumbling" because of their over-familiarity with their fellow villager could possibly be construed as Jesus' break with his own family, let alone how the latter could somehow be paradigmatic for "discipleship." That family members would turn against each other is specific to situations of persecution of members of Jesus' movement who persist in their loyalty (13:9–13).[38]

Far from opposing or abandoning the family, Mark's story includes the family in Jesus' program of societal renewal. The appearance of independent women such as Mary Magdalene is likely a reflection of the deteriorating conditions for family and village life at the time. To hear these episodes more appropriately we must again attend to the historical social context. The fundamental social forms of a traditional agrarian society were the patriarchal family and the village community, formed of many such patriarchal families. Such families were also mostly patrilineal, ideally living on ancestral land, the patrimony of the "house(hold) of the father." The husband-father was the head of the family; thus the wife-mother and the children can seem to modern Western observers almost as his property. Correspondingly, the village "elders" would be the heads of the most prominent families (such as the "head of the assembly," Mark 5:22–23). The principal symbolization of social relations in the village communities that comprised such a society (e.g., relative status and authority) was in terms of kinship, primarily those of family relations.

The advent of Roman imperial rule in Palestine brought acute pressure on the viability of the patriarchal family and a breakdown in patriarchal authority. In their conquest and reconquest (see chapters 2 and 6 above), the Roman armies would have killed or enslaved a disproportionate number of young men. The pressure for tribute and taxes on top of tithes and offerings from the various layers of rulers required peasant families to borrow, leading them ever more heavily into debt. It became increasingly difficult for fathers of families to avoid having a family member taken into debt-slavery or to avoid forfeiting control of the ancestral family land. Herod Antipas's building of two capital cities within twenty years in the tiny area of Lower Galilee, which required massive numbers of laborers, also disrupted traditional patterns of family and village life. Jesus' parables provide evidence for large numbers of day laborers available locally, and the historian Josephus indicates that many thousands of workers labored in the reconstruction of the Temple in Jerusalem for nearly eighty years (Matt. 20:1–16; *Ant.* 20.219). The breakdown of traditional patriarchal family life under the pressure of these interrelated political-economic factors would have brought a sense of shame and frustration to many a father-husband head of household and undermined their authority—with all the attendant detrimental effects on women and children and implications for local family life. Mark's episodes dealing with marriage and family must be heard in this context.

Jesus' Teaching on Marriage in a Dispute with Pharisees (Mark 10:2–9, 10–12)

In this controversy with the Pharisees, Jesus speaks from and for the Galilean popular Israelite tradition in opposition to the representatives of the "great tradition" cultivated in Jerusalem, as discussed in chapter 7. The Pharisees serve as a foil for Jesus' teaching. And "the question put before Jesus is totally androcentric and presupposes patriarchal marriage as a 'given.'"[39] The Pharisees' reply to Jesus' question about what Moses had commanded about divorce indicates that they not only allowed divorce, but allowed it at the (dis)pleasure and discretion of the husband—a man could simply give his wife a certificate of dismissal. But the Pharisees in Mark are caricatured representatives of the Jerusalem elite, not of a putative "Judaism." Mark's Jesus is not somehow challenging or breaking through the patriarchal practices of "Judaism," but is rather deeply rooted in what was probably the view of the vast majority of Judean as well as Galilean villagers, that marriage was fundamental to social life and virtually inviolable and unbreakable. As in most agrarian societies, so in Galilee and Judea, the husband and wife were at the center of the basic productive unit of the society, often working side-by-side in the fields or on the threshing floors.

Jesus' teaching about divorce and remarriage, moreover, is part of a larger covenantal "charter" aimed at the renewal of village community life on the basis of Mosaic covenantal commandment, as explained in chapter 8. The issue of marriage cannot be separated from other covenantal issues. The stability of marriage and family as the most fundamental social unit was essential for the ongoing life of the village community. Indeed, most of the basic covenantal commandments of God can be seen as fundamental principles designed to maintain the viability of the fundamental social-economic unit, the family. Thus in this teaching on marriage and divorce, Jesus can be seen as restoring or renewing the most fundamental Israelite principles of marriage and family integrity. Mark's Jesus here does not create a new basis for a less patriarchal marriage in opposition to a more patriarchal "Jewish" practice, but defends covenantal Israelite marriage and family against the permissive "Pharisaic" policies that may have been instrumental in allowing wealthy and powerful elite families to consolidate their economic power.

It would be anachronistic to make Mark's Jesus into a feminist opponent of patriarchal marriage. His renewed covenantal teaching on marriage, however, does indeed pointedly place marriage on a less patriarchal basis than the permissive divorce practices of the Herodian elite. The appeal to "the beginning of creation" insists that God did not intend and does not approve of the permissive patriarchal prerogative of "putting way" a wife with a simple certificate of dismissal. Far from approving of such practices, God created human beings as male and female, apparently on an equal footing. The citation from the end of the second creation story would appear to be a pointed reference to the then-current "patrilocal" practice: It is not woman who is given into the power of man in order to continue "his" house and family line, but it is man who shall sever connections with his own patriarchal family and "the two shall become one *sarx*."[40] "Flesh" in this case does not refer to humanity as sinful or to sex, but to body or person or humanity. Nor does it refer to some androgynous primal man, but to the unity of the female and the male in marriage. The last saying, "therefore what God has joined together let a human not separate," finally, makes marriage grounded in God's creation the first principle of the renewed covenantal order (see previous chapter). Thus, not only does Mark's Jesus insist upon marriage and family as the basis of a renewed covenantal society, but he gives marriage a more egalitarian basis in God's creation than was current in scribal discussion and elite social practice.[41]

The continuation of Jesus' teaching in the form of covenantal case law (10:10–12) reinforces the importance of marriage as the basis of family life in this sustained covenantal subsection of Mark's story. The issue is now clearly divorce for the purpose of remarriage, apparently precisely what the elite were practicing in order to consolidate economic power. Jesus now explicitly appeals to the covenantal commandment against adultery, which protects the integrity of the family/household as the fundamental social unit. The paired statements allow divorce but proscribe remarriage, thus taking a stand against divorce for purposes of remarriage. The standard understanding of adultery was that it was another man's offense against the woman's husband as head of the family unit. The formulation in Mark (10:11–12) considers cases of initiative by the woman/wife parallel to those of initiative by the man/husband.[42] As in Jesus' appeal to creation, Mark's story again appears to place women on an equal footing with men, to treat them equally.[43]

Jesus' Dispute with the Sadducees (Mark 12:18–27)

Jesus's sharp debate with the Sadduccees in Mark 12:18-27 also deals with the issue of marriage, or more precisely patriarchal marriage. This episode produces nothing but puzzlement to interpreters because it establishes no link with Jesus' resurrection and because Jesus' reply to the Sadducees query does not offer a good argument for the resurrection.[44] Our effort to hear each episode in the context of the whole story, however, may open our ears to some possibilities in this case. First, as in Jesus' disputes with the Pharisees, such as their question about hand washing and divorce, Jesus shifts the focus. In this case he changes the issue from resurrection to (levirate) marriage. Second, the narrative context is Jesus' series of confrontations with the Jerusalem ruling groups over their religiously legitimated economic exploitation/oppression of the people. The chances are, therefore, that for Mark's Jesus the issue at stake in this episode also has something to do with the rulers' exploitative economic practices. Third, the question of women's position and roles in Mark's story cannot be separated from the question of economic exploitation, as we have already seen in the case of the hemorrhaging woman and the widow who gave away her whole household, apparently at the encouragement of the scribes.[45]

The Sadducees present the hypothetical case of repeated levirate marriage as posing an impossible situation for future resurrection life, supposedly as a continuation of existing social relationships such as patriarchal marriage. Like the Pharisees' question about divorce, the Sadducees' question presupposes patriarchal marriage. In the traditional Israelite practice of "levirate" marriage, when an (older) brother died without a son, the (younger) brother would marry his widow in order to produce an heir (Deut. 25:5–6). The traditional practice of levirate marriage, while providing economic security for the widow (the Tamar story, Gen. 38), had the purpose of securing the continuation of the patriarchal family line and the family inheritance ("house," lands, etc.). At the time of Jesus and Mark's story, however, such a practice was hardly of much benefit to impoverished peasants living under the threat of losing their family inheritance because of multiple layers of taxes and spiraling debt. The only people with a stake in levirate marriage and other laws designed to ensure patriarchal inheritance were the wealthy priestly families and their Herodian allies—who were also the creditors taking over peasants' land for their debts.[46] It is also important to remember that while the Sadduccees insisted that only the *written* Law of Moses was valid, the more liberal Pharisees attempted to adjust and apply the Law to new historical conditions in their oral "traditions of the elders."

Jesus' sharp reply to the Sadduccees' question is a blunt criticism of the high priests' and other rulers' use of patriarchal marriage laws to consolidate wealth (including control of land). He appeals to future resurrection life in order to relativize patriarchal marriage as only a temporary institution. It was not ordained by God for all time. To declare that in the resurrection "they neither marry nor are given in marriage" (12:25) undermines the principal legal basis on which the wealthy families depended for their retention of wealth and power. Over against the wealthy Sadducees' obsession with inheritance from the dead, Jesus places God's revelation to Moses in the burning bush story— that he is the God of the living (12:26–27)—in the very scripture which the Sadducees appealed to for their self-legitimation. Heard with such attention to who would have been pressing patriarchal marriage laws and for what purpose, this episode fits with the other episodes in Jesus' prophetic attack on the Jerusalem rulers and their representatives. In the overall context of Mark's story the issue here is not resurrection but levirate marriage laws as an example of how the ruling elite use patriarchal marriage as a manipulative device in consolidating control over land and other resources. But while their obsession with patriarchal inheritance from the dead means death for the people, the God revealed in their scripture is concerned for the life of the living.

My Brother and Sister and Mother (Mark 3:31–35)

Finally we must examine closely an episode that many have taken as Jesus' rejection of the family, and that others have read as Jesus' rejection of patriarchy in general (3:31-35). Removed from its place in Mark's story, this episode was susceptible of unwarranted speculation. It was often claimed that this episode, in connection with Jesus' "rejection in his hometown" (6:1–6), signals Jesus' break with his family. Neither episode, however, implies anything of the sort. In the episode in Jesus' "hometown," not his family but other villagers "stumble" at him. The point is that he can do no deed of power when the people are not responsive. This comes immediately after the episode of the hemorrhaging woman's healing because she had such faith. In the episode earlier in Mark's story (3:31–35), Jesus uses his "mother and brothers" to serve as a foil for the point about "doing the will of God," but that does not suggest that he is breaking off relations. Indeed, his mother is one of the three faithful women who witness his crucifixion and the empty tomb (see 6:3; 15:40; 16:1).

   Nor can the point of the episode be reduced to the simple conclusion that, over against Jesus' family or the family in general, Jesus' inner or intermediate circle of followers are his (or the) "true family." This episode and its function in Mark's story are more complex and subtle than that. Nor is the point of the episode that the call to join the "family of Jesus/God" supersedes the demands of one's own concrete family. Nor is it warranted to argue that in the symbolic narrative of this episode Jesus' followers form a new "household," the family being outside the "house." These and other questionable uses of Mark 3:31–35 have depended upon a (mis)reading of 3:19b–21 as referring to Jesus at "home" with "his family." But "those around/with him" (the disciples?) went out to restrain him. Since 3:19b–21 does not refer explicitly to "home" and "family," it seems doubtful that we should find a "sandwich" pattern in Mark 3:19b–21, 22–30, 31–35.[48] The episode in 3:31–35 does not mention "house." The mother and brothers are simply outside, in contrast to "those seated around him." Indeed, nothing in the episode suggests any opposition to or rejection of the fundamental social unit of the family, and nothing suggests the formation of a new, supposedly communal household or family.

The most striking feature of this episode also fits the circumstances of patriarchal families disintegrating under the tightening economic pressures outlined a few pages back. The pronouncement that Jesus delivers, as the point of this episode, is also the summarizing statement of the first main step of the Gospel story: "Whoever does the will of God is my brother and sister and mother." That is a remarkable formulation for a pronouncement addressed to people who would simply have assumed a patriarchal social structure and culture. As is evident in other Gospel materials and the letters of Paul, the androcentric term *adelphoi*/"brothers" was commonly used as an inclusive term including women (e.g., Matt. 5:22–24; 7:3–5; hence the paraphrase/translation "brothers and sisters" or "neighbor" in NRSV). The addition of "sisters" in this pronouncement thus pointedly emphasizes the importance of women in Jesus' movement. The inclusion of "sisters" in the pronouncement then makes all the more striking the omission of "fathers," normally the most important member in the family. Jesus' declaration of the future renewal of households, with fields, also includes sisters but omits "fathers" from the list of family members (10:30). In these pronouncements of Jesus, Mark's story is clearly signaling something significant.

Overinterpretation of this remarkable formulation has been tempting. It is often suggested that "fathers" are omitted because, after Jesus introduced a more direct and intimate relation to God, his followers understood God as the "true father." However, referring to God as Father was hardly original with or distinctive of Jesus, and the notion that Jesus' followers did not use "father" with reference to people comes from Matthew's Gospel (23:9). In Mark's story, on the other hand, Father is not a prominent term for God for Jesus' followers. Except for the generalized reference to "your Father" that appears to be a late addition to the story (11:25), "the Father" occurs only in connection with "the son (of man)" (8:38; 13:32). Only in his prayer in Gethsemane does Jesus himself address God as "Abba, Father." So deference to God as the "true father" cannot be the reason for omitting "fathers" from the list of "family" members. It is also difficult to imagine that the omission of "fathers" from "the family" signifies that the movement Mark addresses excluded fathers (it certainly included husbands, as indicated by 10:2–9, 10–12). And it may be going too far to claim that this omission means that the Jesus' movement had formed (completely) egalitarian familial communities.

The formulation of the pronouncement, however, does appear to be a challenge to the norm of the patriarchal family under a male head—except insofar as Jesus or God in effect replaces fathers as the male authority figure. Such a move toward a less patriarchal family and familial community would be particularly understandable and particularly appropriate in circumstances where patriarchal authority in families and village communities was beginning to break down under severe economic-social pressures. In any case, the final statement of the first step of Mark's story of Jesus' renewal of Israel as the manifestation of the kingdom of God presents an image or model of familial community that is pointedly lacking a paternal authority figure as a guide for covenantal social relations and interaction.

It would be unreasonable to claim that a story derived from the patriarchal society of the ancient world somehow managed to embody egalitarian ideals that have come to prominence only in recent times. Yet Mark's story appears to make some significant breaks with the standard patriarchal patterns known from ancient cultures in general. Jesus' teaching on marriage addresses women as well as men. In grounding marriage in God's creation of humanity as male and female, with a pointed jab at the prevailing patrilocal pattern, he seems also to be countering normative predominance of the man's rights and prerogatives over the woman's. At the very least, his emphasis on the inviolability of marriage would have protected women's economic rights, which would have been particularly important in circumstances of extreme economic pressure on peasant families and the threat of their disintegration. The ideal of a nonpatriarchal familial community in Jesus' pronouncement about whoever does the will of God being his brothers, sisters, and mothers provides a complementary principle of Jesus' program of societal renewal. This principle appears to press the communities of the movement to respond supportively as family to the needs of women and children who were left vulnerable by family disintegration.

Women as Paradigms of Faithful Ministry

With a clearer sense of particular episodes involving women and of other episodes particularly pertinent to women's lives, we can better appreciate the importance of the women subplot in Mark's overall story. Except for Jesus' first healing, of Simon's mother-in-law, women are absent from the beginning of the story when the twelve are called and appointed as the implied leaders and representatives of the renewed Israel. In the middle sections of the story, however, the woman who had been hemorrhaging for twelve years and the twelve-year-old woman who is almost dead appear as figures representative of Israel experiencing renewal in Jesus' exorcisms and healings. The hemorrhaging woman is the most conspicuous paradigm of faith and bold initiative in the Gospel. The Syrophoenician woman, moreover, is the only figure in the story who bests Jesus in debate, in the process eliciting Jesus' confirmation that other peoples are to be included in the renewal of Israel in the fulfillment of history.

Although they almost disappear again from the story until its climax in Jerusalem, women then step into key roles as the twelve betray, deny, and disappear. The dominant Western Christian reading of Mark's Gospel as focused on discipleship has obscured the importance of the women in the climactic events of the story. Far from serving as a mere foil for the high priests who are about to capture Jesus, the woman who anoints Jesus plays a role every bit as important as that of Judas who betrays him. She, and not a male figure, is the prophet who performs the essential prophetic act of designating Jesus as the (martyr-) messiah, when she anoints him—for burial.

While the betrayal, denial, and flight of the twelve command more narrative attention than the women's actions, the women who remain near, looking on from a distance at the crucifixion, and who go to the tomb after the Sabbath play two crucial, central roles in the story. First, in contrast to the twelve, the women are the only examples of persistence in following and serving, the models for the movement Mark addresses. Although Jesus is described as feeling godforsaken, he does not die totally abandoned. The women are nearby. Representing those who have experienced the liberating and empowering divine power mediated through Jesus, the women sustain a patient caring presence during Jesus' crucifixion, a presence that can be wounded but not denied. Having marked the site of his burial, they return to anoint him.[49] Second, they are the only witnesses to Jesus' death and to the empty tomb and announcement that Jesus is going ahead into Galilee (where the movement is presumably to continue).[50] The women would therefore by implication have been the first to proclaim the "good news" of the vindication of the martyr-messiah and the ones to lead the way in the continuation of the movement back in Galilee and beyond.

A review of key episodes in the middle of the story and of what might seem a theme of secondary importance in the story confirms the importance of the women as paradigms of faith, following, and service, in contrast to the twelve as paradigms of misunderstanding of and inability to follow Jesus' mission. In the third, and therefore surely most telling, of the twelve disciples' utter misunderstandings of Jesus' mission that would entail a martyr death, James and John request positions of power at his right hand and left hand, as exalted rulers, when he comes into his glory. This evokes Jesus' final covenantal teaching, on the politics of his movement. In contrast to the other peoples, who have rulers and tyrants lording it over them, in the renewed Israel, "whoever wishes to become great among you must be your servant." The leaders of Jesus' movement must serve the others in the movement.

The theme of serving/servant—or better, "ministering"—does not occur often in Mark's story, but is highly significant when it does. The Greek term *diakonos* can have connotations of menial domestic service. In Mark, Paul, and other New Testament literature, however, it refers to service in the *ministry* of the movement. Central in the story, of course, is that Jesus himself will serve or minister to others in becoming a ransom for (the liberation of) many, in a statement juxtaposed with his admonition to the disciples who seek rulership. And the divine messengers minister to Jesus in the wilderness testing. The paradigms of persistence and continuity in service or ministry to others, however, are the women, from Simon's mother-in-law to the women who—according to the general announcement immediately after the death (ministering) of Jesus—had followed and served/ministered all along. In retrospect, the hearers realize at the end of the story that when the twelve, who stubbornly persisted in their pursuit of power, were admonished by Jesus to become servants or ministers of the others, he was urging them to do as the women in the movement had been doing all along and faithfully persisted in doing to the end.

Mark's portrayal of women as paradigms of service has been highly problematic in Christian interpretation. It has been turned into the virtual opposite of Jesus' pointed admonition to James and John, and through them to the hearers of the Gospel. Men with power and authority in the church and society have regularly laid upon women with neither power nor authority the role and ideal of self-denying service. For readers who do not keep Mark's whole story in mind, certain episodes are susceptible of such exploitation. Mark's model of service seems to be derived from the gendered division of labor in a typical traditional patriarchal society. Taken out of the overall story, Simon's mother-in-law's domestic service toward the beginning of the story could easily be made into a paradigm of service in menial and domestic tasks. Indeed, a shift from leadership as a general *service* (or *ministry*) of the communities in the movement to service at meals took place early in the development of "early Christianity," as represented in the book of Acts. In Paul's letters, the earliest evidence for movements of Jesus-believers, it is clear that "ministers/servants" were the leaders of the communities and the overall movements, and that such "ministers" included women, as did Paul himself, and Apollos at Corinth, and Phoebe, "minister" at Cenchreae (1 Cor. 3:5; Rom. 16:1; cf. Acts 1:17, 25).

The twelve under the leadership of Peter decide to devote themselves to the "service/ministry of the word," relegating "service" at table to lower ranking "ministers" (Acts 6:1–6).

If anything, Mark's Gospel is a protest against the tendency for the leadership of the Jesus movement to become figures of power and authority in imitation of models from the dominant social-political order. An extremely difficult problem faced by popular movements of protest and renewal that are striving to create an alternative to the dominant social order is the lack of an alternative model. The only model of humanity available for oppressed people is their image of their oppressors, as the great educator Paolo Freire has pointed out. In a patriarchal society the only model of leadership in the village community is the male head of household. The only model of leadership beyond the local community is the people's image of how their wealthy and powerful rulers operate. The latter is precisely what James and John have in mind when they ask Jesus to appoint them to positions of power and authority when he comes into his glory. This and Mark's sharp criticism of the twelve generally suggests that in Mark's view the twelve have themselves begun to operate on such a model of leadership in setting themselves up as the heads of the Jesus movement(s) in Jerusalem.

It is precisely over against this hierarchical model of leadership that Mark presents the women as paradigms of "following" Jesus and service in the movement. The women's faithful response to Jesus' program, their "following" in the "way" he had led, and their service stand starkly opposite the failure and misunderstanding of the twelve. Mark's story in general, and explicitly so in 10:35–45, pointedly demands that those with power, the twelve, serve those without it, the rest of the movement. The discussion with James and John in particular and Mark's broader theme of service do not present an ideal of general social behavior as selfless menial service. It is rather a demand that a movement striving to realize an alternative social order not fall back into the patterns they are struggling against. Similarly, the self-denial in Jesus' calls for "taking up your cross" is not an idealization of submission to those in authority (e.g., women to men, slaves to masters, subjects to rulers), but suffering for a political cause, the goal of which is the ending of submission and suffering.[51] The related principle of "receiving the kingdom of God as a little child" (10:15), moreover, "is not an invitation to childlike innocence and naïveté but a challenge to relinquish . . . domination over others. . . . [The] solidarity from below required by the *basileia* of God . . . challenges those in a position of dominance to become equal with those who are powerless."[52]

Even so, Mark's theme of service, of which the women are paradigms, calls the leadership of the movement to serve the communities of the movement in the broader struggle to renew the social order, in rejection rather than imitation of the model of power and domination under which they have been subjected. In a traditional society dominated by a patriarchal social structure, Mark's story gives voice to a movement that is breaking with certain traditional patterns of power relations and articulating what are relatively more egalitarian principles. Central to the overall story is the subplot of women as paradigms of leadership/service, in contrast to the twelve disciples, who are becoming power-holders in the movement, in contradiction to the teaching of its founder. In its portrayal of the women disciples, over against the twelve who represent the continuation within the Jesus movement of the desire to dominate, Mark's story presents an alternative to the dominant political-economic-religious order. Mark's story presses the hearers to move beyond power-relations in which some dominate and others are powerless to use their newly gained empowerment in service of a movement that can sustain resistance to that dominant order.

10

Prophetic and Messianic "Scripts" in Mark

Since the beginning of our attempt to hear Mark's story anew we have noticed that it portrays Jesus' message, actions, and movement as fulfillment of the history and hopes of the people of Israel. The opening episode in the story presents John's baptism as the fulfillment of Isaiah's prophecy about the messenger who would "prepare the way of the Lord." Through much of the story, Jesus repeatedly performs actions reminiscent of Moses, the founder of Israel, and Elijah, the great restorer of Israel. Like a new Moses, moreover, Jesus restates covenant teaching as a basis for community life and in his last supper with the twelve ceremonially renews God's covenant with the people. At several points the narrative states explicitly that both Jesus' program of renewal and his conflict with the rulers are happening in accordance with and fulfillment of "the scriptures." The hearers of Mark get the sense that the story was "scripted" in Israel's history and cultural tradition.

The Dangers of Proof-Texting Mark's Christology

Theological interpreters, however, have again diverted attention from Mark's larger story in two interrelated ways, by focusing on Mark's interpretations of isolated scriptural texts, and by finding Mark's "christology" in those interpretations.

First, biblical scholars were only too eager to take up the task of delineating precisely how the writer of the Gospel of Mark "interpreted scripture." They simply assumed that, in effect, events and their interpretation were somehow separate steps or processes. The standard scenario is that early Christians, under the powerful impact of Jesus' ministry and inspired with a new perspective by the resurrection, were led by the Spirit to come up with an adequate interpretation of the events they had just experienced. They did this by studying the scriptures, pondering prophecies, and examining texts carefully. Jesus did many miracles. Later, in retrospect, by examining texts, early Christian writers portrayed those miracles with allusions to scriptural stories about Moses. Jesus was beaten and crucified by the Romans. Only later did early Christians interpret his suffering and death in terms of the scriptures such as Psalm 22. Jesus was resurrected from the dead and appeared to his disciples. Only later did early Christians use Psalm 110:1 to portray their exalted Lord as seated "at the right hand of God" and Daniel 7:13 to portray the exalted Jesus as "the Son of Man coming with the clouds of heaven." As the first evangelist to write a Gospel, Mark supposedly represents a certain maturation of this early Christian interpretation of scripture.[1]

Second, modern interpreters whose primary concern is christology not surprisingly found that Mark's principal concern in scriptural interpretation was also christology. Mark supposedly specialized in "messianic" or "christological exegesis," as indicated in the titles of recent books. These interpreters simply assumed a synthetic Christian christology in which "Christ/Messiah," "Son of God," "Son of Man," and "Suffering Servant" were all interrelated "christological titles" present in a variety of Jewish texts, interpretations, and "messianic expectations" that were fulfilled in Jesus' divine incarnation, ministry, crucifixion, resurrection, and parousia. They then found these interrelated elements of synthetic Christian christology in—or rather read them into—words, phrases, and verses of Mark.[2]

These interrelated practices of analyzing the details of Mark's exegesis of scriptural texts and finding there his christology are both highly problematic. Focusing on how isolated passages in Mark conflate and interpret isolated passages from "scripture" tends to abstract and divert attention from a dynamic sequential narrative full of multiple conflicts, subtleties, and ironies. Moreover, Mark is imagined as a scriptural scholar engaged in a task so complex that he could realistically have accomplished it only if he were working on a high-capacity computer loaded with multilingual files of multiple versions of the scriptures in Hebrew, Aramaic, and Greek, along with Jewish Pseudepigrapha, Targums, and Talmuds. Further undermining the credibility of the claim that Mark is "quoting" and interpreting scripture, the "quotations" usually turn out to be at most a few words of allusion, often combined with another few words of allusion to another passage.[3] And the hypothesis of Mark engaged in interpretation of scripture is based on what we now recognize as unwarranted assumptions that literacy was widespread and scrolls readily available and that a well-defined canon of scriptures existed already in Mark's historical situation.

Focusing narrowly on christology also diverts attention from the dynamics of the overall story and obscures the more complex ways in which the story may be rooted in Israelite tradition. To search for christology in Mark, moreover, may be a questionable historical enterprise. It is not at all clear that terms such as "son of man," "son of God," "son of David," and "messiah" were what could be called "titles" yet. It is certainly not obvious that they function as titles in Mark's story.

In attempting to understand how Mark's story presents Jesus' program of renewal of Israel in opposition to the rulers as the fulfillment of Israel's history, cultural tradition, and scripture (which is written!), we must obviously come to grips with the implications of the oral communication environment sketched in chapter 3. We must also take fully into account the difference and yet interaction between the "great tradition" and the "little tradition" discussed in chapter 7. Jesus, his movements, and the performers of Mark's story would have had a very different relation to the Israelite cultural tradition and to the scripture than that assumed by modern scholars accustomed to print culture and well-stocked libraries. However illiterate they may have been, Galilean and Judean villagers would have known and actively cultivated Israelite tradition. The Israelite tradition cultivated by villagers, however, would have been their own popular Israelite tradition, parallel to but distinctively variant from the "great tradition" cultivated by the literate elite in Jerusalem (including the scripture). Jesus and his followers would have known and built their movement upon the popular Israelite tradition. Mark's story, which developed in communities of Jesus' movement, similarly would have worked primarily out of the popular tradition.

Because of the probable interaction between the great tradition, including the scripture, and the popular tradition, villagers would also have known about and would have heard and known some of the contents of the great tradition. As explained in chapter 7 above, it seems likely that the Hasmoneans and their successor high-priestly rulers in Jerusalem would have pressed "the laws of the Judeans" on the Galileans, at least with respect to the relations of the villagers to the Jerusalem temple-state. Indeed, the Pharisees may have been active in Galilee precisely in this capacity of pressing "the laws of the Judeans," including some of the contents of scripture (the Mosaic Law, etc.) on the Galileans. Moreover, because writing was held in great awe and had a certain aura among the villagers, it had authority among the common people who could not have read it. The written version of Israelite tradition, the scripture, therefore, also had a certain awe and authority for Galileans. For a movement such as Mark's, moreover, that stood in conflict with the Jerusalem elite who controlled the scripture, it was all the more important to appeal to the authority of scripture in defense of its own position that opposed those with "authority" (e.g., the scribes and Pharisees in Mark 1:21–28; 2:23–28; 7:1–13; 10:2–9; 12:28–37).

Given limited literacy and the limited availability of scriptural scrolls in a predominantly oral communication environment, however, the developers, composers, and performers of Mark's story would not have known the text of scripture in any precise sense. They would have been familiar with terms, phrases, and certain key passages. And they had a sense of its general authority, especially because the scribal and priestly elite who held power in the society appealed to it regularly. That is precisely the sense one gets from listening to Mark's story attentively. Some of the most important appeals to "the scripture" are vague and general in the extreme. The scripture in general, never mind what passages in particular, was being fulfilled in Jesus' betrayal, arrest, and execution, as stated in Mark 14:21 and 14:49. In this very general reference to authority of scripture generally, Mark parallels the early "creed" of another branch of the Jesus movement, recited in 1 Corinthians 15:3–5, where Jesus is said to have died for our sins and to have been raised on the third day "in accordance with the scriptures." Where Mark's story does make reference, explicitly or implicitly, to particular brief phrases or perhaps a whole line from scripture, they are not "quoted" with any precision from a manuscript, as discussed just above. And related phrases from other scriptural books tends to be conflated or linked with one attributed to a particular prophet, as in Mark 1:2–3.

The fulfillment of Israelite history and tradition so prominent in Mark's story, however, is carried only to a very limited extent by recitations of particular prophecies from scripture. Far more important in Mark are the many references and allusions to key figures, themes, and patterns from Israelite tradition that figure prominently at any number of points in Israelite tradition, scriptural and extrascriptural. Examples of these have cropped up throughout the chapters above, whether the allusions to Moses' sea crossing and feeding in the wilderness, Jesus' appeal to the basic commandments of God in arguments with the Pharisees, or the broad allusions to the Mosaic covenant and covenant themes. In their "scribal" mentality focused on isolated verses, sayings, and "pericopes," modern biblical scholars tend to impose their own assumption of print culture onto the way in which Jesus movements and "Christian" writers appropriated Israelite tradition. But that has obscured the more important ways that Israelite tradition influenced life in a traditional society where oral communication predominated, i.e., through the broader patterns implicit in the cultural tradition out of which the people had lived for generations.[4]

Attending to those broader patterns embedded in Israelite tradition that influenced the Jesus movement, which in turn produced and cultivated Mark's story, requires a number of interpretive innovations beyond the standard assumptions and methods of biblical studies. Recognizing that Mark's story focuses on and was addressed to imperially subjected people forces us to recognize also how different the historical context of the story was from our own. If Mark's story was originally performed orally before communities of a popular movement, then the overall story was far more important than the "meaning" of individual sayings and episodes within the story. Also, the story would have communicated by resonating with its hearers through repeated referencing of the cultural tradition out of and against which they were listening. That would require us to become as familiar as possible with that very cultural tradition in order to also "hear" the story ourselves, and for it to communicate something to us—so that we do not simply domesticate the story into something we (want to) hear from our basis in our own culture. If we also attempt to take the Gospel whole, moreover, and not reduce it to a message of individual discipleship, we must attend to the complex plotting of the story around the historical struggle of Galileans and others to attain the liberation of their own community life from the multiple layers of rulers whose domination diminished and disintegrated their personal, familial, and communal existence.

From a number of angles in the explorations in earlier chapters, it is clear that Mark's story presents the renewal of Israel under the enabling kingdom of God spearheaded by Jesus as the fulfillment of the history and hopes of the people of Israel. The complex plotting of the story, and perhaps the historical movement that Mark's story recounts as well, therefore, must arise out of the cultural tradition of Israel that is supposedly being fulfilled. If we can hold these various facets together in listening to the story, then we can perhaps hear broader patterns of resonance with Israelite tradition in the episodes and overall plotting of Mark's story.

Two broader patterns deeply rooted in Israelite popular tradition are audible if we have ears to hear the overall story as well as its component episodes. The pattern of a popular prophet leading the renewal of Israel against its rulers seems clear both in its particulars and its broad outline. The other pattern, that of a popular messiah who becomes a martyr for the kingdom of God, seems ambiguous in Mark's story, and one suspects some ambivalence about whether and in what way Jesus is presented as the messiah. The term "scripts" may be useful in reference to these broad patterns in Israelite tradition in two interrelated ways. First, while playing on the term "scripture," yet purposely placed in quotation marks to indicate that in fact it was not written, the term "script" points to cultural contents that were deeply embedded in the memory and oral practices of the Judean and Galilean people in ways that went far beyond what was written in the scripture. Second, the term "script," again in quotes to remind us that it existed primarily in memory and oral practices, not in written form, suggests something like the script of a play or movie. In that sense popular movements would have been informed by and following or adapting a cultural "script" deeply embedded in Judean and Galilean culture.

The Origins and Manifestations of the Prophetic "Script"

Twice in the story Mark refers to the impression that Jesus was making on the people: "Jesus' name had become known. Some were saying 'John the Baptist has been raised from the dead; and for this reason these powers are at work in him.' But others said, 'It is Elijah.' And others said, 'It is a prophet, like one of the prophets of old'" (6:14–15; cf. 8:28). In these passages Mark indicates that people who had heard of Jesus had fairly vivid memories from their cultural tradition of Israelite prophets, Elijah in particular, which Jesus seemed to match. As suggested in connection with the conflicts between Jesus and the Pharisees, the people would have derived those vivid images of the prophets from their own popular tradition. We moderns have no direct access to that popular tradition in texts (except for the Gospels themselves), however, because the ordinary people, who could not read and write, left no written records. We have only indirect and very fragmentary evidence for the popular Israelite tradition from two kinds of sources. The written great tradition provides occasional windows onto popular traditions; and the elite who do write (e.g., Josephus) occasionally give accounts of popular behavior or movements that seem to be rooted in and manifestations of popular tradition.

Prophetic Movements in Israelite Tradition

There were at least two different types of prophets in Israelite tradition.[5] Prophets of the one type, such as Isaiah or Jeremiah, delivered oracles. Having overheard what Israel's God Yahweh was saying in the heavenly council, they repeated those judgments, usually indictments and punishments of the kings and their officials for exploiting the people in violation of the Mosaic covenant. The other type of prophet, while also receiving and delivering the word of God, led movements of liberation from or resistance against unjust oppressive foreign and/or domestic rulers. The prototypical prophet-leader in Israelite tradition, great and little, was the larger-than-life figure of Moses. Inspired through visions and direct communication with Yahweh, he led the liberation of the people from hard bondage under the Egyptian Pharaoh. Rallying a despairing people to trust Yahweh and performing many "signs and wonders along the way, he led Israel across the Sea and through the wilderness with miraculous supplies of food and drink. On the way, at Sinai Moses mediated the covenant with Yahweh that provided the fundamental guidance for Israelite social-economic-political life. This story was carried not only in written form in the book of Exodus, but in many oral recitations such as victory songs, psalms, and covenant renewals, as we can detect from the way those other media were later taken up into texts, such as Exodus and the Psalms.

As Moses' protégé and successor, Joshua picked up the role of the charismatic leader of the people in the struggle against the Canaanite kings, again with wondrous events of Yahweh's acts of deliverance for the people. He also mediated the renewal of the covenant. After Joshua came a succession of "liberators" such as Gideon and Deborah the prophetess, who led a revival of commitment to the covenant and reassertion of the people's independence under the rule of Yahweh. Again we can discern clearly that popular traditions such as the age-old "Song of Deborah" (Judges 5) must have been sung among the people for centuries before being taken up into a written history by the later elite editors of the Deuteronomic history.

After the emergence of monarchy in Israel, the prophets/liberators no longer led the people in battle against foreign kings. They continued their double function of communication with God and leadership of the people, only now against oppressive kings of Israel. The most famous of these were Elijah and his protégé Elisha. The stories of Elijah and Elisha provide remarkable illustrations of how legends of popular prophets were taken up from the "little tradition" into the official (Deuteronomic) history of the kings of Judah and Israel (1 Kings 17–19, 21; 2 Kings 1–9).[6] We must assume that the stories of popular prophets such as Elijah and Elisha continued to be told orally among Israelite villagers, particularly in northern areas such as Galilee, where the stories have their setting—even though the only access we now have is the official (Deuteronomic) royal history into which some of them were incorporated.

These prophets were messengers who delivered Yahweh's will to king and people in oracular pronouncements (1 Kings 17:1; 2 Kings 6:8–10, 18). But they were primarily leaders of popular movements of renewal in Israel in resistance to or rebellion against the monarchy, which under king Ahab had become intensely oppressive under foreign influence. As an integral part of their leadership of popular renewal and resistance to oppressive monarchy, Elijah and Elisha performed healings and "miracles" such as multiplication of food. They also worked with dozens of other prophets, apparently in local revival and organization of the people.

In perhaps the most dramatic and ominous episode, Elijah led a great "revival" meeting at which he constructed an altar of twelve stones, obviously representing the twelve tribes of Israel, in a contest of Yahweh with the Canaanite god Baal, "Lord Storm," to prove which god really did control the destiny of the people. The event then flowed into a rebellion of the newly inspired Israelites, who took the opportunity to kill the thousands of "prophets of Baal" who had been brought in by Ahab to bolster his control of the realm (1 Kings 18).

The legends of Elijah also link him closely with Moses. As other prophets were being hunted down by the regime of Ahab and Jezebel, he withdrew to the wilderness of Sinai-Horeb, the very mountain of revelation. There God both renewed his personal strength and commissioned him to return to his people and "anoint" a new king, i.e., to spearhead a rebellion against Ahab's oppressive regime (1 Kgs. 19). In another vivid episode, Elijah and Elisha, accompanied by fifty other prophets, went out on Yahweh's instructions to the Jordan River: "Then Elijah took his mantle, and rolled it up, and struck the water, and the water was parted to the one side and to the other, till the two of them could go over on dry ground (2 Kgs. 2:8). Then after Elijah was taken up by a whirlwind into heaven, and Elisha had assumed his mantle, he in turn "struck the water, and the water was parted and Elisha went over." These are clearly prophetic signs of deliverance for the people reminiscent of Moses and the crossing of the sea in the exodus and of Joshua and the crossing of the Jordan into the promised land.

Memories of Moses and Elijah were prominent in Israelite tradition, at both the elite scribal level and the popular level. The whole Torah or Law, of course, ostensibly stemmed from Moses and the bulk of its contents consists of Moses' leadership of the exodus and particularly the covenant and covenantal law that he mediated. As we know from the Gospels themselves, covenant and covenantal law continued to serve as the basis of societal life among the villagers of Galilee, as evident in Jesus' ministry and movement. The prominence of Moses in exodus and covenant law in the "great tradition," moreover, would have strongly reinforced his importance in the "little tradition," including the popular differences which were important to reaffirm against the prestige and aura of what stood "written." It would have been utterly inappropriate and therefore impossible for a "new" Moses to "update" the Law among ruling circles who based their own power and position on the already established and authoritative "great tradition." Nevertheless, in at least a minimal indication of the provisional character of their law code, the book of Deuteronomy includes an indication that a new Moses-like prophet (from among the people!) would be necessary: "I will raise up from them a prophet like you from among their brethren; and I will put my words in his mouth, and he shall speak to them all that I command him" (Deut. 18:18).

Although Judean literature includes virtually no indication of any expectation of an "eschatological prophet,"[7] even elite circles had adopted Elijah as a paradigmatic leader of the restoration of the people Israel. Perhaps because, according to the legends, Elijah had not died but been taken up into heaven, he is expected to return to set things right (Mal. 3:1–3; 4:4–6). The second-century B.C.E. scribe Ben Sira, in a recitation of the great heroes of the past, presents what looks like a common expectation that Elijah, who had performed wondrous deeds and "sent kings down to destruction," would return "to restore the tribes of Jacob" (Sirach 48:1–10). Because of the general lack of sources for the centuries before the time of Jesus, we have little evidence for either prophetic expectations or prophetic movements. The handful of references to Elijah, however, indicate that memories and expectations at least of Elijah were still very much alive even in scribal circles—and if alive in scribal circles, all the more so in popular circles.

Popular Prophetic Movements Contemporaneous with Jesus and Mark's Gospel

Suddenly, right around the time of Jesus, several popular movements led by prophets emerged in Judea. Their sudden appearance at this time may be due partly to the fact that we have written sources for this time. But it also has to do with the worsening circumstances of the people under Roman, Herodian, and high-priestly rule during the first century C.E. (as sketched above in chapter 2). Of special importance for understanding Jesus and Mark's story, these popular prophetic movements are clearly reminiscent of earlier Israelite prophetic movements, such as those led by Moses, Joshua, and Elijah. It seems that memories of God's great acts of deliverance under Moses and his successors in Israel's history must have been alive among the people, providing a virtual "script" for new movements focused on God's renewed acts of deliverance and renewal.

The Judean historian Josephus writes disparagingly of several such movements that occurred in the mid-first century.[8]

> Impostors and demagogues, under the guise of divine inspiration, provoked revolutionary actions and impelled the masses to act like madmen. They led them out into the wilderness so that there God would show them signs of imminent liberation. (*J.W.* 2.259; the parallel in *Ant.* 20.168: For they said that they would display unmistakable signs and wonders done according to God's plan.)

It is not difficult to detect, behind Josephus' hostile account, that these were large popular movements inspired by prophetic figures who, like Moses of old, led their followers out into the wilderness to experience God's acts of deliverance with attendant signs and wonders, as in the exodus and wilderness wandering toward the promised land. Josephus recounts three movements of special significance. The first occurred under the Roman governor Pilate among the Samaritan people, who were of Israelite heritage like the Judeans and who cultivated a parallel tradition of Moses as the great liberating prophet.

> A man commanded the Samaritans to go up with him to Mount Gerizim, which is for them the most sacred mountain. He promised to

show them the holy vessels buried at the spot where Moses had put
them. . . . But Pilate, with a contingent of cavalry and armed infantry,
attacked those who had assembled beforehand in the village, killed
some, routed others, and took many into captivity. From this group
Pilate executed the ringleaders as well as the most able among the
fugitives. (*Ant.* 18.85–87)

A decade later, around 45 C.E., in a movement also mentioned in Acts 5:36
but mistakenly dated forty years earlier,

> A charlatan named Theudas persuaded most of the common people to
> take their possessions and follow him to the Jordan river. He said he
> was a prophet, and that at his command the river would be divided and
> allow them an easy crossing. . . . But [the Roman governor] Fadus sent
> out a cavalry unit against them, which killed many in a surprise attack,
> though they also took many alive. Having captured Theudas himself,
> they cut off his head and carried it off to Jerusalem. (*Ant.* 20.97-98)

Yet another decade later, around 55 or 56 C.E., in a movement confused
with the terrorist "Dagger Men" in Acts 21:38,

> A certain man from Egypt arrived at Jerusalem (cf. *J.W.* 2.261—in the
> countryside), saying he was a prophet and advising the mass of the
> common people to go to the Mount of Olives, which is just opposite
> the city. . . . He said that from there . . . at his command the walls of
> Jerusalem would fall down and they could then make an entry into the
> city. But when Felix [the Roman governor] learned of these things, he
> attacked the Egyptian and his followers, killed four hundred of them
> and took two hundred alive. (*Ant.* 20.169–71)

It is significant that all of these particular movements follow the same general pattern. A popular prophet, inspiring a large following among the peasantry, leads them to a significant location where they will experience a new act
of God's deliverance resembling one of God's great acts of deliverance in the
origin of Israel under Moses and Joshua. That the followers are from the
"masses" or "the countryside" or gather at a "village" indicates that these were
definitely movements among the peasantry. That they involve the "majority"
or "30,000 people" suggests just how large they were and why they appeared
to pose a threat to the Roman order, such that the Roman governor in every
case sent out considerable military force and slaughtered hundreds of the participants. That they were taken by surprise and easily killed indicates that they
were not armed rebellions but nonviolent movements expecting divine deliverance. That the people brought their possessions indicates that they were not
simply out on a holiday. And finally, in each case the expectation of the new

act of deliverance is patterned after one of the great acts of deliverance under Moses or Joshua: Theudas was taking the role of a new Moses or new Joshua leading the people out into the wilderness at the Jordan to experience a new exodus or a new entry into the promised land (or a combination of both). The "Egyptian" Jewish prophet was a new Joshua leading a new battle of Jericho, where "the walls came tumbling down" (Josh. 6:15–20).

If Josephus reported only one such movement or if his accounts construed them as exactly alike, they might not be so striking. But since there were apparently several such movements, all concentrated in mid-first-century Judea and Samaria, and since they are different in particulars while so similar in general pattern, that common pattern must be taken seriously as historical evidence. The similarities of these movements point to a broader pattern embedded in Israelite culture in first-century Judea and Samaria, rooted in the memory of earlier prophetic movements known in Israelite tradition. And that pattern in the multiple prophetic movements in Israelite cultural tradition was sufficiently alive so that it *informed* new movements among a people desperate for deliverance from their circumstances under Roman rule. Potential prophetic leaders and their potential followers alike, from their cultural memories, were well acquainted with several particular variations on a general "script" of a prophetic movement of deliverance from oppression by their rulers and restoration and renewal of their people.

A Parallel Prophetic "Script" Evident in the Dead Sea Scrolls

Just when New Testament scholars were being forced to admit that the supposedly standard "Jewish expectation" of "the Messiah" had little basis in Judean literature just before the time of Jesus, along came the discovery of the Dead Sea Scrolls, attesting to, not just one, but two messiahs and a future prophet as well. Scholars began to comb the scrolls for new proof texts showing that, after all, the Jews did have "expectations" of "the Messiah" and related savior figures. The scrolls, produced by a literate priestly-scribal community off in exile in the wilderness, do display a kind of "proof-texting" of their own. We are no longer looking for proof texts, however, but for broader patterns in Israelite tradition that might inform the broader pattern of Jesus and his movement as portrayed in Mark's story or of the Righteous Teacher and the Qumran community he headed. In this regard, the Scrolls present a fascinating supplement to the evidence of the popular prophetic movements for the prominence of a "script" of a "prophetic movement" in Israelite tradition in late Second Temple times.

At first glance the Dead Sea Scrolls seem to differ from the Gospels with regard to how they portray their founding heroes. Whereas the Gospels, collectively at least, seem to apply a number of images of leader- and savior-figures to Jesus as their fulfillment or epitome, the scrolls do not apply images such as "the messiah of Aaron" or the "teacher at the end of days" or "a prophet like Moses" to the Righteous Teacher.[9] On the other hand, however, in relation to his followers the scrolls present the Righteous Teacher as a new Moses in his basic functions. The Righteous Teacher and his followers not only launched a new exodus into the wilderness but founded a renewed covenant community. The renewed covenant community, moreover, was guided by a council consisting of twelve men and three priests. That indicates that the renewed covenant community at Qumran was a reconstitution of Israel (albeit a priestly-scribal version). It has been suggested that the restoration of Israel was a "militant messiah's" mission separate in Judean literature from the renewal of justice and holiness among the people by a "prophet like Moses."[10] But that appears to be a misreading of the Scrolls, which portray the Qumran community led by the Righteous Teacher as both, i.e., a restoration of Israel (at least provisionally) precisely to a life of holiness and justice.[11]

At first glance the "script" of a new Moses leading a prophetic movement at Qumran might appear fundamentally different from the "script" informing the popular prophetic movements led by Theudas and "the Egyptian." That is, in the former the prophet leads both a new exodus and a renewed covenant community, whereas in the latter the prophet leads only a new exodus or new entry into the promised land. And the former involved literate scribes and priests, whereas the latter occurred among the peasantry. Two considerations, however, suggest that the "new Moses" parallel in the scrolls may be closer to the popular prophetic "script" than appears as first. First, whereas the priestly-scribal community at Qumran was able not only to go out into the wilderness but to establish a community as well, the popular prophetic movements were militarily suppressed before they had a chance to realize their vision. Presumably a new exodus or wilderness sojourn would have aimed at a new settlement on the land. Fairly clearly, the logic in a new battle of Jericho was to again enjoy an independent life on the land, free of Roman (and/or high priestly) domination. By implication, the popular prophetic movements were also aiming at a renewal of Israel, presumably including renewed covenantal community life.

Second, although we cannot automatically assume that documents produced by scribal circles such as Qumran are good sources for what ordinary people were thinking and doing, the Qumran literature may bear greater similarities to popular views than other scribal literature. In their sense of oppression by domestic and foreign rulers, the Qumranites had come into a position vis-à-vis the established rulers similar to the perpetual position of the peasantry.[12] And the whole tradition of exodus and covenant stood against hierarchical order and centralized rule, particularly oppressive foreign rule. When Judeans celebrated the Passover festival, commemorating their ancestors' liberation from bondage under Pharaoh, it often led to demonstrations clamoring for independence of Roman rule. The priests and scribes at Qumran, who previously would have depended on the royal and priestly Zion traditions and Moses as author of the written Torah, suddenly turned to the more subversive tradition of Moses. Suddenly, in a relationship to the rulers similar to the one that the peasants were always in, they acted out the Mosaic exodus and covenant tradition.

The "script" of a new Moses leading a new exodus and a renewed covenant evident behind the Righteous Teacher in the Dead Sea Scrolls should thus be taken more as a supplement to the "script" of prophetic movements. It does not so much differ from as provide a more complete picture of that prophetic script derived from Israelite tradition that would have been operative among the peasantry—a script that may help us understand the broader pattern that informs Mark's story.

The Origins and Manifestations of the Messianic "Script"

In Mark's story the Roman governor Pontius Pilate orders Jesus crucified on the charge of being "the king of the Judeans." Pilate, however, was not the only Roman official in first-century Palestine to deal with a popular Israelite leader who was viewed as "king of Israel/the Judeans." Both before and after Jesus of Nazareth, there were several popular leaders who were acclaimed "king" by their followers. Judging from the accounts of the historian Josephus, one particular social form taken by popular rebellions around the time of Jesus was a large group of followers led by one of their number that they looked upon as their chosen or anointed king. Even from a cursory knowledge about David's rise to the kingship in ancient Israel, we may suspect that, parallel to the tradition of popular prophets and prophetic movements, there was another tradition in Israelite culture, that of popular messianic movements, that lay behind the multiple messianic movements contemporary with Jesus and Mark.

Messianic Movements in Israelite Tradition

In order to understand popular "messiahs" and "messianic" movements in Israelite tradition, we need to cut through the vague and composite Christian concept of "the Messiah."[13] The term "Christ" results from the Greek translation of the Hebrew *messiah* (*mašiaḥ*). The Christian understanding of Jesus as the Messiah or Christ is a creative synthesis of several originally separate strands of Israelite expectation and Greek philosophical concepts. The image of a "messiah" was originally separate from other figures and terms from Israelite tradition such as "prophet," "son of man," "son of David." At the time of Jesus, moreover, there was no uniform concept and usage of "messiah," let alone a standard expectation of "*the* Messiah." Indeed, the term is relatively rare in Judean literature prior to the time of Jesus. It is not even clear that *messiah* was used (by itself) as a title in those rare occurrences.[14] This makes all the more important the many concrete movements focused on a popularly acclaimed "king" in the generations immediately before and after Jesus.

It is necessary also to distinguish clearly between the more imperial concept and tradition of kingship that dominates the Hebrew Bible as we have it and the tradition of popular kingship that can be discerned here and there. Much of the previous Christian construction of "the Messiah" and "messianic expectations" has focused on the official Judean royal ideology. God's covenant with David had guaranteed the Davidic monarchy unconditionally to last forever (2 Samuel 7). Borrowing from ancient Near Eastern imperial kingship, the royal Psalms, such as Psalms 2 and 110, acclaimed the Davidic monarch as the "anointed" of God and designated God's "son" at his coronation and seated at the right hand of God in his imperial power. Some of the principal "messianic" prophecies were rooted in that imperial monarchic tradition (e.g., Isa. 9:2–7).

"Underneath" that imperial royal ideology, as it were, in the stories of the origin of kings and kingship in Israel's history, is a resilient tradition of popular kingship. The prototypical popular king, of course, was David himself. In the struggle to resist domination by the Philistine kings, David had become a well-known warrior under Saul, the first king of Israel, and then the chieftain of a large band of brigands. Eager to find a champion to lead them against the Philistines, "all the men of Judah *anointed David king* over the house of Judah." Then "all the elders of Israel *anointed David king* over Israel" (2 Sam. 2:4; 5:3). If we look closely at these accounts and consider them in the historical situation, three interrelated aspects of the prototypical popular kingship stand out clearly. First, the very way the term *messiah* ("anointed") is used, indicates that the people themselves make David king *by popular acclamation* or election. Second, popular kingship was *revolutionary*. The point of acclaiming David king was for him to then lead Israel in establishing their independence of the domination of the Philistines. Third, popular kingship was *conditional*. If the people elected/anointed David for a particular limited purpose, they could also withdraw their recognition if he failed or overstepped the conditions of his election. And that is precisely what happened after David conquered Jerusalem with his own mercenary troops as a capital city from which to rule over Israel and became overly comfortable with his concubines. The Israelites mounted two massive rebellions against their "anointed," who proceeded to conquer the people with his own professional royal troops (2 Samuel 15–20).

The tradition of popularly anointed ("messiahed") kingship remained alive under David and his successor Solomon. Solomon's son Rehoboam, assuming that the Israelites would simply acquiesce to his kingship, arrogantly refused to agree to the people's demand to lighten the burden of forced labor Solomon had imposed. The ten northern tribes of Israel, understanding kingship as conditional, rebelled and proceeded to acclaim Jeroboam as king to lead their rebellion against the imperialistic Davidic kingship of Rehoboam (1 Kings 12). For three more generations in Israel, when sons of previously popularly acclaimed kings attempted to succeed their fathers and thus establish a dynasty, Israelites and/or the army rebelled and acclaimed another leader as king. The last recorded movement led by a popularly acclaimed king came after Ahab had temporarily succeeded in establishing a dynasty. In this case, the prophets Elijah and Elisha touched off the rebellion by "anointing" Jehu as the new popular king (1 Kgs. 19; 2 Kgs. 9). We have no records of subsequent messianic movements among the people. The tradition of popularly "messiahed" kings, however, had become well established among the people, as is evident in its persistence for several generations.

Popular Messianic Movements in the Generations before and after Jesus

Movements headed by popularly acclaimed "kings" erupted after the death of the tyrannical Herod the Great in 4 B.C.E. and then during the great revolt in 66–70. Josephus's accounts are far too elaborate to quote at length. Most important are the clear reminiscences of the earlier messianic movements led by David et al. Following are three excerpts from Josephus's *Antiquities* (17.271–81).

> Judas, son of the brigand-chief Hezekiah, organized a large number of desperate men at Sepphoris in Galilee and raided the fortress/palace. He armed his followers and made off with all the goods that had been seized there, . . . in a zealous pursuit of royal rank, . . . by advantage of his superior strength.
>
> Simon, an imposing man in both size and bodily strength, . . . having organized some men, . . . was proclaimed king. . . . After setting fire to the royal palace in Jericho, he carried off the things that had previously been taken (and stored) there. He also set fire to numerous other royal residences.
>
> Athronges, . . . an obscure shepherd, yet remarkable for his stature and strength, dared to aspire to kingship. . . . Putting on the diadem,

> Athronges held council on what was to be done. . . . He held power
> for a long time, having been designated king. . . . He and his [four]
> brothers] pressed hard in the slaughter of both the Romans and the
> Herodian troops . . . in guerrilla warfare.

Like the prophetic movements, these messianic movements display a common pattern. Most striking perhaps is the motif familiar from the stories of the young king David. The movements are headed by popularly acclaimed "kings." Josephus, who writes history in Hellenistic style, obviously avoids using Israelite language of *messiah*, anointed. But that would be the way these figures, who were proclaimed by, their followers as king, would have been designated in Israelite Palestine. The people, far from looking to the aristocratic families for leadership, focused on charismatic figures of humble origins. One was the son of a brigand-chief, another a shepherd—both reminiscent of David. Perhaps the impressive physical stature and strength of these figures was also reminiscent of David, who had been a fierce warrior. And of course, like the earlier messianic movements in the people's tradition, these movements were clearly rebellions against oppressive (foreign and domestic) rule. Like the ancient Israelite movements, moreover, these new movements were of considerable size yet were relatively well organized. And they were relatively successful, at least temporarily, before the Roman troops could completely suppress them. Indeed, the movement led by Athronges effectively controlled certain areas of Judea for about three years.

Again during the great revolt against Roman rule in 66–70 C.E., and sixty years later, popular messianic movements emerged, one on a massive scale. Simon bar Giora and his movement displayed a number of features reminiscent of earlier Israelite movements, particularly the one led by David. Beginning in Acrabatene to the northeast of Jerusalem, Simon gathered a following, "who obeyed him like a king," in villages throughout the hill country of Judea, "proclaiming freedom of (debt-) slaves and reward for the free" (*J.W.* 2.652–53; 4.507–13). He then moved into Idumea, establishing a base at Hebron, where David was first "messiahed" king (4.529–34). After he took over much of the city of Jerusalem, he was the leader of the largest fighting force against the Roman siege. When the Romans finally captured Jerusalem, Simon, dressed in the purple cape of royalty, was taken prisoner and later formally executed in the great triumphal procession in Rome as "the enemy's general"—i.e., as the "king of the Judeans" leading the revolt (7.29–31, 36, 153–55). The final Judean revolt against Roman rule was led by Bar Kokhba, whom none other than the revered radical rabbi Akiba acclaimed "This is the king, the messiah" (*y. Ta'an.* 4.8 [68d 48–51]). However dormant the popular messianic tradition had been in earlier centuries, it played a highly significant role for a century and a half, as popular messianic movements emerged as the principal social form assumed by Galilean and Judean rebellion against Roman domination. Attempting to set things right, these kings and their movements took back the excesses of wealth that their rulers had taken by exploiting their labor. And they sustained prolonged guerrilla warfare against the overwhelming military might of the Roman legions so that they could again be free to live directly under the rule of God.

The Prophetic "Script" in Mark's Story

In several connections in the preceding chapters we have found Mark's story portraying Jesus as following the prophetic "script" in his program of renewing the people of Israel. Like Theudas and "the Egyptian," and like Elijah of old, Jesus is leading Israelite peasants. His vision and his movement, moreover, aim to achieve freedom from the Roman and Jerusalem rulers, just as the prophetic movements in Israel's tradition sought liberation from oppressive foreign or domestic rule. Whereas Theudas and "the Egyptian," like Moses or Joshua, led the people in an action of deliverance away from their (previous) homes, Jesus and his assistants, like Elijah, Elisha, and their scores of "prophets," focused on revitalization of faith and obedience to God's rule in Israel's village communities, in opposition to their rulers. Like the Qumran community, the movement Jesus leads is portrayed explicitly as a new exodus and its communities are called to live in a renewed covenant. Like the popular prophets who pose as the new Moses or new Joshua, Jesus is portrayed as and is associated repeatedly and explicitly with Moses and Elijah. Mark's story is full of, indeed permeated with, images, references, actions, and teachings that suggest that it is fully informed by the prophetic script that was so prominent among the people in first-century Palestine.

Having noted and discussed many key aspects of this "script" in the chapters above, it now remains to examine Mark's Gospel more closely to discern just how extensive and central they are in the story. It will become evident that the prophetic broader script seems implicit and often explicit at every step throughout the story. Particular images, references, and teachings vary in how allusive and implicit or explicit they appear. But aspects of the prophetic script seem to permeate the whole story.

The opening of Mark's story portrays Jesus as the new Moses and Elijah and his movement as the new exodus. The explicit recitation of "Isaiah" presents John the Baptist as the messenger who prepares "the way of the Lord," that is, the new exodus of the people from bondage like that of ancient Israel under Egyptian domination. At Jesus' baptism the Spirit came upon Jesus, endowing him as a prophet for his mission (cf. Isa. 42:1; 61:1–11), and drove him out into the wilderness for testing as the (Moses- and Elijah-like) prophet who will lead the renewal of Israel.[15]

Clear reminiscences of Moses' founding and of Elijah's renewal recur through the first section on Jesus' inaugural mission in Galilee. Like Moses designating Joshua and Elijah summoning Elisha, Jesus calls those who will assist in his program of renewal. This program becomes unmistakable when he appoints them as the twelve representative heads of the renewed Israel (cf. Elijah's making an altar of twelve stones, representing the twelve tribes of Israel). Meanwhile, Jesus' declaration of forgiveness of sins and pronouncement about doing the will of God signal the renewal of the Mosaic covenant.

Unmistakable reminiscences of Moses' leadership of the exodus and Elijah's miraculous restorative deeds form the very infrastructure of the next main section of the story. Jesus performs two sequences of liberative actions in almost the same order that signal and constitute a renewal of Israel. The "typological" pattern resembles that inherent in the contemporary popular prophetic movements. As Moses engaged in sea crossings and wilderness feedings, so did Jesus. As Elijah healed people and brought a virtually dead child back to life and multiplied food, so did Jesus. The healings of the two women in particular, representative of Israel insofar as the one had been hemorrhaging for twelve years and the other was almost dead just at twelve years of age, clearly indicate that Jesus is engaged in a renewal of Israel as a people (and note the "twelve" baskets of broken pieces left over at the first wilderness feeding). With all these clear parallels to Moses and Elijah, it is no surprise at all when Mark relates that people generally believed Jesus was a prophetic figure— either John the Baptist raised from the dead or Elijah or "a prophet like one of the prophets of old" (6:14–16; 8:27–28)—and that Jesus refers to himself as a prophet (6:4). His commissioning of the twelve to preach and exorcize in village communities cannot help but remind those familiar with Israelite tradition of Elijah's commissioning of Elisha and his working with and through the scores of prophets. And Jesus insists, versus the scribes and Pharisees, on the basic "commandment of God" as the fundamental principle guiding social and economic relations in Israel, referring explicitly to the covenantal principles and prefiguring the covenant renewal in the next section of the story.

While the next section of the story is structured by the three announcements that "the son of man" must suffer, be killed, and rise again, the contents of much of the section is Jesus' prophetic role in the renewal of Israel, including the renewal of the Mosaic Covenant. The appearance of Moses and Elijah with Jesus transfigured on the "mountain" confirms that in all these episodes Jesus is acting as a Moses- and Elijah-like prophet of Israel's renewal while transcending their paradigmatic historical roles. This episode is rich with (metonymic) references to Moses and three of his close assistants ascending a mountain where Moses was transfigured and a divine voice came from a cloud. Indeed, the command to "listen to him" is a direct allusion to God's promise to raise up a prophet like Moses (Deut. 18:15). With these clues clearly in mind, we can then also catch the allusions to Jesus' debates with the scribes and Pharisees, the professional interpreters of the laws of Moses in Jerusalem. Jesus is speaking as the people's prophet defending the basic "commandments of God" given through Moses in the covenant. Prominently positioned in the narrative just prior to his heading into Jerusalem for direct confrontation with the rulers, Jesus reestablishes the Mosaic covenant in the sequence of episodes on marriage, economic relations, and political relations and leadership in the communities of his movement.

These last two sections of Mark's story include an important aspect of Jesus as prophetic leader that usually goes unnoticed. Both in the overall story and in the introduction to the episode of the killing of John the Baptist, Jesus' role and destiny are closely linked and paralleled with John's. John proclaimed a baptism of repentance = renewal of covenant, was delivered up and executed by a ruler. In the overall story Jesus proclaims renewal of Israel and covenant, is delivered up and executed by the rulers. Jesus is so closely associated with John as to be taken as John raised from the dead. The suggestion is that prophets, who oppose the rulers, are killed—but that they keep being vindicated and they keep coming back. Following the transfiguration on the mountain in the next main step of the story, in response to the question about the scribes' teaching about Elijah coming first, Elijah is identified, in effect, with John the Baptist, who had just been executed because of his prophesying. The point of Jesus' reply to the question is again the parallel between "the son of man," apparently Jesus, and John, now identified as Elijah returned. What goes unnoticed is that it is because of Jesus' prophetic role and program that "the son of man" is to suffer and be killed, just as Elijah was hunted by the monarchs and John was jailed and beheaded by "king Herod." Interpreters usually associate Jesus' martyr death with his role as "messiah." This is surely because of the juxtaposition of Peter's answer in 8:29 and Jesus' first announcement of the death of "the son of man" in 8:31, as well as his sentencing and execution as "messiah" and "king of the Judeans." But Jesus' primary role and program throughout this section of the story—structured as it is by the three announcements of his death and rising again, as in the story as a whole—is prophetic. Mark's story focuses on a martyr-prophet as much as or more than on a martyr-messiah.

Once he enters the Jerusalem Temple, Jesus delivers one prophetic demonstration and declaration after another against the Temple, the high priests, and their scribal representatives. Mark's story now adds to the earlier direct allusions to Moses and Elijah some direct references to the prophetic condemnation of the Temple by Jeremiah and a prophetic oracle against the

Jerusalem rulers by Isaiah as well as the prophecy of Daniel. Mark sustains the rich and multiple allusions to Moses, Elijah, and other prophets throughout most of the story. Like Elijah, the Teacher of Righteousness, and perhaps also "the Egyptian," Jesus condemns the expoitative, oppressive rulers on the basis of the Mosaic covenant and its values and provisions ("love your neighbor"). Right on into the climactic section telling of the arrest, trial, and crucifixion, Jesus continues his role as the new Moses. At the Passover, celebrating the exodus liberation of the people, he solemnly ceremonially renews the covenant at the last supper.

The Messianic "Script" in Mark's Story

By contrast with the prominence of the prophetic script at every step in Mark's story, the story's relation to the messianic script is extremely unclear. As a man of the people he was acclaimed by the people, but not as a king. Peter acclaims him as "the messiah," but Mark in effect rejects the acclamation. He is associated with the Davidic kingdom, but Mark seems ambivalent about that. He opposes the Roman and Jerusalem rulers, but as a prophet, not a popular king at the head of a revolt. And he is identified as "the king of the Judeans/Israel" at the end of the story, but only by the rulers in sarcastic mockery of his "failure."

The term "messiah" is by no means the only indicator of the messianic "script," but its rare and peculiar usage in the story is surely an indicator of how reticent Mark is about the "script." Mark has characters refer to Jesus as messiah only at two or three points: perhaps at the very beginning, briefly with serious qualification at the middle, and more prominently but very ambiguously at Jesus' trials and execution at the end. The "superscript" referring to "Jesus messiah" was probably not part of the original story, but was added later in the manuscript tradition. The reference to Jesus as "my son," i.e., the son of God, by the voice at his baptism (1:11) is often taken as an indication that he is the messiah. But it is difficult to find Judean or other texts prior to the time of Jesus that suggest that "son of God" had a specifically "messianic" nuance.[16] Christian interpreters often take "son of God" in Mark as a reference to or synonym for "the messiah." But that appears to be reading back into Mark an identification that was made only later, when various roles, images, and terms ("titles"?) used in connection with Jesus became synthesized into an emergent "christology." We should therefore hesitate about hearing messianic overtones when the unclean spirits call Jesus "son of God" (3:11; 5:7).

Thus Mark's story has no reference to Jesus as "the anointed one" until the middle of the story, when Peter declares "You are the messiah" (8:29). But when he then objects to Jesus' announcement that "the son of man" must suffer and be killed by the rulers, Jesus rebukes him as "Satan." Peter's declaration is the closest Mark's story comes to Jesus' being acclaimed as messiah by his followers, as Judas in Galilee and Athronges in Judea were popularly acclaimed "king." But in the subsequent narrative sequence Mark is either rejecting or strongly qualifying what that declaration would appear to signify.

Perhaps the closest Mark's story comes to portraying Jesus as a popular messiah at the head of a movement comes at his entry into Jerusalem. Just before Jesus enters Jerusalem the blind Bartimaeus refers to Jesus as "Son of David," a designation often closely linked with "anointed one," since David was the prototypical messiah in Israelite tradition. And Jesus' entry into the city appears to be a "staged" demonstration featuring Jesus in the role of a peasant messiah riding on a donkey, in allusion to a prophecy (in Zech. 9:9, where the king, while triumphant, is "humble and riding on a donkey"). Also, Jesus' followers cry out for "the coming kingdom of our ancestor David."

In his prophetic confrontation with the rulers and their representatives, however, Jesus then refutes the official scribes' view that "the Messiah is the son of David." There is little evidence before or around the time of Jesus that "Son of David" was a "messianic title."[17] The identification of a messiah as "son of David" would have derived from the great tradition of Jerusalem, where centuries earlier the kings of the Davidic dynasty had been designated as "anointed" at their coronation. After David himself, the popular kings were definitely not "son of David," since they were either leading rebellions against the Davidic kings or leading rebellions in the northern kingdom of Israel no longer controlled by the Davidic kings in Jerusalem. The popular messiahs around the time of Jesus, as inauspicious shepherds or sons of bandit-chiefs, would have been only figuratively "sons" of David at best. Not surprisingly, it is the scribal *Psalm of Solomon* 17 that provides the principal reference to the messiah as "the son of David." That reference does suggest that the scribes at the time of Jesus did indeed think of a divinely "anointed" king and one who would be derived from a legitimate family with proper credentials, as opposed to the utterly illegitimate Idumean strongman Herod, who had been appointed by the Romans. Mark has Jesus pointedly reject just this identification of the messiah toward the end of his sustained confrontation with the Jerusalem rulers—by means of a clever device of pointing out who is speaking of whom in an imperial "royal psalm" (Ps. 110:1).[18] The point is clearly to reject any notion of the messiah-king as an imperial ruler (just as Jesus had rejected James and John's aspiration after imperial power and prestige in 10:35–45). But does Mark have Jesus reject an imperial messiah in order to clear the way for Jesus as a popular messiah? If anything, the insistence that the messiah is not the son of David would appear to suggest that both Bartimaeus and Jesus' followers at his entry into Jerusalem got it wrong: if Jesus is a messiah, he is definitely not the son of David.

References to Jesus as "messiah" and "king" become prominent in the
climactic passion narrative. But the narrative displays considerable ambivalence or uncertainty about just what Jesus' being messiah means—or perhaps
about whether he is properly understood as the messiah. When the unnamed
woman, assuming the role of a prophet, anoints Jesus, i.e., designates him as
"messiah," Jesus himself states explicitly that she has "anointed my body for
its burial"—i.e., apparently rejecting or downplaying the standard understanding of a messiah as the divinely designated and/or popularly acclaimed
leader of the people's liberation. At his trial before the chief priests, elders, and
scribes the high priest asks point blank, "Are you the messiah?" (14:61) Then
the Roman governor Pilate asked, "Are you the king of the Judeans?" (15:2).
In both trials Jesus remains silent throughout except for one brief response.
To Pilate's question "Are you the king of the Judeans?" he replies, "You say
so." With regard to the High Priest's question, "Are you the messiah?" the
canonical text of Mark 14:62 (followed by NRSV and other modern English
translations) has Jesus offer what seems like a weak affirmative or perhaps even
a questioning answer ("I am?") before immediately calling attention to "the
son of man . . . coming" in judgment. As suggested by Matthew's and Luke's
common agreement against canonical Mark's text at 14:62, however, along
with Jesus' reply to Pilate in all three Gospels, the earlier version of Mark
known by Matthew and Luke almost certainly had Jesus reply "You say so" to
the high priest as well as to Pilate. Thus it seems likely that in Mark's story
before it became a canonical text, Jesus never claims to be "the messiah" and
never even admits the designation as appropriate.

In referring to him as "the king of the Judeans" (15:9, 18) the Roman governor Pilate and his soldiers seem to be indicating that Jesus is the messiah, yet
Mark indicates explicitly that they are mocking him.[19] Similarly the chief
priests and scribes refer to the crucified Jesus as "the messiah, the king of
Israel," but again completely in mockery. Only in complete irony can Jesus be
"the messiah, the king of Israel." Finally, the centurion apparently in charge
of Jesus' execution says of the now dead Jesus, "Truly this man was a son of
god," again apparently in mockery and sarcasm, or at least ironically, and in a
phrase that may not be an allusion to the messiah at all.[20]

Mark' story thus includes few references to Jesus as messiah, particularly in
the passion narrative. Even in those references, moreover, it is not at all clear
whether Mark is presenting Jesus as a messiah or implying that only others
called him "the messiah," and only in misunderstanding. Peter clearly misun-
derstands what "messiah" might mean when applied to Jesus. Jesus' followers
at his entry into Jerusalem do not seem to understand what is happening any
better than Peter. The woman-prophet who anoints him for burial seems to
have it right, whatever that is. In the trials and crucifixion, however, only the

rulers who are condemning and torturously executing him refer to him as king/messiah. And we cannot help but notice another curious matter. Mark seems to superimpose Peter's and the Jerusalem and Roman rulers' designation of Jesus as the messiah upon, or insert them into, his more sustained and consistent portrayal of Jesus as a prophet engaged in the renewal of Israel over against the rulers.

For a century now scholars have debated the "messianic secret" in Mark's Gospel. It appears that the messianic secret in Mark is that Jesus is not very messianic—or is messianic only in a highly qualified and ironic sense. Mark's Jesus rejects the aspirations to power of the twelve, he twists the significance of the woman's prophetic anointing, and he never accepts the "charge" of the high priests who condemn him or the Romans who crucify him.

In sum, in order to hear Mark's story in its relation to Israelite tradition, we modern listeners must become more fully acquainted with the "scripts" of leaders and movements embedded in Israelite culture at the time of Jesus and Mark. Mark does occasionally make reference to scripture, mainly in order to claim its authority in opposition to its scribal and Pharisaic proprietors. But the scripture was only the written, hence visible, "tip of the iceberg" of Israelite tradition. The much weightier and more influential part of Israelite tradition is ordinarily hidden from our view in the popular tradition that was cultivated orally among the people. With the occasional windows that the written great tradition provides onto the popular tradition, we can discern clear "scripts" of two types of movements among the people that aimed to restore or renew the people's life independent of rulers they experienced as overly oppressive, one led by prophets like Moses and Elijah, the other led by popularly acclaimed ("messiahed") kings like David. Those "scripts" remained alive, if dormant, in the popular memory. In a time of new oppression and crisis for the people, however, those "scripts" were available for leaders-and-followers to follow or adapt in attempting again to renew their society. That is what happened repeatedly at the time of Jesus in the popular prophetic and messianic movements, which thus attest the vitality of these particular "scripts" in Judean and Galilean society precisely during the time of Jesus and his movement and the development of Mark's story. Attending to these "scripts" embedded in Israelite popular tradition can enable us to hear Mark's story with much greater appreciation of how it resonated with the subjected people to whom it was originally addressed. We are thus listening not to figure out "who precisely was Jesus as an individual person," which is an ahistorical modern Western question. We are listening rather to discern what "scripts" were being addressed to the people who identified with and lived out of a particular cultural tradition, a highly relational historical question.

Appendix 1

Both the additive and the repetitive features of Mark's narrative can be appreciated by viewing and especially by sounding out (or getting someone who knows Greek to read aloud) the following transliteration of one episode, Mark 1:21–28. It is readily evident to the ear, aided here by the eye, that virtually every clause, except some of those in direct dialogue, begins with Kai (= and). And the repetition of phrases, terms, and even sounds can be seen by the lines under words or syllables.

Kai eisporeuontai eis Kapharnaoum;
kai euthus tois sabbasin eiselthōn eis tēn synagōgēn edidasken.
Kai exeplēssonto epi tē didachē autou;
ēn gar didaskōn autous hōs exousian echōn,
kai ouch hōs hoi grammateis.
Kai euthus ēn en tē synagōgē autōn anthrōpos en pneumati akathartō,
kai anekraxen legōn:
Ti hēmin kai soi, Iēsou Nazarēnē?
Ēlthes apolesai hēmas?
Oida se tis ei, ho hagios tou thou.
Kai epetimēsen autō ho Iēsous:
phimōthēti kai exelthe ex autou.
Kai sparaxan auton to pneuma to akatharton
kai phōnēsan phōnē megalē exēlthen ex autou.
Kai ethambēthēsan hapantes,
hōste syzētein autous legontas:
ti estin touto?
Didachē kainē kat' exousian;
kai tois pneumasi tois akathartois epitassei,
kai hypakouousin autō.
kai exēlthen hē akoē autou euthus pantachou
    eis holēn tēn perichōron tēs Galilaias.

(Mark 1:21–28)

And they went to Capernaum;
and when the sabbath came, he entered the synagogue and taught.
And they were astounded at his teaching,
for he taught them as one having authority,
and not as the scribes.
And immediately there was in their synagogue a man with an unclean spirit,
and he cried out,
"What have you to do with us, Jesus of Nazareth?
Have you come to destroy us?
I know who you are, the Holy One of God."
And Jesus rebuked him, saying,
"Be silent, and come out of him!"
And the unclean spirit, convulsing him
and crying with a loud voice, came out of him.
And they were all amazed,
and they kept on asking one another,
"What is this?
A new teaching—with authority!
And he commands even the unclean spirits,
and they obey him."
And at once his fame began to spread
    throughout the surrounding region of Galilee.

(Mark 1:21–28 NRSV, with the *and*s restored)

Notes

Chapter 1: Getting the Whole Story

1. For centuries Mark was simply not read at all! Most people, of course, could not read, the Bible was not translated into vernacular languages until early modern times, and books were not readily available even in the West until modern times. Mark was the first Gospel composed, according to the standard theory about the relation between the Gospels, but it was then followed and incorporated by both the Gospel of Matthew and the Gospel of Luke. In Christian tradition, however, Matthew was thought to be the first Gospel and, since nearly all of Mark was included in Matthew, no one bothered to read Mark. As St. Augustine commented: "Mark follows [Matthew] closely and looks as if he were his servant and epitomist (breviator)" (*De Consensu Evangelistarum* 1.2(4)).

2. The pioneers in reading the whole Gospel of Mark as a story were Werner H. Kelber, in a series of lectures to a general audience, published as *Mark's Story of Jesus* (Philadelphia: Fortress Press, 1979); and David Rhoads and Donald Michie, *Mark as Story: An Introduction to the Narrative of a Gospel* (Philadelphia: Fortress Press, 1982). Cf. Frank Kermode, *The Genesis of Secrecy: On the Interpretation of Narrative* (Cambridge, Mass.: Harvard University Press, 1979).

3. This is argued by the literary critic Stanley E. Fish, *Is There a Text in This Class? The Authority of Interpretive Communities* (Cambridge, Mass.: Harvard University Press, 1980), who insists that meaning is made possible only through the communal reading strategies used to actualize a text. Thus, in effect, meaning precedes both text and reader, a sobering practical thought for biblical interpreters.

4. Recently, commercial publishers, realizing the great profits to be made in the religious and biblical studies "market," have paid teams of scholars to contribute to "Study Bibles" that they then sell mainly to students as "texts" for college and university courses.

5. This is still true in many mainline Protestant churches, where lessons from the Gospel of Mark are read in the worship services on two out of three Sundays throughout the year, every three years, in the "lectionary cycle."

6. Besides being traditional, the custom of hearing the Gospel in fragments of scripture lessons is presumably convenient and manageable for people who cannot

summon the time to listen to a medium-length story that would take an hour and a half and may not appear entertaining. Yet most people will spend two or three hours going to a new movie or listening to a TV movie or sports event. And the Gospel story has plenty of violence, particularly toward the end, when Jesus throws things around in the Temple and is then captured by a paramilitary band as if he were an ancient Robin Hood, then mocked by the soldiers and nailed to a cross between two (other) "bandits."

7. Another example: In many churches the "lesson" purposely chosen for "Pledge Sunday," when church members are asked to make their pledges of financial support for the work of the church for the coming next fiscal year, is the episode in which the poor widow, out of her poverty, gave "everything she had, her whole living" (Mark 12:41–44). In the context of Mark's ongoing story, however, Jesus does not approve of her supreme sacrifice. Rather, he uses her sacrifice as an illustration of how the scribes "devour widow's households (livings)," and he announces that the Temple, in which they are based, is about to be destroyed! (12:38–40; 13:1–2; cf. 11:15–18).

8. In *The Quest of the Historical Jesus*, Albert Schweitzer exposed just how problematic were the many lives of Jesus written primarily on the basis of Mark during the nineteenth century.

9. That these are called *pericopae*, or "cuttings," in the field indicates at least some awareness that particular lessons are being "taken out of context."

10. Rhoads and Michie, *Mark as Story*, has been particularly influential.

11. See, e.g., David Rhoads, Joanna Dewey, and Donald Michie, *Mark as Story*, 2d ed. (Minneapolis: Fortress Press, 1999).

12. However, one important introduction to "Mark as story" (Rhoads et al., *Mark as Story*, 2d ed., 5–6) suggests that this be avoided.

13. For an accessible orientation, see Jane P. Tompkins, "An Introduction to Reader-Response Criticism," in *Reader-Response Criticism: From Formalism to Post-Structuralism* (Baltimore: Johns Hopkins University Press, 1980). The most influential "reader-response" theorist in the United States is Wolfgang Iser. See his *The Implied Reader* (Baltimore: Johns Hopkins University Press, 1974) and *The Act of Reading* (Baltimore: Johns Hopkins University Press, 1978). The fullest "reader-response" treatment of Mark is by Robert M. Fowler, *Let the Reader Understand: Reader-Response Criticism and the Gospel of Mark* (Minneapolis: Fortress Press, 1991). See also his shorter introduction, "Reader-Response Criticism: Figuring Mark's Reader," in *Mark and Method: New Approaches in Biblical Studies*, ed. Janice Capel Anderson and Stephen D. Moore (Minneapolis: Fortress Press, 1992), 50–83. Critical assessment of the adaptation of the reader response to biblical studies is found in Stephen D. Moore, *Literary Criticism and the Gospels: The Theoretical Challenge* (New Haven, Conn.: Yale University Press, 1989), chaps. 6–8.

14. See further Fowler, *Let the Reader Understand*, 41–49; Moore, *Literary Criticism*, 81–88.

15. Fredric Jameson, *The Political Unconscious: Narrative as a Socially Symbolic Act* (Ithaca, N.Y.: Cornell University Press, 1981), 9.

16. In his inaugural lecture at Oxford, George Gordon, one of the first professors of the new field of English Literature, declared that "England is sick, and . . . English literature must save it. The Churches (as I understand) having failed, and social remedies being slow, English literature has now a triple function: still, I suppose, to delight and instruct us, but also, and above all, to save our souls and heal the State." Cited by Chris Baldick, *The Social Mission of English Criticism* (Oxford:

Oxford University Press, 1983). From the outset of the new field of English Literature, "the emphasis was on solidarity between the social classes, the cultivation of 'larger sympathies,' the instillation of national pride and the transmission of 'moral' values," according to Terry Eagleton, *Literary Theory: An Introduction* (Minneapolis: University of Minnesota Press, 1983), 27.

17. Eagleton, *Literary Theory*, 21.

18. The incisive critical discussion by Edward W. Said, *Culture and Imperialism* (New York: Alfred A. Knopf, 1993), set the terms for recent discussion of literary criticism's practice of separating literature from political affairs.

19. Amos N. Wilder, *Jesus' Parables and the War of Myths* (Philadelphia: Fortress Press, 1982), 18.

20. For fuller critical discussion, see Moore, *Literary Criticism*, 60–66.

21. Jameson, *The Political Unconscious*, 17. For a fuller and highly suggestive discussion of a "political reading" of Mark, see Ched Myers, *Binding the Strong Man* (Maryknoll, N.Y.: Orbis Books, 1988), chap. 1.

22. Fuller discussion can be found in *The Postmodern Bible*, by members of "The Bible and Modern Culture Collective" (New Haven, Conn.: Yale University Press, 1995). For example, "Once reading conventions are acknowledged as the site of meaning production for both the text and for the reader-critic, then the formation of those conventions and the interests involved in their maintenance or change must be considered primary factors in the reading process" (57–58).

23. In the discussion below, I will often refer to episodes or parts of the story without chapter and verse references, where the reference may be clear by itself, in order to encourage getting to know the story without those distracting references by numbers. But when less obvious or more precise references are necessary, I reluctantly resort to the chapter and verse numbers.

24. A videotape of the sensitive, moving, and highly suggestive performance of Mark by David Rhoads can be rented or purchased.

25. Fowler, *Let the Reader Understand*, 138–39, comments that "the intertwining of incongruent (paradoxical?) plot lines in Mark gives the story great dramatic power, but it has puzzled modern interpreters, who, following Aristotle, presume that good plots must be 'complete and whole,' although Mark's is neither."

26. Rhoads, Dewey, and Michie, *Mark as Story*, 39–47; Fowler, *Let the Reader Understand*, 65.

27. Moore, *Literary Criticism and the Gospels*, 27.

28. Fowler, *Let the Reader Understand*, 76.

29. See further Fowler, *Let the Reader Understand*, 163–94.

30. The historical realization of the "kingdom of God" now underway and soon to be implemented "in power" (1:14–15; 8:34–9:1) would mean independence and self-government by egalitarian communities, as indicated clearly in Mark 10:17–45, on which see chapter 8 below.

31. So, e.g., Mary Ann Tolbert, *Sowing the Gospel: Mark's World in Literary-Historical Perspective* (Minneapolis: Fortress Press, 1989). But the only characters who really can be made to fit one of the types of hearers of the word in Mark 4:13–20 are the disciples. Fowler, *Let the Reader Understand*, 183 n. 38, similarly suggests that Tolbert takes this interpretive scheme too far.

32. Helmut Koester, *Ancient Christian Gospels: Their History and Development* (Philadelphia: Trinity Press International, 1990), 1–43.

33. The possibility of discerning such an intermediate stage, however, should not be dismissed.

34. Lawrence M. Wills, *The Quest of the Historical Gospel* (London and New York: Routledge, 1997), 8–9.
35. David Aune, *The New Testament in Its Literary Environment* (Philadelphia: Westminster Press, 1987), 33. Christopher Bryan, *A Preface to Mark* (Oxford: Oxford University Press, 1993), 37.
36. Similarly, Adela Yarbro Collins, *The Beginning of the Gospel: Probings of Mark in Context* (Minneapolis: Fortress Press, 1992), 25–26.
37. As Aune (*New Testament*, 57) admits.
38. Similarly, in contrast to Hellenistic-Roman lives and hero-narratives—and to Matthew and Luke as well—Mark presents no miraculous birth or remarkable youth. And unlike Hellenistic-Roman heroic biographies, Mark clearly rejects any cult of a risen Jesus at the tomb, instead summoning the followers back to Galilee, where Jesus' story, by implication, continues. Also, in contrast to Plato's and Xenophon's portrayals of Socrates, Mark does not represent Jesus primarily as gathering and teaching disciples, but as manifesting the kingdom of God in preaching and healing, which work the disciples are commissioned to expand (cf. Vernon Robbins, *Jesus the Teacher* [Philadelphia: Fortress Press, 1984]). Wills, *The Quest of the Historical Gospel*, 11, points out that "there is still a distance between [Mark] and the social level and literary attainments of the Greek novels," which were inappropriately characterized as "popular" literature, and therefore a closer literary analogy to Mark than ancient biographies. Cf. Tolbert, *Sowing the Gospel*.
39. Alastair Fowler, *Kinds of Literature: An Introduction to the Theory of Genres and Modes* (Oxford: Oxford University Press, 1982).
40. Collins, *Beginning of the Gospel*, 24–27, also arguing that Mark's story must be understood as history, seeks an ancient generic model in the "historical monograph." Mark is decisively different, of course, insofar as it focuses on ordinary people. It is refreshing also to have an expert on apocalyptic literature pointing out that it also deals with history. While picking up a few motifs that may derive from Judean apocalyptic literature, however, Mark's story displays more prophetic than apocalyptic features, as discussed in chapter 6 below.
41. It is sobering to reflect on the criticism by Eagleton, *Literary Theory*, 50, that New Criticism was "a recipe for political inertia, and thus for submission to the political status quo."
42. Rhoads et al., *Mark as Story*, 4, advocate reading "Mark as story rather than as history" in the sense of not looking "through Mark as a window into history." Point well taken. But given the limited information available in a short story such as Mark taken out of historical context, it is not clear that we will find clarity on something we do not initially understand simply by rereading the story as uninformed readers.
43. We need think only of the cost in terms of the Christian anti-Judaism that has found confirmation in continuously misinformed assimilation of Mark's story to a certain Christian view of history.

Chapter 2: Submerged People's History

1. For sharp summary statements of the Bible as colonizing text, the added impact of imperial strategies of assimilatist Bible reading, and nascent efforts at "reading for decolonization," see Justin S. Ukpong, "Rereading the Bible with African Eyes," *Journal of Theology for Southern Africa* 91 (1995): 3–14; and Musa W. Dube,

"Toward a Postcolonial Feminist Interpretation of the Bible," *Semeia* 78 (1997): 11–26.

2. See the critical treatment in Eric R. Wolf, *Europe and the People without History* (Berkeley: University of California Press, 1982).

3. See the recent surveys of the provenance of Mark's Gospel by E. Earle Ellis, "The Date and Provenance of Mark's Gospel," and John R. Donahue, "The Quest for the Community of Mark's Gospel," both in F. Van Segbroek et al., eds., *The Four Gospels 1992: Festschrift Frans Neirynck*, vol. 2 (Leuven: Leuven University Press, 1992), 801–15 and 817–38, respectively; and Joel Marcus, "The Jewish War and the Sitz im Leben of Mark," *SBL* 111 (1992): 441–62.

4. For a full critical discussion of Israelite history and textual representation in the Hebrew Bible, see now Norman K. Gottwald, *The Politics of Ancient Israel* (Louisville, Ky.: Westminster John Knox Press, 2001).

5. A standard presentation of Judean apocalyptic literature in its historical context is John J. Collins, *The Apocalyptic Imagination* (New York: Crossroad, 1983).

6. For a recent critical review of the history of the Israelite people under foreign empires, particularly as it bears on the Galileans, see Richard A. Horsley, *Galilee: History, Politics, People* (Valley Forge, Pa.: Trinity Press International, 1995), chaps. 1–4.

7. A fuller, documented presentation of Galilee under Hasmonean rule and Roman and Herodian conquests will be found in Horsley, *Galilee*, chap. 2; see esp. pp. 54–56 for Galilean resistance to Herod's conquest.

8. Fuller presentation of these revolts, esp. those led by popular kings, is given in Richard A. Horsley with John S. Hanson, *Bandits, Prophets, and Messiahs* (new ed.; Harrisburg, Pa.: Trinity Press International, 1998), chap. 3; for more fully documented and detailed analysis, see Horsley, "Popular Messianic Movements around the Time of Jesus," *CBQ* 46 (1984): 471–93; and "The Zealots: Their Origins, Relationships, and Importance in the Jewish Revolt," *NovT* 28 (1986): 159–92.

9. Critical analysis and presentation is given in Horsley, *Galilee*, chaps. 3, 5, 7, 12; and Richard A. Horsley, *Archaeology, History, and Society in Galilee: The Social Context of Jesus and the Rabbis* (Valley Forge, Pa.: Trinity Press International, 1996), chaps. 2, 3, 5.

10. See the fuller treatment in *Bandits, Prophets, and Messiahs*, chap. 4. We will return to examine these popular prophetic movements that occurred right around the time of Jesus for what they may reveal about the particular Israelite tradition and distinctive Israelite social form that informed much of the material in the Gospel of Mark.

11. See further *Bandits, Prophets, and Messiahs*, chap. 5; and Richard A. Horsley, *Jesus and the Spiral of Violence* (San Francisco: Harper & Row, 1987; Minneapolis: Fortress Press, 1993), chap. 3.

12. See the discussion of the implications of archaeological evidence to date for ancient "synagogue" buildings in Galilee for reconstruction of social circumstances and social history in Horsley, *Galilee*, chap. 10, and *Archaeology, History, and Society*, chap. 6; cf. Lee I. Levine, "The Nature and Origin of the Palestinian Synagogue Reconsidered," *JBL* 115 (1996): 425–48.

13. On these and related Synoptic Gospel materials, see further Horsley, *Jesus and the Spiral of Violence*, chap. 10. Tat-siong Benny Liew, *Politics of Parousia: Reading Mark Inter(con)textually* (Leiden: E. J. Brill, 1999), 64–93, in a primarily rhetorical-critical analysis, surveys Jesus' attack on the "Jewish authorities" in Mark's narrative, although without linking it with the focus, early in Mark's story, on Jesus' activity in village communities and without attention to Mark's historical context.

14. For an analysis of the sources and critical discussion of the "Dagger Men," see Richard A. Horsley, "The Sicarii: Ancient Jewish Terrorists," *JR* 59 (1979): 435–58.

15. See further Horsley, *Jesus*, 306–17.

16. The "son of man" in the dream-vision of Daniel 7 is interpreted in the second half of the chapter as referring to "the saints of the Most High," i.e., it is a symbol for the people collectively. There is no reason to believe that this collective meaning had disappeared in Mark's story. Mark is apparently leaving his various references to "the son of man" purposely indefinite.

17. That the dominant language can be used for purposes of resistance and subversion is much discussed; see, e.g., Ania Loomba, *Colonialism/Postcolonialism* (London: Routledge, 1998), 91–94.

18. The long-standing Christian view that Mark is about the origins of Christianity from Judaism is attested in its various facets by many studies. A very influential insistence that the referral of the disciples back to Galilee is a symbol for the "Gentile mission" is found in Norman Perrin, *The New Testament: An Introduction* (New York: Harcourt Brace Jovanovich, 1974), 150–51.

19. The criticism of Mark's narrative presentation of Jesus as the new authority figure and of the implied pessimism regarding the possibilities of "agency" articulated by Liew, *Politics of Parousia*, 93–108, 109–32, must be taken seriously. Such criticism, however, may pertain as much or more to the modern Western Christian apocalyptic reading of Mark than to Mark's story itself, with its martyred authority figure and lack of anything like a full-blown parousia. It is worth noting that the "son of man" in Mark 13:26–27 does not "annihilate" anyone, but sends out messengers to gather in the elect (see further chapter 6 below). And what can we make of the "agency" of a protagonist who pursues his program of renewing Israel and attacking the local and imperial rulers in full awareness that it will lead to his death—a confidence in the purposes and possibilities of agency that clearly does not take its cue from politics as the pragmatic art of the possible. In this connection we would have to explore the relationship between vision, contingency, and agency.

20. On the mechanisms in peasant societies designed to maintain the economic viability of each household in the village, see James C. Scott, *The Moral Economy of the Peasant* (New Haven, Conn.: Yale University Press, 1976). These mechanisms in Israelite society are reflected in Leviticus 25 and parallels in the covenant code of Exodus 21–23 and Deuteronomy—devices such as the sabbatical cancellation of debts, sabbatical release of debt-slaves, and redemption of land by the next of kin.

21. See, for example, the review of recent studies of popular resistance movements against the British in India by Rosalind O'Hanlon, "Recovering the Subject: *Subaltern Studies* and Histories of Resistance in Colonial South Asia," *Modern Asian Studies* 22 (1988): esp. 192–93.

Chapter 3: Mark as Oral

1. Werner Kelber has been the pioneer in New Testament studies challenging the field to take seriously how the assumptions of print culture have limited and skewed modern interpreters' ability to discern how communication and transmission of Jesus traditions worked in a predominantly oral communication environment. See his groundbreaking work *The Oral and the Written Gospel: The*

Hermeneutics of Speaking and Writing in the Synoptic Tradition, Mark, Paul, and Q (Philadelphia: Fortress Press, 1983), esp. chaps. 1–2 on pre-Markan materials; and his more recent reflections in "Jesus and Tradition: Words in Time, Words in Space," *Semeia* 65 (1994): 139–67, esp. 140–41.

2. William V. Harris, *Ancient Literacy* (Cambridge, Mass.: Harvard University Press, 1989), esp. 114, 264, 13, 22. Cf. Mary Beard, ed., *Literacy in the Roman World* (Ann Arbor, Mich.: Journal of Roman Archeology, 1991).

3. H. C. Youtie, "Petaus, fils de Petaus, ou le scribe qui ne savait pas écrire," *Chronique d'Égypte* 81 (1966): 127–43. See also Youtie, *"Aggrammatos:* An Aspect of Greek Society in Egypt," *Harvard Studies in Classical Philology* 75 (1971): 161–76; *"Bradeos grafon:* Between Literacy and Illiteracy," *Greek, Roman, and Byzantine Studies* 12 (1971): 239–61; *"Hypografeus:* The Social Impact of Illiteracy in Graeco-Roman Egypt," *Zeitschrift für Papyrologie und Epigraphie* 17 (1975): 201–21; and Harris, *Ancient Literacy,* 202, 277, 280–81.

4. Harris, *Ancient Literacy,* 248–53.

5. Harris, *Ancient Literacy,* 198–99, 201.

6. Ironically, although recent studies of Jesus and early Christianity acknowledge the extremely limited levels of literacy in ancient Greek cities and the Roman empire, they continue to trust generalizations about high rates of Judean or diaspora Jewish literacy that preceded recent critical studies of literacy in antiquity. See, e.g., Martin Hengel, *Judaism and Hellenism* (2 vols.; Philadelphia: Fortress Press, 1974), 1.78–83; S. Safrai, "Education and the Study of the Torah," in *The Jewish People in the First Century* (Compendia Rerum Iudaicarum ad Novum Testamentum, sec. I.2), ed. S. Safrai and M. Stern (Philadelphia: Fortress Press, 1976), 2.945–70, esp. 952, 954. "According to Josephus, in first-century Judaism it was a duty, indeed a religious commandment, that Jewish children be taught to read. . . . [R]abbinic sources suggest . . . there is little question that by the first century C.E. Judaism had developed a strong interest in basic literacy and that even small communities had elementary schools." Harry Y. Gamble, *Books and Readers in the Early Church* (New Haven, Conn.: Yale University Press, 1995), 7.

7. "To learn *grammata*" in *C. Ap.* 2.204 in the context of study of the law suggests not learning to read (so the Thackeray translation in the Loeb edition), but learning "scripture," which is done through public oral teaching, as indicated earlier at 2.175.

8. *Pace* Martin Goodman, *State and Society in Roman Galilee, A.D. 132–212* (Totowa, N.J.: Rowman & Allanheld, 1983), 72, whose discussion of "education" (pp. 71–81) does not appear to apply to village culture.

9. Meir Bar-Ilan, "Illiteracy in the Land of Israel in the First Centuries C.E.," in *Essays in the Social Scientific Study of Judaism and Jewish Society,* ed. Simcha Fishbane and Stuart Schoenfeld (Hoboken, N.J.: KTAV, 1992), 46–61.

10. Rosalind Thomas, *Literacy and Orality in Ancient Greece* (Cambridge: Cambridge University Press, 1992), 102–3, 120–23.

11. Thomas, *Literacy and Orality,* 118, 123–24; and J. Herington, *Poetry into Drama: Early Tragedy and the Greek Poetic Tradition* (Berkeley and Los Angeles: University of California Press, 1985).

12. Pierre Hadot, "Forms of Life and Forms of Discourse in Ancient Philosophy," *Critical Inquiry* 16 (1990): 497–98.

13. Botha,"Greco-Roman Literacy," 201.

14. Thomas, *Literacy and Orality,* 48–50, 122–23.

15. Harris, *Ancient Literacy,* 223–28.

16. Ibid., 227–28. This raises questions about the thesis of Mary Ann Tolbert, *Sowing the Gospel: Mark's World in Literary-Historical Perspective* (Minneapolis: Fortress Press, 1989), 59–79.

17. Thomas, *Literacy and Orality*, 4.

18. Susan Niditch, *Oral World and Written Word* (Louisville, Ky.: Westminster John Knox Press, 1996), 104–6. The "documentary history" recounted in Ezra 1–6 of the Persian imperial authorization of the rebuilding of the Temple in Jerusalem illustrates both the memorial character of the Persian imperial decrees, which prove difficult to locate in the imperial "archives" (6:1–2), and the magical-religious function of (some of) the writing. In the decree authorizing support from the imperial revenues for sacrifices to God and prayers for the emperor in the rebuilt Jerusalem temple, Darius also pronounces a curse on anyone who would dare to alter his edict (6:6–12): he would be impaled on a beam from his own house, which would be turned into a manure heap!

19. By analogy with the *Didache*, "there is nothing in this *didache* that the reader does not already know"; Ian Henderson, "*Didache* and Orality in Synoptic Comparison," *JBL* 111 (1992): 292.

20. Paul J. Achtemeier, "*Omnes verbum sonat:* The New Testament and the Oral Environment of Late Western Antiquity," *JBL* 109 (1990): 26–27 makes the general point that since written scrolls in antiquity were so difficult to "read," given the lack of breaks between words, the lack of markings of divisions, and the cumbersome unrolling and rolling of the scroll, that "references were therefore much more likely to be quoted from memory than to be copied from a source." The opening of the Mishnah tractate *Abot* certainly gives the impression that the rabbis believed that the tradition of (the?) Torah had been oral all along, as Moses handed it on to Joshua, Joshua to the elders, etc., in the "chain of tradition."

21. Martin S. Jaffee, "Writing and Rabbinic Oral Tradition: On Mishnaic Narrative, Lists and Mnemonics," *Journal of Jewish Thought and Philosophy* 4 (1994): 126, 143–44.

22. Vernon K. Robbins, "Oral, Rhetorical, and Literary Cultures," *Semeia* 65 (1994): 79.

23. On the cultivation of Israelite tradition orally among Galilean and other villagers, see further the investigations in Richard A. Horsley, *Galilee: History, Politics, People* (Harrisburg, Pa.: Trinity Press International, 1995), 148–56; 245–51; and in Horsley and Jonathan Draper, *Whoever Hears You Hears Me* (Harrisburg, Pa.: Trinity Press International, 1999), 98–122, 135–50.

24. To say "Old Testament," as is often done in Christian New Testament interpretation, of course, is an anachronism, since there was no such thing yet as the "New" Testament at the time Mark and other Gospels were produced.

25. For example, when in discussing John and Baptist in Luke 7:27 and its parallel in Matt 11:10 (which must come from Q) Jesus says "it is written," it is unclear exactly what "text" he is "citing." It makes more sense to understand the term "as it is written," here and in the Q story of the testing (Luke 4:1–13 and its parallel in Matt. 4:1–11), as a reference to the authority of the scripture rather than a citation formula or reference to a particular written text.

26. Only in explaining the events that were difficult to accept and understand, such as the betrayal, arrest, and crucifixion of Jesus and the desertion of the disciples, does Mark appeal to the general or particular authority of the scripture (14:21, 27, 49). His procedure here is similar to the way the creed Paul cites in 1 Corinthians

15:3–5 refers to the general authority of "scripture" (with no particular references) to authorize the death and resurrection of Christ.

27. The observation by Achtemeier, *"Omnes verbum sonat,"* 7, that "the sheer act of committing traditions to writing did not eliminate their continued transmission in non-written forms," while making somewhat the same point, is in effect an understatement, for transmission was embedded and effected in repeated performance.

28. Modern biblical scholars, concerned with the sacred words of the word of God, have labored assiduously to "establish" the precise wording of the text on the basis of the best (i.e., critically established) manuscript evidence. The best manuscripts date from several generations, even centuries after the origin of Mark's story. And those manuscripts were produced in the context of an ongoing oral performance of the story. Because of certain patterns of variation between the *canonical* text (version) of Mark (i.e., the one that teams of scholars have decided to have printed in editions of our Greek New Testament) and the canonical texts of Matthew and Luke, who both supposedly copied the same text/version of Mark, it has been suggested that canonical Mark is a secondary development from Matthew's and Luke's Mark (see esp. Helmut Koester, *Ancient Christian Gospels;* Philadelphia: Trinity Press International, 1990, 273–86). That there were different versions of Mark's story in circulation is highly likely considering the relationship between ongoing performance of stories such as Mark and written manuscripts of such stories. It may be the chimera of the modern print-culture-based scholarly imagination that a single prototype of Mark ever existed. In any case, what we have in the canonical Mark in our Bibles is a particular English translation of a written copy, probably a second- or third-generation written copy, of a narrative that was regularly performed orally. That is, we have a secondary transcript of one performance of the story. We have one textual rendition of an otherwise living oral tradition. The canonical text of Mark in front of us thus provides a window onto one performance in an ongoing performance tradition of Mark.

29. His comments are paralleled by Seneca (Achtemeier, *"Omnes verbum sonat,"* 10). Well into the second century, the Gospels that became canonical were not yet widely distributed (Birger Gerhardsson, *Memory and Manuscript: Oral Tradition and Written Transmission in Rabbinic Judaism and Early Christianity*, ASNU 22 [Lund: C. W. K. Gleerup; Copenhagen: Ejnar Munksgaard, 1961], 200).

30. Helmut Koester, *Synoptische Überlieferung bei den Apostolischen Vätern* (Berlin: Akademie-Verlag, 1957).

31. Thomas, *Literacy and Orality*, 104.

32. "Reading was . . . oral performance *whenever* it occurred and in whatever circumstances. Late antiquity knew nothing of the 'silent, solitary reader'"; Achtemeier, *"Omnes verbum sonat,"* 17, contra Havelock (see note 41 below).

33. Kelber, "Jesus and Tradition," 155.

34. The following sketch of how meaning occurs in oral performance is heavily indebted to John Miles Foley, *Immanent Art: From Structure to Meaning in Traditional Oral Epic* (Bloomington, Ind.: Indiana University Press, 1991); and *Singer of Tales in Performance* (Bloomington, Ind.: Indiana University Press, 1995); and to M. A. K. Halliday, *Language as Social Semiotic: The Social Interpretation of Language and Meaning* (London: Edward Arnold, 1978). For a more developed statement of a theory of performance-and-hearing in connection with the speeches of Jesus in Matthew and Luke's Gospels known as "Q" see Horsley, "Recent Studies of Oral Derived Literature and Q," in Horsley and Draper, *Whoever Hears You Hears Me,*

chap. 7. The sociolinguistic theory of Halliday has been applied to Mark (though not to its oral performance) by Brian K. Blount, *Go Preach! Mark's Kingdom Message and the Black Church Today* (Maryknoll, N.Y.: Orbis Books, 1998).

35. Foley, *Immanent Art*, 5.
36. Werner H. Kelber, *The Oral and Written Gospel* (1983), pioneered exploration of the implication of orality for the development of Jesus traditions in general. The first explorations of Mark as (rooted in) oral performance were Joanna Dewey, "Oral Methods of Structuring Narrative in Mark," *Interpretation* 53 (1989): 32–44; and Pieter J. J. Botha, "Mark's Story as Oral Traditional Literature: Rethinking the Transmission of Some Traditions about Jesus," *Hervormde Teologiese Studies* 47 (1991): 304–31.
37. Joanna Dewey, "Mark as Aural Narrative: Structures as Clues to Understanding," *Sewanee Theological Review* 36 (1992): 47.
38. Kelber, *Oral and Written Gospel*, chap. 2, provides a very creative and illuminating analysis of the oral storytelling behind Mark's Gospel.
39. In this connection I again recommend viewing/hearing the highly suggestive dramatic performance of Mark's story in English by David Rhoads (see note 24 of chapter 1).
40. The groundbreaking work on Homeric epic, drawing upon comparative material from twentieth-century Bosnian and Serbian epic singers was carried out by Milman Parry and Albert Lord. It is most accessible in Lord's *Singer of Tales* (Cambridge, Mass.: Harvard University Press, 1960). Very suggestive and helpful analysis of Native American stories has been done by Dell Hymes, "Discovering Oral Performance and Measured Verse in American Indian Narrative," reprinted in his *"In Vain I Tried to Tell You": Essays in Native American Ethnopoetics* (Philadelphia: University of Pennsylvania Press, 1981), 79–141.
41. Eric Havelock, *Preface to Plato* (Cambridge, Mass.: Harvard University Press, 1963), 180.
42. Walter Ong, *Orality and Literacy* (London: Methuen, 1982), 34.
43. In the following transliteration, one can again attempt to hear, with the aid of the eye, the repetition of (sequences of) words and sounds in Mark 1:40–45.

     Kai erchetai pros auton   lepros
     parakalōn auton kai gonypetōn kai legōn autō hoti ean thelēs dynasai me katharisai.
     Kai orgistheis ekteinas tēn cheira autou hēpsato
                                        kai legei auto: thelō,   katharisthēti.
     Kai euthys apēlthen ap' autou hē lepra,   kai ekatharisthē.

44. In the following transliteration, one can attempt to hear the repetition of (sequences of) words and sounds in Mark 7:29–31.

     Kai eipen autē:
     Dia touton ton logon hypage,   exelēlythen ek tēs thygatros sou   to daimonion.
     Kai apelthousa eis ton oikon autēs
              heuren to paidion beblēmenon epi tēn klinēn kai to daimonion exelēlythos.

45. Havelock, "Oral Composition," 182.
46. Ibid., 183. Ong, *Orality and Literacy*, 39, points out that oral narrative is "redundant or 'copious.'" Writing establishes a line of continuity outside the mind. But in oral narrative, there is nothing to backloop into outside the mind, for the oral

utterance has vanished as soon as it is uttered. Hence the mind must move ahead more slowly, keeping close to the focus of attention much of what it has already dealt with. Redundancy, repetition of the just-said, keeps both speaker and hearer surely on the track.

47. The function of this story as a major turning point in the story should not be overblown. The hearers already know, from the very outset (from their belonging to the movement that has produced and regularly hears this story) that if Jesus was a messiah at all, he was a martyred messiah. In the overall Markan narrative therefore this story functions more as a key indication of how Peter and other disciples are doing in their struggle to "see" and "hear" what is happening.

48. The echoes and other connections even include details of motif and theme. The healing of the blind man in Bethsaida in 8:22–26 happens in two stages, as does the preceding healing story of the deaf and dumb man in 7:31–37. In both Jesus uses spittle in the healing (the only occurrences of the motif in Mark) and commands silence, and verbal echoes between the two stories abound. The hearers, who during the previous section 4:35–8:21 have just heard two parallel stories of a sea crossing, an exorcism, a mass feeding in the wilderness, and a first healing, now finally hear the parallel to the story of the second healing. The healing in 7:31–37 deals with hearing and that in 8:22–26 with seeing. In between, Jesus asks the disciples pointedly, "Having eyes do you not see, and having ears do you not hear?" (8:18).

49. Ong, *Orality and Literacy*, 34.

50. Dewey, *Markan Public Debate*, 144.

51. Walter J. Ong, *Interfaces of the Word* (Ithaca, N.Y.: Cornell University Press, 1977), 282.

Chapter 4: Disciples Become Deserters

1. Much of the burgeoning number of studies by theologically oriented "redaction critics" is surveyed in C. Clifton Black, *The Disciples according to Mark: Markan Redaction in Current Debate* (JSNTSS 27; Sheffield: Sheffield Academic Press, 1989), in which much of the critique focuses on what seem to be "straw men." The work of Ernest Best has been focal, the most accessible being his *Following Jesus: Discipleship in the Gospel of Mark* (JSNTSS 4; Sheffield: JSOT Press, 1981).

2. An influential early exploration was Robert Tannehill, "The Disciples in Mark: The Function of a Narrative Role," *JR* 57 (1977): 386–405. The following paragraph is based on this article, with references, respectively, to pp. 396–97, 392–93, and 395.

3. David Rhoads, Joanna Dewey, and Donald Michie, *Mark as Story: An Introduction to the Narrative of a Gospel* (2d ed.; Minneapolis: Fortress Press, 1999), 128–29.

4. Mary Ann Tolbert, *Sowing the Gospel: Mark's World in Literary-Historical Perspective* (Minneapolis: Fortress Press, 1989), 223–25.

5. Brief critique of the individual spiritual quest driving the discipleship reading of Mark is found in John R. Donahue, S.J., *The Theology and Setting of Discipleship in the Gospel of Mark* (Milwaukee, Wis.: Marquette University Press, 1983), 30–31.

6. E.g., Stephen H. Smith, *A Lion with Wings: A Narrative-Critical Approach to Mark's Gospel* (Sheffield: Sheffield Academic Press, 1996), 52–59.

7. Jack Dean Kingsbury, *Conflict in Mark: Jesus, Authorities, Disciples* (Minneapolis: Fortress Press, 1989), 6–13; Smith, *Lion with Wings*, 61–62.

8. Despite Tolbert's cautionary comments (*Sowing the Gospel*, 76–77), literary critics still apply character theory derived from modern novels to Mark, e.g., Elizabeth

Struthers Malbon, "The Jewish Leaders in the Gospel of Mark: A Literary Study of Marcan Characterization," *JBL* 108 (1989): 259–81; "Narrative Criticism: How Does the Story Mean?" in *Mark and Method: New Approaches in Biblical Studies* (Minneapolis: Fortress Press, 1992), 28–30; and Smith, *Lion with Wings*, chap. 2; and Tolbert herself presented an article with a title that, given her cautionary comments, must be intended as ironic, in "How the Gospel of Mark Builds Character," *Int.* 47 (1993): 347–57.

9. Rhoads, et al., *Mark as Story*, 99–100. Similarly, Elizabeth Struthers Malbon, "The Major Importance of the Minor Characters in Mark," in Malbon and Edgar J. McKnight, eds., *The New Literary Criticism and the New Testament* (JSNTSS 109; Sheffield: Sheffield Academic Press, 1994), 58–85, indicates at points (e.g., 69, 73–83) that the plot is the controlling factor in an approach that tends to flatten the story by abstracting from the plot. This holds also for Peter, who is portrayed as a more distinctive individual character than the others. The recent attempt by Timothy Wiarda ("Peter as Peter in the Gospel of Mark," *NTS* 45 [1999]: 19–37) to find "significant elements of individual human experience" in Mark's characterization of Peter ignores not only the plot that Mark's characterization serves but also the historical context in which the story was plotted.

10. Tolbert, *Sowing the Gospel*, 77.

11. Tolbert, "How the Gospel of Mark Builds Character," *Interpretation* 47 (1993): 349.

12. Rhoads et al., *Mark as Story*, 99. Not surprisingly, therefore, when these literary critics are ostensibly presenting Mark's "characterization" of the disciples (123–27), they basically explore the (sub) *plot* of the conflict between Jesus and the disciples.

13. By far the most influential statement has been Gerd Theissen, *The Sociology of Early Palestinian Christianity* (Philadelphia: Fortress Press, 1978).

14. See esp. John H. Elliott, "Social-Scientific Criticism of the New Testament and Its Social World: More on Method and Models," *Semeia* 35 (1986): 1–34; and Richard A. Horsley, *Sociology and the Jesus Movement* (New York: Crossroad, 1989), chaps. 1–3; and Jonathan A. Draper, "Wandering Charismatics and Scholarly Circularities," in Richard A. Horsley and J. A. Draper, *Whoever Hears You Hears Me: Prophets, Performance, and Tradition in Q* (Harrisburg, Pa.: Trinity Press International, 1999), 29–45.

15. For an interpretation of Jesus and the disciples as similar to an ancient philosopher and his students, see Vernon K. Robbins, *Jesus the Teacher: A Socio-Rhetorical Interpretation of Mark* (Philadelphia: Fortress Press, 1984).

16. This and the next two quotations are from Tannehill, "The Disciples in Mark," 396–97, 399, and 400, respectively.

17. As claimed by Tolbert, *Sowing the Gospel*, esp. 59–75. Cf. the more recent assessment of ancient "novels" by Lawrence Wills, "The Depiction of Slavery in the Ancient Novel," *Semeia* 83/84 (1998): 113–32.

18. Robbins, *Jesus the Teacher*. See now the reworking of some of the same comparative material in Whitney T. Shiner, *Follow Me! Disciples in Markan Rhetoric* (SBLDS 145; Atlanta: Scholars Press, 1995).

19. See further the fuller discussion by Richard A. Horsley in *Whoever Hears You Hears Me*, 233, 242–48; and Jonathan A. Draper, "Wandering Radicalism or Purposeful Activity? Jesus and the Sending of Messengers in Mark 6:6–56," *Neotestamentica* 29 (1995): 183–202.

20. Observed by Donahue, *Theology and Setting of Discipleship*, 31.

21. Cf. Tolbert, *Sowing the Gospel*, 22.
22. There seems little point in discussing a passing phase in the interpretation of Mark in terms of a hypothetical conflict in theologies or Christologies. According to one line of theological interpretation with considerable scholarly cachet thirty years ago, in criticizing the disciples Mark was opposing a "divine man" *(theios anēr)* Christology of Jesus as a glorious wonder-worker, portrayed in the first half of the Gospel, replaced in the second half by emphasis on the suffering and crucifixion of Jesus, which a "disciple" should imitate. See esp. Theodor J. Weeden Sr., *Mark—Traditions in Conflict* (Philadelphia: Fortress Press, 1971). The synthetic modern scholarly construct of the "divine man" and its application to New Testament materials was convincingly laid to rest by David L. Tiede, *The Charismatic Figure as Miracle Worker* (SBLDS 1; Missoula, Mont.: Scholars Press, 1972), and Carl R. Holladay, *Theios Aner in Hellenistic Judaism: A Critique of the Use of This Category in New Testament Christology* (SBLDS 40: Missoula, Mont.: Scholars Press, 1977); and Howard C. Kee, "Aretalogy and Gospel," *JBL* 92 (1973): 402–22.
23. Briefly discussed by Graham Stanton, *The Gospels and Jesus* (Oxford: Oxford University Press, 1989), 47.
24. Werner Kelber is the principal scholar who, taking seriously the severity of Mark's portrayal of the disciples, has interpreted the Gospel as an argument against what they represented historically in the early Jesus movement(s)—in three different books with three different emphases on the issues dividing Mark from Peter, James, and the Twelve: *The Kingdom in Mark: A New Place and a New Time* (Philadelphia: Fortress Press, 1974); *Mark's Story of Jesus* (Philadelphia: Fortress Press, 1979); and *The Oral and the Written Gospel* (Philadelphia: Fortress Press, 1983). Attempts to argue against his historical interpretation of Mark's portrayal of the disciples tend to downplay the severity of Mark's portrayal, e.g., Elizabeth Struthers Malbon, "Text and Contexts: Interpreting the Disciples in Mark," *Semeia* 62 (1993): 81–102.
25. See, for example, Robert P. Meye, *Jesus and the Twelve: Discipleship and Revelation in Mark's Gospel* (Grand Rapids: Eerdmans, 1968).
26. See further Neil Q. Hamilton, "Resurrection Tradition and the Composition of Mark," *JBL* 84 (1965): 415–21, followed by John Dominic Crossan, "Empty Tomb and Absent Lord (Mark 16:1–8)," in Werner Kelber, ed., *The Passion in Mark* (Philadelphia: Fortress Press, 1976), 135–52.

Chapter 5: Getting the Whole Story

1. More in a line with traditional theological interpretation, David Rhoads, Joanna Dewey, and Donald Michie, *Mark as Story: An Introduction to the Narrative of a Gospel* (2d ed.; Minneapolis: Fortress Press, 1999), 77, and others suggest that God is establishing rule "over the world." Usage of the phrase in Mark's narrative, however, almost always has a social-political sense, as in Mark 10:15, 23–25. For a presentation of Jesus' proclamation of the kingdom of God as meaning the social-political renewal of Israel in Markan and other Synoptic Gospel materials, see Richard A. Horsley, *Jesus and the Spiral of Violence* (San Francisco: Harper & Row, 1987), chap. 7.
2. The two sets of miracle stories were delineated by Paul J. Achtemeier, "Toward the Isolation of Pre-Markan Miracle Catenae," *JBL* 89 (1970): 265–91. He then explained their origin in terms of Hellenistic Jewish texts and their significance in connection to celebration of the Eucharist in the Hellenistic church in "The

Origin and Function of the Pre-Marcan Miracle Catenae," *JBL* 91 (1972): 198–221. As we are finally beginning to recognize, of course, traditions of Israel's origins were also cultivated orally in popular circles in Galilee and Judea, as explored in Richard A. Horsley, *Galilee: History, Politics, People* (Valley Forge, Pa.: Trinity Press International, 1995), 148–56; and "Israelite Traditions in Q," chap. 5 in Horsley and Jonathan Draper, *Whoever Hears You Hears Me* (Harrisburg, Pa.: Trinity Press International, 1999).

3. Werner Kelber, *Mark's Story of Jesus* (Philadelphia: Fortress Press, 1979), 30–35; debated by Robert M. Fowler, *Loaves and Fishes: The Function of the Feeding Stories in the Gospel of Mark* (SBLDS 54; Chico, Calif.: Scholars Press, 1981), 61–65; Elizabeth Struthers Malbon, "The Jesus of Mark and the Sea of Galilee," *JBL* 103 (1984): 363; and Ched Myers, *Binding the Strong Man* (Maryknoll, N.Y.: Orbis Books, 1988), 187–89, 194–95.

4. Jesus' authority over the sea in these Markan episodes should not be taken as a separate plot line or subplot, but an integral feature in his Moses- or Elijah-like actions taken in renewal of Israel. Cf. Rhoads et al., *Mark as Story*, 83.

5. The Greek term identifying Jairus as an *archisynagōgos* has often been mistranslated as a "ruler" of the synagogue. But just as a "bandit chief" (*archilēstēs*) is not a "ruler" but a leader of the band, so an "assembly chief" is not a ruler; hence this episode cannot be understood in terms of class relations. Cf. Myers, *Binding the Strong Man*, 200. See now the general review essay by Lee I. Levine, "Synagogue Leadership: The Case of the Archisynagogos," in Martin Goodman, ed., *Jews in a Greco-Roman World* (Oxford: Clarendon Press, 1998), 195–213.

6. Burton L. Mack, *A Myth of Innocence: Mark and Christian Origins* (Philadelphia: Fortress Press, 1988), 222–24, while discerning the popular Galilean-rooted tradition on which they draw, interprets the sets of pre-Marcan miracles in individualistic terms and over against "the Jewish point of view" as representing the formation of a "new congregation" of an "unlikely mixture" or "socially marginal, . . . 'unclean' people," so that Jesus is not the Mosaic renewer of Israel but "the founder of a new society." Mark's Jesus, however, is not establishing "a new social order" (so Rhoads, *Mark as Story*, 85) or a new discipleship community (so Myers, *Binding the Strong Man*), but is working in village communities and households to renew or revitalize Israelite society. Thus what might be taken as separate plot strands of community building, healing and exorcism, and political conflict (so, e.g., Myers, 138), are all aspects of the renewal of Israel over against its rulers.

7. Typical examples in standard journals are Elizabeth Struthers Malbon, "The Jewish Leaders in the Gospel of Mark: A Literary Study of Marcan Characterization," *JBL* 108 (1989): 259–81; and Terence J. Keegan, O.P., "The Parable of the Sower and Mark's Jewish Leaders," *CBQ* 56 (1994): 501–18.

8. Various aspects mentioned in the following several pages are discussed and documented in my *Jesus*, chaps. 1–4; *Sociology and the Jesus Movement* (New York: Crossroad, 1989), chaps. 4–5; (with John Hanson) *Bandits, Prophets, and Messiahs* (new ed.; Harrisburg, Pa.: Trinity Press International, 1999); and "High Priests and the Politics of Roman Palestine," *Journal for the Study of Judaism* 17 (1986): 23–55.

9. See Josephus's accounts of the "Fourth Philosophy" and critical discussion in Horsley with Hanson, *Bandits, Prophets, and Messiahs*, 190–99; and Horsley, *Jesus*, 77–89.

10. See further my *Galilee*, chaps. 3 and 7; and *Archeology, History, and Society in Galilee:*

The Social Context of Jesus and the Rabbis (Valley Forge, Pa.: Trinity Press International, 1996), chaps. 1–2. On the legend of John the Baptist's beheading, see Gerd Theissen, *The Gospels in Context* (Minneapolis: Fortress Press, 1991), 81–96.

11. On the high priesthood and its opposition, see further Horsley, "High Priests and Politics," in *Jesus*, 286–92; *Galilee*, 128–37; and Martin Goodman, *The Ruling Class of Judea* (Cambridge: Cambridge University Press, 1987), 9.

12. Josephus's accounts of the *Sicarioi* are critically discussed in my *Bandits, Prophets, and Messiahs*, 200-216; *Jesus*, 39–43; and esp. "The Sicarii: Ancient Jewish Terrorists," *Journal of Religion* 59 (1979), 435–58.

13. Cf. Rhoads et al., *Mark as Story*, 77–78. For yet another indication of how Jesus' condemnation of Temple and high priesthood fits the historical-cultural context, see the recent article by Johannes C. De Moor, "The Targumic Background of Mark 12:1–12: The Parable of the Wicked Tenants," *Journal for the Study of Judaism* 29 (1998): 63–80.

14. On the following facets of Galilean history and circumstances, see further my *Galilee*; and *Archaeology, History and Society in Galilee*.

15. See the extensive discussion of Galilean village life in Horsley, *Galilee*, chaps. 8–10; on indebtedness, see *Sociology and the Jesus Movement*, 88–90.

16. See the examination of the archaeological and textual evidence in Horsley, *Galilee*, chap. 8.

17. For suggestive discussion of the "little tradition" versus the "great tradition," see James C. Scott, "Protest and Profanation: Agrarian Revolt and the Little Tradition," *Theory and Society* 4 (1977): 1–38, 211–46. On Israelite popular tradition, see further Horsley, *Galilee*, 148–56; and "Israelite Traditions in Q," in *Whoever Hears You Hears Me*, chap. 5; and *Bandits, Prophets, and Messiahs*, chaps. 3–4.

Chapter 6: The Struggle Against Roman Rule

1. In a textbook widely used in introductory New Testament courses, Norman Perrin, *The New Testament: An Introduction* (New York: Harcourt Brace Jovanovich, 1974, and subsequent editions), subtitles the chapter on the Gospel of Mark "The Apocalyptic Drama."

2. For a fuller survey and analysis, see Richard Horsley, "Wisdom and Apocalypticism in Mark," in *In Search of Wisdom: Essays in Memory of John G. Gammie*, ed. Leo G. Perdue, Bernard Brandon Scott, and William Johnston Wiseman (Louisville, Ky.: Westminster/John Knox Press, 1993), 223–44.

3. Two critical surveys are John J. Collins, *The Apocalyptic Imagination* (New York: Crossroad, 1984); and George W. E. Nickelsburg, *Jewish Literature between the Bible and the Mishnah* (Philadelphia: Fortress Press, 1981).

4. See further Richard A. Horsley, *Jesus and the Spiral of Violence* (San Francisco: Harper & Row, 1987), 129–31.

5. See further Horsley, "Wisdom and Apocalypticism," 228–30.

6. A fuller treatment, with different emphasis, is givien in Richard A. Horsley, "The Kingdom of God and the Renewal of Israel: Synoptic Gospels, Jesus Movements, and Apocalypticism," in *The Encyclopedia of Apocalypticism*, vol. 1: *The Origins of Apocalypticism in Judaism and Christianity*, ed. John J. Collins (New York: Crossroad, 1998), 304–9, 326.

7. The following paragraphs are dependent on previous treatments in Horsley, "Wisdom and Apocalypticism in Mark," and "The Kingdom of God and the Renewal of Israel."

8. From the vast literature on the "son of man," one might consult Adela Yarbro Collins, "The Origin of the Designation of Jesus as 'Son of Man,'" *HTR* 80 (1987): 391–407; John R. Donahue, "Recent Studies on the Origin of 'Son of Man' in the Gospels," *CBQ* 48 (1986): 484–98; Douglas R. A. Hare, *The Son of Man Tradition* (Minneapolis: Fortress Press, 1990).

9. A review of earlier scholarly discussion is in G. R. Beasley-Murray, *Jesus and the Last Days: The Interpretation of the Olivet Discourse* (Peabody, Mass.: Hendrickson, 1993; orig. 1954).

10. Lars Hartman, *Prophecy Interpreted: The Formation of Some Jewish Apocalyptic Texts and of the Eschatological Discourse in Mark 13 Par.* (Lund: Gleerup, 1966), lays out the prophetic background of many of the motifs in Mark 13.

11. That is, although Jesus' speech is drawing on imagery of theophany used previously in prophetic announcements of God's imminent defeat of foreign rulers, it focuses only on the deliverance of dispersed Israelites, without apparent reference to destruction of the imperial forces that are causing the suffering unprecedented since the beginning of creation. Jesus' speech here articulates liberation from, but not any annihilation of, imperial power. Cf. the recent rhetorical analysis of Tatsiong Benny Liew, *Politics of Parousia: Reading Mark Inter(con)textually* (Leiden: Brill, 1999), 107.

12. Note the similar image of the future restoration of Israel in the Synoptic Sayings Source Q, Matt. 8:11–12 // Luke 13:28–29. For a demonstration that the latter passage, and by implication Mark 13:27, does not refer to the Gentiles, as often claimed by Christian interpreters, but to the ingathering of Israelites, see Dale C. Allison Jr., *The Jesus Tradition in Q* (Harrisburg, Pa.: Trinity Press International, 1997), 176–91.

13. Burton L. Mack, *A Myth of Innocence: Mark and Christian Origins* (Philadelphia: Fortress Press, 1988), esp. 353–76.

14. So also Adela Yarbro Collins, *The Beginning of the Gospel: Probings of Mark in Context* (Minneapolis: Fortress Press, 1992), 75–76, 82.

15. See chaps. 2 and 5 above. More extensive, documented discussion of the history and particular events and movements in this prolonged conflict will be found in Horsley with Hanson, *Bandits, Prophets, and Messiahs*; Horsley, *Jesus and the Spiral of Violence*, 26–58; Horsley, *Sociology and the Jesus Movement* (New York: Crossroad, 1989), chaps. 4–5. As is surely already evident, my analysis of "Jesus'" speech in Mark 13 in historical context is an attempt to cease working on the basis of modern scholarly assumptions (such as that Mark can be analyzed separately from the rest of the Gospel or that Mark viewed the Temple positively) and anachronisms (such as "nationalism" and "Judaism") and synthetic constructs (such as "the Zealots" or "Davidic Messianism"). For a suggestive recent analysis of Mark 13 that still works with many of these standard assumptions and constructs, see Joel Marcus, "The Jewish War and the Sitz im Leben of Mark," *JBL* 111 (1992): 441–62.

16. Horsley, *Jesus and the Spiral*, 28–49.

17. Moreover, for those in Judea, fleeing toward the mountains would mean fleeing in the direction of Jerusalem, which lay in the center of the mountains. That is precisely where many Judean peasants fled during the great revolt in 67–68, particularly those who formed fighting forces. But if the narrator of Mark were attempting to warn his hearers about getting caught in the firestorm during the Roman reconquest from 67–70, flight in that direction would not have made sense. Here is another factor suggesting that the speech in Mark 13 addresses

(and should be heard as reflecting) a situation sometime during the decades of conflict that led up to the great revolt, but not after the revolt became centered in Jerusalem.

18. Working on the assumption that the exorcisms in Mark are integral to and inseparable from the overall story, our procedure will be almost the virtual opposite from the standard form-critical analysis, which isolates each exorcism story from its wider literary context and then compares it with extrabiblical Hellenistic stories mainly for formal characteristics.

19. The following terminological analysis is based on Howard Clark Kee, "The Terminology of Mark's Exorcism Stories," *NTS* 14 (1968): 232–46. *Horkizein*, one of the usual terms in Hellenistic exorcism stories, is used in Mark only at 5:7 where the demon says "I adjure *(horkizō)* you by God, do not torment me"—i.e., the demon tries to exorcize Jesus!

20. Translation is from Geza Vermes, *The Complete Dead Sea Scrolls in English* (London: Penguin Books, 1997), 178.

21. This conclusion paraphrases Kee's conclusion about *ga'ar*, "Terminology," 234–35, who writes "the commanding word." But in the Qumran passages and Psalms passages cited, more than a word is involved. Perhaps "word" is a carryover from the translation "rebuke" that Kee is insisting is too weak. Indeed! Both God's action in the Qumran and biblical passages and Jesus' action in Mark are more than verbal! As Kee says, 235–36, *ga'ar* means to overcome God's enemies and to bring them under God's rule.

22. The demon's question is the central statement in the chiastic oral pattern of 1:21–29a.

23. Kee, "Terminology," 243.

24. Ibid., 239–41.

25. Howard Clark Kee, "Aretology and Gospel," *JBL* 92 (1973): 419.

26. For a convincing treatment of the "rebuke of the storm" episode belonging with exorcism stories in terms of structure, especially "the interaction between the characters," see Antoinette Clark Wire, "The Structure of the Gospel Miracle Stories and Their Tellers," *Semeia* 11 (1978): 88–92.

27. It is worth noting that only the scribes' accusation and Jesus' reply in this episode, and not any of the exorcism episodes themselves, connect the demons with a broader struggle between God and Satan.

28. See the linguistic evidence in E. C. B. MacLaurin, "Beelzeboul," *NovT* 20 (1978): 156–60.

29. John Dominic Crossan, *The Historical Jesus* (San Francisco: HarperCollins, 1991), 319, suggests that Beelzebul "is the voice, surely, of the Little Tradition, an attack that bespeaks a village environment." But the name is spoken by the scribes from Jerusalem, not by a villager, and such a suggestion does not take seriously that the sources examined to ascertain the background of the name are all (by definition as written texts of inscriptions) from representatives of the "great tradition," either Canaanite or Judean.

30. We should note the parallel to the breaking into Satan's royal house and plundering his goods (if possessed people, then he has taken them by force from their rightful houses) in the popular insurrections led by popularly acclaimed "kings" after the death of Herod in 4 B.C.E. In Galilee Judas broke into the royal fortress at Sepphoris (near Nazareth) and, besides seizing the arms stored there, "made off with all the goods that had been seized [from people's houses and taken] there" (*Ant.* 17.271). Similarly the popular "king" Simon burned the royal palace

at Jericho and plundered "the things that had been seized [and taken] there" (274). Just as these popular kings are *taking back* from the royal fortresses what the oppressive king Herod's soldiers had taken from the people, so Jesus is taking from Satan's house what his demons had seized from the people's houses.

31. Crossan, *Historical Jesus*, 315, calls attention to a remarkable cross-cultural parallel to the demon named "Legion." Barrie Reynolds, *Magic, Divination, and Witchcraft among the Barotse of Northern Rhodesia* (Berkeley: University of California Press, 1963), 133–35, found among the Luvale people a recent form of possession that differed from the traditional ailment called *mahamba*, involving ancestral spirits. Those who suffered from *bindele*, the word for "European," were apparently believed to be possessed by the spirit of (a) European.

32. J. Duncan M. Derrett, "Contributions to the Study of the Gerasene Demoniac," *JSNT* 3 (1979): 5–21.

33. Frantz Fanon, *The Wretched of the Earth* (New York: Grove Press, 1968; French original, 1961). The parenthetical numbers in the following paragraphs refer to pages in the 1968 edition. Paul W. Hollenbach, "Jesus, Demoniacs, and Public Authorities: a Socio-Historical Study," *JAAR* 49 (1981): 567–88, explored the social-psychological and ideological relevance of Fanon's account of colonial Algeria for Jesus' exorcisms in historical context. The political-historical dimensions of the analogy, i.e., the colonial/imperial situation, remain to be explored.

34. The Greek term for "power/authority" in Jesus' first public act/exorcism, (1:22, 27), and again in the dispute over "power/authority" (11:27–33), is *exousia*. This term is closely related in Mark's story to the term for divine "power," *dynamis* (12:24; 13:26; 14:62; 9:1), which Mark also uses for Jesus' acts of power, such as healings and exorcism (5:30; 6:2, 4, 14; cf. 9:38–41). Jesus' acts of power, such as exorcisms, are direct manifestations of divine power in a way that the mere "signs and wonders" (*sēmeia* and *terata*) performed by the "false prophets" and "false messiahs" (13:21–22) are not.

35. For a political reading of the Mark that virtually identifies the Jerusalem rulers and Temple with the demonic forces, see Myers, *Binding the Strong Man.*

Chapter 7: Jesus vs. the Pharisees: Contesting the Tradition

1. See further Anthony J. Saldarini, "Delegitimation of Leaders in Matthew 23," *Catholic Biblical Quarterly* 54 (1992): 659–80; and "Boundaries and Polemics in the Gospel of Matthew," *BibInt* 3 (1995): 239–65.

2. Jacob Neusner, *From Politics to Piety: The Emergence of Pharisaic Judaism* (Englewood Cliffs, N.J.: Prentice-Hall, 1973).

3. See further Steve Mason, *Flavius Josephus on the Pharisees* (Leiden: Brill, 1991); and Richard A. Horsley, *Galilee: History, Politics, People* (Valley Forge, Pa.: Trinity Press International, 1995), 149–52.

4. Burton L. Mack, *A Myth of Innocence: Mark and Christian Origins* (Philadelphia: Fortress Press, 1988), 41–44, 95.

5. See further Horsley, *Galilee*, 52, 58, 149–52.

6. Ibid., 233–35; and see further my *Archaeology, History, and Society in Galilee* (Valley Forge, Pa.: Trinity Press International, 1996), chap. 6, and the references cited there.

7. Mack, *Myth of Innocence*, 43, 94, 195–98.

8. Shaye J. D. Cohen, *From the Maccabees to the Mishnah* (Philadelphia: Westminster Press, 1987), 221.

9. On these matters see Gary Porton, "Midrash: Palestinian Jews and the Hebrew Bible in the Greco-Roman World," in *ANRW* II.19.2, 113–15.

10. Saldarini, "Boundaries and Polemics," 250.

11. James C. Scott, "Protest and Profanation: Agrarian Revolt and the Little Tradition," *Theory and Society* 4 (1977): 3–32, 159–210, presents an analysis that is very suggestive for Gospel materials and Jesus movements. I attempted to adapt the distinction between great and little traditions for interpretation of the popular prophetic and messianic movements and for Jesus movements in late Second Temple times. See Richard A. Horsley, "Popular Messianic Movements around the Time of Jesus," *CBQ* 46 (1984): 471–95; "'Like One of the Prophets of Old': Two Types of Popular Prophets at the Time of Jesus," *Catholic Biblical Quarterly* 47 (1985): 435–63; *Sociology and the Jesus Movement* (New York: Crossroad, 1989), 91–92.

12. Scott, "Protest and Profanation," 5.

13. Ibid., 7.

14. Ibid., 9.

15. Ibid., 10.

16. See Horsley, *Galilee*, 34–52, for an attempt to work cautiously toward a reconstruction of the situation in Galilee following the Assyrian conquest and what happened in connection with the Hasmonean takeover of Galilee in 104 B.C.E. on the basis of extremely fragmentary evidence.

17. See Lawrence H. Schiffman, "Was There a Galilean Halakhah?" in Lee I. Levine, ed., *The Galilee in Late Antiquity* (New York: Jewish Theological Seminary of America, 1992), 143–46.

18. See the rabbinic passages cited and discussed by Schiffman, "Was There a Galilean Halakhah?" One cannot use Josephus's and his co-commanders' and fellow priests' collection of tithes from the Galileans in late 66 C.E. as evidence that the Galileans held to the tithing laws (*Life* 62–63, 80) because (1) this collection was an ad hoc, one-time-only collection and (2) Josephus at least was accompanied by a sizable contingent of Judean troops as well as his own armed bodyguard.

19. Scott, "Protest and Profanation," 15.

20. Ibid., 12.

21. On how the form resembles that of the *chreiai* (necessities) in Hellenistic Roman culture, see Burton L. Mack and Vernon K. Robbins, *Patterns of Persuasion* (Sonoma, Calif.: Polebridge, 1989).

22. E. P. Sanders, *Jewish Law from Jesus to the Mishnah* (Philadelphia: Trinity Press International, 1990), 6–23, surveys scribal-rabbinic views on sabbath observance. Because his agenda is to explain away any seeming conflict between Jesus and the Pharisees, however, his treatment sheds no light on the conflict over sabbath observance in Mark's story.

23. The "unrealistic" aspects of the episode are obvious; e.g.: What would the Pharisees have been doing themselves walking through the fields of villages far from their own homes or accommodations, well beyond the thousand-yard limit for walking on the sabbath?

24. As Daniel Cohn Sherbok, "An Analysis of Jesus' Arguments concerning the Plucking of Grain on the Sabbath," *JSNT* 2 (1979): 31–41, points out, Jesus' defense does not conform to rules of rabbinic argumentation from scripture—yet another indication that Mark's Jesus is rooted in and represents popular tradition over against the great tradition represented by the Pharisees and later rabbis.

25. For example, a manuscript of 1 Samuel found among the Dead Sea Scrolls, 4QSam[b], has words missing from the previously reconstructed Hebrew text of 21:4: ". . . from women, you [pl] may eat of it," i.e., Ahimelech is permitting David and his men to eat the bread. This does not justify the claim, based on assumptions of widespread ancient literacy and possession of scrolls, that "Jesus will have known a text of Samuel similar to that preserved in 4QSam[b]," as Maurice Casey suggests in "Culture and Historicity: The Plucking of the Grain (Mark 2.23–28)," *NTS* 34 (1988): 8–9.

26. This episode does not set up a typological correspondence between David's behavior or David as messiah/king and Jesus' behavior or his role as messiah. Cf. Ched Myers, *Binding the Strong Man* (Maryknoll, N.Y.: Orbis Books, 1988), 160, "David's assertion of his kingly right"; and Morna D. Hooker, *The Gospel according to Mark* (London: A. & C. Black, 1991), 101–4.

27. Maurice Casey, "Culture and Historicity," 11, points out that the later rabbis humanely allowed that anyone suffering from ravenous hunger was to be fed on the Sabbath, even with unclean things, "until his eyes brightened" (*m. Yoma* 8:6). But that simply highlights Jesus' emphasis on David's having satisfied his hunger with supersacred bread taken right off the altar of the Temple.

28. The point is not that Jesus as Son of Man has expropriated authority over the Sabbath, the "debt code," etc. Among recent commentaries, see, e.g., Myers, *Binding the Strong Man*, 160, and Hooker, *Gospel according to Mark*, 105.

29. A rabbinic reference provides what may be a parallel to Jesus' defense of satisfying human needs on the sabbath despite breaking certain scribal regulations. The people of Jericho apparently ignored rabbinic rulings with regard to eating fruit on the sabbath which had fallen under a tree, something they were doing specifically for the benefit of the poor (*m. Pes.* 4:8; *t. Pes.* 2.21).

30. Shaye J. D. Cohen, "*Ioudaios, Iudaeus*, Judean, Jew," in *The Beginnings of Jewishness* (Berkeley: University of California Press, 1999), esp. 71–78; Ross Shepherd Kraemer, "On the Meaning of the Term 'Jew' in Greco-Roman Inscriptions," *HTR* 82 (1989): 35–54.

31. Jacob Neusner, "Mr. Sanders' Pharisees—and Mine," in idem, *Judaic Law from Jesus to the Mishnah* (Atlanta: Scholars Press, 1993).

32. Neusner, ibid., 204–5, offers a succinct summary of the priestly hierarchy of purity and where the Pharisees appear to fit.

33. Jacob Neusner, "'First Cleanse the Inside,'" *NTS* 22 (198): 486–95, provides an incisive, informed discussion of a closely related dispute between Jesus and the Pharisees on purity codes (Q/Luke 11:38–41 // Matt. 23:25–26).

34. Sanders, *Judaism*, 438, observes that later rabbinic debates on whether or not hands should be washed before all meals, regarding it as not compulsory (*t. Ber.* 5:13, 27), "weighs very heavily against the idea that before 70 all Pharisees had washed their hands before every meal." See also Sanders, *Jewish Law*, 31, 35, 39, 229–30. However, on the basis of little evidence, he suggests (39) that the picture of the Pharisees' (and all the Jews') practices in Mark 7:2–4 reflect Jewish communities in the Diaspora.

35. Sanders, *Jewish Law*, 203–4, 230, suggests that discussions in the Tosephta explain key discussions about handwashing (and vessel washing) in the Mishnah in connection with impurity derived from flies ("swarming insects" the size of a lentil). It is tempting to imagine that the Markan narrator in 7:2–4 is alluding to the Pharisees' concern about "fly-impurity" in his caricature of their washing of hands, cups, pots, and kettles.

36. See now A. I. Baumgarten, "The Pharisaic *Paradosis*," *HTR* 80 (1987): 63–77.

37. Lawrence Schiffman, "New Light on the Pharisees," *Bible Review* (June 1992): 30–33, 54, argues that references to "smooth interpreters" in the Dead Sea Scrolls suggests that the Pharisees' views were dominant in Jerusalem for much of the late Hasmonean period.

38. See the lengthy discussion devoted to the variations by Robert H. Gundry, *Mark: A Commentary on His Apology for the Cross* (Grand Rapids: Wm. B. Eerdmans Publishing Co., 1993), 350–51, who also still seeks a textual explanation rooted in the assumption of widespread literacy and the availability of scrolls and codices.

39. A. I. Baumgarten, "*Korban* and the Pharisaic *Paradosis*," *JANES* 16–17 (1984–85): 6, explains that in rabbinic discussion, besides referring to an actual dedication to the Temple, *korban* can also refer, by analogy, to a vow formula by which some object is forbidden to oneself or another person in the same way in which a dedicated animal is forbidden. Like certain rabbinic references, an ossuary inscription found at Jebel Hallet et Turi illustrates the effect of such an oath by which property was forbidden to someone else even it were *korban* only in the sense of "as if it were" dedicated to God: "Everything which a man will find to his profit in this ossuary is an offering to God from the one within it" (in Joseph A. Fitzmyer and Daniel J. Harrington, *A Manual of Palestinian Aramaic Texts* [Rome: Pontifical Biblical Institute, 1978], #69m; discussion and bibliography, 222–23).

40. K. H. Rengstorf, "*korban*," *TDNT* 3.866. Baumgarten, "Korban and the Pharisaic Paradosis," 14.

41. See further J. Duncan M. Derrett, "Marco vii.15–23: il verso significato di 'purificare,'" *Conoscenza Religiosa* (1975): 125–30, 176–83; and Heikki Raisanen, "Jesus and the Food Laws: Reflections on Mark 7.15," *JSNT* 16 (1982): 79–100.

42. R. A. Guelich, *Mark* (2 vols., WBC 34a. Dallas, Tex.: Word, 1989), 1.378–79.

43. Gundry, *Mark*, 539.

44. Cf. Lawrence H. Schiffman, "Was There a Galilean Halakhah?" 145–48, who takes the lack of extant rulings on the different regional customs in Galilee to mean that there was no "Galilean Halakhah." But not only were there no known Galilean "scribes and Pharisees" comparable to those in Judea who would have developed such a "halakhah," there was no need for it if the corresponding contingencies had not arisen because of the persistence of conservative customs in Galilee.

45. On the thrust of the preposition *pros* (= toward, with the purpose or effect of) in this context, see further Gundry, *Mark*, 538, who points out that hardheartedness in biblical discourse usually means stubborn disobedience of God's will.

Chapter 8: Renewing Covenantal Community

1. John R. Donahue, *The Theology and Setting of Discipleship in the Gospel of Mark* (Milwaukee, Wis.: Marquette University Press, 1983), 30, indicts treatments of "discipleship" in Mark for being so individualistic.

2. The most notable was Howard Clark Kee, *Community of the New Age* (Philadelphia: Westminster Press, 1977), who not only noticed Mark's concern for community but utilized sociological approaches in a groundbreaking analysis of the Gospel on which all subsequent studies of the social orientation of Mark have built.

3. For an interpretation that Jesus' proclamation of the kingdom of God entails a renewal of (Israelite) society, see Richard A. Horsley, *Jesus and the Spiral of Violence* (San Francisco: Harper & Row, 1987), chap. 7.

4. Kee, *Community*, 107 n. 10; 111; 153.

5. Stephen C. Barton, *Discipleship and Family Ties in Mark and Matthew* (SNTSMS 80; Cambridge: Cambridge University Press, 1994), 66, 82, 85, 103; cf. "alternative society," 104.

6. Kee, *Community*, 107.

7. Barton, *Discipleship*, 85, 82.

8. Ibid., 104.

9. The assertion by Norman Perrin, *The New Testament: An Introduction* (Harcourt Brace Jovanovich, 1974), 150, that "Mark has a strong concern for Gentiles and the Hellenistic Jewish Christian mission to them" has been influential in recent interpretation of the Gospel. Cf. Werner Kelber, *Mark's Story of Jesus* (Philadelphia: Fortress Press, 1979), 150–51.

10. Perhaps the picture of a new "community formation" in some interpreters' minds derives from previous constructions of Paul's and others' mission in urban areas where they were indeed forming new "voluntary associations," although by building on whole households and not simply by recruiting individuals (see, e.g., 1 Cor. 1:12–16, where several households apparently form the basis of the Corinthian *ekklēsia*).

11. See the fuller discussion in Richard A. Horsley, *Galilee: History, Politics, People* (Valley Forge, Pa.: Trinity Press International, 1995), chap. 10; or the presentation in *Archaeology, History, and Society in Galilee* (Valley Forge, Pa.: Trinity Press International, 1996), chap. 10.

12. For a fuller discussion of the covenant pattern and covenant renewal in the literature of the Qumran community that produced the Dead Sea Scrolls, and its background in Hebrew biblical tradition, see Richard A. Horsley with Jonathan A. Draper, *Whoever Hears You Hears Me: Prophets, Performance, and Tradition in Q* (Harrisburg, Pa.: Trinity Press International, 1999), 201–9.

13. For a more elaborate analysis of the discourse in Luke/Q 6:20–49, see Horsley, *Whoever Hears You Hears Me*, 210–25, and Jesus.

14. Ernest Best, *Following Jesus: Discipleship in the Gospel of Mark* (Sheffield: JSOT Press, 1981), 99, who mentions earlier scholars such as Joachim Jeremias and Eduard Schweizer.

15. Donahue, *Theology and Setting of Discipleship in the Gospel of Mark*, 39.

16. See, e.g., the discussion by Ernst Käsemann, "Sentences of Holy Law in the New Testament," in idem, *New Testament Questions of Today* (Philadelphia: Fortress Press, 1969), 66–81; Kee, *Community*, 140–41. Although these "statements" are closer in form to laws than are the "stipulations" ("you shall not . . .") in the Mosaic covenant, they are substantively principles of social policy, parallel to the Mosaic covenant stipulations.

17. See further the insightful discussion of Mark's treatment of children and the kingdom in Ched Myers, *Binding the Strong Man: A Political Reading of Mark's Story of Jesus* (Maryknoll, N.Y.: Orbis Books, 1988), 266–68.

18. See further the similar discussion of Mark's covenantal economics in Myers, *Binding the Strong Man*, 271–76. See also James C. Okoye, "Reconciliation: Biblical Reflections: II. With Persecutions—Mark 10:30," *New Theology Review* 10 (1997): 34; and George Soares-Prabhu, "Anti-Greed and Anti-Pride: Mark 10:17–27 and 10:35–45 in the Light of Tribal Values," *Jeevadhara* 24/140 (1994): 130–45; in connection with Paulus Kullu, "Tribal Religion and Culture," in the same issue, pp. 89–109.

19. See esp. James C. Scott, *The Moral Economy of the Peasant* (New Haven, Conn.: Yale University Press, 1976).

20. See further Richard A. Horsley, *Jesus and the Spiral of Violence* (San Francisco: Harper & Row, 1987), 242–45.
21. The NRSV and other paraphrases of "those with/around him" is misleading, as pointed out by John Painter, "When Is a House Not Home? Disciples and Family in Mark 3:13–35," *NTS* 45 (1999): 498–513. Thus the episode about Jesus' "mother and brother and sisters" does not begin with 3:19b–21 in a Markan "sandwich" pattern.

Chapter 9: Women as Representative and Exemplary

1. An early historical analysis was that of Winsome Munro, "Women Disciples in Mark?" *CBQ* 44 (1982): 225–41. For critical historical analysis of Markan passages and of Mark's Gospel in the context of a comprehensive constructive feminist historical analysis of women in Christian origins generally, see Elisabeth Schüssler Fiorenza, *In Memory of Her: A Feminist Theological Reconstruction of Christian Origins* (New York: Crossroad, 1983), esp. 137–54, 315–23.
2. Mary Ann Tolbert, "Mark," in *The Women's Bible Commentary*, ed. Carol A. Newsome and Sharon H. Ringe (Louisville, Ky.: Westminster/John Knox Press, 1992), 267–70, emphasizes the importance of the private, domestic sphere as the locus of women's roles in Mark.
3. Thus it may not be significant in analysis to categorize episodes about women according to named and nameless; cf., e.g., Mary Rose D'Angelo, "(Re)Presentation of Women in the Gospels: John and Mark," in *Women and Christian Origins*, ed. Ross Shepard Kraemer and Mary Rose D'Angelo (Oxford: Oxford University Press, 1999), 137–45. As an example of the complications involved in categorizations and judgments, the name "Jairus" (in the NRSV text at 5:22) is missing both in some early manuscripts of Mark and in the parallel to this episode at Matthew 9:18. "Jairus" must have crept into other manuscripts of Mark through influence from the parallel to the episode in Luke 8:41.
4. Schüssler Fiorenza, *In Memory of Her*, 140, 142, saw that patriarchal structures and the poverty of women are closely interrelated and must be considered together. See her later, more elaborated theoretical reflections in *Rhetoric and Ethic: The Politics of Biblical Studies* (Minneapolis: Fortress Press, 1999). See also the critical reflections on feminist and womanist criticism in *The Postmodern Bible* (New Haven, Conn.: Yale University Press, 1995), 235–44; the womanist viewpoint of Delores S. Williams, "The Color of Feminism; Or, Speaking the Black Woman's Tongue," *JRT* 43 (1986): 42–57; Musa W. Dube, "Toward a Postcolonial Interpretation of the Bible," *Semeia* 78 (1997): 11–26; and Chandra Mohanty, "Under Western Eyes: Feminist Scholarship and Colonial Discourses," in *Third World Women and the Politics of Feminism*, ed. Chandra Mohanty, Ann Russo, and Lourdes Torres (Bloomington: Indiana University Press, 1991), 51–80.
5. Sheila Briggs, "'Buried with Christ': The Politics of Identity and the Poverty of Interpretation," in *The Book and the Text: The Bible and Literary Theory*, ed. Regina Schwartz (New York: Blackwell, 1990), 285.
6. Tolbert, "Mark," 268; and more elaborately Marla J. Selvidge, *Woman, Cult and Miracle Recital: A Redactional Critical Investigation of Mark 5:24–34* (Lewisburg, Pa.: Bucknell University Press, 1990); and "Mark 5:24–34 and Leviticus 15:19–20: A Reaction to Restrictive Purity Regulation," *JBL* 103 (1984): 619–23. Rather than single out one or two scholars, however, the point is to

recognize that the field of Gospel studies generally has perpetuated an unhistorical stereotype of legalistic restrictions on women in ancient Jewish society. For example, without referencing ancient sources, widely read recent interpreters of Jesus and the Gospels persist in confusing the distinction between pure and impure with moral, class, and gender distinctions. "Pure and impure got attached to other primary social polities . . . , to the chronically ill and maimed, . . . and associationally to the contrasts between rich and poor, male and female." Marcus Borg, *Jesus in Contemporary Scholarship* (Valley Forge, Pa.: Trinity Press International, 1994), 109–10. So ingrained is the stereotype that it appears even in a book subtitled "Exposing the Roots of Anti-Semitism": "Think about the theological implications of that intercalation, of a purity code in which menstruation is impure so that, from Mark's viewpoint, women start to die at twelve and are walking dead thereafter." John Dominic Crossan, *Who Killed Jesus?* (San Francisco: HarperSanFrancisco, 1995), 101. See further the critical response to Christian theological construction of the situation of women in ancient Jewish society by Ross S. Kraemer, "Jewish Women and Christian Origins," in *Women and Christian Origins*, ed. Ross Shepard Kraemer and Mary Rose D'Angelo (Oxford: Oxford University Press, 1999), 35–49.

7. Joanna Dewey, "The Gospel of Mark," in *Searching the Scriptures: A Feminist Commentary*, ed. Elisabeth Schüssler Fiorenza (New York: Crossroad, 1994), 481; Tolbert, "Mark," 268. A fuller critical response to previous treatment of these Markan episodes is found in Mary Rose D'Angelo, "Gender and Power in the Gospel of Mark: The Daughter of Jairus and the Woman with the Flow of Blood," in *Aspects of the Miraculous in Ancient Judaism and Christianity*, ed. John C. Cavadini (Notre Dame, Ind.: Notre Dame University Press, 2000).

8. Paula Fredriksen, "Did Jesus Oppose the Purity Laws?" *Bible Review* (June 1995): 22.

9. Shaye J. D. Cohen, "Menstruants and the Sacred," in *Women's History and Ancient History*, ed. Sarah B. Pomeroy (Chapel Hill, N.C.: University of North Carolina Press, 1991), 276.

10. Amy-Jill Levine, "Discharging Responsibility: Matthean Jesus, Biblical Law, and Hemorrhaging Woman," in *Treasures Old and New: Recent Contributions in Matthean Studies* (SBLSS 1, ed. David R. Bauer and Mark A. Powell; Atlanta: Scholars Press, 1996), 387, 389, citing Jacob Milgrom, *Leviticus I–XVI*, 936. See further the general discussion of "The Menstruant," in Tal Ilan, *Jewish Women in Greco-Roman Palestine* (Peabody, Mass.: Hendrickson, 1996), 100–105.

11. See further Ross S. Kraemer, "Jewish Women and Women's Judaism(s) at the Beginning of Christianity," in *Women and Christian Origins*, 65–66. "The Gospel story about the woman with a twelve-year discharge . . . does not give any indication that the woman was impure or suffered any degree of isolation as a result of her affliction." Shaye J. D. Cohen, "Menstruants and the Sacred in Judaism and Christianity," 271–99 at 279; see also his "Purity and Piety: The Separation of Menstruants from the Sancta," in *Daughters of the King—Women and the Synagogue: A Survey of History and Contemporary Realities*, ed. S. Groomsman and R. Haute (Philadelphia: Jewish Publication Society, 1992), 106–7.

12. Mary Rose D'Angelo, "(Re)Presentations of Women in the Gospels: John and Mark," in *Women and Christian Origins*, 140.

13. Werner Kelber, *The Oral and Written Gospel* (Philadelphia: Fortress Press, 1983), 44–52, presents a very helpful discussion of the pattern and variations in Mark's healing stories.

14. D'Angelo, "Women in the Gospels," 141.

15. Rita Nakashima Brock, *A Christology of Erotic Power* (New York: Crossroad, 1988), 86. Similarly, the South African woman cited by Malika Sibeko and Beverly Haddad, "Reading the Bible 'with' Women in Poor and Marginalized Communities in South Africa," *Semeia* 78 (1997): 91.

16. Brock, *Erotic Power*, 84, 87.

17. *Pace* Ched Myers, *Binding the Strong Man* (Maryknoll, N.Y.: Orbis Books, 1988), 201–2.

18. Brock, *Erotic Power*, 85: "Behind the two women stand countless others who are encouraged to have courage."

19. Ibid., 86.

20. Albeit rooted in the struggles of some other early Jesus movements, as indicated in Galatians 1–2.

21. Some of the stages in this complex debate are represented by Schüssler Fiorenza, *In Memory of Her*, 136–38; and *But She Said: Feminist Practices of Biblical Interpretation* (Boston: Beacon Press, 1992), 11–12, 96; Tolbert, "Mark," 268; and D'Angelo, "Women in the Gospels," 139.

22. In terms of the emerging (post-Markan) canonical discourse dominated by Greek-speaking non-Israelites and their interests, however, she is far more of an insider, except as a woman.

23. Sharon Ringe, "A Gentile Woman's Story," in *Feminist Interpretation of the Bible*, ed. Letty Russell (Philadelphia: Westminster Press, 1985), 68.

24. Schüssler Fiorenza, *But She Said*, 12, 221 n. 29.

25. Ibid., 160.

26. Ibid., 162. Kathleen E. Corley, *Private Women, Public Meals* (Peabody, Mass.: Hendrickson, 1993), 99–100, explains bluntly that Jesus' response to the Syrophoenician woman's request was insulting.

27. So also Elizabeth Struthers Malbon, "Fallible Followers: Women and Men in the Gospel of Mark," *Semeia* 28 (1983): 29–48.

28. See, e.g., Tolbert, "Mark," 270; Dewey, "The Gospel of Mark," 499; and Elizabeth Struthers Malbon, "The Poor Widow in Mark and Her Poor Rich Readers," *CBQ* 53 (1991): 590–93.

29. Addison G. Wright, S.S., "The Widow's Mites: Praise or Lament?" *CBQ* 44 (1982): 256–65, called attention to the decisive importance of narrative context for interpretation of this episode.

30. Dewey, "The Gospel of Mark," 501.

31. Tolbert, "Mark," 270–71.

32. As Corley, *Private Women, Public Meals*, 93, 102, points out, Mark is simply unconcerned with the ways in which Jesus' appearance at table with women might appear scandalous in (proper, upper-class) Hellenistic-Roman culture. The Gospel of Luke, of course, has moved closer to that more "upscale" Hellenistic-Roman ethos.

33. So also Dewey, "The Gospel of Mark," 501–2; and D'Angelo, "(Re)Presentations of Women," 143.

34. Corley, *Private Women, Public Meals*, 105.

35. Dewey, "The Gospel of Mark," 502.

36. Brock, *Erotic Power*, 97.

37. The most influential statement is Gerd Theissen, *The Sociology of Early Palestinian Christianity* (Philadelphia: Fortress Press, 1978). The hypothesis that Jesus called people to become "wandering charismatics" persists, especially among individu-

alistic American liberal interpreters, despite several severe critiques. For example, John H. Elliott, "Social Scientific Criticism of the New Testament and Its Social World," *Semeia* 35 (1986): 1–34; Richard A. Horsley, *Sociology and the Jesus Movement* (New York: Crossroad, 1989), chaps. 1–3; and Jonathan A. Draper, "Weber, Theissen, and 'Wandering Charismatics' in the Didache," *Journal of Early Christian Studies* 6 (1998): 541–76.

38. "Take up your cross and follow me" is addressed to the same context in Mark 8:34–9:1 as it is in Matt. 10:34–39; 16:24–28 and Luke 9:23–27, where this saying is connected with the sayings about "hating father and mother," a hyperbole for the intensity of commitment necessary in the movement, not a general principle of abandoning family for a vagabond lifestyle. Luke 14:26, in the context of 14:25–33, may well be a more general application of such sayings, although it would then apply to joining a new or different community, not to an itinerant life.

39. Schüssler Fiorenza, *In Memory of Her*, 143. She also pointed out that the issue is not divorce but marriage, and that in patriarchal form.

40. Ibid., 143.

41. Dewey, "The Gospel of Mark," 491.

42. This should now be understood in connection with recently discerned evidence that in late Second Temple times, women could apparently take the initiative in divorce proceedings and/or effectively cause a divorce. See Bernadette Brooten, "Könnten Frauen im alten Judentum die Scheidung betreiben? Überlegung zu Mk 10,11–12 und 1 Kor 7,10–11," *Evangelische Theologie* 42 (1982): 66–80; and Ross S. Kraemer, "Jewish Women and Women's Judaism(s) at the Beginning of Christianity," 59.

43. Dewey, "The Gospel of Mark," 491, 493.

44. Howard Clark Kee, *Community of the New Age: Studies in Mark's Gospel* (Philadelphia: Westminster Press, 1977), 156–57.

45. Schüssler Fiorenza, *In Memory of Her*, 140, 142.

46. The most famous case of a younger brother marrying his brother's widow was the Hasmonean Alexander Janneus and Salome Alexandra, widow of Aristobulus, presumably motivated at least partly in order to keep power in the family. See Josephus, *Ant.* 13.320–21, 400.

47. Dewey, "The Gospel of Mark," 478.

48. See further John Painter, "When Is a House Not Home? Disciples and Family in Mark 3:31–35," *NTS* 45 (1999): 498–513.

49. This interpretation and some of the phrases are from the insightful and sensitive treatment by Rita Nakashima Brock, *Erotic Power*, 98. The women plan to anoint Jesus because, in the "dishonorable burial" of a Roman-executed rebel given him by Joseph of Arimathea, he remains unanointed, as pointed out by Adela Yarbro Collins, *Beginning of the Gospel*, 130–31, 134–35.

50. Carolyn Osiek, "The Women at the Tomb: What Are They Doing There," *Ex Auditu* 9 (1993): 97–107, points out that the rabbinic discussions in the Mishnah do not support the "unexamined scholarly commonplace" that women could not serve as public witnesses. See further the close analysis of the women's role at Jesus' crucifixion and burial by Kathleen E. Corley, "Women and the Crucifixion and Burial of Jesus," *Forum*, n.s., 1 (1998), esp. 203–17.

51. Dewey, "The Gospel of Mark," 488.

52. Schüssler Fiorenza, *In Memory of Her*, 148.

Chapter 10: Prophetic and Messianic "Scripts" in Mark

1. Accordingly, modern scholars construct Mark in their own image: "Mark was a scholar. A reader of texts and a writer of texts. . . . Mark's Gospel was composed at a desk in a scholar's study lined with texts" (Burton L. Mack, *A Myth of Innocence* [Philadelphia: Fortress Press, 1988], 321–23). Undeterred by the inability of their predecessor (Mark) to keep his sources straight (e.g., attributing to Isaiah what came from Exodus and Malachi in 1:2–3) or to cite his texts accurately (shifting from one version to another within single lines or phrases), modern scholars imagine a multilingual scholar with different Hebrew, Aramaic, and Greek texts spread out on his desk from which he would select a phrase here and a word there in composing scriptural conflations.

2. This can be seen particularly in recent treatments of two passages in Mark, one in the baptism episode and one in Jesus' trial before the high priests. The beginning words of the heavenly voice addressing Jesus, "You are my son . . . ," are taken as a citation of Ps. 2:7, which is then interpreted to mean that, in fulfillment of the "royal ideology" in both Ps. 2:7 and 2 Sam. 7:12–13, Jesus is being designated as the messiah who has royal dominion, indeed universal and everlasting royal dominion. See Donald Juel, *Messianic Exegesis: Christological Interpretation of the Old Testament* (Philadelphia: Fortress Press, 1988), 79–80; and Joel Marcus, *The Way of the Lord: Christological Exegesis of the Old Testament in the Gospel of Mark* (Louisville, Ky.: Westminster/John Knox Press, 1992), 69–70. When the high priest presiding at Jesus' trial asks him "Are you the Messiah . . . ?" Jesus answers: "You will see the son of man seated at the right hand of power and coming with the clouds of heaven." The phrase "seated at the right hand" is taken as a quotation of Ps. 110:1, used to interpret Jesus' resurrection as his installation as the royal Messiah at the right hand of God, and the "coming with the clouds of heaven" is taken as a reference to Jesus' parousia. See Juel, *Messianic Exegesis*, 145.

3. On the assumption that Mark was a multilingual scholar with a well-stocked archive of costly and cumbersome scrolls, he is pictured as opening his Gospel with a combination of brief lines from three different "books" (see, e.g., Marcus, *The Way of the Lord*, 12–17). Never mind that he wrongly attributes them all to Isaiah; he firsts conflates "See, I am sending my messenger before your face" from Ex. 23:20 and "who will prepare your way" from Mal. 3:1, then combines them with "the voice of one crying in the wilderness" from Isa. 40:3. Most of the words in Greek are identical with those in the standard Greek translation of the Jewish scriptures of the time, the Septuagint (= LXX). Yet the conflation cannot be wholly dependent on the LXX because the verb "to prepare" in Mark 1:2 differs from "to survey" in the LXX version of Mal. 3:1. So we must resort to the hypothesis that in 1:2b Mark reflects an independent rendering of the Hebrew into Greek. Further into the episode of John's baptism of Jesus, Mark again nimbly manipulates his multiple manuscripts (see e.g., Marcus, *The Way of the Lord*, 48–56). His portrayal of the heavens opening is taken as an allusion to Isa. 63:19 (LXX 64:1), only Mark utilizes the unusual and harsh verb "torn apart" rather than the usual scriptural "opened" in Isa. 63:19, hence he must be dependent on another version of Isa. 63:19, perhaps the Masoretic text of the Hebrew. Although Mark gives no hint that he is quoting from scripture here, in contrast to 1:2–3, we are asked to believe that for the words spoken by the voice from heaven in 1:11 Mark is again combining even tinier text fragments from three different scriptural texts. First, he supposedly took "you are the son my" from the

LXX of Ps. 2:7 despite the different word order ("son my are you"), believable somehow because Heb. 1:5 quotes a whole line "You are my son, today I have begotten you," and because a Western manuscript tradition of the parallel in Luke 3:22 also cites that whole line. "In you I have been pleased," however, supposedly "reflects" the text of Isa. 42:1 despite the lack of common words, because of the association with the Spirit in the context, the similar text Matt. 12:8 is closer to Greek versions of Isa. 42:1 different from the Septuagint, and similarity with the later Aramaic Targum of Isaiah. "The beloved one," more of a problem since it appears in neither Ps. 2:7 nor Isa. 42:1, is speculated to have been suggested by Isa. 42:1 because of its similarity to "the chosen one," or to have come from Gen. 22:2, 12, 16 in the LXX, where Isaac is "the beloved son." To have performed this complicated feat of "word processing" in his first episode, Mark would so far have needed to take extracts from at least six different scriptural texts in multiple versions and languages, as well as to have been influenced by extrabiblical Jewish texts in his choice of variant wording of those texts. The complications begin to strain credulity. The more we become aware of the other possible allusions, the less obvious and distinctive the presumed allusion to the supposed messianic proof text of Ps. 2:7 seems.

4. Mack discerns the complex interweaving of Israelite traditions in Mark's Gospel. Yet he assumes a disconnect between the emerging story of Mark and the scriptures, and he describes the way the connections were made on the assumption that an author, "Mark," had manuscripts in front of him, which he then searched through and examined like a modern scholar working in a print culture. "Mark, or someone in Mark's milieu, spent a considerable bit of time searching the scriptures in the interests of establishing a certain relationship between them and the emerging gospel story of Jesus. . . . His gospel . . . is a highly conscious scholarly effort in fabricating a new text by taking up strands from textual patterns" (*Myth of Innocence*, 323 n 3). I am suggesting that in an oral communications environment, the process was far more "organic." The developing story emerged from patterns present in the Israelite culture in which the movement was grounded.

5. This section and the next depend heavily on my earlier analysis and presentation of prophetic movements in "'Like One of the Prophets of Old': Two Types of Popular Prophets at the Time of Jesus," *CBQ* 47 (1985): 435–63; "Popular Prophetic Movements at the Time of Jesus: Their Principal Features and Social Origins," *JSNT* (1986): 3–27; and, with John S. Hanson, *Bandits, Prophets, and Messiahs: Popular Movements in the Time of Jesus* (Harrisburg, Pa.: Trinity Press International, 1999; orig. 1985).

6. See Robert B. Coote, ed., *Elijah and Elisha in Socioliterary Perspective* (Atlanta: Scholars Press, 1992).

7. Horsley, "Like One of the Prophets," 437–43.

8. The translations of Josephus's accounts that follow are by John S. Hanson, in Horsley with Hanson, *Bandits, Prophets, and Messiahs*, chaps. 3 and 4.

9. John J. Collins, *The Scepter and the Star: The Messiahs of the Dead Sea Scrolls and Other Ancient Literature* (New York: Doubleday, 1995), 102–17.

10. Ibid., 122.

11. The contemporary scribal *Psalm of Solomon* 17, often used as a proof text for a "militant messiah," portrays rather a restoration of (the twelve tribes of) Israel in holiness and justice by a messiah whose militance has been transposed into scribal power—who does not slay with the sword but convicts by the word of his mouth.

12. See the fuller exploration in Horsley, *Jesus and the Spirit of Violence* (San Francisco: Harper & Row, 1987), 129–31.

13. This and the next section depend heavily on my analysis and presentation in "Popular Messianic Movements around the Time of Jesus," *CBQ* 46 (1984): 471–95; Horsley with Hanson, *Bandits, Prophets, and Messiahs*, chap. 3; and Horsley, "Messianic Figures and Movements in First Century Palestine," in James H. Charlesworth, ed., *The Messiah: Developments in Earliest Judaism and Christianity* (Minneapolis: Fortress Press, 1992), 276–95.

14. Marianus de Jonge, "The Use of the Word 'Anointed' in the Time of Jesus," *NovT* 8 (1966): 132–48; Dennis C. Duling, "The Promises to David and Their Entrance into Christianity," *NTS* 20 (1973–74): 68.

15. Adela Yarbro Collins, "Mark and His Readers: The Son of God among Jews," *HTR* 92 (1999), 397, 400-401, also points out that in both his baptism, with the descent of the Spirit, in in his transfiguration, as "beloved son," Mark portrays Jesus as a *prophet*. On the testing of Jesus as prophetic leader of the people, see also Jan Willem Van Houten, "The First Testing of Jesus: A Rereading of Mark 1:2–3," *NTS* 45 (1999): 349–66.

16. So Joseph A. Fitzmyer, "4Q246: The 'Son of God' Document from Qumran," *Biblica* 74 (1993): 153–74, esp. 170–74; but cf. Collins, *Scepter and Star*, 154–72.

17. See the critical survey of terms such as "branch/booth of David" in Collins, *Scepter and Star*, chaps. 2 and 3.

18. As might be appropriate in argument with the scribes, Mark's Jesus here "quotes" the scripture, at Ps. 110:1. The recitation is close to the Septuagint, except for "footstool" (LXX) vs. "under your feet" (Mark) and the omission of the article *ho* before the first *kyrios*. Would the scribes have agreed on the "messianic" reading of this psalm, i.e., that Yahweh/LORD was addressing the Messiah (my lord)? or is Mark's Jesus innovative here? No messianic interpretation of Ps. 110 is attested from Jewish literature of the first century. "David himself says (present tense) him to be lord, so whence is he his son?" Jesus is thus asking for the source of the designation "son of David"; and in light of David's speaking in the Spirit, Jesus is challenging the scribes to produce an inspired scriptural source of "the son of David."

19. It thus seems unwarranted to infer from Mark (and the other Gospels following Mark) that Pilate's order for crucifixion supports "the historicity" of the report that Jesus was executed as a messianic pretender, as do many scholars, recently, for example, Adela Yarbro Collins, "From Noble Death to Crucified Messiah." *NTS* 40 (1994): 427. The Roman governors also executed or slaughtered popular prophets and their movements as threats to the Roman order.

20. On the centurion's phrase "son of god," see now Tae Hun Kim, "The Anarthrous *huios theou* in Mark 15,39 and the Roman Imperial Cult," *Biblica* 79 (1998): 221–41.

Index of Sources

Hebrew Scriptures

Genesis

1:26–31	166
1:27	175–76
2:1–3	166
2:24	175
22:2	283 n.3
22:12	283 n.3
22:16	283 n.3
38	222

Exodus

3–17	31
14:21–28	105
15:1–18	105
15:1–10	141
16	104
18:21	105
18:25	105
19–24	31
20–24	184
20:3–11	199
20:8–11	162
20:12–17	199
20:13	169
21–23	190, 262 n.20
21:26–36	191
21:2	217
21:17	169

22:1–6	190
22:14	190
22:25–27	186, 190, 217
23:4–5	186
23:10–13	190
23:20	60, 283 n.3
24:3–8	111, 200
24:15–18	107
31:14	166
34:21	163

Leviticus

15:19–30	208–9
19:2	186
19:9–18	199
19:17–18	186
19:9	163
19:18	199
24:9	165
25	190, 217, 262 n.20
25:25–28	194
25:47–55	194
27:1–8	170

Numbers

19:11–13	209

Deuteronomy

5:7–15	199

5:12–15	162
5:16–21	199
6:4–5	199
15:1–11	186
17:14–17	176
18:15	249
18:18	238
22:1–4	186
23:24–25	163
23:25	163
24:1–4	174
24:10–13	186
24:14–15	191
25:5–6	222
30:4	130
31:10	57
33.8–11	156

Joshua

6:15–20	241
24	185

Judges

2–9	31
5	160, 237

1 Samuel

10:1	217
16:1–13	217
19–26	165

1 Samuel (continued)
21:1–6   164
21:1–2   164
23:6–11   164

2 Samuel
1   31
2:4   244
5:3   244
7   244
7:9   194
15–20   245
15:35   164
20:25   164

1 Kings
5:13–18   31
11:26–39   218
22   31, 245
17–21   106
2   32, 237
17:1   237
17:8–26   105
18–19   103
18   237
19   103, 238, 245
19:4–9   88
19:11–18   107
19:15–16   218
21   32, 237

2 Kings
1–9   106, 237
2:8–10   106
2:8   238
4:42–44   105
6:8–10   237
6:18   237
9   245
9:1–10   218
12–14   106

1 Chronicles
27:33   194

Ezra
3   264 n.18
1:3   32

6:1–2   264 n.18
6:6–12   264 n.18

Nehemiah
8:1   57
8:4–6   57
10:35–39   32

Psalms
2   244
2:7   283 n.3
8:6–9   166
9:6   137
22   232
68:31   137
78:6   137
80:16   137
107:2–3   130
110   244
110:1   232, 251,
                285 n.18
1–18   109
17   109
118   109

Isaiah
5:1–7   110
5:7–10   110
8:21   130
9:1   180
9:2–7   244
13:13   130
14:30   130
19:2   130
29:13   169
40:3   102, 283 n.3
42:1   247, 283 n.3
43:5–7   130
56:8   130
61:1–11   247
63.19   283 n.3

Jeremiah
23   44
29:14   130
31:8   130
32:37   130
36   54

Ezekiel
5:12   130
31:4–6   104
34   105

Daniel
1   33, 126
7   127
7:9–14   108
7:13–14   44
7:13   128, 130, 232
7:14   166
9:27   130, 132
10–12   126
11:31   126, 130, 132
12:1   130
12:11   130, 132

Zechariah
2:10   130
3:2   137
8:7–8   130
9:9   251
11:5   105
11:17   105

Malachi
3–4   32
3:1–3   238
3:1   60, 102, 178,
                283 n.3
4:4–6   238

Sirach
24:23   157
36:13   88
44:12   168
48:1–10   238
48:10   88

1 Maccabees
1:54   130, 132
6:35   33
6:46   33

2 Maccabees
8:9   194

New Testament

Matthew

4:1–11	264 n.25
4:15	180
5–7	187
5:22–24	224
6:9–11	196
6:10	104
7:3–5	224
8:11–12	272 n.12
8:38	224
9:18	211, 279 n.3
10:5–6	47
10:34–39	282 n.38
11:10	264 n.25
11:25	224
12:8	283 n.3
13:21–22	210
13:32	224
15:1–20	172
16:18–19	30
16:18	83, 90–91, 95
16:24–28	282 n.38
18:17	90
19:30	88
20:1–16	220
23	152
23:9	224
23:25–26	276 n.33
24:15	131
28:19	47

Mark

1:1–13	70, 102–3
1:2–4	101
1:2–3	60, 234, 283 nn.1, 3
1:11	250, 283 n.3
1:12–15	15
1:12–13	88
1:13	206
1:14–3:35	70
1:14–15	14, 23, 28, 48, 71, 89, 259 n.30
1:14	101
1:16–20	15, 71, 79, 92, 119, 181

1:19	80
1:20–10:52	74
1:21–45	72
1:21–29	273 n.22
1:21–28	12, 15, 41, 69, 71, 89, 100, 112, 137–38, 233, 254–55
1:21–22	85
1:21	40, 90
1:22	274 n.34
1:24	138
1:25	92, 189
1:26	138
1:27	274 n.34
1:29–31	206
1:31	206
1:32–34	121
1:34	137, 146
1:36	80
1:39	40, 90, 121, 137, 146
1:40–45	71, 266 n.43
1:41–45	100
1:41–44	109
2:1–3:6	15, 67, 73, 206
2:1–12	49, 73, 100–101, 103, 109, 119, 178, 181
2:2–12	195
2:2–4	210
2:3–5	73
2:5	73
2:6–10	73
2:8	16
2:10	73, 128, 166
2:11–12	73
2:12	73
2:13–17	73, 204
2:13	85
2:15	73, 80
2:16	73
2:17	73
2:18–22	73
2:18	80
2:23–28	60, 73, 162–66, 178, 233

2:23	73, 80
2:24	73
2:27	73
2:27–28	128
2:28	166
3:1–6	73, 100, 155
3:1	40, 73, 90
3:2	73
3:3	73
3:4–5	73
3:5	73, 92
3:6	12, 41, 73, 100, 151
3:7–12	71, 121
3:7	80, 85
3:9	80
3:11	250
3:12	92
3:13–19	15, 71, 79, 92–93, 206, 212
3:13–17	80
3:15	137, 146
3:16	18
3:19–21	195, 224, 279 n.21
3:20–35	72
3:22–30	210
3:22–28	15
3:22–27	139
3:22	47, 100, 137, 151
3:31–35	96, 104, 195–97, 204, 223–25
3:35	196
4:1–34	67, 70, 72, 104
4:1–2	85
4:10–11	80, 206
4:11	15, 79, 123, 127
4:13–20	18
4:16–17	19
4:17	192
4:26–32	127
4:26	18
4:30	18
4:33–34	80

Mark (continued)

4:34 — 79
4:35–10:45 — 15
4:35–8:26 — 67, 70, 71, 104–7
4:35–8:21 — 92, 267 n.48
4:35–41 — 79–80, 138
5:1–20 — 18, 50, 101, 121, 140–41, 181
5:7 — 250, 273 n.19
5:17 — 138
5:18–19 — 119
5:21–43 — 19, 39, 72, 106, 181, 208–12
5:21–24 — 204
5:22–23 — 219
5:22 — 279 n.3
5:24 — 85
5:30 — 274 n.34
5:31 — 80
5:34 — 119
5:35–43 — 95
5:37 — 80, 92
5:42–43 — 119
6:1–6 — 107, 196, 223
6:1–3 — 204, 211
6:1–2 — 59
6:1 — 80
6:2 — 85, 274 n.34
6:4 — 248, 274 n.34
6:6–13 — 107, 119
6:6 — 85
6:7–13 — 15, 40, 65, 79, 89, 92, 181
6:7 — 121
6:10 — 89
6:11 — 89, 189
6:12–13 — 89
6:13 — 121, 137
6:14–29 — 70
6:14–16 — 248
6:14–15 — 236
6:14 — 274 n.34
6:16–29 — 101
6:29 — 94
6:30–44 — 20, 89, 212
6:34 — 85
6:35–44 — 80

6:35–37 — 79
6:37 — 80
6:42 — 215
6:47–52 — 79
6:47–51 — 80
6:52 — 80
7:1–23 — 166–72
7:1–13 — 15, 47, 100, 107, 150, 233
7:1–4 — 210
7:1–3 — 46, 47
7:1 — 151
7:2–4 — 276 nn.34–35
7:2 — 80
7:3 — 48, 105
7:6–7 — 169
7:6 — 60
7:8–13 — 177
7:9–13 — 49, 61, 108–9, 184
7:9–10 — 60
7:10–12 — 172
7:17 — 80
7:19 — 171
7:24–31 — 69
7:24–30 — 122, 180–81, 212–15
7:24 — 41, 51
7:27 — 215
7:29–31 — 266 n.44
7:29–30 — 119
7:31–37 — 267 n.48
8–10 — 75
8:1–21 — 79
8:1–4 — 20
8:4 — 80, 215
8:8 — 215
8:10 — 80
8:11–15 — 150
8:11–12 — 135
8:13–10:52 — 96
8:13–21 — 86
8:14–21 — 20, 80
8:15–21 — 89
8:17–21 — 92
8:18 — 267 n.48
8:19–20 — 179
8:22–10:52 — 70, 186

8:22–26 — 14, 18, 71, 72, 75, 80, 181, 267 n.48
8:26 — 119
8:27–11:1 — 101
8:27–10:52 — 83
8:27–33 — 72, 92–93
8:27–30 — 70
8:27–28 — 248
8:27 — 41, 48, 51
8:28 — 236
8:29 — 5, 15, 249–50
8:31–33 — 70, 79
8:31 — 16, 72, 80, 85, 100, 128, 249
8:32–9:1 — 80
8:32–33 — 79
8:33 — 5, 189
8:34–9:1 — 72, 135, 259 n.30, 282 n.38
8:34–38 — 65, 101, 122, 192
8:34–35 — 86
8:38 — 128
9:1 — 15, 124, 127, 274 n.34
9:2–13 — 44
9:2–10 — 95
9:2–9 — 92
9:2–8 — 80, 107–8
9:9 — 128
9:11–13 — 80
9:12–13 — 60
9:12 — 128
9:14–29 — 122
9:14–18 — 81
9:18 — 137
9:25 — 92
9:30–37 — 72
9:30 — 48, 70
9:31–32 — 79
9:31 — 16, 72, 80, 85, 100, 128
9:32–37 — 80
9:33–41 — 189
9:33 — 48
9:36–37 — 197
9:37 — 20, 189

9:38–41	93, 96, 274 n.34
9:38–40	122
9:47	178
10	172, 186–95
10:1–45	186–94
10:1	14, 48, 85
10:2–45	108
10:2–12	108
10:2–9	15, 49, 100, 150, 172–76, 187, 190, 220–21, 223, 225
10:3–5	61
10:4	60
10:9	196
10:10–12	150, 178, 188–89, 220–21, 225
10:13–16	189–90, 197
10:13	93
10:15	127, 196, 228, 269 n.1
10:16–31	108
10:16–28	50
10:17–45	259 n.30
10:17–31	190–93
10:17–25	43, 49, 127
10:17–22	172, 177, 190
10:19	60
10:23–27	190–92
10:23–25	178, 269 n.1
10:28–31	190, 192
10:28–30	179, 181, 219
10:29–31	119
10:30	123, 224
10:32–40	79
10:32–34	70, 72, 193–94
10:32	15
10:33–34	16, 72, 80, 100, 128, 194
10:35–45	49, 50, 65, 80, 93, 193–94, 228
10:35–40	72
10:42–45	96
10:42–44	194
10:43–44	196
10:45	86, 102, 128, 194

10:46–52	14, 18, 71, 72, 75, 80, 181
10:46	15
10:52	119
11–12	81, 136
11:1–13:2	70
11:1–10	109
11:1	15
11:2–8	60
11:9–10	60
11:11	15
11:12–25	72
11:12–23	18
11:15–24	101
11:15–19	100
11:15–18	19, 41, 258 n.7
11:15–17	110, 216
11:15	148
11:17–18	85
11:17	44, 60
11:18	110
11:23	148
11:27–12:12	46
11:27–33	100, 274 n.34
11:32	110
12:1–12	19, 41, 45, 100, 110, 180
12:10	60
12:12	110
12:13–17	15, 36, 43, 150
12:13	151
12:14	85
12:15	16
12:18–27	61, 95, 175, 222–23
12:24	274 n.34
12:25	223
12:26–27	223
12:28–37	233
12:28–34	195, 197–200
12:28–33	111
12:28–31	177
12:35–44	151
12:35–37	20
12:35	85
12:36	60

12:38–44	170, 184
12:38–40	100, 111, 216, 258 n.7
12:41–44	216–17, 258 n.7
21	xiv, 67, 123–24, 129–36, 272 n.15, 17
13:1–2	15, 19, 41, 100, 110, 216, 258 n.7
13:3–37	70, 81
13:3	92
13:5	123
13:9–13	65, 81, 86, 101, 122, 219
13:9–11	192
13:10	45, 48, 65, 180
13:14–27	122
13:21–22	274 n.34
13:24–26	124
13:26–27	128, 262 n.19
13:26	274 n.34
13:27	272 n.12
13:33–37	81
14:1–16:8	15, 70
14:1–2	15, 100, 109–10, 218
14:3–9	203, 216
14:3–8	72, 217–18
14:9	180
14:10–11	81, 93, 100
14:12	111
14:17–21	79
14:18	81
14:19	93
14:21	128, 234, 264 n.26
14:22–25	65, 111, 195, 200–1
14:24	102, 178
14:25	127
14:26–31	79
14:27–50	81
14:27	264 n.26
14:28	48, 76
14:32–42	79
14:32–50	79
14:41	128, 203
14:43–65	100

Mark (*continued*)
14:43	93
14:49	85, 234, 264 n.26
14:53	81
14:61–64	101
14:61	15, 252
14:62	44, 122, 128, 252,
	274 n.34
14:65	19
14:66–72	79, 81
14:66–70	159
15:1–32	99
15:1	100, 151
15:2	46, 99, 167, 252
15:3–4	151
15:9	46, 167, 252
15:11	171
15:16–20	99
15:18	167, 252
15:20	171
15:25–32	99
15:25	167
15:28	46
15:32	15, 46, 167
15:34	48
15:40–41	205
15:40	33
15:41	218
15:52	72
15:54	72
15:55–65	72
15:66–72	72
16:1–8	33, 72, 95
16:5	108
16:7–8	48, 81
16:8	94

Luke
3:22	283 n.3
4:1–13	264 n.25
4:16–20	59
6:20–49	185–87, 192,
	278 n.13
6:20–22	195
6:27–42	186
7:27	264 n.25
8:41	279 n.3
9:23–27	282 n.38

10:2–16	89
10:5–7	89
10:8–11	89
11:20	140
11:28–41	276 n.33
12:2–31	192
13:28–29	272 n.12
14:25–33	282 n.38
21:20	131
22:28–30	88

John
1:4	178

Acts
1:17	227
1:25	227
1:26	90
2:42	90
4:37	90
5:36	240
6:1–6	228
8:1	90
9:31	90
21:38	240
26:7	88

Romans
11:17	152
16:1	227

1 Corinthians
1:12–16	278 n.10
3:5	227
11:25	177
15:3–8	83
15:3–5	234, 264 n.26
15:4	95
15:5	95

Galatians
1:19	281 n.20
1:17	94
2	180
2:9	94

Hebrews
1:5	283 n.3

Revelation
3:5	108
3:18	108
4:4	108
6:11	108
7:9	108
7:13	108
21:10–14	88

Jewish Literature
Dead Sea Scrolls
CD
4:19–21	176
10:19–20	164
1QGA	137
1QH	58
1QM	
2:2–3	88
4:1–5:16	105
5:1–3	88
14:9–11	138
1QS	184–85
2:21	105
6:3	58
8:1–3	88
8:14	126
9:19	126
1Qsa	
1:14–15	105
1:27–2:1	105
2:21–23	58
1QSb =1Q28b	58
4Q	
159	163
408	58
491	138
503	58
507–9	58
4QM	58
4QS	
184–5	58
4QSam b	276 n.25
11QT	
18:14–16	88
57:17–19	176

2 Baruch
14:18	166

27 130
70:8 130

1 Enoch 126
62 128
90:28–39 114
94–102 32

4 Ezra
9:3 130
13:31 130

Jubilees
2:17–33 163
2:29–30 163

Mekilta
109b 166

Mishnah
m. Abot 264 n.20
m. Ber.
4:3 55
m. Bik.
3:7 55
m. Hag.
2:7 167
m. Ned.
2:4 160
m. Ketub.
1:4–5 174
4:12 174
m. Pe'ah
1:3 163
m. Pes.
4:8 276 n.29
m. Shabb.
1:3 55
7:2 163
m. Sotah
7:8 57
m. Sukk.
3:10 55
m. Yevam.
4:10 174
m. Yoma
8:6 276 n.27
t. Ber.

5:13 276 n.34
5:27 276 n.34
t. Pe'ah
1:6 163
t. Pes.
21:12 276 n.29
y. Shabb.
16:8 159
y. Ta'an.
21:13 246
[68d 48–51]

Psalms of Solomon
11:2–3 130
17 251, 284 n.11

Testaments of the
Twelve Patriarchs
Test. Judah
25:1 88
Test. Moses
10 126–27

Classical Literature
Aristophanes
Acharnians
383–479 56
Thesmophoriazusae
95–265 56

Aristotle
Poetics 82

Augustine
De Consensu Evangelistarum
1.2(4) 257 n.1

Dio Chrysostom
20.20 56

Eusebius
Hist. Eccl.
3.39.4 62

Josephus
Antiquities
1.1–21 133

4.73 170
4.209 55, 57
10.51 168
13.257–58 33
13.296–97 153, 157, 168
13.297 58
13.318 33, 157
13.320–21 282 n.46
13.372–83 153
13.400 282 n.46
13.400–10 153
13.408 168
14:120 33
16.43 55
17:271 34
17.271–81 245
21.17 34, 273 n.30
21.18 273 n.30
17:288–89 34
18:3–9 36
18:23–25 36
18.85–87 240
18.256–309 132
18.273–75 133
20.97–98 240
20:168 239
20:169–71 240
20.219 220

Contra Apionem
1.36 168
1.167 170
2.175 55, 263 n.7
2.178 55
2.204 55, 263 n.7

Life
62–63 275 n.18
18 275 n.18
134–35 58

Jewish War
1.180 33
2.56 34
2.68 34
2.118 36
2.184–203 132
2.229 58

Josephus (continued)		Philo		Pliny the Younger	
2.259	239	*Legatio ad Gaium*		*Epistles*	
2.417	168	19	55	10.96–97	182
2.652–53	246	197–337	132		
4.507–13	246	210	55	Quintilian	
4.529–34	246			*Inst.*	
7.1–4	131	*Mos.*		5.11.19	56
7.29–31	246	2.22	163		
7.36	246			Tacitus	
7.153–55	246			*Histories*	
				5.9.2	132

Index of Authors

Achtemeier, Paul J.   264 n.20, 265 nn.27, 29, 31; 270 n.2
Allison, Dale C., Jr.   272 n.12
Aune, David   260 nn.35, 37

Baldick, Chris   258 n.16
Bar-Ilan, Meir   263 n.9
Barton, Stephen C.   278 nn.5, 7–8
Baumgarten, A. I.   277 nn.36, 39–40
Beard, Mary   263 n.2
Beasley-Murray, G. R.   272 n.9
Best, Ernest   267 n.1, 278 n.14
Black, C. Clifton   267 n.1
Blount, Brian K.   266 n.34
Borg, Marcus   279 n.6
Botha, Pieter J. J.   263 n.13, 266 n.36
Briggs, Sheila   279 n.5
Brock, Rita N.   281 nn.15–16, 18–19, 36; 282 n.49
Brooten, Bernadette   282 n.42
Bryan, Christopher   260 n.25

Casey, Maurice   276 nn.25, 27
Cohen, Shaye J. D.   275 n.8, 276 n.30, 280 nn.9, 11
Collins, Adela Yarbro   260 nn.26, 40; 272 nn.8, 14; 282 n.49, 285 nn.15, 19
Collins, John J.   261 n.5, 271 n.3, 284 nn.9–10, 285 nn.16–17
Coote, Robert B.   284 n.6

Corley, Kathleen E.   281 nn.26, 32, 34; 282 n.50
Crossan, John D.   269 n.26, 273 n.29, 274 n.31, 279 n.6

D'Angelo, Mary Rose   279 n.3, 280 nn.7, 12; 281 nn.14, 21, 33
De Jonge, Marianus   285 n.14
De Moor, Johannes C.   271 n.13
Derrett, J. Duncan M.   274 n.32, 277 n.41
Dewey, Joanna   257 n.2, 259 n.26, 266 nn.36–37, 267 n.50, 267 n.3, 269 n.1, 280 n.7, 281 nn.28, 30, 33, 35; 282 nn.41, 43, 47; 283 n.51
Donahue, John R.   261 n.3, 267 n.5, 269 n.20, 272 n.8, 277 n.1, 278 n.15
Draper, Jonathan   264 n.23, 268 nn.14, 19; 270 n.2, 278 n.12, 282 n.37
Dube, Musa W.   260 n.1, 279 n.4
Duling, Dennis C.   285 n.14

Eagleton, Terry   259 nn.16–17, 260 n.41
Elliott, John H.   268 n.14, 282 n.37
Ellis, E. Earle   261 n.3

Fanon, Frantz   141–44, 274 n.33
Fish, Stanley E.   257 n.3
Fitzmyer, Joseph A.   277 n.39, 285 n.16
Foley, John Miles   265 n.34, 266 n.35

Fowler, Alastair   260 n.39
Fowler, Robert M.   258 nn.13–14, 259
   nn.25–26, 28–29, 31; 270 n.3
Fredriksen, Paula   280 n.8

Gamble, Harry Y.   263 n.6
Gerhardsson, Birger   265 n.29
Goodman, Martin   263 n.8, 271 n.11
Gottwald, Norman K.   261 n.4
Guelich, R. A.   277 n.42
Gundry, Robert H.   277 nn.38, 43, 45

Haddad, Beverly   281 n.15
Hadot, Pierre   263 n.12
Halliday, M. A. K.   265 n.34
Hamilton, Neil Q.   269 n.26
Hanson, John S.   261 n.8, 270 nn.8–9,
   272 n.15, 284 nn.5, 8; 285 n.13
Hare, Douglas R. A.   272 n.8
Harrington, Daniel J.   277 n.39
Harris, William V.   263 nn.2–5, 15; 264
   n.16
Hartman, Lars   272 n.10
Havelock, Eric   265 n.32, 266 nn.41, 45
Henderson, Ian   264 n.19
Hengel, Martin   263 n.6
Herington, J.   263 n.11
Holladay, Carl R.   269 n.22
Hollenbach, Paul W.   274 n.33
Hooker, Morna D.   276 n.26, 28
Horsley, Richard A.   261 nn.6–13, 262
   nn.14–15, 264 n.23, 265 n.34, 268
   nn.14, 19; 269 n.1, 270 nn.2, 8–9; 271
   nn.2, 4–6, 10–12, 14–17; 272 nn.7,
   15–16; 274 nn.3, 5–6; 275 nn.11, 16;
   278 n.3, 11–13; 279 n.20, 282 n.37,
   284 nn.5, 7; 285 nn.12–13
Hymes, Dell   266 n.40

Ilan, Tal   280 n.10
Iser, Wolfgang   258 n.13

Jaffee, Martin S.   264 n.21
Jameson, Fredric   258 n.15, 259 n.21
Juel, Donald   283 n.2

Käsemann, Ernst   278 n.16
Kee, Howard C.   269 n.22, 273 nn.19,

21, 23–25; 277 n.2, 278 nn.4, 6, 16;
   282 n.44
Keegan, Terence J.   270 n.7
Kelber, Werner   257 n.2, 262 n.1, 265
   n.33, 266 nn.36, 38; 269 n.24, 270 n.3,
   278 n.9, 281 n.13
Kermode, Frank   257 n.2
Kim, Tae Hun   285 n.20
Kingsbury, Jack Dean   268 n.7
Koester, Helmut   259 n.32, 265 nn.28,
   30
Kraemer, Ross S.   276 n.30, 279 n.6, 280
   n.11, 282 n.42
Kullu, Paulus   278 n.18

Levine, Amy-Jill   280 n.10
Levine, Lee I.   261 n.12, 270 n.5
Liew, Tat-siong Benny   261 n.13, 262
   n.19, 272 n.11
Loomba, Ania   262 n.17
Lord, Albert   266 n.40

Mack, Burton L.   270 n.6, 272 n.13, 274
   n.4, 275 nn.7, 21; 283 n.1, 284 n.4
MacLaurin, E. C. B.   273 n.28
Malbon, Elizabeth S.   268 nn.8–9, 269
   n.24, 270 nn.3, 7, 281 nn.27–28
Marcus, Joel   261 n.3, 272 n.15, 283
   nn.2–3
Mason, Steve   274 n.3
Meye, Robert P.   269 n.25
Michie, Donald   257 n.2, 258 n.10, 259
   n.26, 267 n.3, 269 n.1
Milgrom. Jacob   280 n.10
Mohanty, Chandra   279 n.4
Moore, Stephen D.   258 nn.13–14, 259
   nn.20, 27
Munro, Winsome   279 n.1
Myers, Ched   259 nn.21, 270 nn.3, 5–6;
   274 n.35, 276 nn.26, 28; 278
   nn.17–18, 281 n.17

Neusner, Jacob   274 n.2, 276 nn.31–33
Nickelsburg, George   271 n.3
Niditch, Susan   264 n.18

O'Hanlon, Rosalind   262 n.21
Okoye, James C.   278 n.18

Ong, Walter   266 nn.42, 46; 267 nn.49, 51
Osiek, Carolyn   282 n.50

Painter, John   279 n.21, 282 n.48
Parry, Milman   266 n.40
Perrin, Norman   262 n.18, 271 n.1, 278 n.9
Porton, Gary   275 n.9

Raisanen, Heikki   277 n.41
Rengstorf, K. H.   277 n.40
Reynolds, Barrie   274 n.31
Rhoads, David   257 n.2, 258 nn.10–12, 259 nn.24, 26; 260 n.42, 266 n.39, 267 n.3, 268 nn.9, 12; 269 n.1, 270 nn.4, 6; 271 n.13
Ringe, Sharon   281 n.23
Robbins, Vernon K.   260 n.38, 264 n.22, 268 nn.15, 18; 275 n.21

Safrai, S.   263 n.6
Said, Edward W.   259 n.18
Saldarini, Anthony J.   274 n.1, 275 n.10
Sanders, E. P.   275 n.22, 276 nn.34–35
Schiffman, Lawrence   275 nn.17–18, 277 nn.37, 44
Schüssler Fiorenza, E.   279 nn.1, 4; 281 nn.21, 24–26; 282 nn.39–40, 45; 283 n.52
Schweitzer, Albert   258 n.8
Scott, James C.   262 n.20, 271 n.17, 275 nn.11–15, 19–20; 279 n.19
Selvidge, Marla J.   279 n.6
Sherbok, Daniel C.   275 n.24

Shiner, Whitney T.   268 n.18
Sibeko, Malika   281 n.15
Smith, Stephen H.   267 n.6, 268 n.8
Soares-Prabhu, G.   278 n.18
Stanton, Graham   269 n.23

Tannehill, Robert   267 n.2, 268 n.16
Theissen, Gerd   268 n.13, 271 n.10, 282 n.37
Thomas, Rosalind   263 nn.10–11, 14; 264 n.17, 265 n.31
Tiede, David L.   269 n.22
Tolbert, Mary Ann   259 n.31, 260 n.38; 264 n.16, 267 n.4, 268 nn.8, 10–11, 17; 269 n.21, 279 nn.2, 6; 280 n.7, 281 nn.21, 28, 31
Tompkins, Jane P.   258 n.13

Ukpong, Justin S.   260 n.1

Van Houten, Jan W.   285 n.15
Vermes, Geza   273 n.20

Weeden, Theodor J.   269 n.22
Wiarda, Timothy   268 n.9
Wilder, Amos N.   259 n.19
Williams, Delores S.   279 n.4
Wills, Lawrence M.   260 nn.34, 38; 268 n.17
Wire, Antoinette C.   273 n.26
Wolf, Eric R.   261 n.2
Wrede, Wilhelm   5
Wright, Addison G.   281 n.29

Youtie, H. C.   263 n.3